THE COLUMBIA HISTORICAL PORTRAIT OF NEW YORK

BOOKS BY JOHN A. KOUWENHOVEN

The Columbia Historical Portrait of New York
Made in America: The Arts in Modern Civilization
Adventures of America, 1857–1900
Partners in Banking: An Historical Portrait of a Great Private Bank
The Beer Can by the Highway: Essays on What's American About America

THE COLUMBIA HISTORICAL PORTRAIT OF NEW YORK

An essay in graphic history

BY JOHN A. KOUWENHOVEN

Icon Editions, Harper & Row, Publishers
New York, Evanston, San Francisco, London

The cover illustration, "Bird's Eye View of the City of New York" (Eno Collection, New York Public Library), was drawn and lithographed by J. Bachmann and published in 1859 by C. Magnus & Co.

THE COLUMBIA HISTORICAL PORTRAIT OF NEW YORK.

 For information address Harper & Row, Publishers, Inc., 10 East 53rd Street, New York, N.Y. 10022. Published simultaneously in Canada by Fitzhenry & Whiteside Limited, Toronto.

STANDARD BOOK NUMBER: 06-430030-7

To the faculty and students
of Columbia University in the City of New York

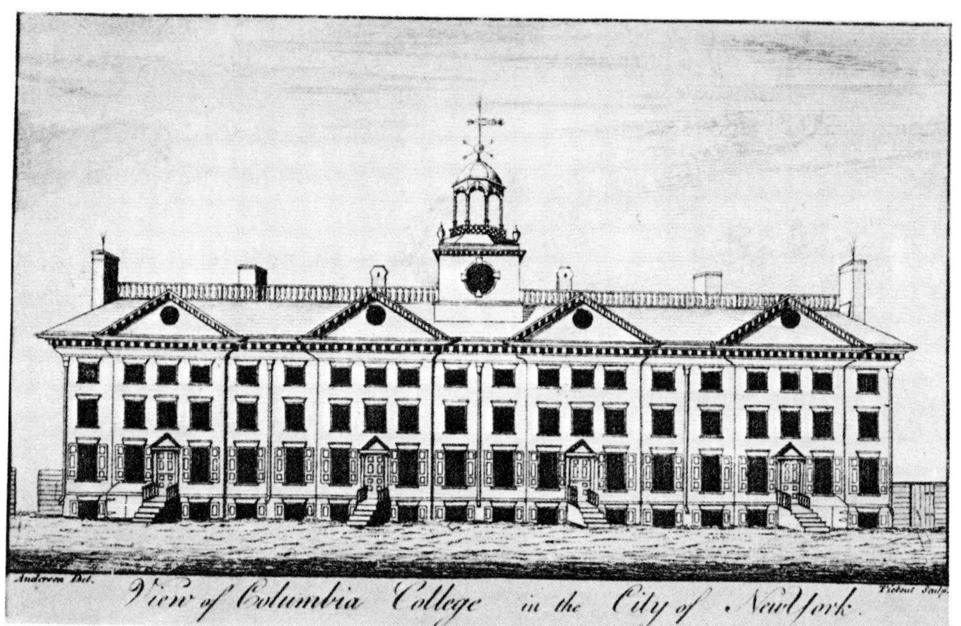

From the New-York Magazine; or, Literary Repository, *May, 1790.*
The J. Clarence Davies Collection, Museum of the City of New York

PREFACE TO THE PAPERBACK EDITION

This book was originally published in 1953, the three-hundredth anniversary of the establishment of the first municipal government in what is now the City of New York (see pages 39 and 41). The word Columbia appears in its title because it was conceived, designed, and written as part of the observance of the bicentennial of the founding of Columbia College (originally King's College) in 1754. The vice-chairman of Columbia University's Bicentennial Committee was Douglas Black, then president of Doubleday & Co., and it was to him that I owed the opportunity to do a book about the pictures of New York as evidence of people's changing visions of urban reality.

There were those who thought a conventional picture book or historical album about Columbia in its urban setting would be a more appropriate undertaking. Yet it seemed to me that a study of the evolution of man's consciousness of the city, as revealed in the visual images he made of it, might be in keeping with the theme of the university's bicentennial celebration: *Man's Right to Knowledge and the Free Use Thereof.*

It was Douglas Black's enthusiastic support of this idea that made the book possible. For one thing, he secured the approval of Columbia's Bicentennial Committee by offering to bring out the book on a nonprofit basis. Doubleday & Co. agreed to turn over all profits on it to Columbia, or absorb whatever losses there might be. Then, to insure the best possible reproduction of the pictures and the handsomest and most readable typographical layout, Mr. Black assigned the job to three of Doubleday's top people: Walter J. Bradbury, the editor; Alma Reese Cardi, the designer; and Leonard Shatzkin, coordinator of production. The story of their unprecedented efforts, in conjunction with George Beck of the Beck Engraving Co., Joseph Schwartz of Westcott and Thomson, and Herman Freund of the Intertype Corporation, was told at length in *Bookbinding and Book Production* (November, 1953). Surely no author ever had so much talented intelligence devoted so imaginatively and intensively to the job of converting his ideas into physical form.

The result was a book that apparently cannot now be republished in its original form except at a prohibitive price. Yet the demand for the book, now out of print, has pushed the price of secondhand copies as high as $80. So I am delighted that Harper & Row has contracted to bring out this inexpensive paperback edition.

They are able to do so by reproducing the original book by the photo-lithographic process. This necessarily involves some loss of detail in the pictures. Even in the original edition it was not easy to see, without the aid of a magnifying glass, that the boy in the photograph at bottom of page 417 was aiming a rifle at (perhaps) a crow in a tree; in this edition all trace of the rifle barrel may have disappeared. Also, the fifteen color plates in the original are here reproduced in black and white. (These are the pictures on pages 40, 58, 67, 96-7, 113, 145, 159, 183, 205, 229, 317, 329, 441, 469, and 501.) Hence the reference in the caption on page 96 to "the large yellow house," for example, will make no sense in this edition. But to compensate for these losses Harper & Row has made it possible for me to correct fifteen errors that got into the original despite my best efforts.

It is the publisher's hope, and mine, that this inexpensive edition will stimulate fresh interest in pictures as "ways of seeing," as evidence not so much of what New York at any time has been as of what the picture maker and his contemporaries thought it was or wanted it to be.

JOHN A. KOUWENHOVEN

Barnard College
June, 1972

CONTENTS

PREFACE

The basic fact of modern civilization is the city. Wherever we may live, city influences surround us. Even in rural areas, city ways and city preoccupations have to a great extent displaced traditional habits and interests. Whether we love the city or are repelled by it, our homes and our clothes, our forms of entertainment and our jobs, our political attitudes and our patterns of social behavior, all directly or indirectly reflect the influence of urban modes and urban methods. For the city is the most dramatic and compelling expression of the creative energies released by the interaction of democracy and industrialism, the twin forces which are reshaping our world. There is no corner of any land, no island in any sea, where the shadow of the city's towers does not fall. There is no human being anywhere who is exempt from the agony and triumph, the despair and aspiration, out of which those towers spring.

As the greatest city to develop since the Renaissance, and as the focal point at which the economic, social, and cultural dynamics of the New World have been concentrated, New York epitomizes the successes and failures of our society. Glorious and absurd, melodramatic and workaday, the first Capital of the World and one of the most provincial towns on earth, New York is as complex and as fascinating as modern civilization itself. At bottom, that is why its ragged and preposterously beautiful skyline has become one of the dominant symbols of that civilization, and why it matters to all of us to understand how that symbol was evolved.

This book, as its title suggests, is an attempt to interpret the evolution of the city in visual terms. It is not, however, a pictorial history of the familiar sort, which attempts to present an ordered sequence of pictures of prominent individuals and significant events. Nor is it simply an album of amusing or striking pictures, though it contains a good many of both sorts. It is a portrait—perhaps it would be more accurate to say a self-portrait—composed of the multiple visions of the city which men have expressed in their pictures of it over a period of more than three hundred years.

Pictures can serve as historical documents in two quite different ways. On the one hand, they are often the source of factual information about topography, manners, and customs which is available nowhere else. On the other, they are a clue to attitudes and interests, to blind spots and perceptions, of which there may be no other surviving evidence.

Without slighting or underestimating the factual aspects of the pictures of New York, this book is primarily intended to explore the other—and less familiar—historical use of such material. The choice of pictures, and the organization of the book, both grow out of the conviction that in our contemporary enthusiasm for picture history and pictorial journalism we too often lose sight of a simple but important truth: that a picture of something is not the thing itself, but somebody's way of looking at it. Even in the most representational pictures, what is shown may tell us less than we can learn from the manner in which it is presented or the point of view from which it is seen.

The book begins, therefore, with an introduction which calls attention to a variety of ways of looking at the city and to some of the pictorial elements which provide us with clues to the interests and preconceptions which those ways imply. Following this, the book itself is arranged in seven groups of pictures representing successive phases in the evolution of the city and of man's consciousness of it. The various groups succeed one another in roughly chronological order but, within each group, chronology is subservient to a sequence which is designed to emphasize and reinforce the dominant attitudes and interests which the pictures of that general period reveal.

A brief essay, commenting on the sequence of pictures, runs through the book at the top of each page. Further comment, together with historical data on each of the nine hundred pictures, will be found in the separate captions.

The book is the result of a prolonged and careful survey of the available pictures of New York from the earliest maps, plans, and views to the infinite variety of photographs, paintings, and illustrations in our own time. Out of this survey came an awareness of certain major changes in man's image of the city, and it is these changes, rather than any preconceived theories of urban development, which have dictated both the choice of pictures and the sequence in which they are presented.

The book's technique is frankly experimental, and the author is aware of many of its imperfections. At best he hopes that it may help to provide those who read it with fresh insights into the problems and the achievements of the civilization in which it is our destiny and our opportunity to live.

John A. Kouwenhoven

Barnard College
Columbia University

OPPOSITE: Manhattan from Brooklyn Heights, 1673 and 1947. Both views show the tip of Manhattan from Wall Street south. "Nieu Amsterdam at New York," showing the city in 1673, is from a line engraving in Carolus Allard's *Orbis Habitabilis,* a sort of pictorial tour of the world published at Amsterdam, Holland, about 1700 (see page 45 for more about this view). The photograph was taken October 12, 1947, from the foot of Cranberry Street when the old brownstone house at 84 Columbia Heights was being demolished. The houses just beneath the woman's basket in the engraved view were at the corner of Wall and Pearl streets (then at the East River shore), one block east of the Bank of the Manhattan Company building and a block south of the Cities Service tower, which are the two tallest structures in the photograph.

Collection of Edward W. C. Arnold; photograph courtesy of Museum of the City of New York

Introduction

WAYS OF LOOKING AT THE CITY

Photograph by Jessie Phelps Kahles, courtesy of Interiors

Pictures of the city are not the city itself . . .

Library of Congress, Division of Prints and Photographs

This photograph of the Flatiron Building was made in 1905 for the Detroit Publishing Co., which specialized in views of cities and employed some excellent photographers. The building, designed by D. H. Burnham & Co., was erected in 1901–2 and at once became a favorite pictorial subject. Because of its odd triangular shape it was for several years the world's most famous skyscraper.

. . . they are ways of looking at it.

Author's collection

This was one of a group of Edward Steichen's photographs which Alfred Stieglitz published in the same issue of *Camera Work* (April, 1906) which announced the opening of the Little Galleries of the Photo-Secession at 291 Fifth Avenue. The Photo-Secession, led by Stieglitz, was organized as a protest against the use of photography as "a purely mechanical means of reproduction," though it never was rigid in its claims for photography as an art. Characteristically, its magazine carried, in this same issue, an article by George Bernard Shaw which warned that, though Whistler's nocturnes were not academic, "the photographer who aims at producing a Whistleresque print is as academic as Nicolas Poussin."

The same place can be seen sentimentally as a background for amusing or pathetic anecdote, or with naïve crassness as a huckster's heaven.

Hudson River Museum at Yonkers

J. Clarence Davies Collection, Museum of the City of New York

Two views of Union Square about 1880. The painting, by William Hahn (1878), is one of many "genre" pictures of the period whose achievement it was to domesticate an urban wilderness in which it was increasingly difficult to feel at home. The other view, with its mobile billboards for Ehret's beer, the A & P, and so on, was one of a popular series of pictorial letterheads published by Charles Magnus. The painting was made from a point just left of the equestrian statue of Washington in the other picture, and shows in the background the Everett House, corner of Seventeenth Street and Fourth Avenue. Farther up Fourth Avenue at Twenty-first Street is Calvary Episcopal Church, whose steeple (later removed) also shows just behind the figure of Washington in the Magnus view.

Seen from a rooftop,
it may be a delicate pattern
of color and light,
while from the pavement
it is a terrifying
onslaught
of traffic.

Smith College Museum of Art

Author's collection

"DEAD MAN'S CURVE"—NEW YORK'S MOST DANGEROUS CROSSING.

Two views of Union Square in 1896. The painting by Childe Hassam, looking southward over the square, was probably sketched from the building of the Century Company, whose magazine published many of Hassam's pictures. The block of buildings at the top center of the canvas are on Fourteenth Street, between Fourth Avenue (at left) and Broadway. The tallest spire against the sky is that of Grace Church, Broadway and Tenth Street. The illustration by W. A. Rogers appeared in *Harper's Weekly,* March 27, 1897, with the title "'Dead Man's Curve'—New York's Most Dangerous Crossing." Looking north toward the old Tiffany & Co. building at Fifteenth Street, it shows the famous double curve around which cable cars were whipped at Broadway and Fourteenth Street. According to the *Weekly,* numerous accidents occurred here in spite of the police and flagmen regularly assigned to guard the crossing.

We can learn much about men's attitudes toward the city from what occupies the foreground of their pictures of it . . .

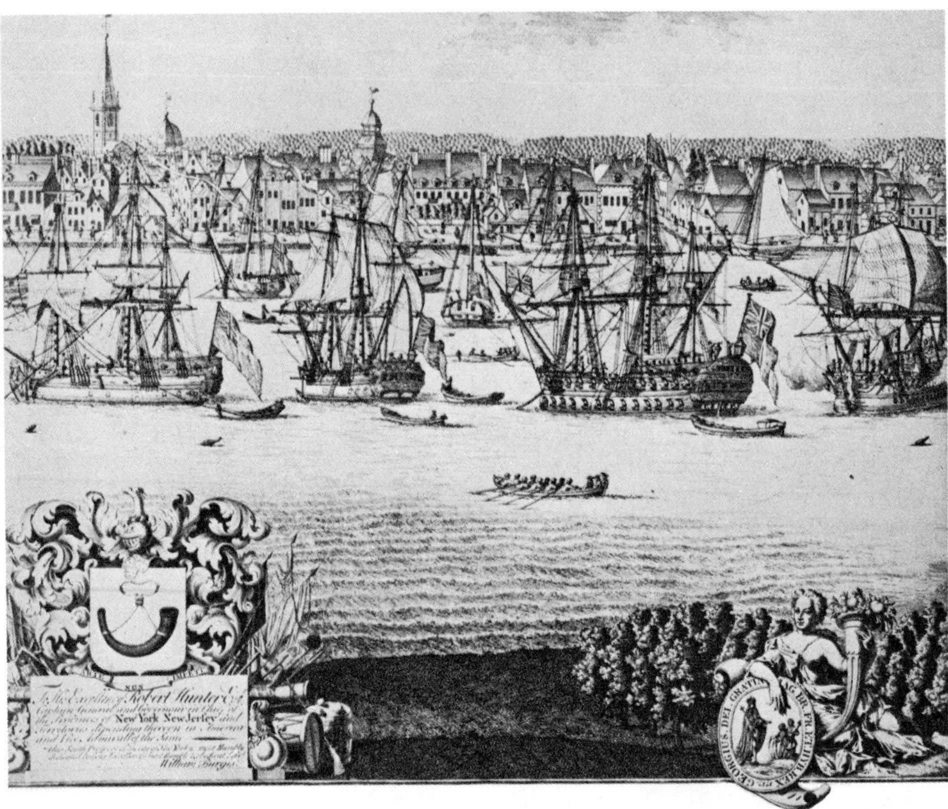

Collection of Edward W. C. Arnold; Photograph courtesy of Metropolitan Museum of Art

Lewis W. Hine Memorial Collection

The upper picture is a detail from the engraved Burgis view of New York (1716–18), which is reproduced and discussed on pages 52–55. Here it is enough to note only the prominence assigned to the coats of arms of the province (at right) and of the royal governor, and to the ships of the Royal Navy at anchor in the East River. The photograph was taken by Lewis W. Hine early in 1931 from the steel framework of the Empire State Building, then under construction. It is noteworthy that Hine had previously made some of our finest photographs of the immigrants who made up the vast majority of the city's laboring classes (see especially pages 459–60). Notice, incidentally, what has become of the Flatiron Building—the lofty subject of the two photographs made thirty years before, pages 14 and 15.

. . . from the way its people are portrayed . . .

Museum of the City of New York

IN THE RAG TRADE

Two ways of looking at one of "New York's Finest." The wood engraving above, by W. L. Thomas, was made from a drawing by the English artist, Arthur Boyd Houghton, and was published in the London *Graphic*, April 9, 1870, as one of his illustrations for a series of articles called "Graphic America." A month later, on May 7, *Harper's Weekly* in New York published the picture below, without mention of Houghton or the *Graphic*. In 1872 the *Weekly* published a couple of Houghton's Western pictures, with due acknowledgment to their creator, and commented on the series of drawings he had made when visiting this country. While admitting that a number of his pictures were "effective and truthful," the *Weekly* asserted that when he was in New York "he either willfully perverted what he saw, or else he had a singular faculty for seeing what was not observable to ordinary eyes."

Author's collection

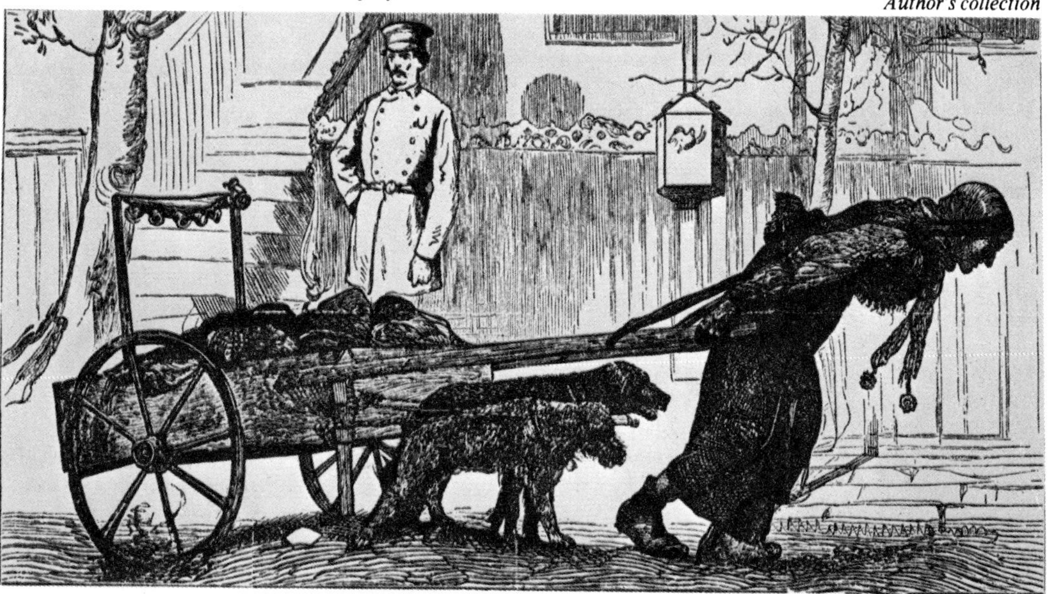

. . . and from the various aspects of city life which, at different times . . .

NDIVI

Author's collection

Beginning in the 1850s and continuing through the next three decades, there was a flood of pictures "revealing" the life of upper-middle-class New Yorkers. The small drawing on this page, by Alfred R. Waud, decorated the initial letter of Chapter I of Thomas Butler Gunn's *The Physiology of New York Boarding Houses* (1857), one of many books which took pride in "unroofing houses, and unveiling to our readers" various aspects of city life. The larger picture, published in *Frank Leslie's Illustrated Newspaper,* July 19, 1879, was entitled "Preparing for the summer exodus—a Fifth Avenue belle superintending the packing of her Saratoga trunk in her dressing-room."

Museum of the City of New York

FRANK LESLIE'S ILLUSTRATED NEWSPAPER.
NEW YORK CITY.—PREPARING FOR THE SUMMER EXODUS—A FIFTH AVENUE BELLE SUPERINTENDING THE PACKING OF HER SARATOGA TRUNK IN HER DRESSING-ROOM.—See Page 335.

. . . have been popular subjects for artists and illustrators.

Museum of the City of New York

Library of Congress, Division of Prints and Photographs

From 1900 to 1930 the destruction of old buildings and the construction of new and taller ones was a favorite subject. At the top of this page is an etching by William C. McNulty entitled "Demolishing Old Madison Square Garden" (1925), recording the end of the famous building designed by McKim, Mead & White and erected in 1890 (see page 441). The photograph of a photographer atop a steel column is from a stereoscopic view published by H. C. White of North Bennington, Vermont, in 1907. It was titled "A Dangerous Position—H. C. White Co. photographer working on column of new building, 250 ft. above ground, New York." The picture was apparently taken from the West Street building, looking down Washington Street to Battery Park, with Governor's Island in the middle distance. The building at left, with scaffolding near the top, is the U. S. Express Co. building, finished in 1907.

As we look at the city's portrait we shall find certain visual themes, such as the canyon streets, recurring through the years . . .

The upper picture is a detail of a large woodcut of "New York in 1849," drawn by E. Purcell, engraved by S. Weekes, and published by Robert Sears. In the portion of the picture here reproduced we are looking down Wall Street from the roof of Trinity Church. The domed building is the Merchants Exchange, designed by Isaiah Rogers and erected in 1836–42. It was later used as the U. S. Customs House, and in 1907 was sold to the National City Bank, which piled another colonnaded structure, designed by McKim, Mead & White, on top of the original building.

Stokes Collection, New York Public Library

Federal Art Project, "Changing New York," from Museum of the City of New York

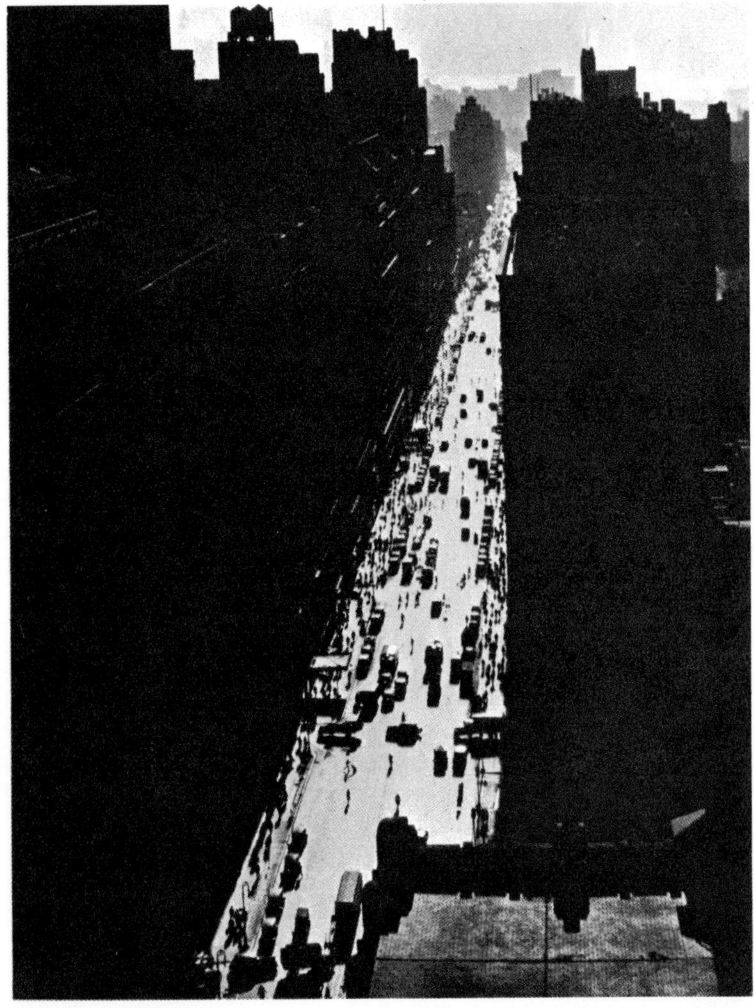

The photograph of Seventh Avenue, looking south from Thirty-fifth Street, was taken December 5, 1935, by Berenice Abbott, a number of whose photographs of the city appear in this volume (see especially pages 484–90).

. . . and others,
like the theme of contrasts,
undergoing significant
and sometimes
amusing changes.

Matthew Hale Smith's best-selling *Sunshine and Shadow in New York* (1868), the frontispiece of which is reproduced here, was only one of a number of popular books which stressed the contrasts between the city's wealth and its poverty. In this anonymous wood engraving the contrast is stated in pictures of storekeeper A. T. Stewart's two-million-dollar mansion on the northwest corner of Fifth Avenue and Thirty-fourth Street (not completed until 1869), and of the Old Brewery at 61 Park Street which had been the original home of the Five Points Mission but had been demolished in 1852 to make way for a more suitable building.

Author's collection

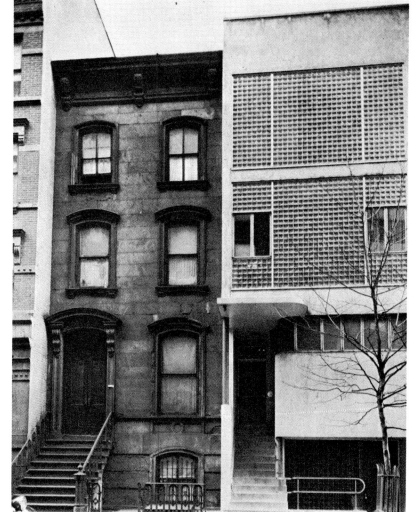

Berenice Abbott's photograph, taken February 1, 1938, contrasts the peeling respectability of a brownstone front at 209 East Forty-eighth Street with the strict efficiency of the glass-front residence and office of architect William Lescaze at 211.

Federal Art Project, "Changing New York," from Museum of the City of New York

We shall see the effects of important changes in the processes of reproducing pictures, ranging from engravings . . .

Collection of Edward W. C. Arnold; photograph courtesy of Museum of the City of New York

The pen and ink drawing above, dated 24 June, 1796, was the original from which the colored aquatint engraving of "New York from Hobuck Ferry House, New Jersey," was made by Francis Jukes in London. According to the inscription on the engraving, which was published in 1800, the picture was drawn by Alexander Robertson, but it may have been done by his brother Archibald, as claimed by Archibald's son in a note written across the bottom of the drawing. Both Robertsons were English-born artists who taught drawing and painting at their Columbian Academy in Liberty Street, New York.

In any event, it is interesting to observe the differences between the engraving and the original. Major changes are freely made for decorative effect. Details, such as the wagon and the date on the house, are omitted, and a tree at right is added for balance even though the profile of the distant city has to be shortened to accommodate it. Yet in other respects the engraver has been scrupulously careful, borrowing the leaves for the plants he inserts at lower left, for example, from the plants in the right foreground of the drawing.

J. Clarence Davies Collection, Museum of the City of New York

. . . to half-tone plates of retouched photographs.

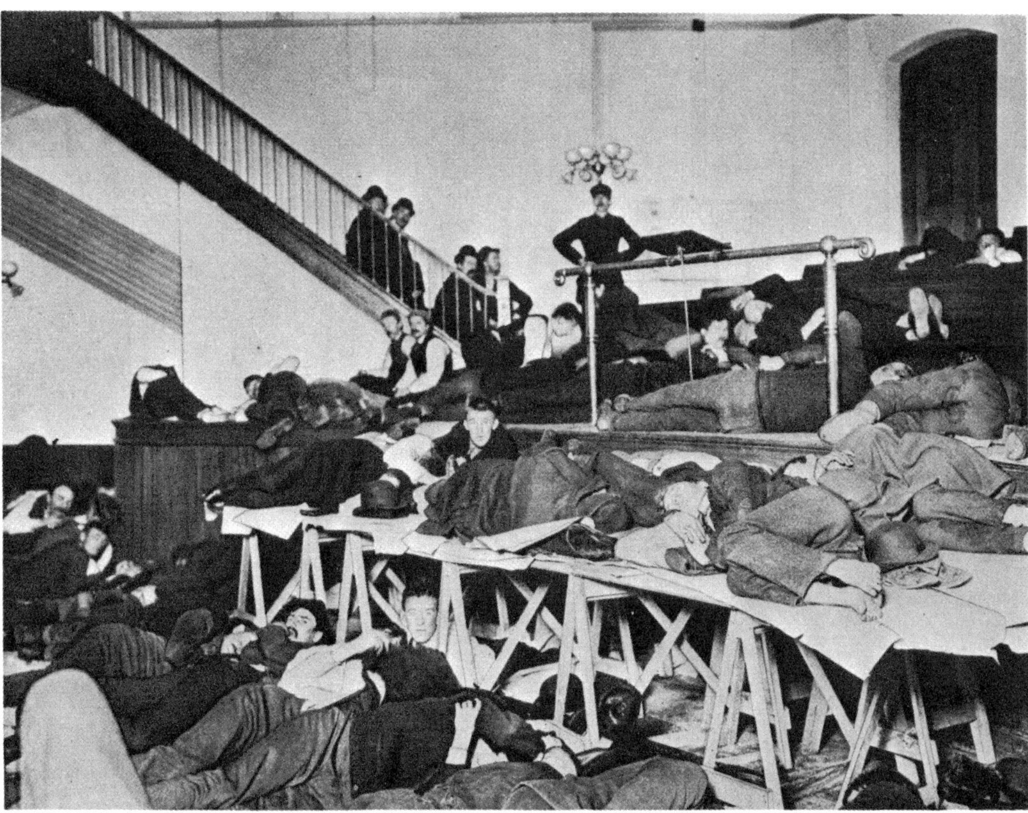

Byron Collection, Museum of the City of New York

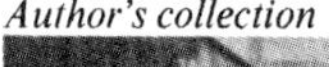

Author's collection

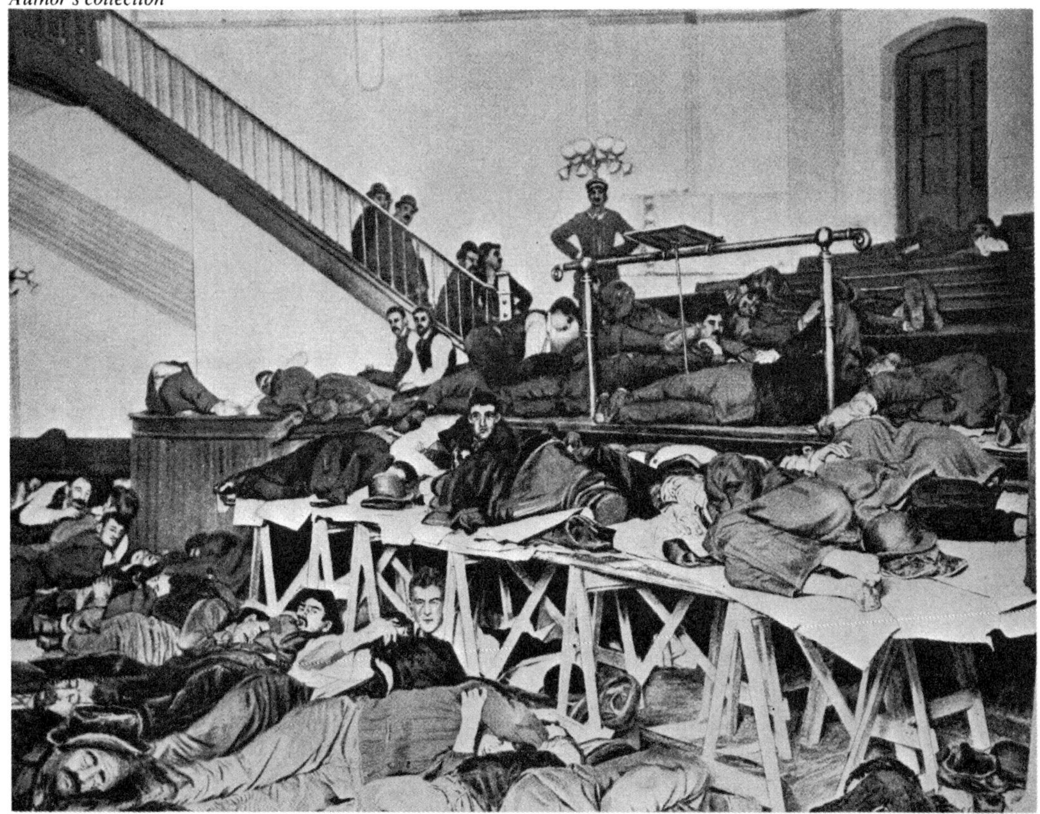

The photograph of the Salvation Army's lodging house in Fourteenth Street was made by Joseph C. Byron in 1897. The print above was made from the original negative, now in the Museum of the City of New York. The version below was published in E. Idell Zeisloft's *The New Metropolis* (New York, 1899) with the caption "Salvation Army Hall thrown open on a hot night to homeless men." As late as 1909 the International Correspondence School course in engraving and printing methods recommended that "to get the best results in the finished cut, the photograph should be painted by an illustrator that makes a specialty of preparing copy for engravers." Notice the faces which have been painted in over the unattached knee at lower left of Byron's photograph.

We shall see how differently city life is reported in different pictorial mediums . . .

On a freezing day in March, 1868, P. T. Barnum's second American Museum, on the west side of Broadway between Spring and Prince streets, was destroyed by fire as its predecessor opposite St. Paul's Chapel (see page 195) had been. The wood engraving, from an on-the-spot sketch by Stanley Fox, was published in the next issue of *Harper's Weekly*. The stereoscopic photograph was probably taken by William B. Holmes.

EXTERIOR OF BARNUM'S MUSEUM AFTER THE FIRE.—[SKETCHED BY STANLEY FOX.]

Author's collection

Collection of H. Armour Smith

. . . and how the various mediums complement and influence one another.

Both pictures on this page from J. Clarence Davies Collection, Museum of the City of New York

The photograph above, probably taken in 1879 after the old Bowery Theater was renamed the Thalia, was obviously the basis for the Magnus letterhead of the "New York Elevated Railroad Station at Bowery and Canal Street." It was only with the aid of photography that wood engravings and lithographs achieved such literal detail and precise perspective. Yet the older mediums retained important advantages. Notice that moving figures in the photograph, such as the man on the roof and the horse in the street, are blurred because of the long exposure required. Notice also that the camera is unable to penetrate the shade of the vine-covered sidewalk café.

The pictorial letterhead was presumably made after an additional story had been built on Atlantic Garden. An undated drawing showing this addition and signed by "Wm. José, Architect," is in the collection of Edward W. C. Arnold.

And if, out of all the pictures that have been made of New York, few until recent years have made any claim as works of art, that too will tell us much about man's awareness of the city.

Photographed by Gottscho-Schleisner, taken from under th Queensborough Bridge about 6 P.M., March 19, 193

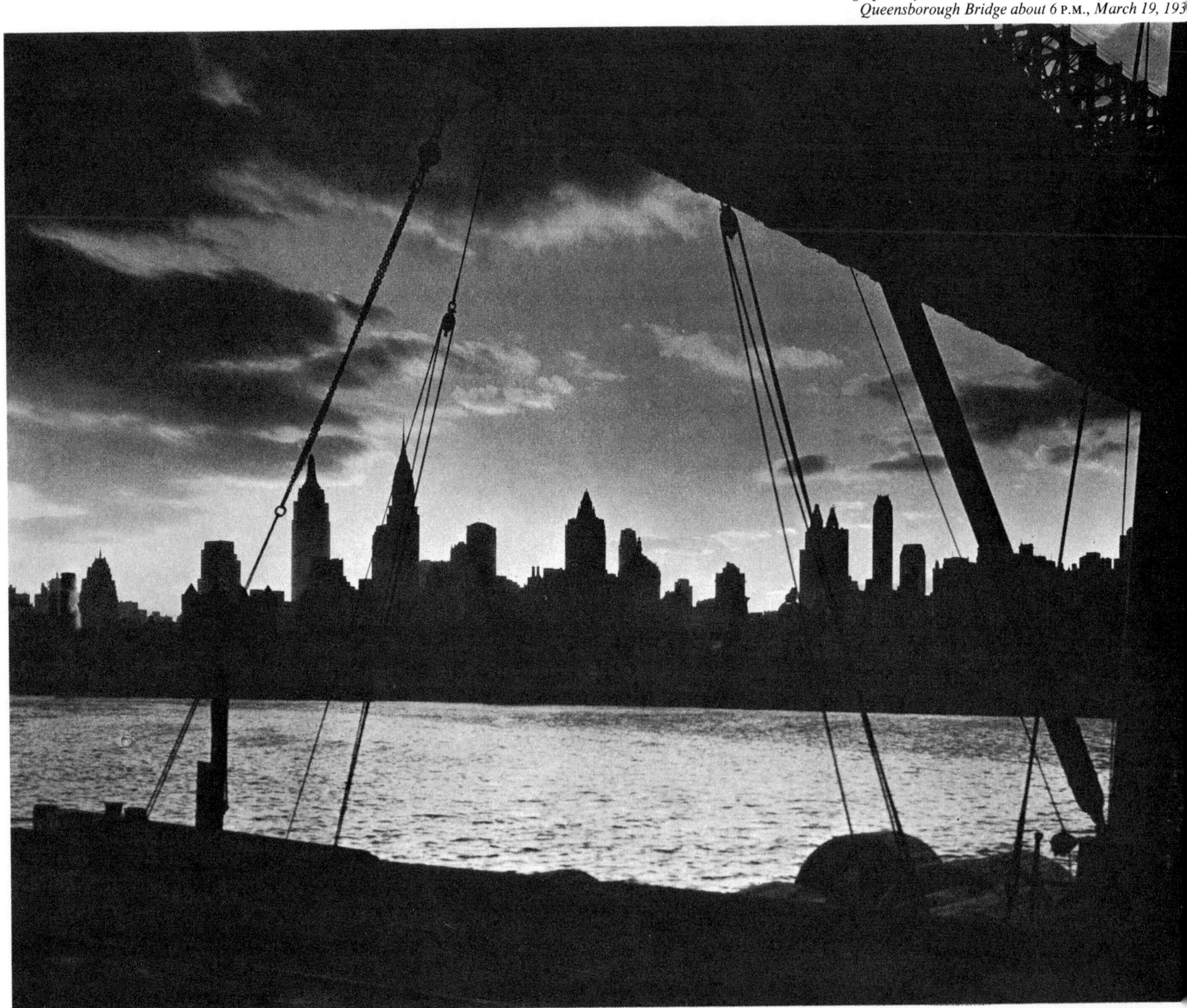

Group One

PLANS AND PROSPECTS 1614-1800

Original in General Government Archives, The Hague, Holland photograph courtesy of Museum of the City of New York

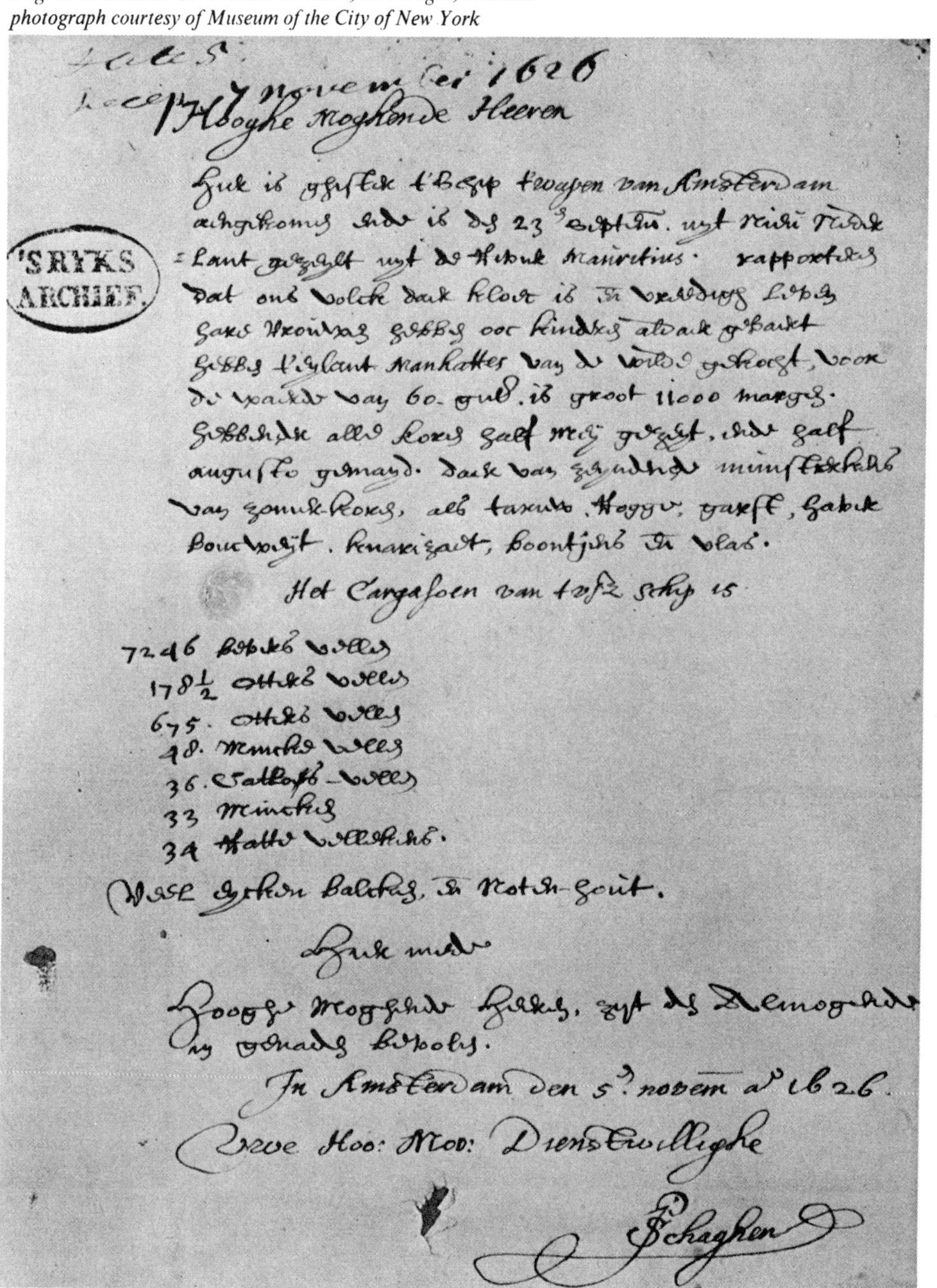

'SRYKS ARCHIEF

Recepi 7 novembri 1626

Hooghe Moghende Heeren

Hier is gisteren 't schip 't Wapen van Amsterdam
aengecomen ende is den 23 septem. uyt Nieu Neder-
=lant gezeylt uyt de Riviere Mauritius. rapporteren
dat ons volck daer kloeck is en vredich leven
haere vrouwen hebben oock kinderen aldaer gebaert
hebben 't Eylant Manhattes van de wilde gekocht, voor
de waerde van 60. guld. is groot 11000 morgen.
hebben alle koren half mey gezayt. ende half
augusto gemaeyd. daer van zijnder monsterkens
van zomerkoren, als tarwe, rogge, garste, haver
boeckweyt. knariezaet, boontjens en vlas.

Het Cargasoen van t'voorsz schip is

7246 bevers vellen
178½ otters vellen
675. otters vellen
48. mincke vellen
36. catlosse vellen
33 minckes
34 hatte vellekens.

Veel eycken balcken, en noten hout.

Hier mede

Hooghe Moghende Heeren, zyt den Almoghende
in genade bevolen.

In Amsterdam den 5e novem ao 1626.

Uwe Hoo: Moo: Dienstwillighe

P. Schaghen

The only record of the original purchase of Manhattan. Letter written in Amsterdam, Holland, November 5, 1626, by Pieter Jansen Schagen, a deputy, to the States-General at The Hague. Translated, it reads:

High Mighty Sirs:
Here arrived yesterday the ship
The Arms of Amsterdam which sailed from
New Netherland out of the Mauritius
[Hudson] River on September 23;
they report that our people there
are of good courage, and live peaceably.
Their women, also, have borne children there,
they have bought the island Manhattes
from the wild men for the value of sixty guilders,
is 11,000 morgens in extent.
They sowed all their grain in the middle of May,
and harvested it the middle of August.
Thereof being samples of summer grain,
such as wheat, rye, barley, oats,
buckwheat, canary seed, small beans, and flax.
The cargo of the aforesaid ship is:
7246 beaver skins, 178½ otter [half-otter?] skins,
675 otter skins, 48 mink skins,
36 wild-cat skins, 33 mink, 34 rat skins.
Many logs of oak and nut-wood.
Herewith be ye High Mighty Sirs,
commended to the Almighty's grace,
In Amsterdam, November 5, Anno 1626.
Your High Might.'s Obedient,
P. Schagen

"It has been said that God made the country and man made the town. So far as this is true, cities and civilization may be regarded as man's irreverent attempt to improve on nature and create a world more after his heart's desire. . . . Cities, and particularly the great metropolitan cities of modern times, so far as they can be regarded as the product of art and design rather than the effect of natural forces, are, with all their complexities and artificialities, man's most imposing creation, the most prodigious of human artifacts. We must conceive of our cities, therefore, not merely as centers of population, but as the workshops of civilization, and, at the same time, as the natural habitat of civilized man."

Robert Ezra Park
The City and Civilization, 1936

The first known picture of what is now New York showed the lonely outpost of European civilization as it was planned to be, rather than as it was.

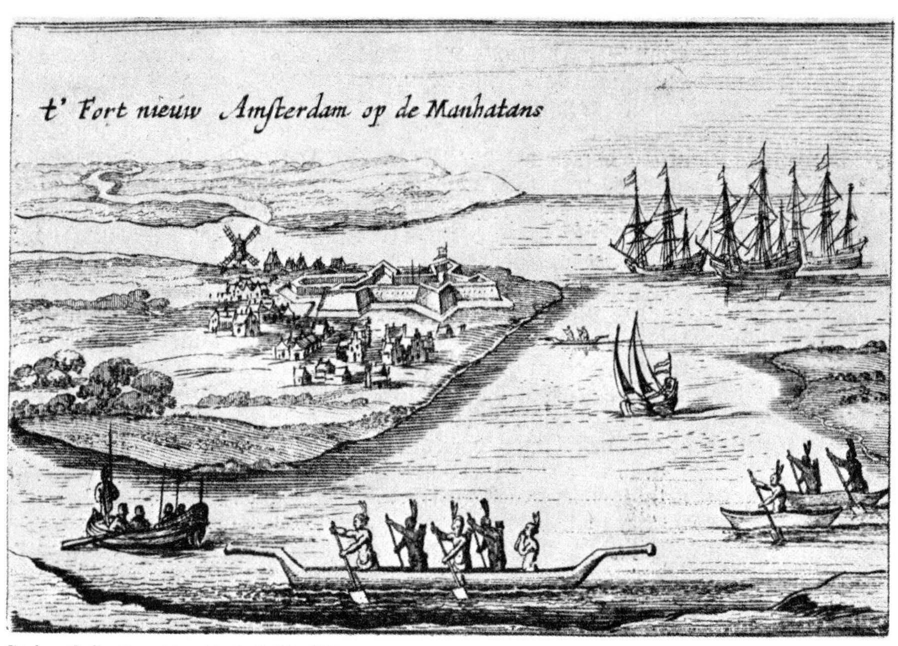

Stokes Collection, New York Public Library

It is possible that the drawing from which this earliest view of New Amsterdam was engraved was made by New York's first city-planner—the engineer Cryn Fredericksz, who had been sent over from Holland in 1625 to lay out a town and a fort for the Dutch West India Company. If so, he probably made it in 1626, just prior to his return to Holland, with the intention of showing the directors how the town would look if his plans were carried out. The thirty-odd houses in the view, and the mill, are almost certainly accurately portrayed, but the five-bastioned fort, which the directors had specified in their instructions to Fredericksz, was never completed. A smaller, four-bastioned fort was built in 1628 but was always being knocked down by pigs and other livestock and was forever being repaired. The engraving (which is reproduced here actual size) was first published by Joost Hartgers, in a compilation of descriptive narratives about the New World entitled *Beschrijvinghe van Virginia, Nieuw Nederlandt, Nieuw Engelandt,* etc. (Amsterdam, 1651). Either the engraving was carelessly made, or the original drawing was made with the aid of a seventeenth-century *camera obscura,* which produced an inverted image, because the topography is reversed. To see the view correctly, with Governor's Island at the left and with the mill on the west shore of Manhattan, where we know it stood, the picture must be looked at in a mirror. Some of the houses had been built before Fredericksz came. Dutch explorers, traders, and garrisons had lived on Manhattan irregularly since 1613. But it was not until 1625 that a permanent community was established, streets laid out, and boweries (farms) established. (It should be noted here that a wild diversity of dates have been assigned in various books to the first permanent settlement on Manhattan. The so-called Van Rappard documents, which establish 1625 as the correct date, were published by the Huntington Library in 1924 and copious extracts were included in the addenda to Stokes' *Iconography* [Vol. VI, 1928]. Yet histories of the city published as recently as 1948 continue to base their accounts of the settlement on material in the first volume of the *Iconography,* written before Stokes had access to these important documents.)

The Old World from which the Dutch colonists had come was a world in which maritime commerce was bursting the rigid patterns of life in the feudal towns . . .

Author's collection

. . . a world which channeled its expanding energies westward from growing seaports like Amsterdam, from which the colonists had sailed.

This is a detail (about four fifths of original size) from an engraved plan of Amsterdam by Balthasar Florensz van Berckenrode, published at Amsterdam by Philip Molenvliet in 1625. The headquarters of the West India Company, which owned and governed New Netherlands from 1621 until 1664, are shown at upper center, near the Brouwer's Graft Canal. At the right is the Prince Graft, leading to the harbor in foreground, and beyond it the newly laid-out part of the city, not yet built up. At the left is the Cingel Canal, with the Herring Packers' Tower at its entrance. A shorter tower on a point of land farther left, outside the scope of this detail, was known as the Schreijerstoren (Criers' Tower), on Schreijer's Hook. From here, emigrants to Brazil, Ceylon, Batavia, or New Netherlands were taken in small boats to larger vessels in the harbor, and here their relatives bade them farewell.

The New World they had come to was still largely unknown; even the coasts were represented very imperfectly on their maps.

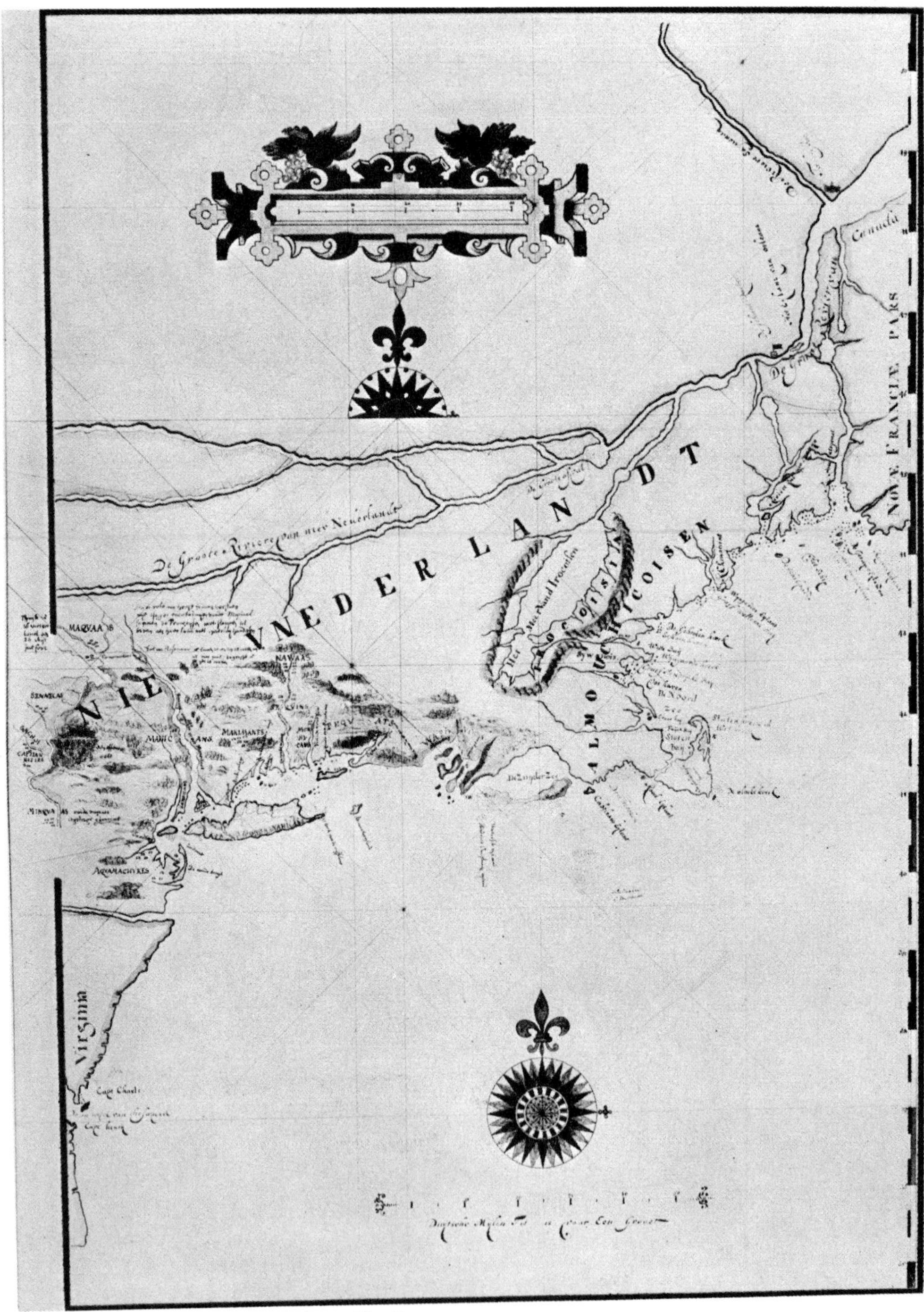

This map, drawn in gold and colors on vellum, was made in 1614 by Adriaen Block, one of the Dutch explorers who followed up Hudson's 1609 discovery of the Hudson River. It is the first map to show Manhattan as an island, and the first to employ the name Nieu Nederlandt.

Original in General Government Archives, The Hague; facsimile in Stokes Collection, New York Public Library

Block's ship, the *Tiger,* burned in the harbor in the fall of 1613, and he and his men wintered on Manhattan while building a small "yacht" which they named the *Onrust* (*Restless*). In this he sailed "through Hellegat [East River] into the great bay [Long Island Sound], and explored all the places thereabouts." It was upon these explorations, plus the earlier maps and records of others, including Hudson, that his map was based.

And yet, almost from the beginning they visualized Manhattan as the focus of the entire region now comprised in Greater New York.

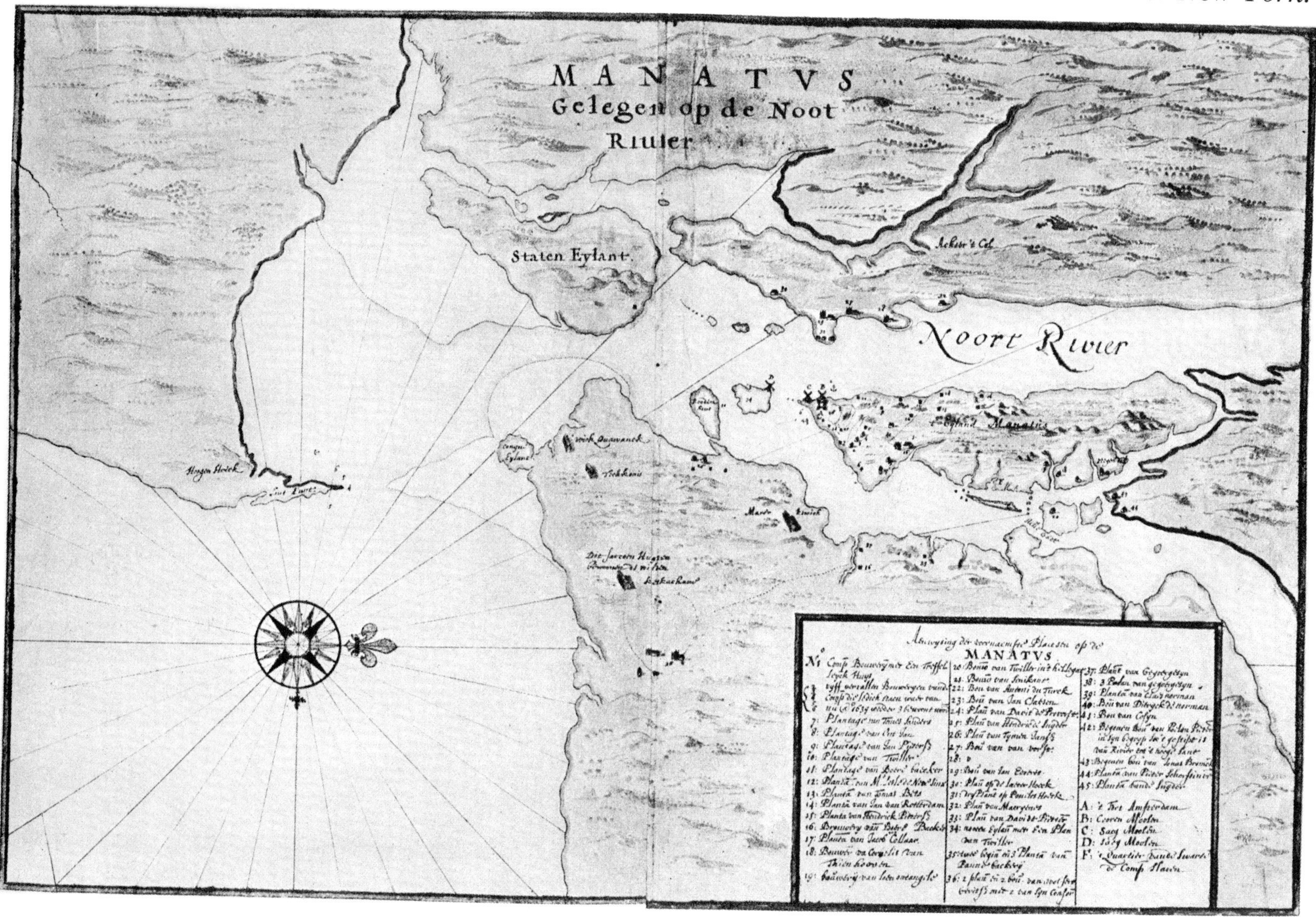

Library of Congress, Division of Maps and Charts

This bird's-eye survey of "Manhattan Lying on the North River" is a copy, made about 1670, of the original Dutch map drawn in 1639 for the West India Company. The original has been lost, but another copy of it, made about the same time and probably by the same draftsman for Cosimo de' Medici, is now owned by the Italian government. The original may have been made by Andries Hudde, who became the first surveyor general of the province. (See F. Van Wyck, *Keskachauge* [New York, 1924], pages 134–69.)

The map was made in the same year in which the West India Company, under pressure from the Netherlands government, began to relax its monopolistic restrictions on trade in New Netherlands and to offer more liberal terms to settlers in an effort to promote colonization. It is interesting to note, in this connection, that the map gives no indication of the trading village which clustered around the fort, but records the bouweries and small farms in detail. Also, as we shall see on the next page, the inset key calls attention to the fact that several formerly deserted farms have been reoccupied and that new buildings are under construction.

Even when there were so few dwellings that they could be individually portrayed . . .

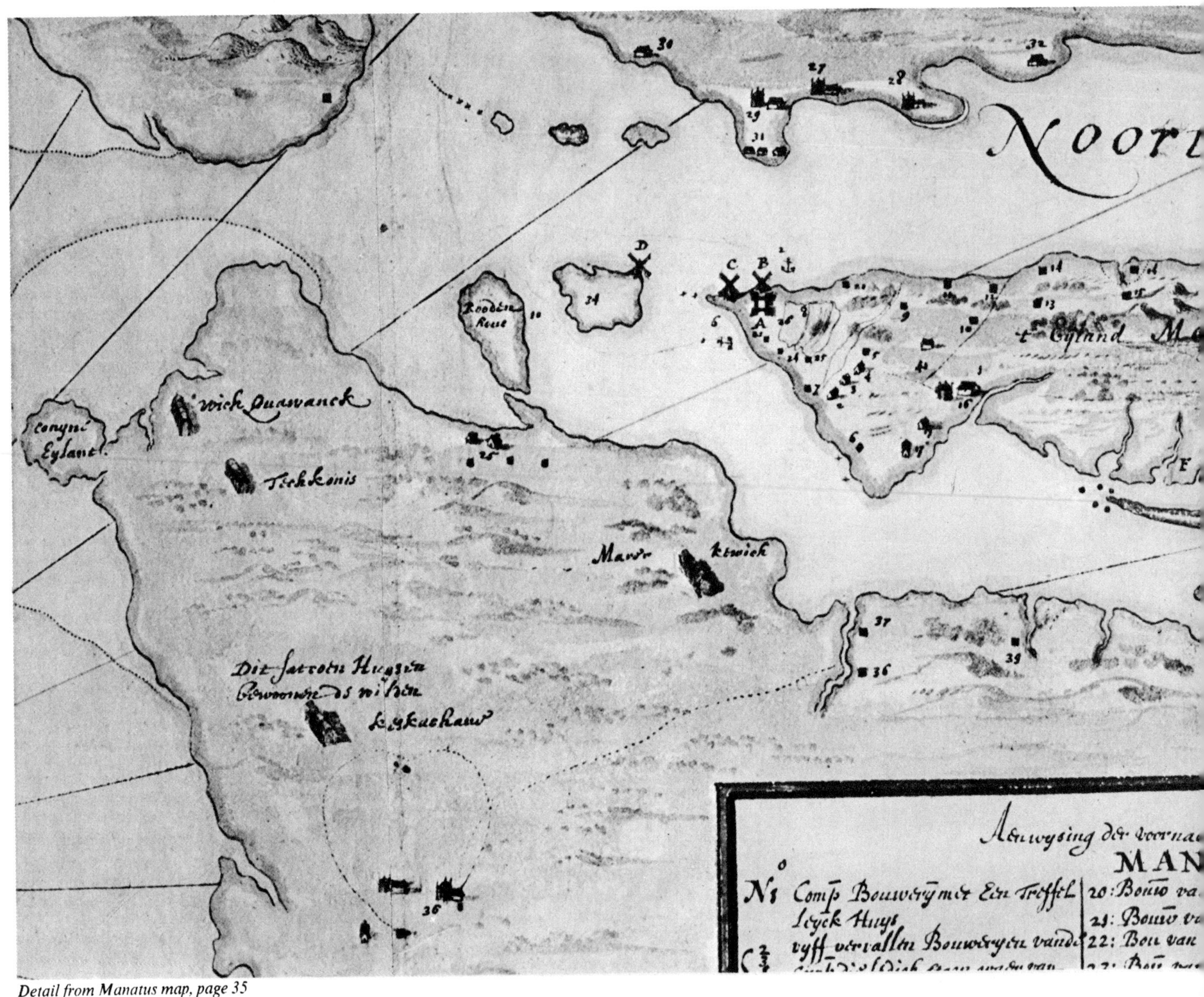

Detail from Manatus map, page 35

This detail from the Manatus map includes all the region in which settlements are enumerated in the inset key. At the right, Nos. 43 and 44 are the two houses on the "recently begun" bouwery of Jonas Bronck, from whom the Borough of the Bronx takes its name. At lower left, No. 36 is the earliest settlement on Long Island, at modern Flatlands, while along the East River we find farms around Wallabout Bay and at Williamsburg. Across the Hudson, in New Jersey, there were settlements where Jersey City, Hoboken, and Weehawken now are, and on Staten Island there is the unnumbered site of the first patroonship there. The Indian longhouses, near Conyné Eylant (Coney Island) and elsewhere, remind us that a good many of the original inhabitants were still around. The bouweries and plantations (smaller farms) of New Amsterdam at this time were usually very simple affairs, sometimes consisting of nothing but a combined house and barn, built in Dutch peasant fashion, and an open-sided shelter for hay or grain. The large bouwery at No. 36, according to an inventory made in 1638, had a house 26′ × 22′, with plank walls and roof and with two garrets, "one above the other," plus a "small chamber on the side with an outlet on the side"; a barn 40′ × 18′ and 24′ high; a "Bergh," or hay-shed, 40′ long; an orchard and garden; about 32 acres of tilled land, sown to summer and winter grain; a wagon, a wheel plow, a harrow, and smaller farm tools; horses, cows, oxen; and a yawl, doubtless for trips to Manhattan and for fishing.

. . . the whole region around the great harbor was seen as a single interrelated community.

KEY TO DETAIL OF MANATUS MAP—1639 (Based on the original inset "Indication of the principal places on the Manatus [Manhattan]," with additions and corrections drawn from contemporary documents and from Stokes' *Iconography*.)

A: Fort Amsterdam. B: Corn (or grist) mill. C, D: Sawmills. E: Hog (now Welfare) Island. F: "The Quarter of the Blacks, the Company's slaves" (of which no other record exists).

1: The West India Co.'s bouwery, "with an excellent house," leased to ex-Governor Wouter van Twiller; later bought by Peter Stuyvesant. (House site: between 1st Ave. and Ave. A, 15th and 16th Sts.)
2, 3, 4, 5, 6: Five run-down bouweries of the Company, 3 of which "are now, in the year 1639," again occupied. These farms, according to Stokes, should be shown stretching along East River. They had originally been assigned to the 5 head farmers of the 1625 settlement, all of whom seem to have left for more favorable localities.
7 (near outlet of Collect Pond on East River): Listed as farm of Tomas Sanders (or Sandersen), was probably Tymen Jansen's. See No. 26.
8: Farm of Old Jan (mistake for Jan Jansen Damen).
9: Farm of Jan Pietersen van Housem, a Danish immigrant.
10 (on the Strand road to the Hudson shore): Farm leased to Wouter van Twiller.
11 (on shore of Hudson): Farm of Barent Dircksen Swart, the farmer-baker: leased at this time to Gerrit Jansen and Volckert Evertsen (see No. 16).
12: Farm of Francis Lesley (or Lesle).
13: Farm of Thomas Betts (or Bets).
14 (two numbers, north and south of the Great Kill, flowing into Hudson at 42nd St.): Farm of Jan Cornelissen von Rotterdam, who moved to Long Island in this year. Willem Willemsen leased the farm July 7.
15: Farm of Hendrick Pietersen van Wesel (or Hasselt).
16: Bouwery of Barent Dircksen Swart, the farmer-baker.
17 (number repeated; probably 16 should be where one of houses marked 17 is): Farm of Jacob van Corlaer (or Curler), from whom Corlaer's Hook takes its name.
18 (on East River, opp. Ward's Island): Bouwery of Cornelis van Tienhoven, provincial secretary, leased at this time to Claes Cornelissen Swits and Jan Claessen Alteras.
19 (written 9 on map): Bouwery of Johannus de la Montagne, a French Huguenot. (Site of house: near McGown's Pass in present Central Park.)
20: Bouwery of Van Twiller in the Hellegat (East River). This is Ward's Island; Randall's Island also belonged to this bouwery. Barent Jansen was resident farmer.
21 (north of mills on Manhattan): Bouwery of the preacher, Domine Everardus Bogardus. This farm (north of Chambers St., between Broadway and the Hudson) later became property of Trinity Church.
22 (east of fort): Bouwery of Antony Jansen, called "the Turk" because he became a Mohammedan while living in Morocco.
23 (number not on map; should be between 22 and 24): Bouwery of Jan Claessen.
24: Farm of Hendrick Jansen, the tailor. (Nos. 24 and 25 are here correctly assigned; in inset key on map they are reversed.)
25: Farm of David Provoost, whose cherry orchard later became the famous Cherry Garden, commemorated in name of Cherry St. The first ferry to Brooklyn ran from this farm.
26: Though listed as Tymen Jansen's farm, this was probably Tomas Sanders' (see No. 7).
27 (on Jersey shore): Bouwery of Cornelis van Vorst at Pavonia in present Jersey City.
28: Farm of Hendrick Cornelissen van Vorst at Hoboken.
29: Bouwery of Jan Evertsen Bout at Pavonia. The house was burned by the Indians in 1643.
30: Farm on Jan de Lacher's (Laughing John's) Hook, where the Indians were massacred by the Dutch in 1643, thus precipitating the war.
31: Three farms on Paulus Hook (at Hoboken). These, with the preceding four, had all been part of Michael Paauw's unsuccessful patroonship of Pavonia. Paauw sold out to the West India Co. in 1634.
32: Farm of Marinus Adriaensen, on site of present Weehawken.
33 (on Staten Island, number lacking): Farm of David Pietersen de Vries, the first proprietor of Staten Island.
34: Nut (now Governor's) Island, with a farm belonging to Van Twiller.
35 (on Long Island, below "Rooden houc [Red Hook]," mistakenly numbered 25 on map): Five farms, 3 completed and 2 begun, of the tile bakers.
36 (in heart-shaped dotted line): Two farms and 2 bouweries of Wolphert Gerritsen van Couwenhoven and 2 partners. This was the first settlement on Long Island, later called Flatlands. The partners were Van Twiller and Wolphert's son Gerrit.
37: Farm of Joris (Georgius) Rapelje, at the Wallabout in Brooklyn.
38 (below 37, erroneously written 36): Three farms of Joris Rapelje.
39: Farm of Claes Carstensen, the Norwegian, at Williamsburg.
40 (lacking on map; should be above and right of 39, on opposite side of Bushwick Creek): Bouwery of Dirck Volckertsen ("the Norman"), another Norwegian. Volckertsen and his brother had been in New Netherlands as early as 1621 on a trading voyage.
41 (on Manhattan): Bouwery of Cosyn Gerritsen van Putten.
42 (number lacking on map; should be by most northerly house on Manhattan, above which is written Zeegendal [Valley of Blessing]): The recently begun bouwery of Jochem Pietersen Kuyter, from Darmstadt (site: north of 124th St., between Lexington Ave. and East River).
43: The recently begun bouwery of Jonas Bronck, a Dane or Swede (house site: railroad depot near corner of Southern Blvd. and Willis Ave.).
44: Farm of Pieter Andriessen, the chimney sweep, who leased it from Bronck.
45 (lacking on map; house indicated just north of No. 18 on Manhattan): Farm of the Snyder (tailor). This house, at foot of present 125th St., was probably the first in Harlem.

From the point of view of the directors at Amsterdam, or their agents voyaging back and forth across the huge Atlantic . . .

This recently discovered painting, showing Domine Everardus Bogardus leaving New Amsterdam on his way to Holland, August 17, 1647, is the earliest known on-the-spot picture of an incident in New York's history. First publicly shown at the Museum of the City of New York while this volume was in press, it is reproduced here for the first time in any book. Technical research (including infrared photographs, X rays, and pigment analysis) supervised by Sheldon Keck of the Brooklyn Museum, and exhaustive historical research by its discoverer, Mr. Thurston Thacher (who plans to publish his findings), leave no doubt that the picture was painted by Augustine Herrman in New Amsterdam contemporaneously with the event depicted. Bogardus, who is shown second from the left in the rowboat (left foreground), was on his way back to Holland to appear before the ecclesiastical tribunal of the Classis of Amsterdam to answer charges brought against him by Director-General Willem Kieft, whose arbitrary and incompetent administration he had criticized from the pulpit and who in turn had accused Bogardus of drunkenness and insubordination. The rowboat is shown leaving the Hudson River shore of Manhattan at a point west of the fort, just above the mill which is marked C on the Manatus map (page 36). It is carrying the domine and others (possibly including two other opponents of Kieft, Jochem Pietersen Kuyter and Cornelis Melyn) out to the ill-fated ship *Princess,* which was anchored out of sight around in the East River, ready to sail. In the center background is Governor's Island, and at the extreme right is one of the houses on Paulus Hook, across the Hudson (No. 31 on Manatus map). The *Princess,* which also had Kieft himself aboard, on his way back to try to defend the Indian massacres and other scandals of his administration, went on the rocks in a gale off the coast of England, and eighty of her crew and passengers—including both Bogardus and Kieft—were drowned. Melyn and Kuyter were among the few survivors.

. . . the little settlement at the sea's edge was lonely under a huge sky, its outskirts fading into a limitless unknown landscape on all sides.

Original in General Government Archives, The Hague; facsimile in Museum of the City of New York

This lovely water color, known as the Prototype view, represents New Amsterdam three hundred years ago, at just about the time when, on February 2, 1653, the first municipal government was established. Manhattan Island still remained the personal property of the West India Company, and the director general of the province retained ultimate authority. But the new court of burgomasters and schepens (aldermen) was an important step toward self-government for the city.

Though this water color was made after the English captured the city in 1664 as indicated by the title ("New Amsterdam now New York on the Island of Man[hattan]"), it was made from an earlier drawing (now lost) which was also the basis of views used as insets on the famous Visscher map (c. 1655) and in the 1656 edition of Vander Donck's *Description of New Netherland.* The view was taken from a point off the tip of Manhattan, and shows the Hudson River shore up to present Rector Street and the East River shore almost to Coenties Slip. In the foreground, on Schreijer's Hook (named after the one in Amsterdam, page 33), is the little wharf where all passengers and goods were landed and embarked; behind it, the weighing beam and the crane. Just right of the windmill is the fort, containing, besides the barracks and jail, the church and, just behind and to the right of it, the governor's house. The three tall buildings just right of center (above the largest ship) are storehouses, one of which was the Company's, where goods and merchandise were received and dispatched. The large building on the shore at the right was the former city tavern, taken over in 1653 as the Stadt Huys (City Hall) where the burgomasters and schepens met.

Throughout the Dutch period, even in the carefully detailed surveys made for those responsible for the city's growth . . .

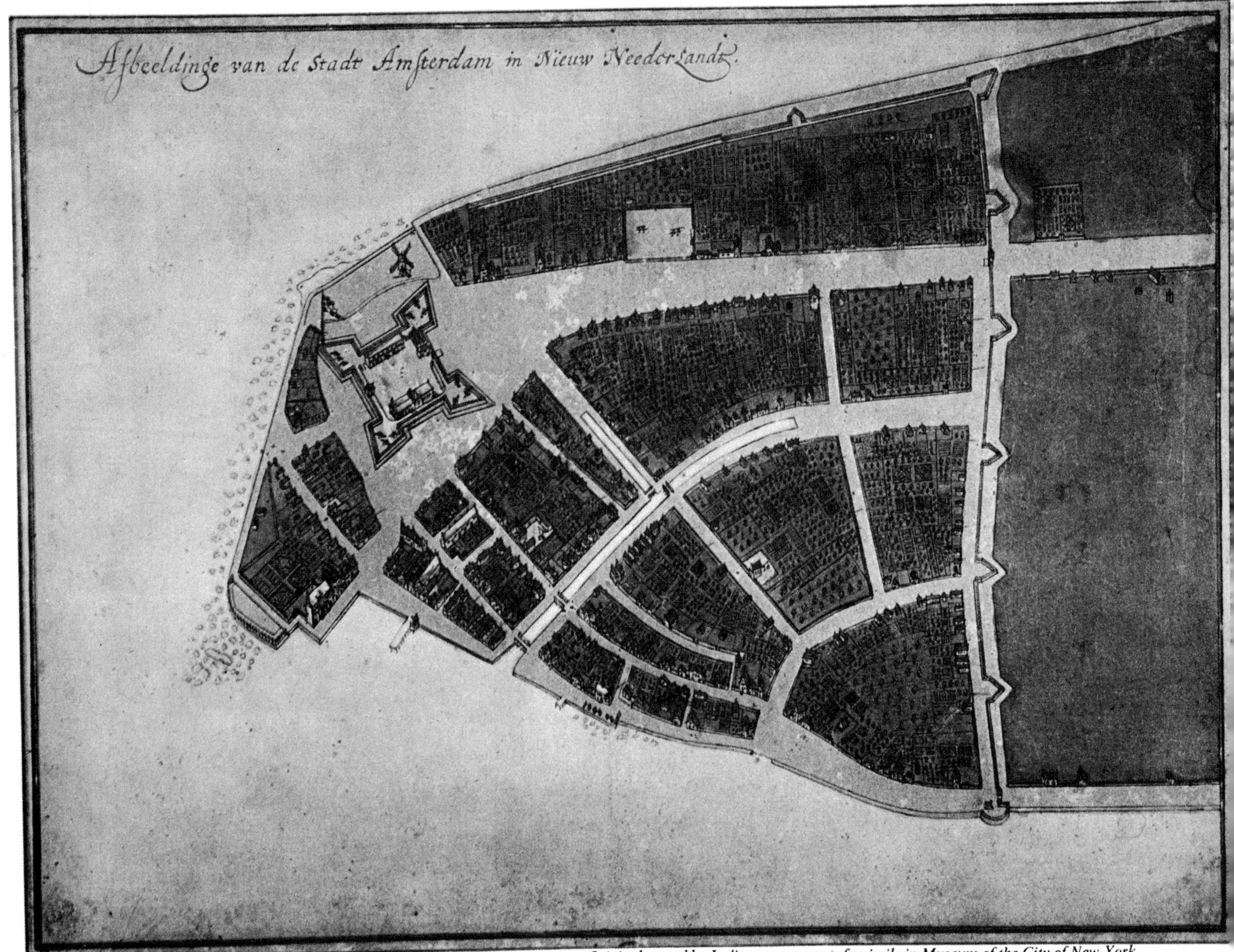

Original owned by Italian government; facsimile in Museum of the City of New York

This bird's-eye view (original 25″ × 18⅝″) is known as the Castello Plan, from the name of the villa near Florence in which it was discovered. Like the Manatus map (page 35), it is a copy, made about 1670, of an earlier Dutch drawing. The original was drawn in 1660 by Jacques Cortelyou, who was directed by the burgomasters on June 7 to survey and prepare a plan of the city. The reason for the survey was that the city fathers were hard pressed to find house sites for newcomers to the growing city, largely because "many spacious and large lots" had not been built upon, their owners preferring to use them as gardens or orchards while waiting for land values to rise. In October, Stuyvesant sent Cortelyou's plan to the directors at Amsterdam, and in December they acknowledged receipt of it but observed that "according to our opinion too great spaces are as yet without buildings . . . where the houses apparently are surrounded by excessively large plots and gardens." (Compare the bird's-eye plan of Amsterdam, p. 32.) Made only four years before the English captured New Amsterdam, this is the only plan of the city which has survived from the Dutch period. A rectified redraft, supervised by I. N. Phelps Stokes, was published in the *Iconography* (Vol. II), giving supplementary details derived from other sources. In style and manner, however, the redraft is affectionate and cozy, with a kind of antiquarian charm quite unlike the factual linear directness of the original plan.

... the perspective is westward,
and the burgers' houses seem to be facing Europe.

Drawn for this book by Sigman-Ward, New York City
Stippling indicates blocks and
streets of modern city

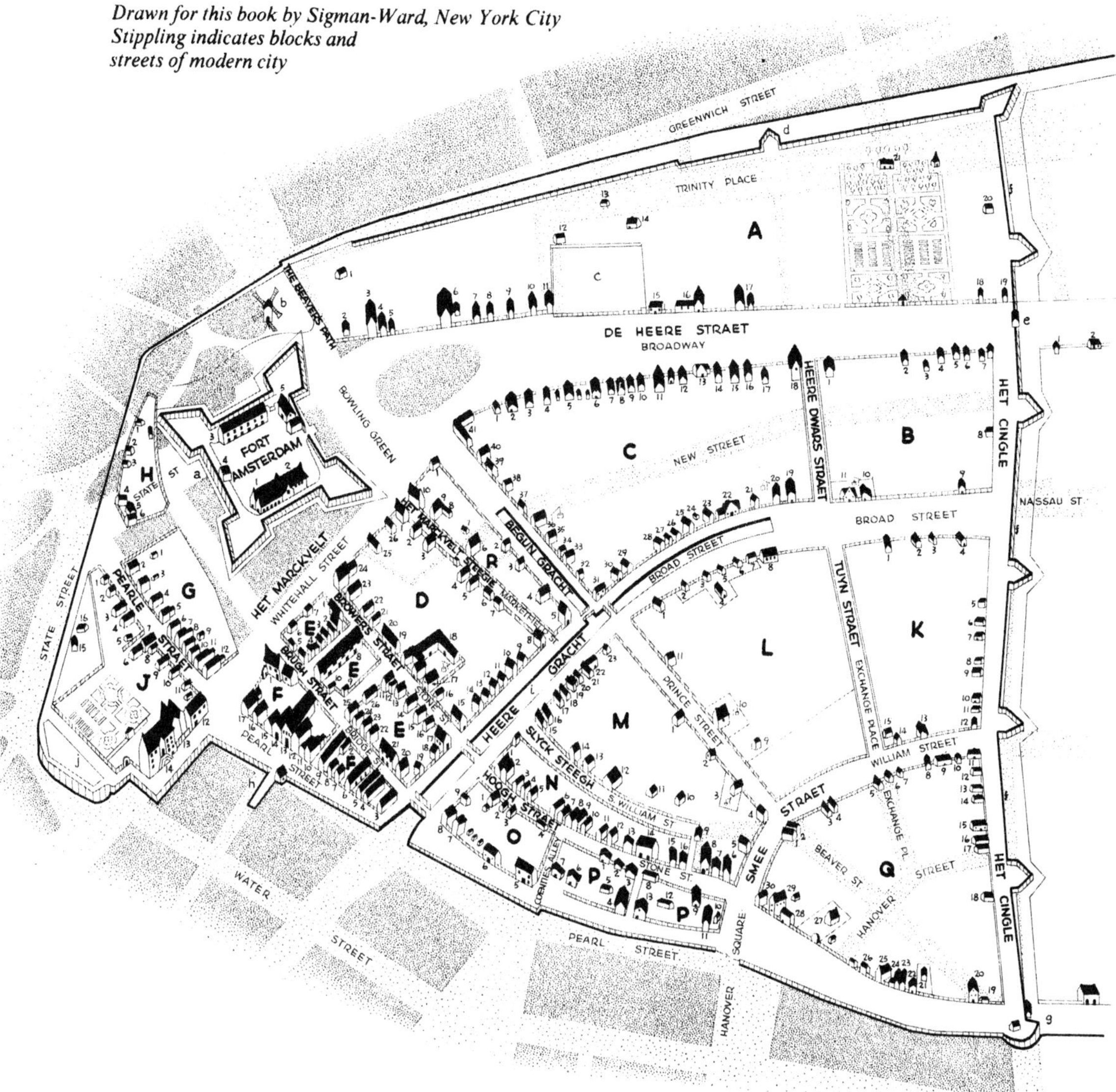

By an earlier survey, made in 1656, the streets of the little city had been "set off and laid out with stakes." At that time there were about 120 houses; now, four years later, there were over 300, most of which are identified in the key on this and the following page. An anonymous English "Description of ye Towne of Mannadens," dated just a year after this plan was made, tells us that it is "seated between New Engld and Virginia, commodiously for trade" and that it "hath good air, and is healthy, inhabited wth severall sorts of Trades-men and marchants and mariners." It was from this merchant-trader class that the officials of the first municipal government had been chosen in 1653. Of the first two burgomasters, Arent van Hatten had returned to Holland before 1660, but Martin Cregier, the tavernkeeper and captain of the burger guard, lived comfortably at the site of No. 3 Broadway (Block A, No. 3). Of the first schepens (or aldermen), Paulus Leendersen vander Grift (A-15 and 16) was a sea captain and trader whose warehouse (F-14) had been an important feature of the town in the Prototype view (page 39); William Beeckman lived outside the city wall at Corlaer's Hook; Pieter Wolphertsen van Couwenhoven, the brewer, lived near the fort (G-12) though his brewery was uptown (B-10); Maximilian van Gheel had left town by 1660, but had lived while a schepen at the house (E-2) now occupied by the wine and tobacco merchant, Frederick vanden Bergh; and Allardt Anthony, one of the first lawyers in town, lived in a large house (F-9) which had been "an ornament to the city" when built by Isaac de Forest in 1657.

KEY TO THE CASTELLO PLAN
(Based upon material in Stokes' *Iconography* and upon the key to the scale model of New Amsterdam in the Museum of the City of New York.)

PART A: A selected list of structures on the plan, in addition to those mentioned in the caption, a: Fort Amsterdam. Within the fort: 1. Dutch Reformed Church of St. Nicholas; 2. governor's house; 3. barracks for Company's soldiers; 4. guardhouse; 5. officers' quarters or storehouse; 6. Secretary's office. b: The grain mill. c: The cemetery. d: Small fortification, later contemptuously known as Oyster Pasty Mount. e: The Land Gate. f: Wall, built 1653; one of first projects of new municipal government. g: The Water Gate. h: Weighhouse Pier—first commercial pier on Manhattan, built 1659. i: The Heere Gracht, or canal (filled in in 1676). j: Probable site of gallows. Block J, No. 14: Peter Stuyvesant's "Great House." E6: Office of Jacques Cortelyou, surveyor who drew original of this plan. He lived on L. I. (near Fort Hamilton), but regularly worked at this office, one of the first commuters. G3: Home of Jacob Steendam, New Amsterdam's first poet. G1: Home of Trijin Jonas, town's first midwife. F17: House of Dr. Hans Kierstide, town's first regular physician. E9: New hospital, built 1659–60. J10: House of Egbert van Borsum, operator of the ferry to Brooklyn. F1: House of Cornelis Steenwyck, whose portrait is on p. 46. E8: The "five houses" of the West India Co., built before 1633, under single roof. Used as houses for the employees and as storehouses. D17, 18: Residence and brewery of Oloff Stevensen van Cortlandt, burgomaster 1655–65. D20: Offices of Amsterdam firm of Gillis Verbrugge & Co., Dutch traders. D4: Occupied by family Barentzen; house owned by Jan Evertsen Bout. Adriaen vander Donck lived here while writing the *Remonstrance of New Netherland* (1649).
Bout lived in Brooklyn, where he was one of first village schepens in 1646. A6: House of Domine Johannes Megapolensis, who had been the first Protestant missionary to the Indians while at Rensselaerswyck (1642–48). O5: Stadt Huys, or City Hall, converted from the City Tavern in 1653 (see p. 39). M12: House of Evert Duyckingh, glassmaker and limner. On this site (22 S. William St.) in 1729 the first Jewish synagogue in New York was erected. L6: "Trivial School"—elementary Latin school supported by the city. L8: House of Nicasius de Sille, fiscal (secretary) and schout (sheriff) of West India Co.'s colony. His office was E10. Q27, 28: Property of Goovert Loockermans, wealthy merchant, who represented Gillis Verbrugge & Co. (see D20, above). The house was later owned by the famous pirate, Captain William Kidd (1691–95).

Key to Castello Plan: PART B

BLOCK A

1: Tavern of Lodowyck Pos: captain of the Rattle Watch. 2: Pieter Laurenzen Cock. 4, 5: Jacob de Lang. 7: Lucas Andries. 8: Barent Cruytdop. 9: Dirck Wiggerts. 10: Tavern of Lucas Dircksen. 11: Reindert Jansen Hoorn. 12, 13: Domine Samuel Drisius, the second Dutch clergyman. 14: Laurens Andriessen. 17: Hendrick van Dyck. 18: Jacobus Vis. 19: Cornelis Jansen Pluyvier, innkeeper. 20: Domine Samuel Drisius. 21: West India Co.'s garden.

BLOCK B

1: Augustine Herrman. 2: Pieter Schaefbanck, jailer. 3: Joseph Waldron. 4: Resolveert Waldron. 5: Dirck Siecken. 6: Leandert Aerden. 7: Hendrick Hendricksen. 8, 9: Domine Samuel Drisius. 11: The Latin School.

BLOCK C

1, 2: Residence and tavern of Abraham Pietersen. 3: Gerrit Fullewever. 4: Sergeant Pieter Ebel. 5: Geertie, widow of Andries Hoppen (Hopper). 6: Ensign Dirck Smit. 7: Jan Hendricksen van Gunst. 8: Thomas Fransen. 9: Samuel Edsal, owner. Jan Fries, tenant. 10: Weyntje Elbers, widow of Aert Willemsen. 11: Isaac Grevenraet. 12: Peter Rudolphus. 13: Gabriel de Haas. 14: Boardinghouse of Claes Ganglofs Visscher. 15: Jacobus Kip. 16: Jacobus Vis. 17, 18: Col. Philip Pietersen Schuyler. 19: Deacons' House for the Poor. 20, 21: Jacobus Kip. 22: Pieter Rudolphus. 23: Jan Cornelissen, Weighhouse porter. 24: Jacob Mensen, tailor. 25: Daniel Tourneur, one of early settlers of village of Haarlem. 26, 27, 28: Coenraet Ten Eyck. 29: Dirck Jansen. 30: Boele Roeloffsen. 31: Thomas Fredericksen. 32: Toussaint Briel. 33, 34: Thomas Wandel of Mespat Kill. 35: Probably first poorhouse. 36: Paulus vander Beeck. 37: William Bredenbent. 38, 39, 40: Egbert Woutersen. 41: Jan Jansen from Brestede; Christiaen Pieters, tenant.

BLOCK D

1: Frederick Arentsen. 2: Gerrit Hendricksen from Harderwyck. 3: Nicolaes Boot, trader. 5: Joannes Verveelen. 6, 7: Oloff Stevensen van Cortlandt, who also owned 14, 17, 18. 8: Pieter van Naarden. 9: Coenraet Ten Eyck. 10, 11: Reynout Reynoutsen. 12: Gerrit Jansen Roos. 13: Hendrick Jansen Spiers. 15: Frederick Lubbertsen, of Breuckelen. 16: Abraham de la Noy. 19: Isaac de Forest. 21: Jeronimus Ebbingh. 23: Surgeon Varrevanger (formerly Wooden Horse tavern of Philip Geraerdy). 24: Frederick Philipse. 25: Teunis Tomassen (Quick). 26: Gerrit Hendricksen from Harderwyck.

BLOCK E

1: Hendrick Willems. 3: Warnaer Wessels. Former home of Domine Everardus Bogardus, first permanent clergyman in New Amsterdam. 4: Pieter Jacobsen Buys. 5: Jane, widow of George Holmes, one of earliest English settlers. 7: Frederick Gijsbertsen vanden Bergh. 11: Caspar Steymensen. 12: Jan Jansen from St. Obin. 13: Jacob Kip and Jacob Strycker. 14: Jacob Kip. 15, 16: Isaac Kip. 17: Oloff Stevensen van Cortlandt. 18: Symon Jansen Romeyn. 19, 20: Hendrick Willems. 21, 22: Anthony Jansen van Salee ("Anthony the Turk"). 23, 24, 25, 26: Hendrick Hendricksen Kip.

BLOCK F

2: Tavern of Hendrick Jansen Smith. 3: Tavern of Hans Dreper. 4, 5: Frans Jansen van Hooghten. 6: Bakeshop of Nicolaes Jansen. 7: Hatter's shop of Samuel Edsal. 8: Johannes de Decker. 10, 11: "Van Tienhoven's Great House", property of his heirs and creditors. 12: Warehouse of Augustine Herrman. 13: Pack House (warehouse) of the West India Co. 15, 16: Burgomaster Cornelis Steenwyck.

BLOCK G

2: Annetje Jans Bogardus. 4: Juriaen Blanck. 5: Tavern of Michiel Tadens. 6: Estate of Johannes van Beeck. 7: Claes Claessen Bordingh. 8: Hendrick Hendricksen Obe, city drummer. 9: Claes Jansen. 10: Isaac Gravenraet. 11: Jacques Cousseau.

BLOCK H

1: Jan Dircksen Meyer. 2: Paulus Heymans, of Leyden. 3: James Hubbard, one of founders of Gravesend, L. I. 4, 5: Jan Evertsen Bout, who resided chiefly in Breuckelen. 6: Isaac Gravanraet.

BLOCK J

1: Thomas Lambertsen. 2: Pieter Jacobsen Marius. 3: Nicholas Verlett. 4: Claes Jansen de Ruyter. 5: Lot owned by Jacques Cousseau. 6: François Allard. 7, 8: Sara Pietersen, wife of William Thomas Cock. 9: Gillis Pietersen vander Gouw; Paulus Schrick, tenant. 11: Pieter Cornelissen vander Veen. 12: Nicasius de Sille, probably occupied by his son Laurens. 13: Nicolaes Verlett, brother-in-law of Governor Stuyvesant. Later bought by Jacob Leisler. 15: Tavern of Nichiel Jansen Vreeland. 16: Warehouse of Jacob Stoffelsen.

BLOCK K

1–8: Original grant to Domine Samuel Drisius, who built the four houses on the present Broad St., and the four facing the wall. 9: Jan Jansen, from Languedyck. 10: Abraham Kermell. 11: Hendrick Jansen Sluyter. 12: Cornelis Hendricksen. 13: Arent Lourens. 14: Janneken Bonus, wife of Thomas Verdon. 15: Widow of Albert Jansen.

BLOCK L

1: Douwe Hermsen. 2: Jan Swaen, of Stockholm. 3: Jacob Strycker. 4: Jacob Luybeck. 5: Jacob Strycker and Secretary Cornelis van Ruyven. 7: Thomas Wandel. 9: Augustine Herrman; occupied by Pieter Pietersen, the Mennonite. 10: Red Lion Brewery, owned by Isaac de Forest, Joannes Verveelen, and the De la Montagnes. 11: Albert Pietersen.

BLOCK M

1: Robert Roelantsen; William Abrahamsen (Vander Borden), tenant. 2: Pieter Gysen. 3: Brewhouse of Michiel Jansen (Vreeland) of Communipaw. 4: Geertje Jans Stoffelsen. 5: Meindert Barentsen. 6: Dirck Jansen van Deventer. 7: Thomas Wandel. 8, 9: House and warehouse of Rutger Jacobsen; occupied by Abraham de Lucena, prominent Jewish merchant. 10: Domine Johannes Megapolensis. 11: Jan Reyndersen. 13: Joost Goderus. 14: "The house of the Company's negroes." Built by the West India Co., before 1643, to house its slaves. 15: Tavern of Adriaen Vincent, a Walloon. 16: Skipper Tomas Davidts. 17, 18: John Vincent and Anna Vincent, children of Adriaen Vincent. 19, 20: Abraham Jansen. 21: Tavern of Jan Rutgersen. 22: Jacobus Backer. 23: Jochem Beeckman.

BLOCK N

1, 2: House and brewery Jacob Wolphertsen van Couwenhoven. 3: Claas Carstensen, a Norwegian. 4: Grietje Dircks, wife of Barent Gerritsen. 5: Magdalena Waele, wife of Gysbert Teunnissen. 6: Thomas Wandel. 7: Tavern of Pieter Andriessen. 8, 9, 10: Nicolaes de Meyer of Holsteyn. 11: Tielman van Vleck. 12: Tavern of Aris Otto. 13, 14: Skipper Wessel Evertsen. 15: Asser Levy. 16: David Jochemszen.

BLOCK O

1: Adolph Pietersen. 2: Jan Cornelissen van Hooren. The three small sheds fronting Pearl St. were probably fishermen's sheds. 3: Sybrant Jansen de Galma. 4: "The Hall on High St. in back of the Stadt Huys." Possibly a storehouse. 6: Rem Jansen. 7: Sybout Claessen. 8: Hendrick Jansen vander Vin. 9: Cornelis Melyn.

BLOCK P

1, 2: Charles Bridges, an Englishman, known as Carel van Brugge. 3, 4: House and tavern of Solomon La Chair. 5, 6: Charles Bridges (Carol van Brugge). 7: Tavern of George Wolsey. 8: Richard Smith. 9: Evert Duyckingh (see Part A, M-12). 10, 11: Abraham Martens Clock. 12, 13: Richard Smith.

BLOCK Q

1, 2: The stillhouse and smithy of Burger Jorissen (see No. 30). 3: Estate of Govert Loockermans. 4: Metje Juriaens. 5, 6, 7: Jacob Hendricksen Varravanger. 8: Tavern of Andries Rees. 9: Ide Cornelissen van Vorst. 10: Immetje Dircks, widow of Frans Claessen. 11: A double house owned by Teuntje Straatmans and her husband, Gabriel Carpesy. 12: Albert Cornelissen Wantenaar. 13: Pieter Jansen Trinbolt (the Norman). 14: Pieter Andriessen. 15: Jacob Jansen Moesman. 16: Arien Dircksen. 17: Abraham de la Noy, the younger. 18: Lambert Huybertsen Mol. 19: Tryntje Scheerenburgh. 20: Tavern of Sergeant Daniel Litschoe. 21: Jacob Jansen Flodder. 22: John Lawrence. 23: Andries Jochemsen, occupied by Agatha vander Donck. 24: Andries Jochemsen, occupied by Claes Claesen Smith. 25: Tavern of Andries Jochemsen. 26: Willem Pietersen. 29: Johannes van Brugh. 30: Burger Jorissen.

BLOCK R

1: Tobacco warehouse of Albert Andriessen. 2: Hendrick Egbertsen. 3: Hendrick van Bommel. 4, 5: Willem Cornelis. 6: Tavern of Pierre Pia, a Frenchman; owned by Joannes Verveelen. 7: Jan Jansen Hagenaar. 8: Andries Claessen. 9: Claes van Elslant. 10: Albert Andriessen.

BEYOND THE WALL

1: Sybout Claessen. 2: Jacques Pryn. 3: Lysbet Tyssen, widow of Maryn Adriaensen.

To many people in Europe, of course, facts about New Amsterdam were of no importance. A completely fictitious view would do, if it matched their idea of what a city was.

Collection of Edward W. C. Arnold; photograph courtesy of Museum of the City of New York

This fantastic engraved view, dated 1672 and signed by the French engraver Jollain, was undoubtedly part of a series or collection of plans and views of cities, of which a number were issued in Europe in the seventeenth century. Though dated when the English had control of the city, the title and description refer to Dutch times. The artist has apparently used as his model a view of Lisbon, Portugal, issued many years earlier. Certainly the view has nothing to do with New Amsterdam. Notice Quebec perched on the thumb-shaped hill at upper right, and the busy Place de la Bourse at left center. The description, in Latin and French, tells us the city is "famous for its grandeur, its commerce, and the large number of its inhabitants, the length and excellence of its harbor, the beautiful structure of its churches and fine buildings, and for its admirable situation." In the French, but not in the Latin, there is a final clause saying it is a place "where the discontented often betake themselves."

To the Dutch and the English, however, New Amsterdam was a key to the vast, savage interior of the continent— a key worth fighting for.

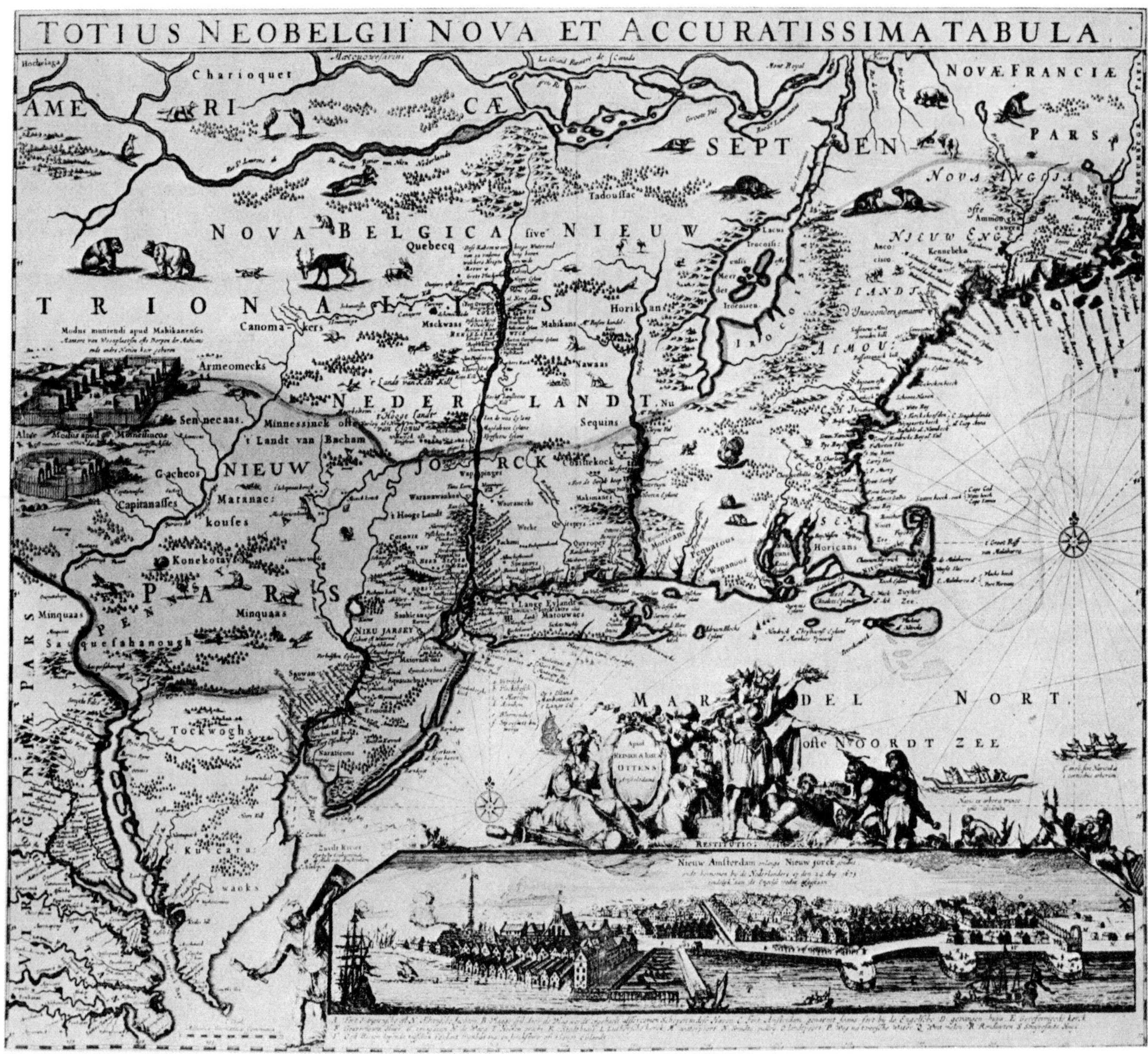

J. Clarence Davies Collection, Museum of the City of New York

This so-called "Restitutio Map and View" takes its name from the word engraved beneath the central figure in the allegorical group (lower right), which was designed to celebrate the recapture of the city by the Dutch in 1673 and the restoration (for a few months) of Dutch rule. The fleet of Admiral Cornelis Evertsen, who recaptured the city, is shown off the south coast of Long Island.

The copy reproduced here is a late state of the map, which was originally published (and probably engraved) by Carolus Allardt in Holland.

As for the people who lived there, or the lives they led, we have almost no visual record except for the absurd little figures scratched on the engraved views of the town . . .

Inset view from map on page 44

The Restitutio view of "New Amsterdam formerly called New York and now retaken by the Netherlanders on the 24 August 1673" was probably drawn soon after the Dutch reoccupied the town. (This late state of the view has the added words "finally again surrendered to the English," but is in other respects identical with previous issues.) As was so often the case with early views of the city, this one served as the prototype of a whole series, including the Carolus Allardt view reproduced on page 13. There are many inaccuracies in the picture, the most noticeable of which is the exaggerated size of the fortified roundout batteries, and it is possible that the view was worked up in Holland from rough sketches made on the spot or from verbal descriptions.

Detail from above view, one and one half times original size

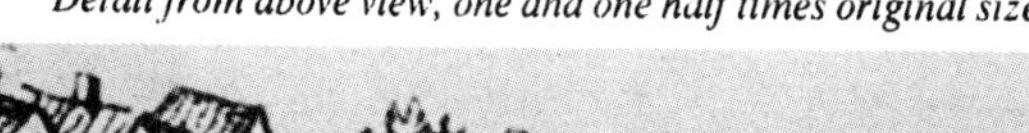

. . . and a few portraits of prominent burgers, painted after the English captured the city.

New-York Historical Society

It is not known whether this portrait of former Burgomaster Cornelis Steenwyck (c. 1668) was painted in this country or in Holland. In any case, it undoubtedly shows us the man as he liked to be seen. There is a touch of elegance in the heraldic device at the top of the painted frame (Steenwyck served as mayor under English rule in 1668 and 1669); but there is Dutch plainness in the firmly modeled face, and the textures of cloth and lace do not distract our attention from it. The inset view of New Amsterdam (based, apparently, upon the Prototype view, page 39) emphasizes his long association with the town's development.

Not until 1679, when this crude drawing was made, did anyone attempt to depict the city from any but an external, westward-looking point of view.

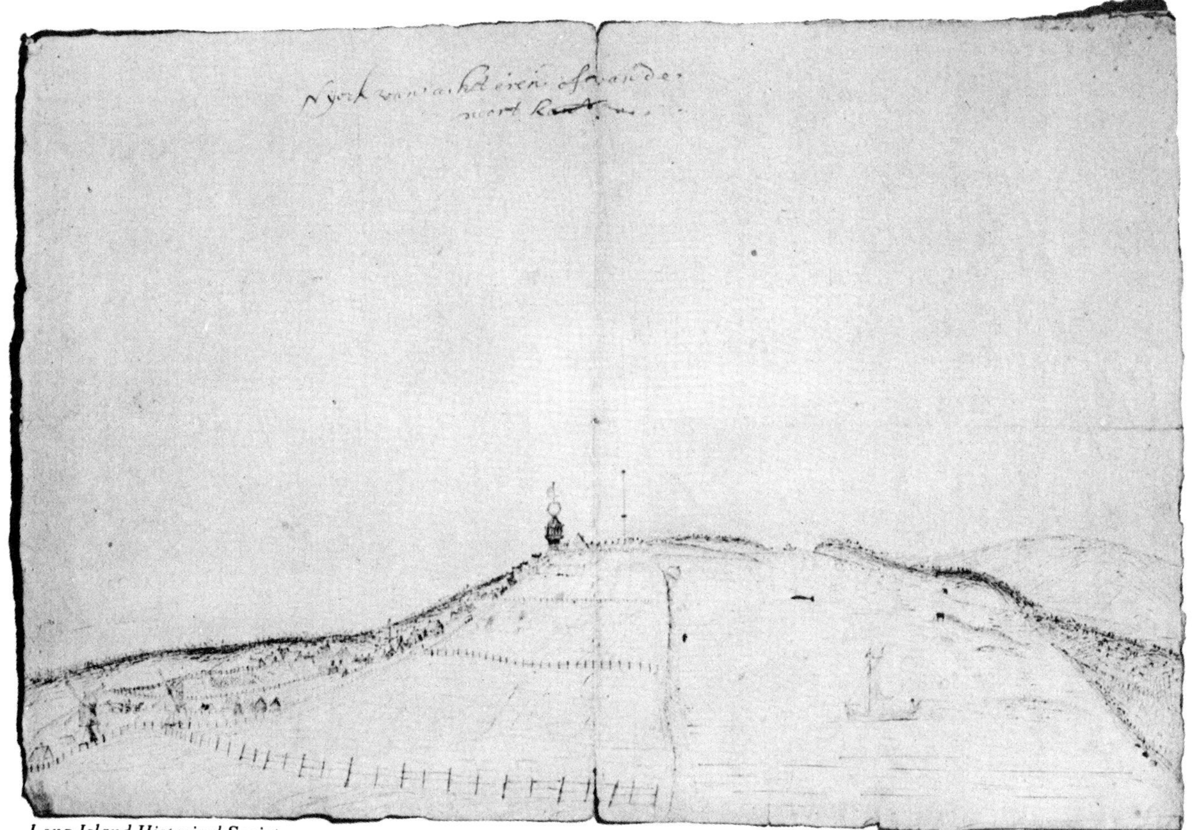

Long Island Historical Society

This view of "N ÿork from behind or from the north side" is the only known picture of the city made from a point on Manhattan Island in the seventeenth century, and the only one to show the west shore of the island, except the Herrman painting on page 38. It is one of three pen and ink drawings of the city contained in a manuscript *Journal of a Voyage to New York* (1679–80), by Jasper Danckaerts and Peter Sluyter, two Hollanders who were looking for a suitable place to establish a colony of the Labadist sect to which they belonged. Danckaerts was the scribe and probably the artist of the *Journal,* and for all his shortcomings as a draftsman his pictures are obviously honest attempts to record exactly what he saw.

This sketch was made from a point close to the Hudson shore (that *is* the river at right of center, with the boat and the spouting whale in it), probably near present Duane Street. The bulbous tower is, of course, a greatly exaggerated version of the tower on the church in the fort, with the flagpole to its right. Broadway runs diagonally from the fort toward the windmill, lower left, which stood in present City Hall Park, just south of Chambers Street. The wagon between the two mills is the earliest known picture of a horse-drawn vehicle in the city.

By that time the city wall and the roundout batteries, which had seemed so important in the view made during Dutch-English hostilities . . .

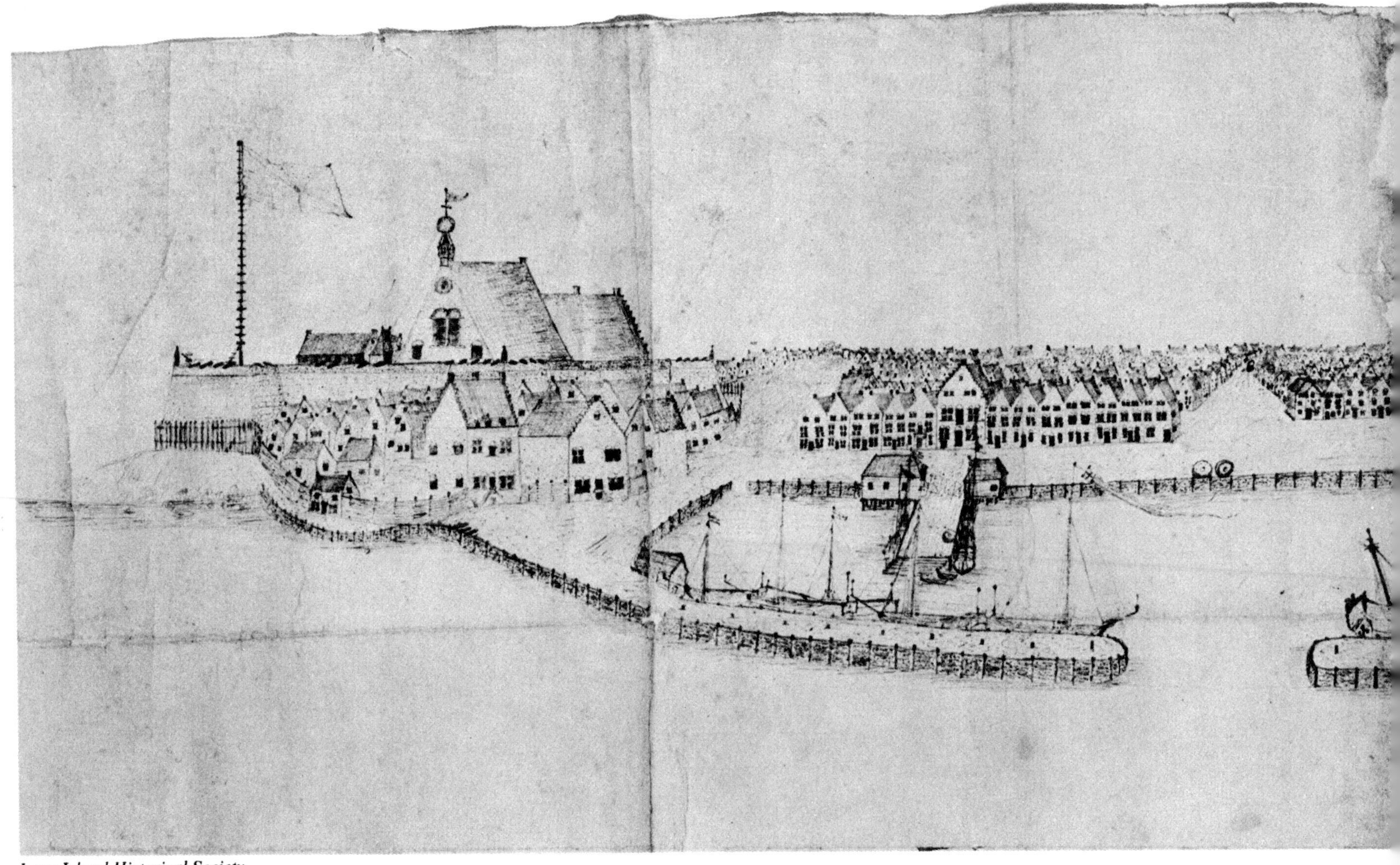

Long Island Historical Society

The largest and most ambitious of Danckaerts' drawings was this general view of the city in 1679–80. Made from Brooklyn Heights, it shows the city from the southern tip to a point beyond the outlet of the Fresh Water (or Collect) Pond, which lay east of Broadway, north of present City Hall Park. Notice that this view shows us much farther into the interior of the town than any earlier view; we can see down Whitehall Street (at left), for example, to the houses on the far side of Broadway, facing modern Bowling Green.

Danckaerts and Sluyter found New York "a pretty sight" as their ship approached it from the Narrows, but were troubled by the "wild worldly" character of its inhabitants when they landed. One day, after watching a militia muster, Danckaerts described the drill in his *Journal.* "Some were on horseback, and six small companies were on foot," he wrote. "They were exercised in military tactics, but I have never seen anything worse of the kind." Clearly, as the principal features of his picture suggest, martial matters were secondary to those of expanding commerce.

. . . have dwindled to insignificance, in the eyes of an inquiring visitor, compared with the new commercial dock and the growing settlement beyond the wall.

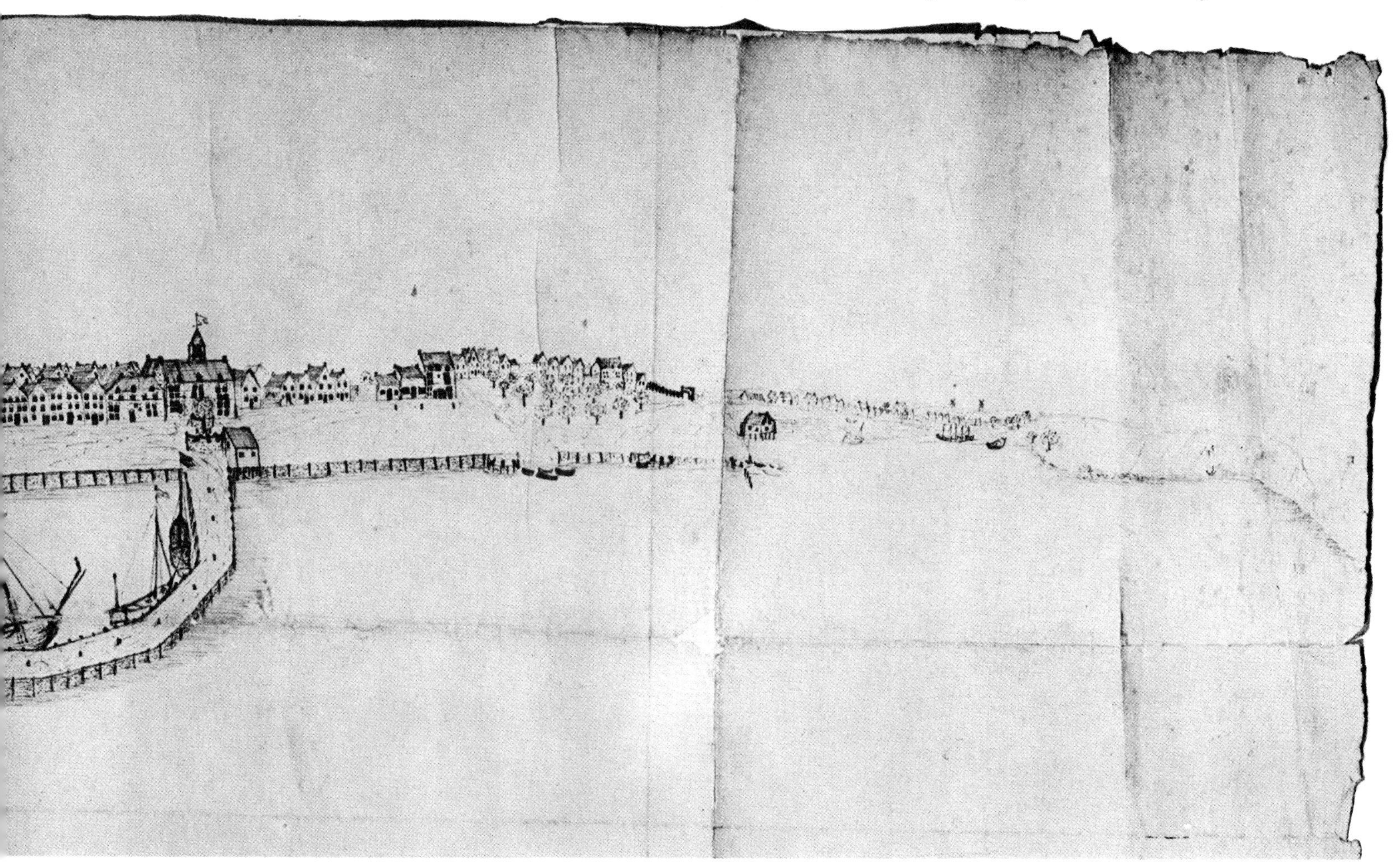

The principal physical changes in the town, in the five years since the English took permanent possession, were all in the nature of urban improvements. Most of the old landmarks remained. The fort, renamed Fort James, was in other respects little changed. Stuyvesant's Great House, on the shore just below the church in the fort, was still the grandest house in town, and was lived in at this time by Captain Thomas Delavell, the mayor of the city. The old West India Company warehouse still stood on Pearl Street, at the head of the wharf, though it was now known as the King's Warehouse and Custom House.

Of the new structures, the most impressive was the recently completed Great Dock, extending from Whitehall to Coenties Slip, in front of the City Hall. (One of the roundout batteries is just visible at the City Hall end of the dock.) A new Market House, built (1677) on piles over the water, can be seen left of the wharf, across from the Weighhouse. Uptown, beyond the wall, is the newly constructed Slaughterhouse, built out over the water away from other houses. Farther right, along the Smith's Vly (Flats), is a row of houses, in one of which Danckaerts and Sluyter stayed. Beyond and behind them are the two new mills which appear in left foreground of the view on page 47.

With the change to English rule, life in New York came under more courtly influences . . .

New-York Historical Society

When Indian sachems were received at court in London and had their portraits painted, by order of Queen Anne, in the conventional poses of aristocratic portraiture, it was only natural that the fashion should spread to wealthy colonials. This is a mezzotint engraving, made by John Simon, of a portrait of Tee Yee Ho Ga Row, "Emperor of the Six Nations," which was painted in London by John Verelst in 1710. Many of these mezzotints were sent to America for sale in the colonies.

Tiyonoga, as he was usually called, was a Mohawk chief who was one of the five Indian kings taken to London by Colonel Peter Schuyler in an effort to impress them with England's power.

. . . though the strong Dutch middle-class tradition was still reflected in the inelegant honesty with which even well-to-do citizens were sometimes portrayed.

New-York Historical Society

This portrait of Mrs. David Provoost, whose son became mayor of the city in 1699, was made about 1700 by an unknown artist, relatively untouched by the "dash and glitter" of the fashionable English portrait style. Here are reflected the solid bourgeois qualities which still persisted, side by side with the increasing elegance fostered among the wealthy merchants and gentlefolk by the example of the royal governors. David Provoost was a baker, the son of the David Provoost whose farm was shown at No. 25 on the Manatus map (page 36).

By the second decade of the eighteenth century, pictures of the city reflected a mixture of pride in the increasing elegance of its façade . . .

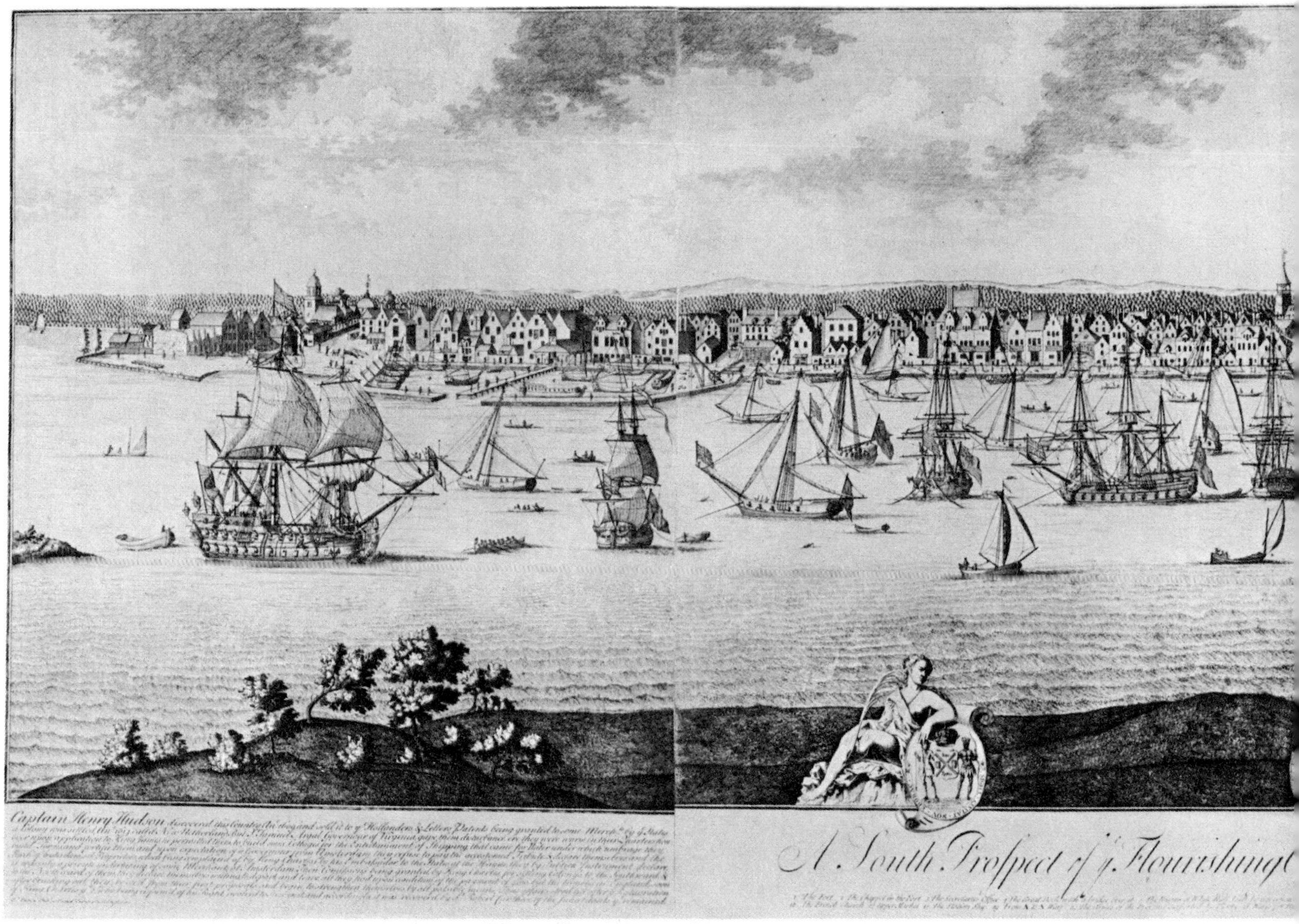

Collection of Edward W. C. Arnold; photograph courtesy of Metropolitan Museum of Art

"A South Prospect of the Flourishing City . . ." as it was mistakenly called (since it was from the east), was drawn by William Burgis about 1717. It is a six-foot panorama (77″ × 20½″) printed from four separate copper plates engraved by John Harris of London. Like the earlier views on pages 45 and 48–49, the drawing was made from Brooklyn Heights, but here for the first time the Brooklyn ferry landing is shown and the landscape of the Jersey shore is clearly depicted in the background. The presence of so many ships in the East River, two of which are firing salutes, suggests that the view was intended to celebrate some special occasion, possibly King George's birthday on May 28, 1717. In any event, the prominence assigned to the vessels of the Royal Navy, to the seals of the city and province, and to the elaborately ornamented dedicatory panel (see page 18), all bespeak pride in the city's role as a provincial capital. At this period New York was the third largest city in the colonies, with a population in 1720 of about 7000. (Boston and Philadelphia, both founded after New Amsterdam, had populations of about 12,000 and 10,000 respectively. If these figures seem small, it should be remembered that even in England there were only a few larger towns at this period. Urbanization had scarcely begun.)

. . . and an urban interest in the life and occupations of its inhabitants. Here for the first time our attention is called . . .

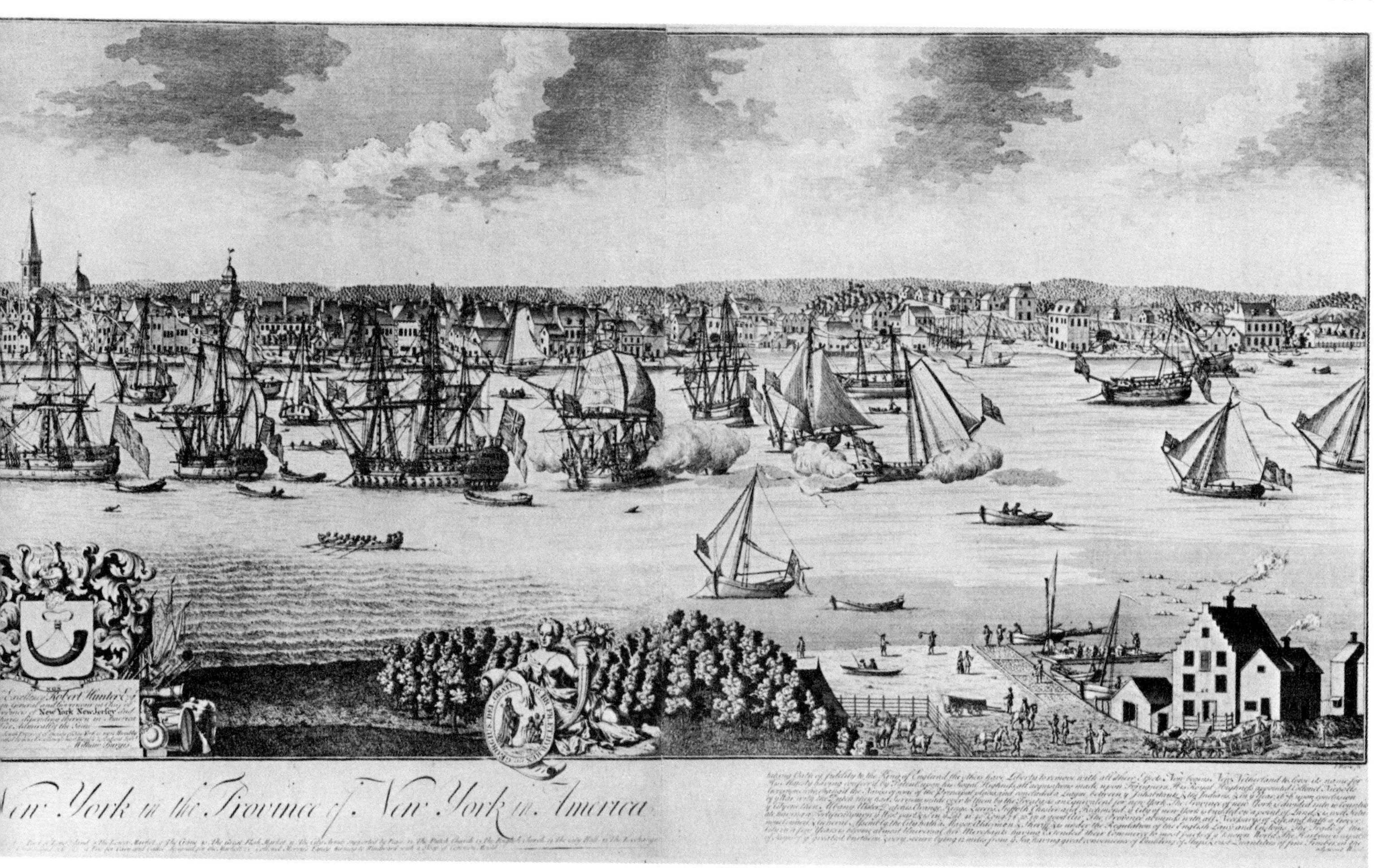

ew York in the Province of New York in America

The city as Burgis saw it was assuming a new and more modern appearance. The medieval Dutch architecture of the old city below Wall Street, with its stepped gables and steep roofs, gave place in the upper town to Renaissance styles popular in England at the time. Even in the old part of town there were significant changes. Stuyvesant's "Great House," more recently known as Whitehall, was a burned-out shell, and the old Stadt Huys, at the north end of the Great Dock, had been torn down. The peak of the city's skyline is no longer the church in the fort (now Fort George), but has moved uptown to the vicinity of Wall Street where the first Trinity Church (1696–98; steeple 1711) may be seen just right of the center fold, flanked to the south by the Dutch Church (1692–96) and to the right by the new City Hall (on site of present Sub-Treasury) and the Eglise du St. Esprit on Pine Street (1704).

The entire waterfront of the lower city has been moved out into the East River, so that the houses on Pearl Street, which fronted the river in earlier views, are now a block inland and are hidden from view by newer structures. Among the most conspicuous houses are those of such merchant-aristocrats as Philip van Cortlandt (with two stepped-gable dormers to the right of the pier), Tobias Ten Eyck (behind the fish market shed at Coenties Slip), Robert Livingston (who owned the house with the enormously tall chimneys, which had formerly belonged to his associate, Captain Kidd, the pirate), Colonel Abraham de Peyster (the second of the two large houses with gardens, just north of the French church), and Abraham Wendell (at extreme right, site now inland at Cherry and Catherine streets).

. . . by gestures as unhurried and stylized as those of the courtly gentlemen in the picture itself, to scenes of urban life . . .

Detail of Burgis view, pages 52–53, about two thirds original size

The gentlemen on the ferry landing in Brooklyn
are pointing out to their ladies
the ferry house, built in 1700, where James Harding
kept the "publick house of Entertainment"
required by his franchise as ferryman;
the farmer's ox-drawn cart bringing produce
from a Long Island farm for the city's market;
and the ferry for livestock on the way
to Johannes Beeckman's new slaughterhouse,
standing on piles at the shore directly across the river
(see large view).

The detail at left looks down Wall Street,
over the roof of the Exchange (established in 1670),
to Trinity Church and the City Hall (1699).

At lower right is the first picture of a New Yorker's
private yacht, Colonel Lewis Morris' *Fancy*.

Details, actual size

. . . and we become Addisonian "spectators" of activities in the city streets, on the Exchange, in the shipyards, and at the ferry.

Details, actual size

When the Huguenot John Fontaine came to New York from Virginia in 1716, he noted in his *Journal:* "There are but two coaches belonging to this province, because of the badness of the roads, though there are many rich people." And there are two coaches in the Burgis view, one proceeding westward on Whitehall Street, past the old church and the governor's house, and the other standing on the bluff (left) above the shipyard at the intersection of Pearl and Cherry streets (then Queen and Sackett).

Detail, actual size

The four shipyards along the East River shore (five, if you count the vessel drawn up on the shore at Whitehall) remind us that the city lived almost wholly by trade with the West Indies and Britain. From 1717 to 1720 an average of about 225 vessels cleared the port every year.

New York was more than a century old, however, before any pictures showed it as it might look to someone walking its streets. Significantly, the first of these . . .

This engraved view of the New Dutch Church was drawn, and possibly engraved, by William Burgis late in 1731. So far as we know, the print reproduced here is the only surviving copy. The church, later known as the Middle Dutch Church, was erected 1727–31. It stood on the east side of Nassau Street, between Crown (now Liberty) Street and Little Queen (now Cedar) Street. The coach, proceeding eastward on Crown Street, may have been intended to represent Rip van Dam's, since the view was dedicated to him, but coaches were fairly common among wealthy New Yorkers by this time. The church in the right background of the view was the Eglise du St. Esprit on King (Pine) Street. Services in the Dutch Church were still performed in Dutch for a generation after this time, but by 1756 there were signs that a change was due. In an account of the city written in that year, William Smith, author of the first history of the city, warns that although the Dutch congregation is still the most numerous in the city, "as the language becomes disused, it is much diminished; and unless they change their worship into the English tongue, must soon suffer a total dissipation." Eight years later, exactly one hundred years after Stuyvesant's surrender of New Amsterdam, English preaching was finally introduced in this and the other Dutch Reformed churches in the city.

Metropolitan Museum of Art

. . . proudly calls attention to such symbols of urban prosperity as a new church, a coach, and a paved street, while the second earnestly records that most pressing of urban problems, fire.

Stokes Collection, New York Public Library

This view of an unidentified New York street is an enlarged detail reproduced from a notice-of-meeting of the Hand-in-Hand Fire Company, which was probably engraved about 1750.
Fire had threatened the community from the start (there had been a "general conflagration" in 1626!), and the city records bear witness to the increasing concern with fire control after 1648 (when the first fire wardens were appointed).
In 1737 the legislature had authorized the Common Council to select forty-two "strong able Discreet honest and Sober Men" as "ffiremen of the City of New York," thus establishing the fire department. The first two fire engines in the city had been brought over from England in 1731, and by 1750 there were six engines.
The engraved view shows the firemen passing buckets of water from the well-pump (left) to be poured into the engine, where six men, three on a side, work the pump which forces the stream through the nozzle held by the fireman on top of the engine. The people at right are carrying things from the burning house in sacks and baskets. The chief, right of engine, is shouting directions through his trumpet.

By then a native portraiture was developing, whose naïve and exuberant energy disrupted the formal patterns of imported English styles.

Colonel A. C. M. Azoy, owner; courtesy of Metropolitan Museum of Art, American Wing

This painting of "Eva and Katherine de Peyster" was painted about 1728 by an unidentified artist (possibly Pieter Vanderlyn) who was one of a group identified by James Thomas Flexner as the "Patroon Painters." These painters, who met the demand for decorative portraits among wealthy New York families in the 1720s and 1730s, worked closely with one another to produce what Flexner calls "the first recognizable school in American art." With sweeping lines and gay colors, they translated the symbols of the cosmopolitan English style into terms which were suited to a region accustomed to homely Dutch realism. The De Peyster family symbolized the merging influences. Abraham de Peyster, who died in 1728, was the son of one of the early Dutch burgers, and had served variously under the English as mayor, chief justice, chairman of the King's Provincial Council, and acting governor. His house is shown on page 53.

But views of the city still showed it as the English saw it— a colonial outpost defended by His Majesty's ships and men.

Collection of Edward W. C. Arnold; photograph courtesy of Museum of the City of New York

This "View of Fort George with the City of New York" is the first known view of the city from the west. Drawn sometime between 1731 and 1736, probably by a naval officer, it was engraved by John Carwitham and published in London as one of a collection of *Views of Cities.* The eight steeples, or towers, are numbered, indicating that there was originally an accompanying descriptive text. They are, left to right: Trinity Church (see page 54); the Lutheran Church (erected 1727–29, southwest corner Broadway and Rector); the New Dutch Church (see page 56); Eglise du St. Esprit (see page 53); City Hall; Old Dutch Church (on Garden Street); the secretary's office in the fort; and the rebuilt chapel in the fort. The governor's house appears in the view as an extension of the chapel. To the right of the fort may be seen the roof of the DeLancey mansion, later Fraunces Tavern (southeast corner Broad and Pearl).

The middle years of the eighteenth century produced few pictures of the city, but many surveys, charts, and descriptive works.

Eno Collection, New York Public Library

Collection of Allen S. Davenport

The mariner's chart, from the *English Pilot* (1749), was one of a number of similar drafts of the harbor made in this period. William Bradford, New York's first printer, published one in 1735, and a very similar one was engraved in the same year by Carwitham, who had done the "View of Fort George" (page 59). Bradford and Carwitham also did plans of the city itself at about this time, the former's based upon the survey by James Lyne.

These were prosperous times for the port of New York. From 1747 to 1762 the number of ships owned by New Yorkers increased from 99 to 447, and the number of seamen employed rose from 755 to 3552. A large share of the port's activities do not appear on official records of imports and exports, however, since many of its vessels were engaged in smuggling and privateering. A letter in a New York newspaper, June 6, 1748, protested that "scarce a Week passes without an illicit Trader's going out or coming into this Port . . . who are continually supplying and supporting our most avowed Enemies [the French]."

Culturally the city was also making progress. The New York Society Library, the oldest in the city, was founded in 1754, the same year that King's College (now Columbia) was established.

All that survives is an occasional view, such as this painting, done in the mode if not the spirit of the earlier engraved prospects . . .

New-York Historical Society

This anonymous painting (60″ × 37½″), made about 1757 by someone with a sign painter's eye for detail, clearly owes something of its vision of the city to the engraved Burgis view (pages 52–53). But it was done by someone whose point of view was far less closely identified with the interests of the royal governor and his circle. Here is the city as it would appear to one of those "mechanicks and tradesmen" whose influence was beginning to be felt in local politics, in opposition to the court party. There is a cart in the view, but no coach, and the genteel ladies and courtly gentlemen have been replaced by merchants and dock workers and a shambling militia company.

Compare this painting also with the Carwitham view (page 59), in which the officers and men from the ships in the foreground dwarf the tiny citizens at the landing place. There is a ship's boat in the foreground here, also, and the painter is obviously interested in the ships (probably privateersmen, with a captured French prize); but the sailors are less than half the size of the distant figures on the waterfront.

. . . and some affectionate memory images, recorded long afterwards . . .

Both pictures lent by Miss Ethel M. Howell to Museum of the City of New York

This painting purports to show the south side of John Street between William (left) and Nassau streets in 1768. It was painted by Joseph B. Smith, probably in 1817 just before the demolition of Wesley's Chapel (center), the first Methodist church building erected in America. (The present John Street Methodist Church is the third to occupy the site.)

Smith made several pictures of the old church. In the water-color self-portrait at left, made about 1868, he sits before an easel bearing another John Street picture which was engraved for subscribers in that year. He holds a list of subscribers headed by the name of ex-Mayor James Harper, a loyal Methodist who founded Harper & Bros. publishing house. On the wall behind him is another of Smith's popular subscription pictures, "The Mechanic's Own," representing a clipper ship built in 1849 for an association of New York mechanics.

. . . by a man who knew his public's growing sense of history.

Details

John Street in 1768 was a quiet, middle-class neighborhood inhabited by painters, chairmakers, grocers, bookbinders, and the like. No. 34 was the home of William Colgate, tallow chandler, founder of the Colgate soap business. Most of the figures in Smith's painting are portraits from memory, including that of Wesley's disciple, Captain Thomas Webb (wearing a patch over the eye he lost at the siege of Louisburg in 1758), and that of Peter Williams, the Negro sexton who later went into the tobacco business and made enough money to finance the building of New York's first Methodist Church for Negroes (1800).

The steeple in the detail at right is that of the Middle Dutch Church, down Nassau Street at Liberty. The smaller steeple in the large picture was the First German Reformed Church (1765) on Nassau Street, south of John. The houses at extreme right were on west side of Nassau.

Increasing colonial self-consciousness in the years preceding the Revolution had already awakened interest in the city's past . . .

Library Company of Philadelphia

Pierre Eugène du Simitière was a Swiss-born artist and naturalist who devoted years of travel and study to compiling and collecting material for a history of North America. Among his "Papers relating to N. England N. York &c," there is a 1769 memorandum on old houses in the city with dates "marked by large irons." The oldest one he found was 1678, though he was certain there were older buildings in town. This pen and ink sketch was one of several he made while living in New York.

Ten years later Du Simitière offered for sale a number of "pictures, chiefly painted in oils, on boards . . . of those kinds the Dutch settlers brought a great many of with their furniture." He had found them in New York garrets where, as he put it, they had been "confined as unfashionable when that city was modernized." He had also collected a good deal of material on New Amsterdam, which is now among his manuscripts in the Free Library of Philadelphia and the Library of Congress.

. . . just as it had awakened the merchant citizen's pride in New York as his family home.

Lent by the Misses Shippen to Museum of the City of New York

In the years immediately preceding the Revolution there was a great increase in the number of portraits commissioned by New Yorkers. Throughout the American colonies, foreign and native-born artists were warmly encouraged, and many a European painter who had been unable to make a go of it at home found full employment over here. Among these was William Williams, an Englishman who successfully practiced all branches of the art in Philadelphia, including scene painting for the first theater in America, and who also wrote a novel and taught music. It was Williams who started young Benjamin West on his road to the Royal Academy.

Williams worked in New York in the early seventies, at which time he did this group portrait of "The Denning Family" (57¼″ × 40¾″). The picture was painted in 1772 at William Denning's Wall Street home. The colossal urn and pedestal are, of course, trappings which Williams carried over from scene painting into portraiture, but the little glimpse of landscape undoubtedly shows the spire of Trinity Church at the head of Wall Street.

A new and self-confident generation was even ready to see itself through the forthright eyes of Copley, without any background garniture whatever.

Metropolitan Museum of Art

When John Singleton Copley, the greatest of our colonial painters, came down from Boston in 1771 he found "so many that are impatient to sit" that he was busy every moment. What is more, he found discriminating clients; he could not hurry his work, he wrote to a friend back home, because "the Gentry of this place distinguish very well, so I must slight nothing." His portrait of "Samuel Verplanck" (1771) shows us a descendant of one of the early Dutch settlers, whose family had amassed considerable wealth and who were prominent in local affairs. Verplanck was a member of the first class to graduate at Columbia (then King's) College. Four years after his portrait was painted he served as one of the delegates to the first New York Provincial Congress. His house is shown on page 83.

It is to officers of the British forces,
sent over to police the increasingly rebellious colonies,
that we owe the pictures . . .

Columbiana Collection, Columbia University

This southeast view of the city was drawn "on the spot" by Captain Thomas Howdell of the Royal Artillery, and engraved by P. Canot. It was published in 1768 as one of the plates in *Scenographia Americana, or, A Collection of Views in North America and the West Indies, neatly engraved . . . from drawings taken on the spot, by several officers of the British Navy and Army,* a handsome collection issued by Thomas Jeffreys of London.

The view shows the city as seen from a point near the present intersection of Varick and Beach streets. (One must assume that the engraver, not the captain, supplied the palm tree.) The large building in the center of the view was the new King's College, on the site now bounded by Murray, Barclay, Church, and Chapel streets. The cornerstone had been laid in 1756, but it was not until 1760 that the building was ready for the faculty and students "to Lodge and Diet" in it.

The engraving was uncolored in its original state but, like many prints of the period, was subsequently colored by hand.

. . . and maps which record the rapidly expanding city . . .

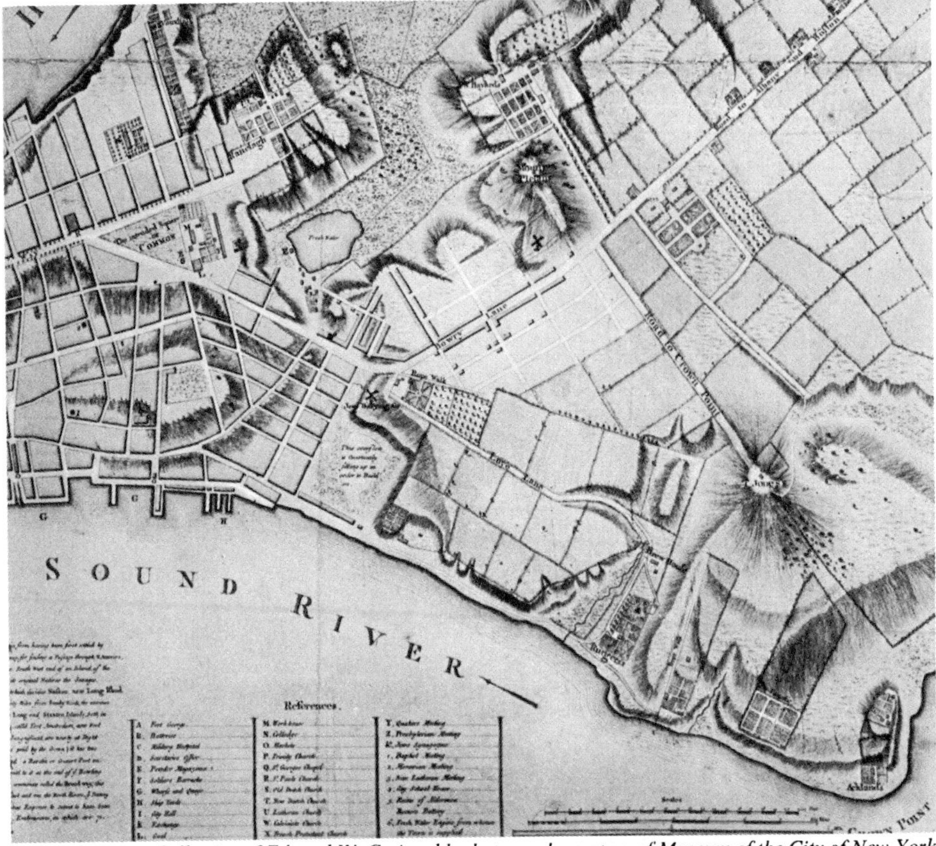

Collection of Edward W. C. Arnold; photograph courtesy of Museum of the City of New York

Stokes Collection, New York Public Library

The maps on this page show the changes which occurred in the upper part of the city (i.e., above present City Hall Park) in the course of a single year. At the top of the page is a section of the Montresor Plan, engraved by P. Andrews from a survey made in the winter of 1765–66, during the Stamp Act riots, by John Montresor at the behest of General Thomas Gage, commander in chief of His Majesty's forces in North America. Below is a comparable section of the plan drawn about a year later by Bernard Ratzer, an army officer, who also drew, shortly thereafter, the more inclusive map of the city and its environs, with a view of the city from Governor's Island, which is reproduced on the OPPOSITE page. (Both the plan and the map were engraved by Thomas Kitchen. By an engraver's error Ratzer's name is given as Ratzen on the smaller plan.)

In the year between Montresor's survey and Ratzer's many new streets have been laid out, notably in the area between King's College (upper left) and the Hudson, and between the Fresh Water and Corlaer's Hook, where Division Street marked the line between the Rutgers estate and the property of James DeLancey. The large estate shown above and to the right of the Rutgers house on both maps was Mount Pitt, then owned by the Loyalist historian of New York, Thomas Jones (see pages 96–97).

. . . of the seventeen-sixties and early seventies.

Eno Collection, New York Public Library

Several of the most interesting views of the city were published in conjunction with admiralty charts.

Both pictures from collection of Edward W. C. Arnold; photographs courtesy of Museum of the City of New York

The so-called "Wooded Heights View," above, is an aquatint engraving, drawn, engraved, and published by Joseph F. W. Des Barres as one of the plates in the *Atlantic Neptune,* a collection of charts, plans, and views for the use of the Royal Navy. It shows the west shore from a point above Liberty Street to the Battery, and was probably drawn in 1772. At this period the shore line was at Greenwich Street, so that the walled garden between the two sailboats was in the rear of Nos. 59–63 Broadway.

The view of Hell Gate in 1777, by W. A. Williams, is part of an inset panel on a large engraved "Chart of the Coast of New England and New York" by Captain Holland, published in London by Laurie & Whittle in 1778. A key identifies the numbered items as follows: 1: Horn's Hook, 2: the Gridiron, 3: Hancock's Rock, 4: the Mill Rock, 5: Morrisania, 6: Bahanna's (or Barren, now Ward's) Island, 7: Pinfold's Place, 8: Hallett's Point, 9: the Pot, 10: the Hog's Back, 11: the Frying Pan. Mill Rock is still there, though many of the obstructions were blasted out of the channel between 1869 and 1876 (see page 380).

When war came,
the British moved on the city
at once . . .

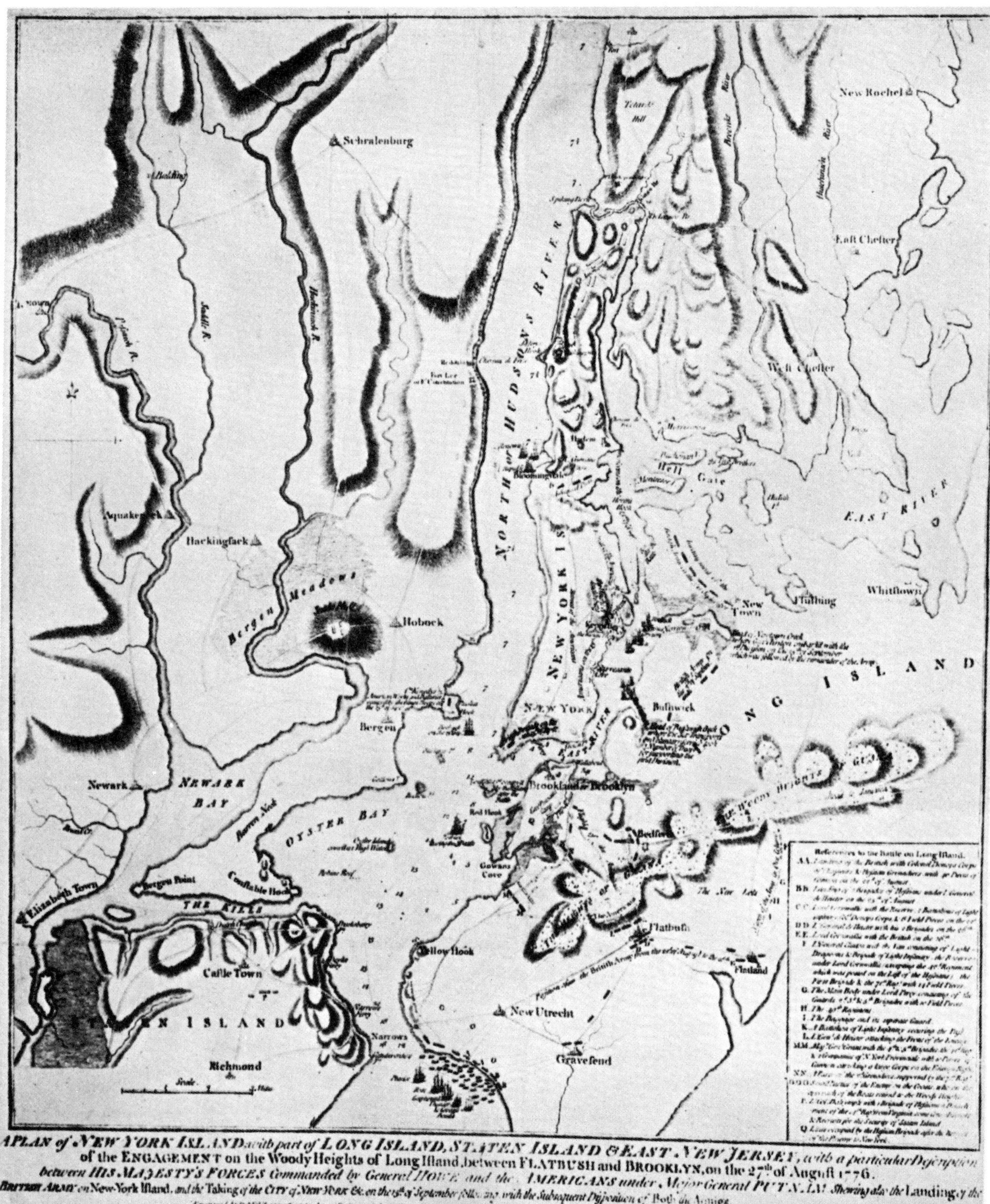

Collection of Edward W. C. Arnold; photograph courtesy of Museum of the City of New York

This map, known as the "Howe War Plan," was published by William Faden in London in 1776, and was issued both separately and bound up with Faden's *North American Atlas* (1777). There are several states of the engraving, of which this is the fifth.

Below the map, on the original, there is a detailed account (not reproduced here) of the Battle of Long Island, taken from General Howe's account of his successful attack and the Americans' retreat.

. . . and Washington's army had to abandon it, after brief resistance.

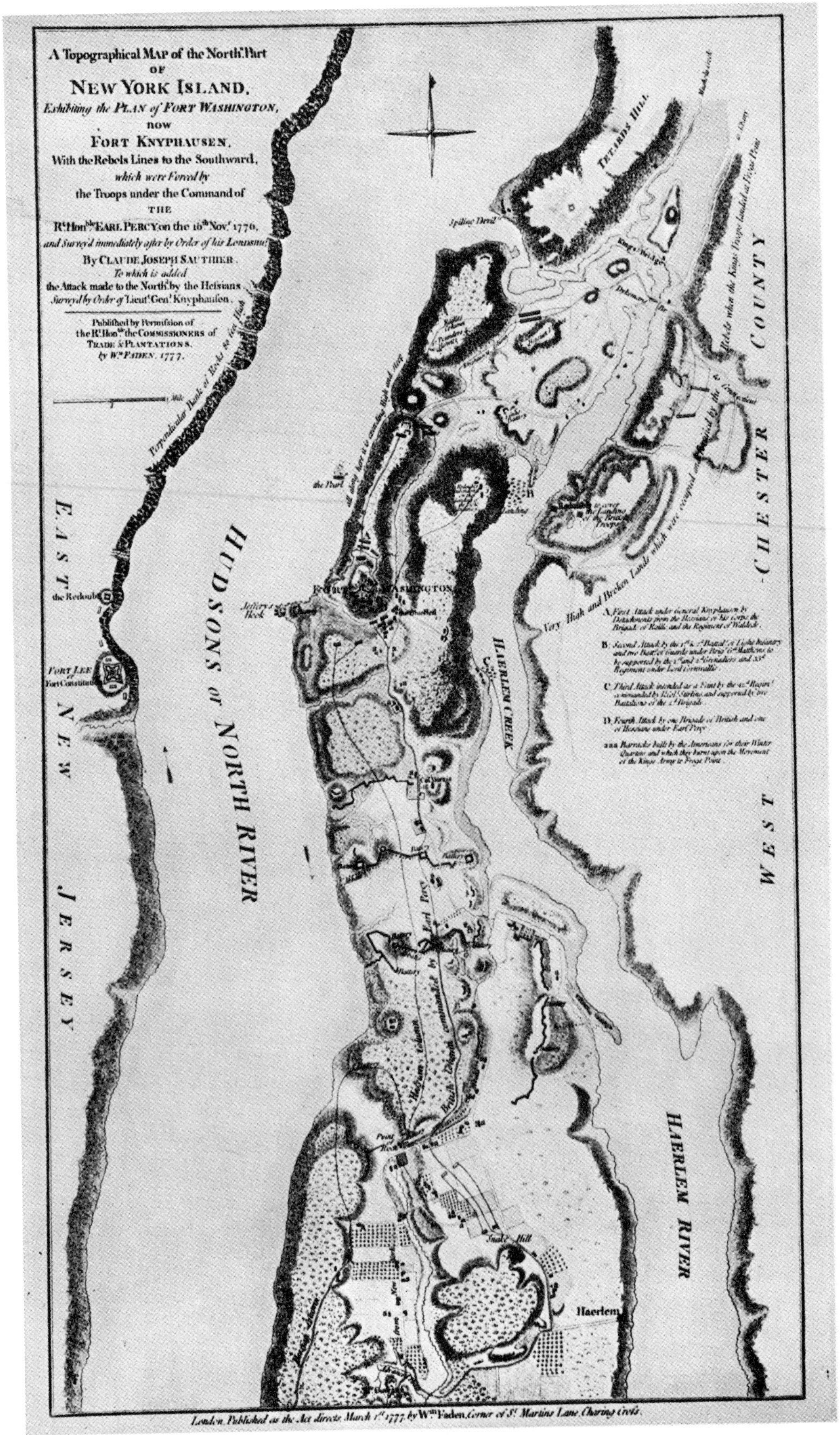

This map of the northern end of Manhattan was drawn by Claude Joseph Southier from a survey made right after the British and Hessian troops captured Fort Washington. Like the map on the preceding page, it was engraved on copper and published in London by William Faden.

The map shows the roads and houses, as well as the topographical features of the island, from McGown's Pass (at the north end of present Central Park) and Harlem to Kingsbridge. Near the center of the map is the house built by Colonel Roger Morris about 1765, now known as the Jumel mansion (see page 74). Jeffrey's Hook, projecting into the river just below Fort Washington, is the present site of the Little Red Light House and the east tower of the George Washington Bridge. Fort Washington itself stood just west of present Fort Washington Avenue, about on the line of 183rd Street, at the highest natural elevation (267.75 feet) on Manhattan. Part of the site is now included in Bennett Park. For a picture of the landing operation at B on the map, see page 74.

Collection of Edward W. C. Arnold; photograph courtesy of Museum of the City of New York

The only pictures we have of the war itself, in and around New York, are the leisurely drawings . . .

Spencer Collection, New York Public Library

This water-color drawing is one of a series made during the war by Captain Archibald Robertson, a Scot who served with British headquarters troops as an engineer officer and deputy quartermaster general. (He is not to be confused with the painter of the same name who worked in New York after 1791.) It is inscribed, in Robertson's hand: "View of the Narrows between Long Island and staaten Island w^t our Fleet at Anchor & Lord Howe coming in —taken from the height above the Water^g place Staaten Island 12th July 1776." The ships are part of a fleet of 52 warships and 427 transports which the British concentrated at New York preparatory to launching their attack. These ships, with the 34,000 troops encamped on Staten Island, composed the largest expeditionary force of the eighteenth century.

The view was probably made from the vicinity of present Rosebank, looking east-southeast toward the sea gate between Fort Hamilton (at left) and Fort Wadsworth (at right). The arm of land reaching out from Long Island behind Lord Howe's ship is Coney Island.

. . . of talented British officers who occasionally . . .

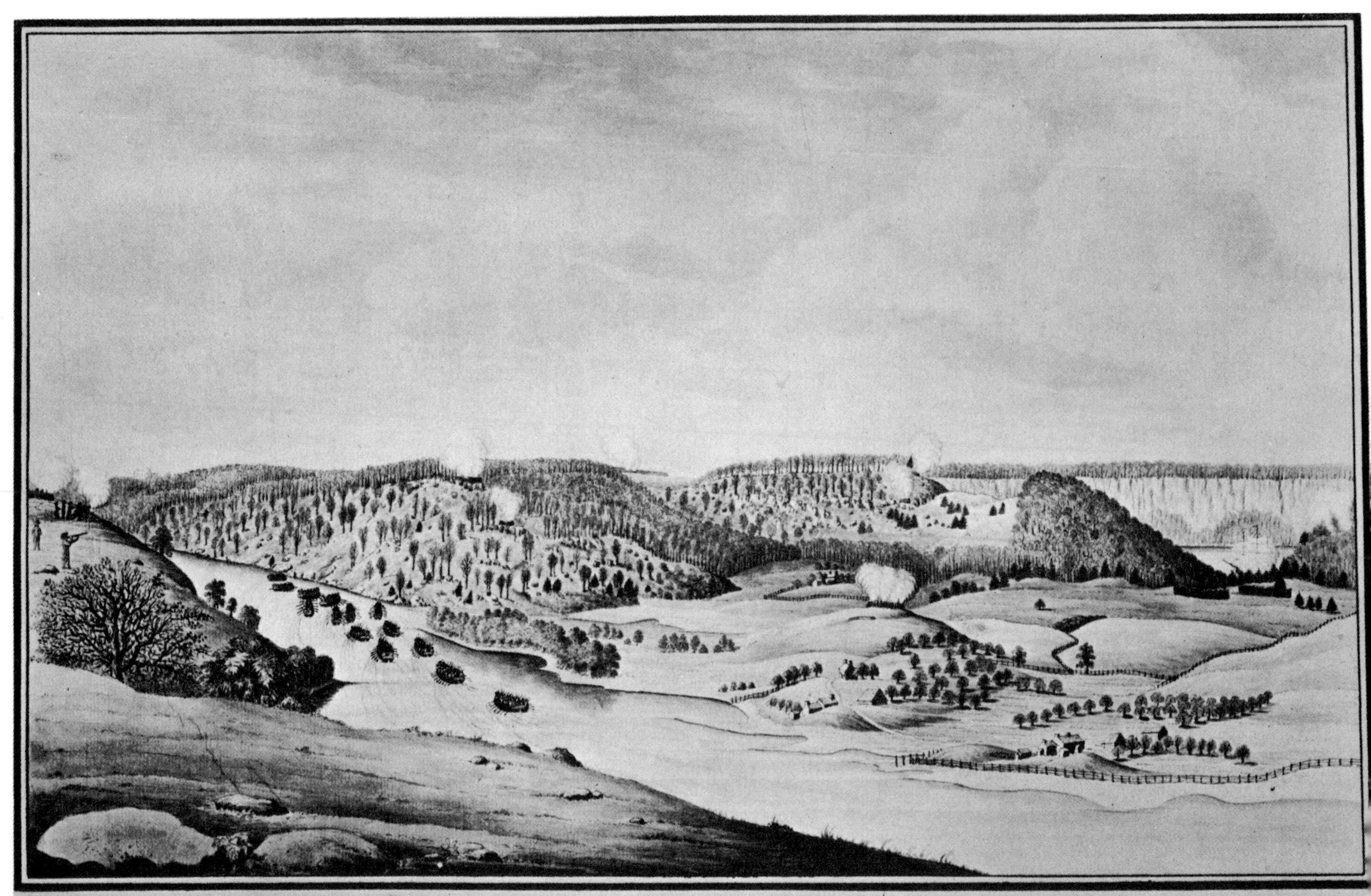

A View of the Attack against Fort Washington and Rebel Redouts near New York on the 16 of November 1776 by the British and Hessian Brigades

Stokes Collection, New York Public Library

Captain Thomas Davies of the Royal Regiment of Artillery made this water-color drawing of the attack against Fort Washington, November 16, 1776, from what is now the campus of New York University, on University Heights in the Bronx. Davies commanded a battery of twelve-pounders which covered the landing of the troops here shown beetling across the river. On the skyline at the left of the view is the Morris (Jumel) mansion. At the right, in the gap now spanned by the Henry Hudson Bridge from Inwood to Spuyten Duyvil, the British frigate *Pearl* lies at anchor where the Harlem River meets the Hudson. Fort Washington is on the high ridge in the center of the view. The house on the Harlem River shore, lower right, was the Nagel homestead, built by John Nagel in 1736 at what is now the intersection of Ninth Avenue and 213th Street. It was demolished in 1907.

The Landing of the British Forces in the Jerseys on the 20th of November 1776 under the command of the Rt. Honble. Lieut. Genl. Earl Cornwallis

Emmet Collection, New York Public Library

Though it has been attributed to Lord Rawdon, afterwards the first Marquis of Hastings, who was an officer on Cornwallis' staff, this water color of the British landing at Alpine, New Jersey (at the foot of the Palisades opposite Yonkers), was probably made by the same Captain Davies who drew the previous picture.

Cornwallis' move forced the Americans to abandon Fort Lee, down-river opposite Fort Washington, and precipitated Washington's long retreat through New Jersey to Philadelphia.

. . . and then, during their occupation of the city, indulged their topographical interests with "something in the landskip way."

Both drawings from Spencer Collection, New York Public Library

Two more drawings from the series by Captain Archibald Robertson (see page 73).

ABOVE: "View of North River looking toward Fort Washington, October 16, 1781." This must have been made from a point just north of where Grant's Tomb now stands. The low point on the shore line in the foreground is where 125th Street now crosses under the Riverside Drive viaduct to the abandoned Fort Lee ferry slips.

BELOW: "View North over Harlem Valley." The church which shows at center right is the Dutch Reformed Church, built in 1686, which stood between 124th and 125th streets, west of First Avenue. It was badly damaged during the war.

But New York, in the minds of most Americans, was a conventional image of the commercial port, not a particular place . . .

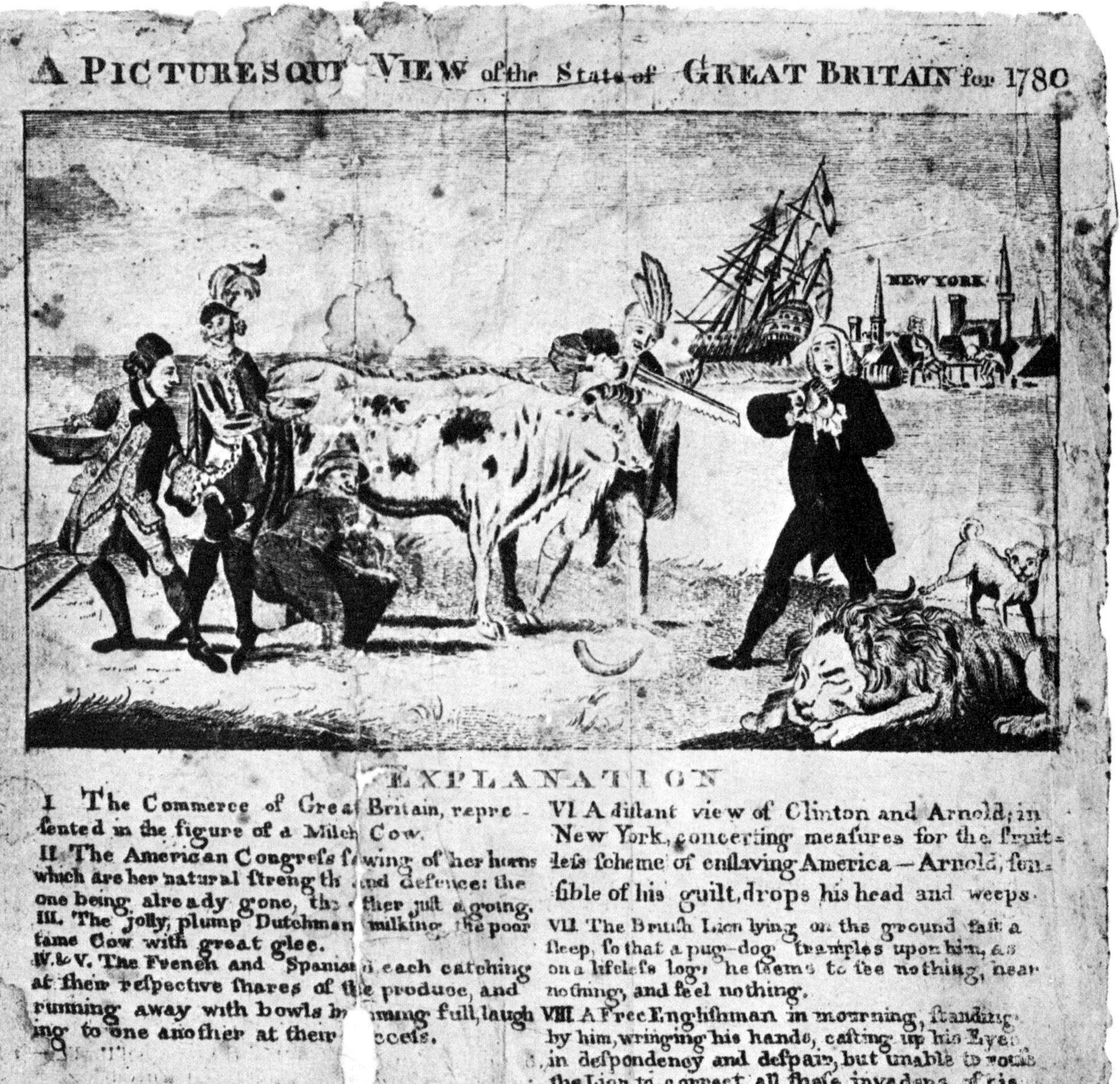

A PICTURESQUE VIEW of the State of GREAT BRITAIN for 1780
NEW YORK
EXPLANATION
I The Commerce of Great Britain, repreſented in the figure of a Milch Cow.
II The American Congreſs ſawing of her horns which are her natural ſtrength and defence: the one being already gone, the other juſt a going.
III. The jolly, plump Dutchman milking the poor tame Cow with great glee.
IV. & V. The French and Spaniard each catching at their reſpective ſhares of the produce, and running away with bowls b mming full, laughing to one another at their ccess.
VI A diſtant view of Clinton and Arnold, in New York, concerting meaſures for the fruitleſs ſcheme of enſlaving America — Arnold, ſenſible of his guilt, drops his head and weeps.
VII The Britiſh Lion lying on the ground faſt aſleep, ſo that a pug-dog tramples upon him, as on a lifeleſs log, he ſeems to ſee nothing, hear nothing, and feel nothing.
VIII A Free Engliſhman in mourning, ſtanding by him, wringing his hands, caſting up his Eyes in deſpondency and deſpair, but unable to rouſe the Lion to correct all theſe invaders of his Royal Prerogative and his ſubjects' property

Collection of Edward W. C. Arnold;
photograph courtesy of Museum of the City of New York

An engraved cartoon, attributed to Paul Revere, the Boston patriot and silversmith, who also engraved and published the famous print of the Boston massacre (1770).

. . . while in Europe,
where the events culminating in the American Revolution
had awakened renewed interest in America . . .

Collection of Edward W. C. Arnold; photograph courtesy of Museum of the City of New York

One of a series of "peep show" views of New York engraved and published in Augsburg by Balthazar Frederic Leizelt in 1775 or thereabouts. Like the earlier Jollain view (page 43), these were purely imaginary conceptions, bearing no more relation to reality than many earlier and later descriptions of the New World by Europeans who had not (and some who had) seen it.

. . . any pictures of the city were acceptable, no matter how blatantly trumped up.

Museum of the City of New York

This fictitious view of the destruction of the statue of George III, which stood in Bowling Green at the foot of Broadway, was one of another series of "peep show" views, this one engraved by François Xavier Habermann and published in 1776. Like the earlier series, it was published at Augsburg. Other prints in this series purported to show British troops entering the city, the Great Fire of 1776, and other events of the war.

With victory, and the evacuation of the city by the British, New York became the first capital of the new nation . . .

J. Clarence Davies Collection, Museum of the City of New York

A symbolic design, drawn by Charles Buxton, M.D., engraved by Cornelius Tiebout, and published at New York in 1783 by Charles Smith, who dedicated it "with due Respect" to the Congress of the United States. The view framed in the panel behind Washington shows the fort, Bowling Green (with the pedestal from which the statue of George III had been torn, July 9, 1776), and the Kennedy house, No. 1 Broadway, where Washington had lived during the early days of the Revolution and where Sir William Howe and other British officers lived during the occupation.

The classical elements of Dr. Buxton's design, we may note in passing, were a promise of the classic revival which was soon to sweep through American architecture.

. . . whose new Constitution it celebrated in a splendid banquet pavilion, designed by Major L'Enfant.

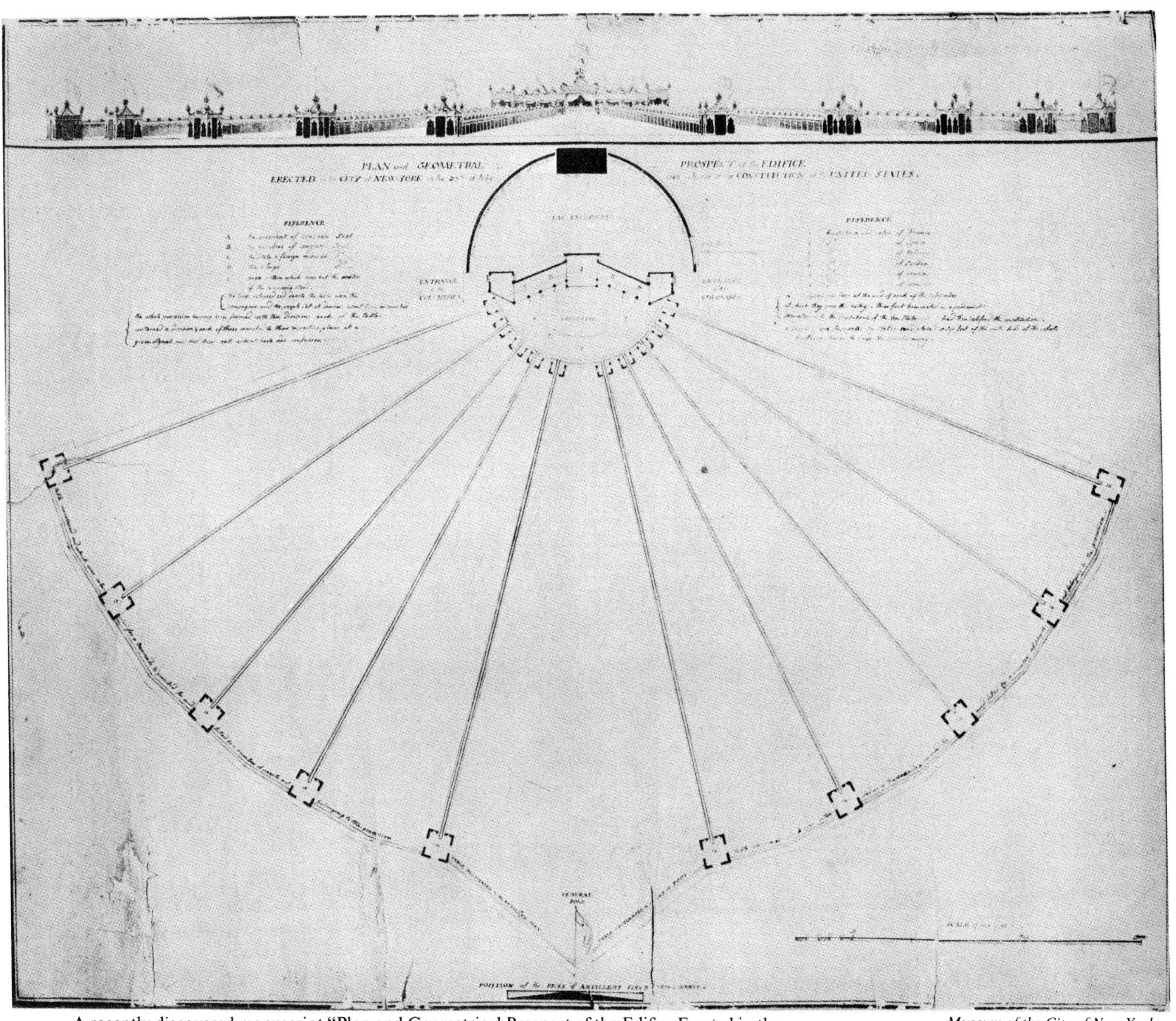

A recently discovered manuscript "Plan and Geometrical Prospect of the Edifice Erected in the City of New-York on the 23d of July 1788 in honor of the Constitution of the United States," reproduced here for the first time. It was drawn by Major Pierre Charles L'Enfant, one of the heroes of Lafayette's army, who was in charge of the celebration and designed the structure. After a day of parades, more than 6000 people assembled at the long tables provided in L'Enfant's pavilion, to dine and listen to speeches from the members of Congress and other dignitaries at the head table. "Two oxen were roasted whole, and several cows and sheep" together with "hams &c. &c.," as contemporary accounts inform us. The pavilion was built on Bunker Hill (called Mount Pleasant on the Montresor plan, page 68) near the present intersection of Grand and Centre streets.

This is L'Enfant's first important designing job in America. A few months later he was commissioned to remodel and enlarge the City Hall for use as Federal Hall (see pages 83–85), and a few years after that drew up the plans for the new federal city of Washington, D.C.

Museum of the City of New York; photograph courtesy the Bland Galleries

And yet, except for this engraving of Washington's inauguration, there were no contemporary pictures of the historic events of the time.

Peter Lacour delin.
A. Doolittle Sculpt.
FEDERAL HALL
The Seat of CONGRESS
Printed & Sold by A. Doolittle New Haven 1790

Collection of Edward W. C. Arnold; photograph courtesy of Museum of the City of New York

The pictures that were made were of important buildings, especially the remodeled City Hall . . .

A Perspective View of the City Hall in New York taken from Wall Street

Collection of Edward W. C. Arnold; photograph courtesy of Museum of the City of New York

A view down Wall Street toward Trinity Church, showing the City Hall as remodeled by Major L'Enfant in 1788–89. Drawn and engraved on copper by Cornelius Tiebout (c. 1791–93), it shows the wing at the rear, which was one of L'Enfant's additions.
The house at the extreme right is the Verplanck mansion (see page 66). The one at the left, partly obscuring the new Trinity Church (replacing the one destroyed by fire in 1776), belonged to Nathaniel McKinley and stood on the southwest corner of Wall and Broad streets. From its stoop Alexander Hamilton spoke in defense of the Jay Treaty to angry crowds who attacked him with oaths and stones.

OPPOSITE: This view of Federal Hall at the time of Washington's inauguration was drawn by Peter (or Pierre) Lacour, a French painter and designer who visited America after the Revolution, and was engraved on copper by Amos Doolittle of New Haven, who published it in 1790. (The original print is almost twice as large as this reproduction.)

. . . which stood commandingly in Wall Street, at the head of Broad Street . . .

Detail of engraving on page 83

. . . as an example of the first attempt to create an "American" order of architecture.

As Talbot Hamlin has pointed out, the choice of L'Enfant as architect of Federal Hall was a sign of a widespread cultural movement in America—a turning away from English ideals and tastes. Yet L'Enfant's design, in spite of such "French" influences as the ironwork in front of the windows, has a monumentality and simplicity unlike that in the current classic buildings of either France or England. These qualities, more than the stars and eagles employed as decorative elements in the modified Doric façade, prefigured the distinctively American classic revival architecture which flowered under the aegis of Jefferson.

Many of the city's older houses had been destroyed in the Great Fire of 1776, but Broad Street was a jumble of old and new.

Stokes Collection, New York Public Library

This water-color drawing by George Holland is the only contemporary view of the upper end of Broad Street in the eighteenth century. It was made in 1797 from a point just south of Exchange Place (then Garden Street).

The spire to the left of the old Federal Hall (now City Hall again, since the federal government had removed to Philadelphia in 1790) is St. Paul's Chapel six blocks up Broadway. Farther left, over the roof of the three-story house, is the cupola of the First Presbyterian Church on the north side of Wall Street, halfway between City Hall and Broadway.

The Dutch gabled house dated 1698 was occupied at this time by James Bryson, merchant, and Moses Smith. It had been built by John Hendricks de Bruyn, and was one of the last Dutch buildings to survive in this part of the city (see page 138).

From the Hudson the shabby parts of the city didn't show, and the town had an elegant and spacious look.

View of NEW YORK from LE JUPITER of 74 Guns. Lying at Anchor in the NORTH RIVER.

Collection of O'Donnell Iselin; photograph courtesy of Museum of the City of New York

The Archibald Robertson who signed this water-color drawing (dated August 20, 1793) had come to New York in 1791. With his brother Alexander, he opened the Columbian Academy of Painting at 89 William Street in 1793, just a few months after this drawing was made. A colored engraving based upon the drawing was published a few years later, and several manuscript variants (presumably made by Robertson's pupils) also exist. The large building in the center of the view is the new Government House, facing Bowling Green at the foot of Broadway on the site of Fort Amsterdam. Erected in 1790, it was originally intended as the residence of the President, but when the federal government moved away it became the governor's mansion, and was at this time occupied by Governor George Clinton (see also page 88). The house at extreme left, beyond Trinity Church, is the Van Cortlandt mansion (9–11 Broadway), owned at this time by Cornelius Ray (see page 102). The large block of buildings right of the ship's shrouds are on the west side of Broadway south of Exchange Place. The two middle ones had been President Washington's official residence in 1790.

At closer range, however, even Government House lost some of its dignity, thanks to the lounging cattle, though the fenced-off Battery made a pleasant park.

New-York Historical Society

C. Milbourne's 1797 water color shows Government House during Governor John Jay's occupancy (see page 90). The next year, it became the Elysian Boarding and Lodging House, and was subsequently used as the Custom House. It was torn down in 1815. The present U. S. Custom House occupies the site. Bowling Green's fence appears at left.

The view of the Battery, with its flagstaff that Washington Irving likened to a gigantic churn, was drawn by John Drayton, an urbane South Carolinian who visited New York in 1793. (The engraving, by S. Hill, is one of the illustrations in Drayton's *Letters Written during a Tour through the Northern and Eastern States* [Charleston, 1794].) The ship sailing by, according to Drayton, is the *Ambuscade,* a French frigate "having a liberty cap on the fore-top-gallant-mast head," which had brought Citizen Genêt to this country as minister from France.

Stokes Collection, New York Public Library

Civic improvement was sponsored by many worthy citizens, whose portraits in this period . . .

Museum of the City of New York

ABOVE: James Duane, first mayor of New York after the Revolution (1784–89), is here portrayed in a miniature by John Ramage, the most successful portrait painter in town. The miniature was probably made in 1789, in which year Ramage also painted one of Washington. Duane had been a delegate to the Second Continental Congress, was a warden of Trinity and a leader in re-establishing Columbia College after the Revolution.

New-York Historical Society

RIGHT: John Vanderlyn's portrait of Robert R. Livingston, Jr., was painted in 1804 in Paris, where Livingston was serving as minister to France and Vanderlyn (who had studied painting in Robertson's school [page 87]) was saturating himself with the solemn and solid neo-classicism of David and his followers. Livingston had served in the Continental Congress and was the first chancellor of New York State. He was president of the Society for the Promotion of Agriculture, Manufactures, and Arts, and a patron of the New York Academy of Fine Arts.

. . . reflect some of the fashionable neo-classic influence . . .

Joseph Wright, who painted John Jay's portrait in 1786, was the son of a local waxworks proprietress, Mrs. Patience Wright.

Born in New Jersey, he studied painting in London and Paris, and maintained a studio in Pearl Street for several years after 1786.

His dry-point etching of Washington was the first "painter-etching" made in this country.

Jay was an able conservative patriot, author of the Jay Treaty, first Chief Justice of the U. S. Supreme Court, and a governor of New York.

Both portraits from New-York Historical Society

It had been Aaron Burr, whose portrait Vanderlyn painted in 1809, who provided the funds to send Vanderlyn to Paris to study in 1793. Burr's trial for treason and the tragic duel in which he killed Hamilton have overshadowed the otherwise brilliant and effective leadership he provided in local and national affairs. The organizing genius of Tammany as a political force, and founder of the Bank of the Manhattan Co., he was long a prominent figure in New York.

. . . which was also reflected in the buildings they erected.

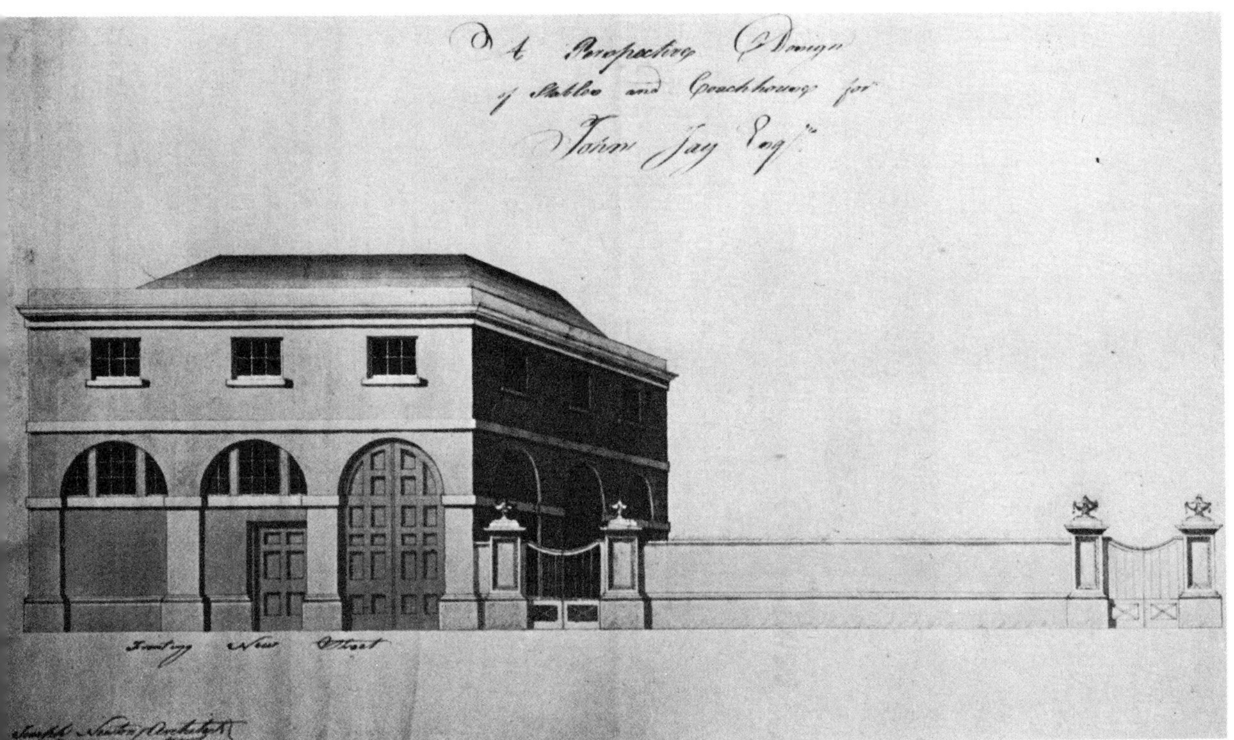

Museum of the City of New York

LEFT: Architect's perspective design for "Stables and Coachhouse for John Jay Esq.," by Joseph Newton, architect, Bowery, New York. Jay's house, built in 1786, was at 52 Broadway, but the property ran through to New Street, on which the stables fronted.

BELOW: Richmond Hill, pictured here in an engraving by Cornelius Tiebout for the June, 1790, issue of the *New-York Magazine,* was a country estate a mile and a half outside the city where Charlton and Varick streets now intersect. Built in 1767, it was occupied by Vice-President John Adams in 1789–90, acquired on a sixty-nine-year lease from Trinity Church by Aaron Burr in 1797, and sold to John Jacob Astor in 1803. It was moved in 1813, was used for a while as a theater, and was finally demolished in 1849.

J. Clarence Davies Collection, Museum of the City of New York

Elaborate urban estates were planned by the new federal aristocracy, while dispossessed Loyalists moved to more modest quarters.

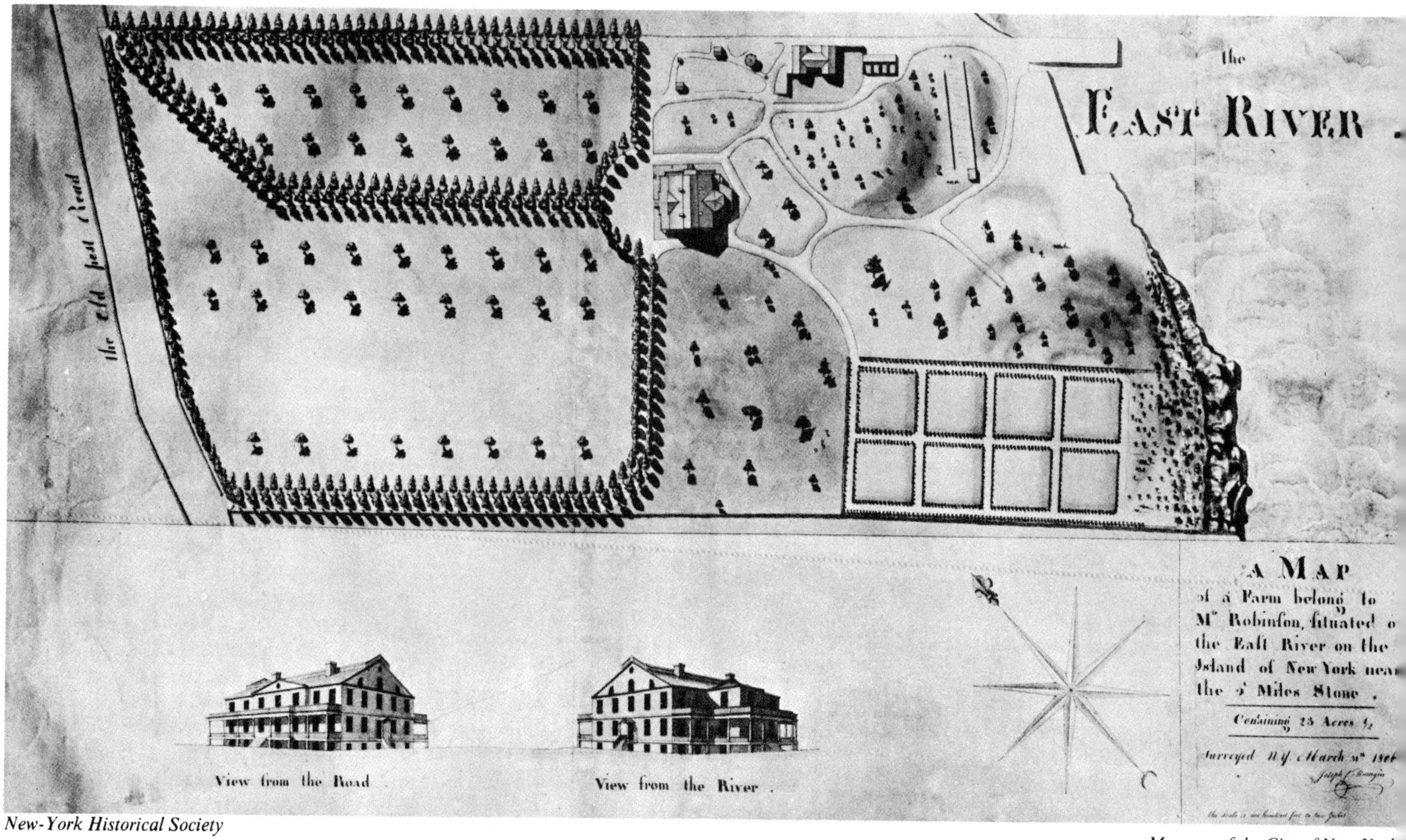

the Old post Road

the EAST RIVER

View from the Road

View from the River

A MAP
of a Farm belong to
Mr Robinson, situated o
the East River on the
Island of New York nea
the 5 Miles Stone.
Containing 25 Acres ½
Surveyed N.Y. March 1806
Joseph F. Mangin

New-York Historical Society

Museum of the City of New York

Mount Vernon, or "Smith's Folly" as it was also called, was planned, and started in 1795, by Colonel William Stephens Smith and his wife Abigail (daughter of John Adams). Reverses in fortune compelled Smith to sell the place, and it was acquired by William T. Robinson, who completed it in 1798–99. In 1806, when Joseph F. Mangin surveyed and drew the above manuscript plan, it was one of the finest estates on Manhattan. The house burned in 1826, and was not rebuilt, but the stable shown at the top of the plan still stands on its original site and is now the headquarters of the Colonial Dames of America at 421 East Sixty-first Street (see page 472). "Union Hill" in Fordham, shown at right in an anonymous water color of about 1790, was built after the Revolution by Mrs. Peter DeLancey, whose large estate at West Farms (where the Bronx Zoo now stands) had been confiscated because of her Loyalist sympathies.

Everyone (including those who made pictures) apparently enjoyed getting out of town . . .

Collection of Edward W. C. Arnold; photograph courtesy of Museum of the City of New York

Belvedere House was one of the first "country clubs" in America.
It was built in 1792 by the "thirty-three gentlemen"
who belonged to the Belvedere Club, on grounds bounded by the present
Montgomery, Clinton, Cherry, and Monroe streets.
The house contained private rooms for the club,
together with rooms for public entertainment, including a ballroom,
dining room, bar, cardroom, and bedchambers.
The grounds were ornamented with gardens and a bowling green.

The drawing by J. Anderson, engraved by John Scoles,
was published together with an article about the club
in the *New-York Magazine,* August, 1794.
The house shown left of Belvedere
was probably the Rutgers mansion, on the site now bounded
by Cherry, Jefferson, Madison, and Clinton streets.
Both places can be clearly seen on the map on pages 104–5,
above the eastern extremity of Cherry Street.

. . . to skate at Lispenard Meadows, or to dine at a tavern up in Harlem . . .

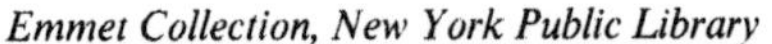

Stokes Collection, New York Public Library

ABOVE: A wash drawing by Alexander Anderson, the wood engraver, of Lispenard Meadows about 1798. View from a point on Broadway near Spring Street looking toward the Hudson.

Emmet Collection, New York Public Library

LEFT: Pen and ink drawing by Archibald Robertson, "In Harlem Lane." The Kimmel Tavern, at left, stood on northeast corner of present Eighth Avenue and 120th Street.

. . . or just to stroll in the country lanes beyond the Fresh Water (or Collect) Pond.

Collection of Edward W. C. Arnold; photograph courtesy of Museum of the City of New York

This water-color drawing (probably by Archibald Robertson) dated March, 1798, is the only known contemporary view of the Collect, or Fresh Water —one of the most interesting topographical features of Manhattan in the early years. The pond covered the area north of present Foley Square where the Department of Health and New York State buildings now stand, its overflow running through the marshes of Lispenard Meadows to the Hudson. The view was probably made from a point near the present intersection of Canal and Centre streets. The spire at left is that of St. George's Chapel (corner of Beekman and Cliff streets); the one at right, St. Paul's on Broadway between Fulton and Vesey streets. Just left of St. Paul's is the Bridewell, or city prison, just west of the site where City Hall now stands (see page 111). The small buildings on the south shore of the pond were probably connected with the rope yard and tanneries which clustered there. It was on the Collect that John Fitch had carried out his experiments with his steamboat a year or two before this drawing was made (see page 118). In 1803 the work of filling in the pond began, and by 1811 the hills around it had been leveled and no trace of it remained. A sewer now drains the still living springs which fed the pond.

From the porch of a suburban estate out near Corlaer's Hook . . .

This "View of the City and Harbour of New York, taken from Mount Pitt, the Seat of John R. Livingston, Esqre" was drawn and engraved by Charles-Balthazar-Julien Fevret de Saint-Mémin, a young French refugee who had arrived in New York in 1793 and whom Livingston befriended. Mount Pitt (see page 68) was, as Livingston himself described it, "a charming house, situated outside New York, dominating the town, and from which one enjoyed a superb view which on one side included the entire harbor." The view, made while Saint-Mémin was staying at the house in 1794, was probably drawn from the porch. Grand Street, then a country lane, runs across the foreground just in front of the house. The boy and child are walking down Clinton Street toward Division Street, along which the coach is traveling northeast. The large yellow house at right stood at the junction of Clinton (then Arundel Street, north of Division), Hester (then Eagle), and Division streets (see map, pages 104–5). The roof of the Rutgers mansion (see page 93) shows at the left.

Collection of Irving S. Olds

. . . the distant city looked dainty and charming, however shabby and sordid parts of it might be . . .

. . . and the rural atmosphere was scarcely disturbed even by the growing settlement around the Navy Yard.

Detail of preceding picture

The buildings on the shore of the East River, at the center of the Saint-Mémin view, were clustered along Cherry Street from Rutgers Street to Catherine Street (where Knickerbocker Village now stands in the shadow of the Manhattan Bridge). Beyond them, in the harbor, lies Governor's Island, separated from Red Hook in Brooklyn by Buttermilk Channel, and in the distant background Staten Island.

In the preface to Vol. I of the *Iconography of Manhattan Island* (1915), the most magnificent collection of New York pictures ever yet, or ever likely to be, published, I. N. Phelps Stokes remembered that it was while looking at Saint-Mémin's picture, at the house of a friend in 1908, that "something in the aspect of the little group of houses clustering along the river bank . . . combined with something in the attitude of the two figures in the foreground and in the appearance of the coach hurrying along the road in the middle distance, suggested to me the idea of writing a book on the history of New York prints."

Over in Brooklyn, too, one could live among rural pleasures, going to the city only for work.

Columbiana Collection, Columbia University

This water color of New York from Brooklyn is inscribed "Drawn by Archibald Robertson my father, Andrew J. Robertson." It was probably made in 1796.

The large house at right was the Cornell mansion later owned by Hezekiah Pierrepont. During the Battle of Long Island it had served as Washington's headquarters.

Moreau de St. Méry, a French exile who lived in New York in 1794, wrote appreciatively of Brooklyn as a place of residence. Just south of the village and overlooking the river, he noted, "is a small chain of hills, on which are the country houses of many New Yorkers. Its proximity to New York leads many New Yorkers to rent the houses and send their families there during the hot season. The men go to New York in the morning, and return to Brooklyn after the Stock Exchange closes.
The elevated situation of these country residences, in addition to being healthy, gives them the advantage of a charming view which includes New York and the nearby island . . . and is constantly enlivened by the passing of the boats which ply on both rivers."
An eight-room house over here, with a piazza, stable, and six acres of land, rented, he tells us, for three hundred dollars a year.

Of the business and manufactures upon which New Yorkers depended for a living . . .

THE

DEED OF SETTLEMENT

OF THE

Mutual Affurance Company,

FOR INSURING HOUSES FROM LOSS BY FIRE IN NEW-YORK.

MUTUAL ASSURANCE COMPANY

PROTECTION

NEW-YORK:

PRINTED BY WILLIAM MORTON.

MDCCLXXXVII.

Stokes Collection, New York Public Library

Though there had been previous unsuccessful attempts to found fire insurance companies, the first successful enterprise was the Mutual Assurance Co., whose constitution and by-laws were published in 1787 in the pamphlet whose cover is reproduced here. The company was incorporated in 1798, and in 1845 changed its name to the Knickerbocker Fire Insurance Co.

The engraving of the fire-fighting scene was done by Peter Rushton Maverick, whose son Peter was also an engraver and was one of the founders of the National Academy of Design.

An air furnace for iron casting was built on the Hudson shore by Peter Curtenius, Gilbert Forbes, Richard Sharpe, and Thomas Randall in 1767. It stood between Greenwich Street and the shore north of Provost (now Franklin) Street, as indicated on the map, pages 104–5. The accompanying engraved view (slightly enlarged here) was printed at the head of a broadside advertisement which was printed for Peter Curtenius & Co. by J. McLean in 1787. The furnace turned out pots, stoves, forge hammers, plow plates, and other products.

New-York Historical Society

. . . or of their attempts to cope with rising urban problems, we have only the most prosaic pictorial record . . .

No. I.

Charity Extended To All.

State of the *New-York Hospital* for the Year 1797.

Extends 123 ft. 10 In.

GOVERNORS.

Gerard Walton, *President.*
Matthew Clarkson, *Vice-President.*
John Murray, *Treasurer.*
Thomas Eddy, *Secretary.*

Peter Schermerhorn, John Murray, jun. William Edgar, William Minturn, Thomas Buchanan, Robert Bowne, John C. Kunzie, Edmund Prior,

Moses Rogers, John B. Coles, Henry Haydock, jun. Henry Rutgers, John Thurston, John I. Glover, Thomas Franklin, William T. Robinson,

James Kent, Hugh Gaine, William Jauncey, Jacob De La Montagnie, James Watson, John Barrow.

PHYSICIANS.

John R. B. Rodgers, Elihu H. Smith, Samuel L. Mitchell, David Hosack.

SURGEONS.

Richard Bayley, Wright Post, Richard S. Kissam, Samuel Borrowe, Valentine Seaman.

Adolph Lent, *Apothecary,*
Samuel Barnum, *House-Surgeon,*
William Hogsflesh, *Steward,*
Mary Smith, *Matron.*

This Institution was undertaken by private Subscriptions of the Inhabitants of New-York, in the Year 1770, and in Consequence of a Petition to the then Governor, by *Peter Middleton, John Jones,* and *Samuel Bard,* three respectable Physicians of this City, was incorporated by Charter on the 13th of the sixth Month. (June) 1771, under the Stile and Title of, *The Society of the Hospital in the City of New-York, in America.*

The New York Hospital, now housed with the Cornell Medical College in the huge medical center on the East River north of Sixty-eighth Street, had its beginning in 1769 when Dr. Samuel Bard of King's College urged the need for "an hospital for the sick poor of the colony." Chartered in 1771, the hospital was begun, but was destroyed by fire before it was finished. Rebuilt, it became a barracks for troops during the Revolution, and was not finally ready for use as a hospital until 1791.

Account of the Number of Patients admitted in the New-York Hospital, from 31st January, 1797, to 31st January, 1798.

DISEASES.	Remaining 31st Jan. 1797.	Admitted from 31st Jan. '97, to 31st Jan. '98.	Total.	Cured.	Relieved.	Discharged by Desire.	Eloped and discharged disorderly.	Died.	Remaining 31st Jan. 1798.
Amenorhoea,	1	4	5	2			2		1
Atrophia,	1		1						1
Ascites,	1	15	16	9	3		1	3	
Burns,	1	3	4	3					1
Cancers,	1	1	2	1	1				
Diarrhoea,	1	7	8	5	1				2
Febris Intermit,	3	37	40	27			3	9	1
Frozen Limbs,	12	19	31	13	2	5		2	9
Fractures,	5	16	21	9	3			2	7
Gonorrhoea,	1	6	7	3			2	2	
Mania,	4	18	22	4	5	1	1	2	9
Melancholia,	1		1		1				
Ophthalmia,	1	5	6	3			1		2
Palsy,	1	2	3	1	2				
Phelm,	1		1	1					
Pthisis Pulmon,	1	5	6		2	1		3	
Pneumonia,	11	48	59	24		2		13	20
Rachitis,	1		1	1					
Rheumatism,	5	37	42	24	9		4	1	4
Schrophula,	2	3	5	3			1		1
Syphilis,	24	103	127	76	15	1	11	1	23
Tumor,	1	2	3	2					1
Ulcers,	21	68	89	39	10	1	13	3	23
Wounds,	5	13	18	15	2				1
Apoplexy,		2	2					2	
Anasarca,		6	6					5	1
Asthma,		1	1					1	
Colica,		2	2	1				1	
Cataract,		2	2	2					
Catarrh,		1	1						1
Dislocations,		2	2	2					
Dysenteria,		5	5	3	1			1	
Dyspepsia,		5	5		1			2	2
Fistula,		4	4	1	1			1	1
Gravel,		2	2	2					
Hemoptisis,		1	1	1					
Herpes,		2	2	2					
Hepatitis,		2	2	1			1		
Luxation,		9	9	9					
Lumbar Abscess,		2	2			1		1	
Sciatica,		1	1	1					
Scorbutus,		1	1				1		
Tinea Capitis,		1	1	1					
Typhus,		8	8	5	1			2	
White Swelling,		1	1						1
	106	472	578	296	60	12	41	57	112

RECAPITULATION.

Patients Remaining in the Hospital 31st *January*, 1797,		106
Admitted from the 31st *January*, 1797, to 31st *January*, 1798,		472
		578
Discharged.—Cured,	296	
———Relieved,	60	
———By Desire,	12	
———Disorderly and Eloped,	41	
———Died,	57	
		466
Remaining in the Hospital 31st *January*, 1798,		112

—Who were Natives of the following Places,—

America.	England.	Scotland.	Ireland.	France.	Germany.	Spain.	Russia.	Portugal.	Sweden.	Holland.	Denmark.	Italy.	Norway.	Africa.	East-Indies.	West-Indies.	TOTAL.
240	57	25	165	9	20	8	2	1	7	11	3	3	3	8	8	8	578

The hospital's first annual report, two pages of which are reproduced above, was published in 1798. The building stood west of Broadway between present Duane and Worth streets, in the bed of present Thomas Street. (In passing, don't miss the name of the hospital's steward.)

Collection of Edward W. C. Arnold; photographs courtesy of Museum of the City of New York

. . . and of ordinary citizens there is almost no visual trace, even in street views.

One of the physicians at the hospital was Dr. David Hosack, who lived in the house at the extreme left of this picture. The water-color drawing, showing the west side of Broadway from just below Trinity Church to a point north of Murray Street, was made by John Joseph Holland in 1798.

John R. Livingston's town house is the one just north of Dr. Hosack's. Just north of Trinity is the old Van Cortlandt mansion, then owned by Cornelius Ray (see page 87), and beyond it, on the northwest corner of Trinity Place, the Tontine City Hotel. The steeple farther up (shown too far back from the street) was that of St. Paul's.

Parish of Trinity Church in the City of New York; photograph courtesy of the New-York Historical Society

View of the BOTANIC GARDEN of the STATE of NEW-YORK.

Dr. Hosack was also the founder of the Elgin Botanic Gardens, established in 1801 on the site where Rockefeller Center now stands. The land was given by New York State to Columbia College in 1814, and leased by Columbia to the Rockefeller interests in 1929. In the year 2015 the land, with all improvements, will revert to Columbia's control.

The engraving here reproduced was made by W. S. Leney from a drawing made about 1816 by Hugh Reinagle, scenic designer of the Park Theater.

Collection of Edward W. C. Arnold; photograph courtesy of Museum of the City of New York

What people wanted, and made, were pictures of institutions associated in their minds with cultural advance and civic splendor.

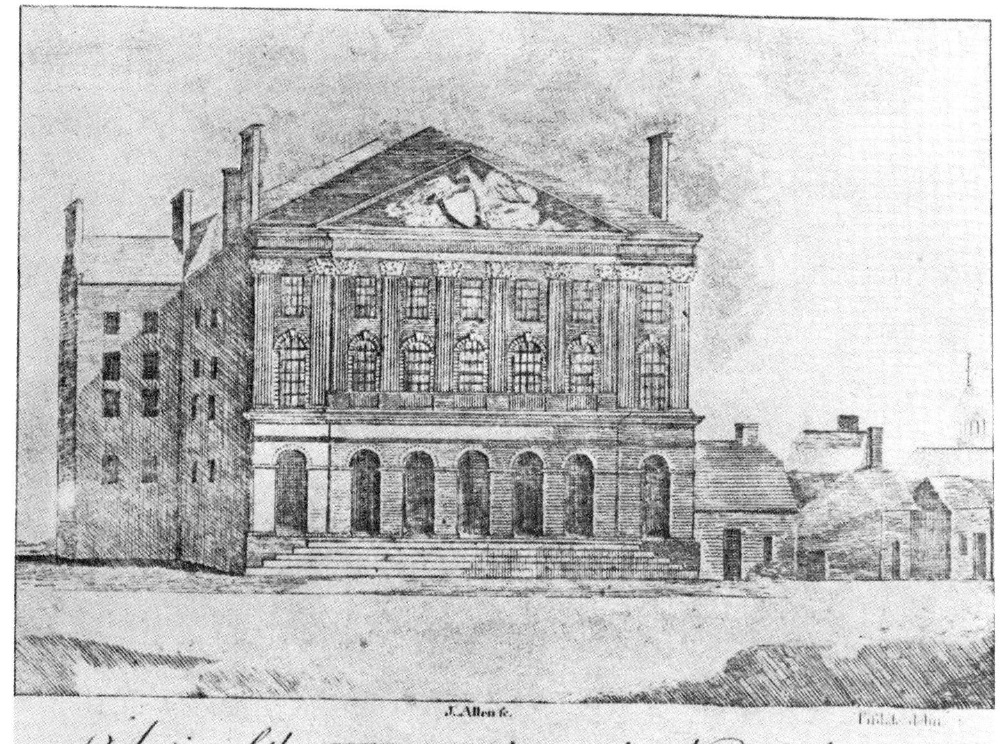

J. Allen fc.
A view of the NEW THEATRE in New York.

The Park Theater, here shown in the frontispiece drawn by E. Tisdale and engraved by J. Allen for Longworth's New York City *Directory* for 1797, was actually opened January 29, 1798, with a performance of *As You Like It*. The architects were the brothers Joseph and Charles Mangin, French refugees, the elder of whom later helped design the present City Hall (page 119).

Both pictures from collection of Edward W. C. Arnold; photographs courtesy of Museum of the City of New York

STATE PRISON, on the Bank of the North River, NEW YORK.

Joseph Mangin was also the architect of the state prison, erected in 1796–97 at Greenwich Village (north of Christopher Street, between Washington Street and the Hudson). The engraving, unsigned and undated, may (as Mr. Harry Bland suggests) have been the work of William Birch, another of whose engravings is on page 106.

At century's end, only such institutions and a few rich men's estates stood out from the solid, anonymous blocks . . .

. . . of houses and shops crowding along both shores
and up the main thoroughfares
in the center of the
wharf-fringed island.

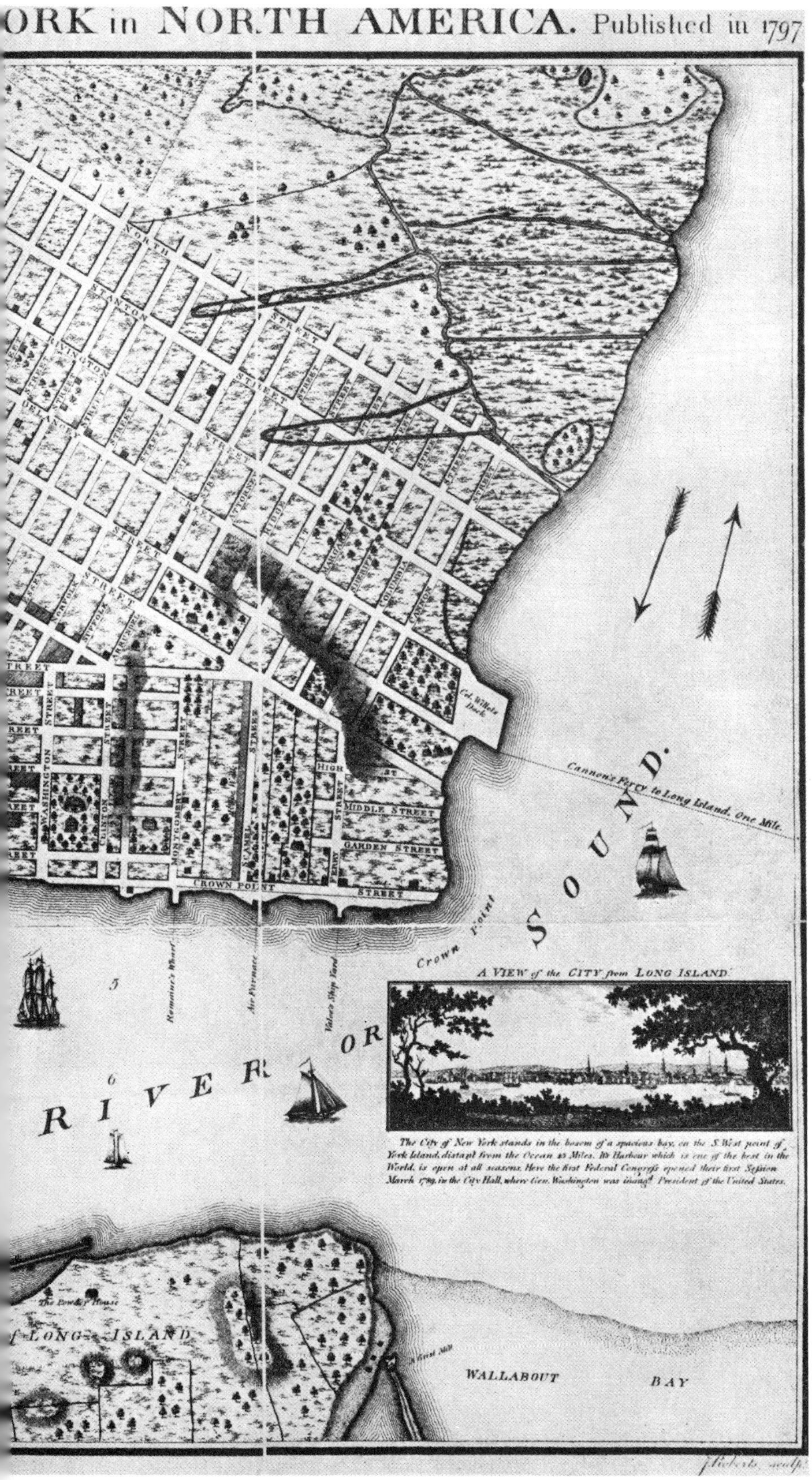

ORK in NORTH AMERICA. Published in 1797

This extraordinarily clear and detailed plan of the city and the built-up portion of Brooklyn in 1796 was drawn by B. Taylor, engraved by J. Roberts, and published in 1797. It is reproduced here slightly more than a third of its original size (36¾″ × 22⅛″). The reader may wish to glance ahead to a recent air view which is reproduced on page 512, of the region from Crown Point (Corlaer's Hook) to the top of the map (about Eighteenth Street).

Stokes Collection, New York Public Library

Only those who kept their distance could preserve the eighteenth-century view of the city as a charming feature of the landscape.

J. Clarence Davies Collection, Museum of the City of New York

This is one of two versions of a "prospect" of the city in 1802, drawn and published by William Birch of Pennsylvania and engraved by Samuel Seymour. A slightly earlier version had a white horse in the foreground instead of the picnic party, and showed a dock on the Long Island shore which is hidden in this version by the clump of trees left of the man with the spyglass.

Why the changes were made, we do not know; but no image in the foreground could express more precisely than this Arcadian picnic the nostalgic persistence of eighteenth-century attitudes toward the urban centers whose turbulence and vitality had already doomed those attitudes to extinction.

THE PEOPLE GET IN THE PICTURE 1800–1845

New-York Historical Society

Francis Guy's paintings of New York (above) and Brooklyn (see next page) marked an important change in ways of looking at the city. For the first time the bustle of human activity in the streets was as interesting as the buildings themselves.

Guy's large (65″ × 43″) canvas of the Tontine Coffee House was painted at the end of the eighteenth century, probably in 1798 or 1799. The Tontine, which is the large building at left, stood on the northwest corner of Wall and Water streets. Built in 1792, it housed the Stock Exchange and the principal insurance offices, and here the important merchants and traders met every day to transact business. Catty-corner across Wall Street was another coffee house (right), known as the Merchants' and beyond, at the foot of Wall Street, was Coffee House Slip.

Quite abruptly, as the nineteenth century opened, the people of the city crowded into the pictures of it . . .

Museum of the City of New York; photograph courtesy of Harry MacNeill Bland

In Guy's paintings we meet for the first time something of that interest in city life which had been so characteristic of the seventeenth-century Dutch painters in Holland though curiously absent from Dutch pictures of New Amsterdam. Guy deliberately aimed, as he put it, "to imitate the ancients in their method of coloring and effect."

During his residence in Brooklyn, from 1817 till his death in 1820, he painted a number of winter and summer scenes. His favorite subject was the view from his second-floor window at No. 11 Front Street, whence he could look down Front (into left background of painting) to Main Street and up James Street (now obliterated by the approach to the Brooklyn Bridge), and to the right along the curve of Front Street to Fulton.

Several versions of the painting exist. The version above, recently acquired by the Museum of the City of New York, may have been copied by another hand, but is identical with one of the versions signed by Guy himself. All of the figures were portraits, and they and the buildings are carefully identified in Henry R. Stiles's *History of the City of Brooklyn* (1869), Vol. II, pp. 88–89.

. . . and trades and occupations which had been beneath notice rivaled important buildings as subjects for illustration.

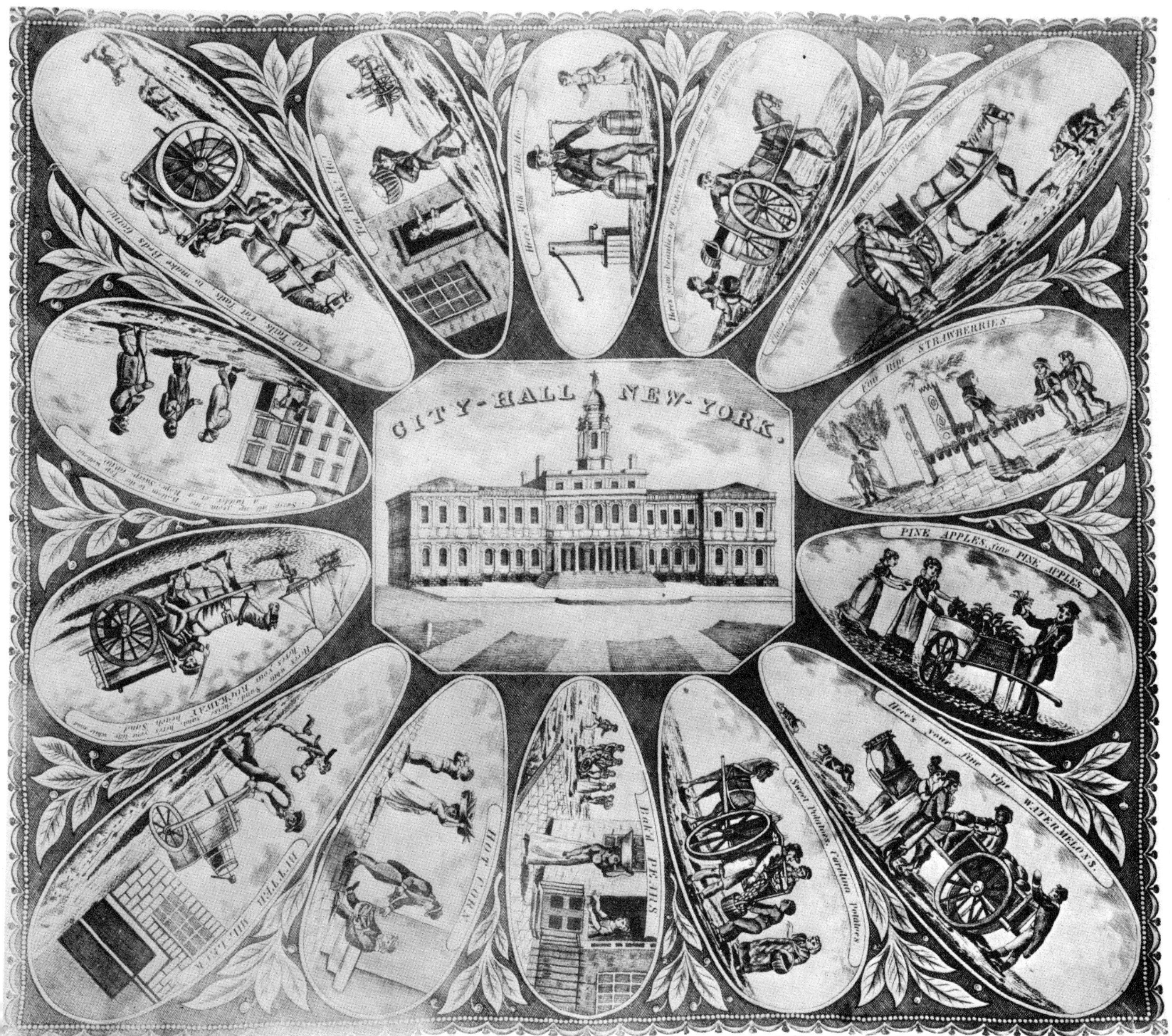

J. Clarence Davies Collection, Museum of the City of New York

This printed toile scarf or handkerchief, with its central panel of the new City Hall, surrounded by vignettes of New York street cries, was probably made about 1814.

Picture books of the city's street cries had been published earlier. One called *The Cries of New York* was first published by Samuel Wood in 1808, though there were later reissues. City Hall, designed by Joseph Mangin and John McComb, was first opened in 1811, though not completed until 1812 (see page 119).

The city, looking forward to almost unlimited expansion . . .

HAMILTON SQUARE.

Corporation Property commonly called the *Dove Lots,*

FOR SALE

On Wednesday, the 8th of April, at the Tontine Coffee-Houfe, at 12 o'clock.

The premises are laid out into 26 lots, containing 62 feet 7 inches front by 365 feet deep; one other lot of 62 feet 7 inches front by 240 feet deep; and one other lot of the same dimensions in front by 225 feet in depth, with a grant in the rear of the last mentioned lots, of a piece of ground of 125 feet 2 inches, by 125 feet, for the purpose of a Church and cademy.

The whole 28 lots front on a parallellogram of 936 feet 2 inches by 250 feet, denominated HAMILTON SQUARE, intersected by Hamilton Avenue, 60 feet wide and surrounded by the Harlem Avenue, or the old Boston Road on the East, 100 feet wide; the Boston Avenue on the West 60 feet wide; and a street on the North and South sides of 60 feet in width.

These lots, subject to an annual quit rent of twenty bushels of wheat, or the value thereof in lawful money, for each lot, will be sold in fee simple to the highest bidder, ten per cent. of the purchase money to be paid at the time of sale, and the remainder in two equal payments, with legal interest, at three and six months credit.

The covenants on the part of the Corporation are, that the square and the circumjacent streets, as delineated in the map, shall be kept open for ever, for public uses; that no more than one dwelling-house, with a stable and out offices, shall be erected on each lot, during the term of 20 years from the day of sale; that each dwelling-house shall recede from and be built up on a line 20 feet from the front of the street, as portrayed in the map. The purchasers of the said lots will be bound to inclose Hamilton Square, agreeably to the plan, and maintain and improve the same, in such style and manner as shall be agreed upon by a majority of their number.

A deed containing the special conditions and covenants will be produced at the time of sale.

The site of Hamilton Square is the most elevated of any land on this island, south of Harlem, and commands a superb view of the East river and the variegated landscape in the vicinity of Hellgate. The steeples of this city are plainly discernible from the ground, and a prospect of the bay and harbour will, in all probability, be commanded from the turrets of the villas, to be erected on the premises. In addition to every other circumstance, the lots have been designedly laid out to attract a genteel neighbourhood, whose wealth and taste will undoubtedly embellish this highly favoured spot, universally acknowledged to be the first on this Island. It is, moreover, the only remaining property, equally extensive, at the disposal of the Corporation.

ALSO, TO BE SOLD,

At the same time and place, on a Lease for Forty-two Years,

Three Lots of Ground adjoining the Harlem Commons; bounded on the West, by the farm formerly of Mr. Apthorp, and on the East by the Albany Avenue, containing about 5 acres each; and one other Lot containing about 4 acres near Anthony Smith's, bounded by the Harlem Commons on the North and by the Harlem Avenue, commonly called the Boston Post Road, on the west.

Maps of the above mentioned property will be exposed at the T. Coffee House until the day of sale, when further particulars will be made known.

BY ORDER OF THE CORPORATION

JOHN S. HUNN.

APRIL 2, 1807. *Street Commissioner.*

PRINTED BY SOUTHWICK & HARDCASTLE, No. 2, WALL-STREET.

RIGHT: Hamilton Square lay between Fifth and Third avenues, from Sixty-sixth to Sixty-eighth streets. Though the corporation promised, in this broadside, that the square would be "kept open forever, for public uses," it was closed and streets were pushed through it in 1869.

BELOW: The official map which laid down the gridiron pattern of New York's growth. Drawn by William Bridges, engraved by Peter Maverick, and published in 1811, it was based upon the survey made in 1807 by John Randel, Jr., for the commissioners who had been appointed by the state legislature "to lay out streets, roads and public squares" in the upper part of the island beyond the built-up portion (which is shaded more darkly on the map). Since the original is almost eight feet long, it is impossible to pick out details on this greatly reduced reproduction, but the reader can easily see how the gridiron disregarded the natural topography of the island.

Collection of Edward W. C. Arnold; photographs courtesy of Museum of the City of New York

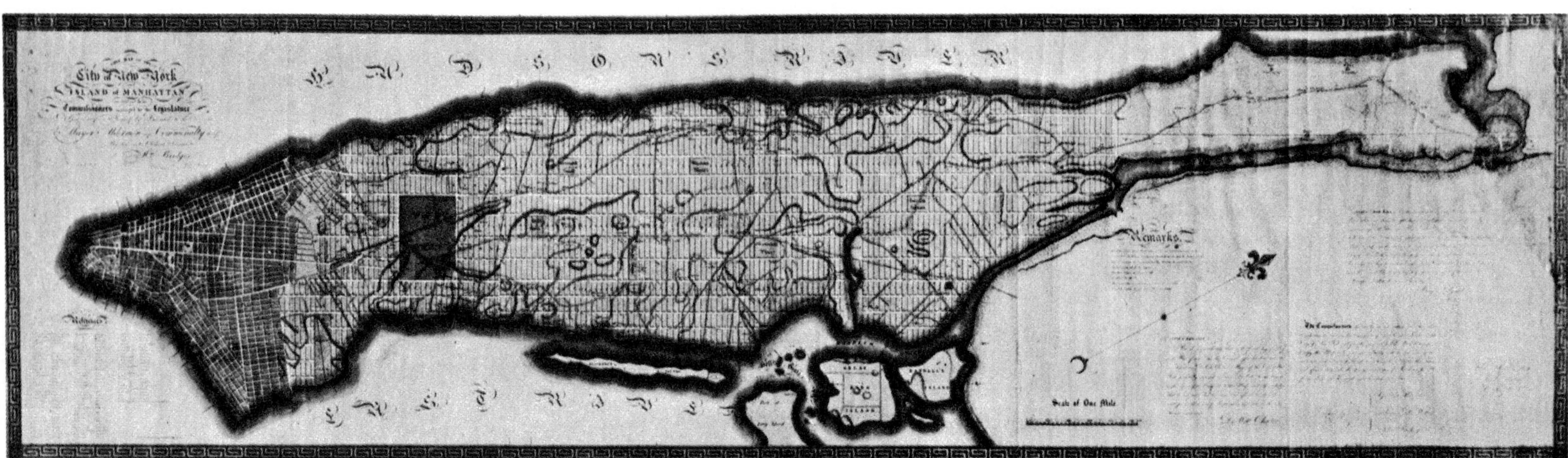

Eno Collection, New York Public Library

. . . was establishing a new municipal center farther uptown . . .

Stokes Collection, New York Public Library

This is one of a group of wash drawings and water colors by the Baroness Hyde de Neuville, who came to New York with her husband in 1807 after being banished from Napoleon's France. After the restoration of the monarchy in 1814, the baron became French minister to the United States.

The drawing was made in February, 1808, looking south from Chambers Street (in foreground) to the Bridewell (see also page 95). To the left appears the unfinished City Hall, above which rises the spire of the Brick Presbyterian Church on the northeast corner of Beekman and Nassau streets. The tall steeple at right is that of St. Paul's, and at extreme right is the cupola of St. Peter's, New York's first Catholic church, built in 1785–86 at the southeast corner of Barclay and Church streets.

In the center foreground is the Charity School, with its playground, which was opened in May, 1807, under the direction of the Free School Society. This former workshop remained the school building until the end of 1809, when the society opened Free School No. 1, on a site near the northeastern corner of present City Hall Park—the first free school in the city to be supported in part by municipal funds (see page 228).

. . . and organizing many new municipal services.

Detail of picture on page 111

The baroness had a nice eye for circumstantial detail, as witness the bedraggled and vagrant pig, and the small boy carrying home a can of beer, in the very shadow of the Board of Health's office at the corner of Chambers Street and Broadway. The board had been organized by the Common Council in December, 1805, to include and expand the functions of the board of three commissioners of health which had been set up in 1797. If one had walked down Broadway and turned right on Warren Street, at the first corner, one would have come after a few blocks to Greenwich Street and the corner shown in the baroness' water color on the next page.

But it was everyday life, at specific times and seasons, which now caught the eye of visitors and residents alike.

Bequest of Mrs. J. Insley Blair, Museum of the City of New York

Like Francis Guy over in Brooklyn (page 108), the Baroness Hyde de Neuville was more interested in the life of the city than in its buildings. Her water-color snow scene of the corner of Warren and Greenwich streets in January, 1809, shows a part of New York which would not conceivably have interested an artist of the Federalist period. These are not the houses of the wealthy, and no public building dominates the view. It is a middle-class neighborhood, slightly down at heel, and ordinary people are shown doing quite ordinary things.

One New Yorker painted a whole series of scenes . . .

William P. Chappel was a self-taught painter who loved to record everyday happenings in the crude but evocative paintings he turned out on cardboard panels approximately 9″ × 6″. On the backs, he wrote detailed titles. The painting above is labeled "House Raisng in Grand St. between 3^{d} Now Elrige & Allen St. 1810 NY." (Third Street became Eldridge Street in 1817.)

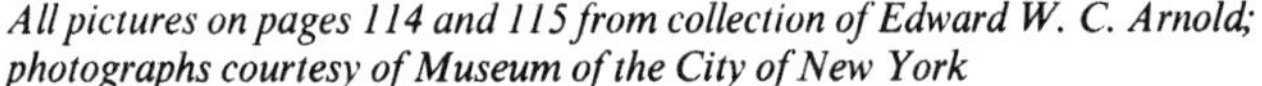
All pictures on pages 114 and 115 from collection of Edward W. C. Arnold; photographs courtesy of Museum of the City of New York

"Intersetion of Bowery Dover Chatham & Catherine St. showing the Old Watch House Wench selling Hot corn on the corner of Dover St. the Stage Waggon by Geo. Hall from Tarrytown North Castle by way of Kings Brige 1810."

. . . affectionately recalling the homely routine of life in unpretentious neighborhoods.

Chappel labeled this "East side of Elizabeth corner of Pump [Canal] st Wm & Groddy Post Paint Mill [at right] Potpye Palmer with his Garbage Cart & Bell 1805." William and Gerardus Post were sons of William Post, who in 1754 established the paint business still carried on in the city by Devoe & Raynolds. The original shop was at 160 Water Street. A recently published history of the company makes no reference to a "paint mill" on the corner of Canal and Elizabeth streets.

In a very long inscription on the back of this panel Chappel noted that it showed one of the City Watch leaving his watch box on patrol. The picture is of the west side of Elizabeth Street, between Canal and Hester streets, in 1809. The house at left was occupied by "an industrious Beadsted Maker Named Ingrist." Set back from the street at right was the Elizabeth Street African Methodist Meeting House where "occasionally preeched the Greatest Learned Doctors."

Others recorded recurrent calamities and disasters . . .

Bequest of Mrs. J. Insley Blair, Museum of the City of New York

A water-color drawing by John Rubens Smith of "St. George's Church after fire of January 5th. 1814." St. George's had been built in 1749–52 and stood on the northwest corner of Beekman and Cliff streets. The fire also destroyed several dwellings and shops in the neighborhood and the African Free School down Cliff Street.

The steeple in the distance is the Brick Presbyterian Church on Beekman at Nassau Street.

. . . the preparations for defense during the war of 1812 . . .

LAUNCH OF THE STEAM FRIGATE FULTON THE FIRST, AT NEW YORK, 29th OCT 1814.

Collection of Edward W. C. Arnold; photograph courtesy of Museum of the City of New York

During the War of 1812 a group of New Yorkers, realizing the defenseless state of the harbor, organized a Coast and Harbour Defense Association. Under their supervision, with financial aid from the federal government, a steam frigate designed by Robert Fulton was built at the shipyard of Adam and Noah Brown at Corlaer's Hook. Originally called the *Demalogos* (Voice of the People), her name was changed to *Fulton the First* in honor of the inventor. The engraved view, drawn by J. J. Barralet "from a Sketch by ——— Morgan, taken on the spot," was published by Cammeyer & Acock, Philadelphia, 1819.

A water-color drawing by John Joseph Holland of Mill Rock and Hell Gate, looking northeast from Fort Stevens, on Hallett's Point. This was one of an important series of views, maps, and plans accompanying a *Report on the Defence of the City of New York* submitted to the Common Council by Brigadier General J. G. Swift, chief engineer of the United States, in 1814. Both Fort Stevens (which stood north of the present site of the Astoria Houses) and the blockhouse on Mill Rock were built in the summer of 1814, chiefly by civilian volunteers. In left background is Manhattan, and at right Ward's Island.

New-York Historical Society

. . . and the great technical achievements of the period.

Stokes Collection, New York Public Library

There are no authentic contemporary pictures of Fulton's first successful steamboat, built at Charles Browne's shipyard near Corlaer's Hook (where the Vladeck Houses now stand), and launched in 1807. The view above, lithographed and published in France, shows the vessel as it appeared after it had been enlarged and completely rebuilt, and was probably drawn sometime between 1810 and 1814. The scenery was almost certainly invented in France.

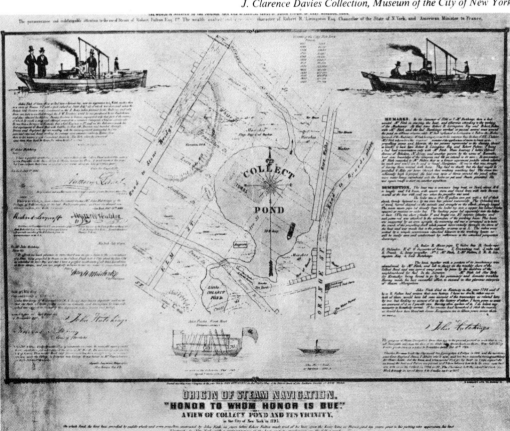

J. Clarence Davies Collection, Museum of the City of New York

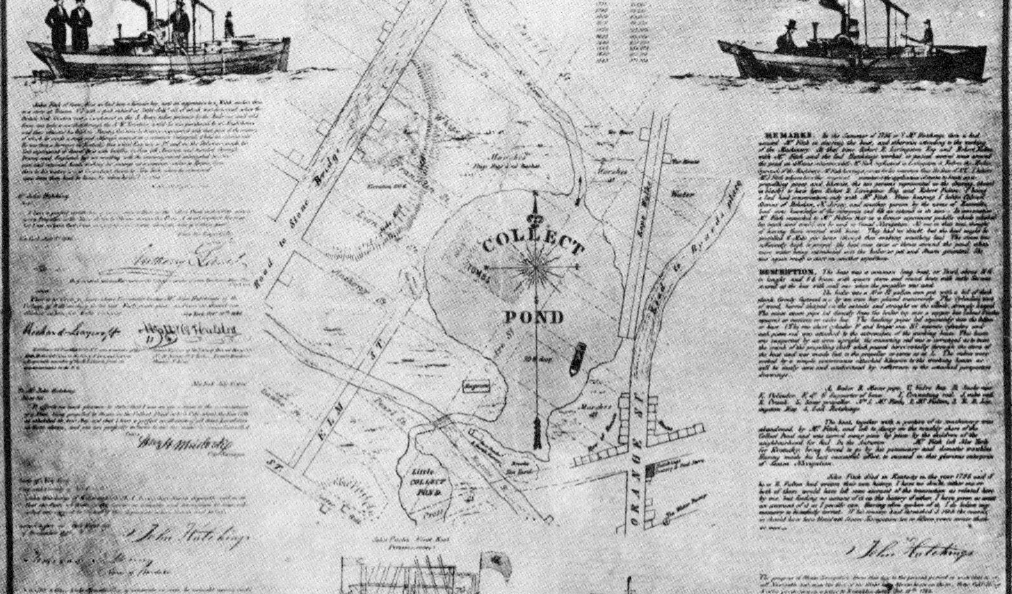

The print at right, drawn by J. Penniman and lithographed by F. Michelin, was published by John Hutchings at Williamsburg, Long Island, in 1846 as a belated attempt to honor John Fitch for his experiments with a steamboat on the Collect Pond in 1796 or 1797. As a boy, Hutchings had helped Fitch during the experiments. (The Hutchings Grocery & Feed Store, shown on the map at the southeast corner of Orange and Cross streets, now Baxter and Park streets, was probably his family's combined home and shop.)

The most animated scenes of city life were those which attracted New Yorkers and visitors alike to Broadway . . .

Bequest of Mrs. J. Insley Blair, Museum of the City of New York

This view of Broadway and the City Hall, looking north from Ann Street, is reproduced from an original water color by the Swedish Baron Axel Leonhard Klinckowstrom, who visited New York in 1818–19. On his return to Sweden, after his American tour, he published two volumes of *Letters about the United States* (1824) accompanied by an *Atlas* in which many of his drawings and sketches (including this one) are reproduced in aquatint engravings. According to the baron, Broadway was the city's most frequented promenade, "where all new fashions can first be admired. In the cool season, and when the weather is fine, the young dandies and the fair sex promenade on the sidewalks between 2 and 3 in the afternoon.
"About a third of the length of the street from the Battery you come across a large 3-cornered place which is shaded by beautiful trees. Here is the City Hall. It is built in a light and very handsome style. As I have made a correct design of this place, and of Broadway and Chatham Street [the picture above] you will get a good idea of this part of New York, which really is pretty. In the same drawing you will see the costumes worn here and also all the vehicles, from the elegant coach down to the modest pushcart, on which the licensed porter is busily transferring the traveller's goods to the harbor."
Beyond St. Paul's (at left) is the old Rutherford house at the northwest corner of Vesey Street, occupied at this time by Elijah Secor, merchant. The second house beyond was John Jacob Astor's.

. . . and the park uptown at City Hall. Many of the pictures were simply stylized generalizations of the urban scene . . .

Bequest of Mrs. J. Insley Blair, Museum of the City of New York

A water-color drawing by Arthur J. Stansbury, made about 1825, shows the rear of the City Hall. It was made from the northwest corner of Broadway and Chambers Street, looking eastward along Chambers (at left) and across the now vacant corner lots which had formerly been the site of the Health Department office and the Charity School (pages 111–12).

The American Museum, originally the Tammany Museum, had been established in 1790, and for many years was housed here in the west wing of the old Almshouse, which also housed the New-York Historical Society and other institutions. In 1830, when the building was taken over for municipal offices, the museum was moved to a new marble building down Broadway at Ann Street, where it was located when P. T. Barnum bought it in 1842 (see page 195).

The domed building beyond the old Almshouse on Chambers Street was the Rotunda, built by the painter John Vanderlyn in 1817 as an "art center" where paintings (including his own vast panoramas of Versailles and Paris) could be exhibited. The two-story building with cupola, in the middle of the picture, was the jail, east of the City Hall on Chatham Street (now Park Row).

. . . but with increasing frequency they are enlivened by the artist's personal response to a particular moment . . .

Both pictures from collection of Edward W. C. Arnold; photographs courtesy of Museum of the City of New York

In Alexander Jackson Davis' 1827 water color, above, we are looking southwest across the park toward St. Paul's Chapel from a point just east of City Hall. Chatham Street (now Park Row) is the other side of the fence at left. The houses shown between St. Paul's and City Hall are on the west side of Broadway from Vesey Street to Park Place. Just north of Barclay Street is the American Hotel, opened that year. North of the hotel, the house with the arched doorway was the residence of Philip Hone, mayor of the city for one term (1825–26) and the author of a diary which gives an unparalleled picture of the city's life from 1828 to 1851.

The wash drawing was made by the engraver John Hill on the back of a fragment of his famous aquatint of City Hall (not reproduced in this volume; see Stokes, *Iconography,* Vol. III, Plate 97). It bears the penciled inscription, "View from my Work-Room Window in Hammond St by J. Hill —1825—." Hammond is now West Eleventh between Greenwich Avenue and the West Side Highway.

. . . or to a specific episode. New attitudes and new interests were beginning to break down many of the formalities inherited from the previous century.

Chicago Historical Society

"Half past Eight O'clock. The Cook enrag'd at the Steerage Passengers being late with their Breakfast on Board the Ship *Acasta,* Decr 1824" —so reads the caption at the bottom of this painting. And a note across the top, on the edge of the sail, labels it "A Hasty Sketch taken by J. Gear on his Voyage to America."

Gear apparently went on to the West soon after landing. But many of the 4889 German and Irish and Scandinavian immigrants who landed in New York that year stayed in the city.

The city's growth in the early twenties, in spite of three years of postwar depression, was astonishing. Population increased thirty per cent, from 123,706 in 1820 to 166,806 in 1825. More than 1600 new houses were built in the year 1824 alone.

Although engraved views of the city retained many eighteenth-century mannerisms (supplied by the engraver if they were absent from the originals) . . .

Stokes Collection, New York Public Library

Collection of Edward W. C. Arnold; photograph courtesy of Museum of the City of New York

The above view of "New York from Heights near Brooklyn" (published in 1823) was engraved by John Hill (see page 121) from a water color by William G. Wall, a portion of which is reproduced at left. Wall advertised this and a companion print of "New York from Weehawk" as pictures made from points of view which afforded "the most favorable view" of the city and conveyed "the most correct impression of the beauties of the Bay and the surrounding scenery." In this connection, note the differences in the foreground landscape of the engraving and the original, as well as the added figures.

The view was made from Bergen Hill (since leveled, near present Carroll Park). The windmill on the shore, center right, was at Pierrepont's old Anchor Gin Distillery, at the foot of Joralemon Street. The Cornell mill and houses are on the point of land this side of the distillery, and on the hill above it is the Remsen house.

. . . a cheaper and more rapid technique of reproducing pictures, better suited to romantic sketches of "the picturesque" . . .

AMERIQUE SEPTENTRIONALE — ETAT DE NEW-YORK

Interieur de New York, rue de Provost et Chapel — No. 3 — Interior of New York, Provost Street and Chapel

Das Innere von New York, Strasse Provost and Chapel.

J. Clarence Davies Collection, Museum of the City of New York

The four lithographs reproduced on this and the following page were printed in France from drawings made about 1820 by J. Milbert, a Frenchman who came to New York in 1815. The two on this page are from his *Itinéraire Pittoresque du Fleuve Hudson* (Paris, 1825), for which the lithographs were made by Villeneuve. Lithography had been invented by Senefelder in 1798 and by 1809 there were seven lithographic establishments in Munich. By 1816 the new process had been established in Paris, and by 1822 in London. New York's first lithographer began publishing in 1825 (see page 129).

Collection of Edward W. C. Arnold; photograph courtesy of Museum of the City of New York

The view above, of Provost Street (now Franklin) and Chapel (now West Broadway), was the one which Milbert considered most typical of the city. It is noteworthy that he, like the Baroness de Neuville a decade earlier (see page 113), chose such an unpretentious neighborhood for his "typical" view.

At left is a nearer view of Pierrepont's Anchor Gin Distillery in Brooklyn, shown also in the Wall view on the preceding page.

. . . was already popular in Europe and was soon to be widely available here.

J. Clarence Davies Collection, Museum of the City of New York

Milbert's pictures on this page were part of a set of fourteen lithographs published in Paris in 1825 as *A Series of Picturesque Views in North America.* The one above, entitled "View of the Tavern on the Road to King's Bridge Near Fort Washington," shows the Blue Bell Tavern, which had been built before the Revolution on the west side of Broadway north of present 181st Street and was not torn down until 1880 (see map, page 72).

This view of "Lydick's Mill & House on Bronx River, West Farms" shows a part of the Lydig property which is now the site of the zoo in Bronx Park. The Lydig family acquired the property in 1802 and remained in ownership until 1884, when the park was established.

Collection of Edward W. C. Arnold; photograph courtesy of Museum of the City of New York

Meanwhile the city's expanding commercial life continued to be recorded chiefly in crude woodcuts . . .

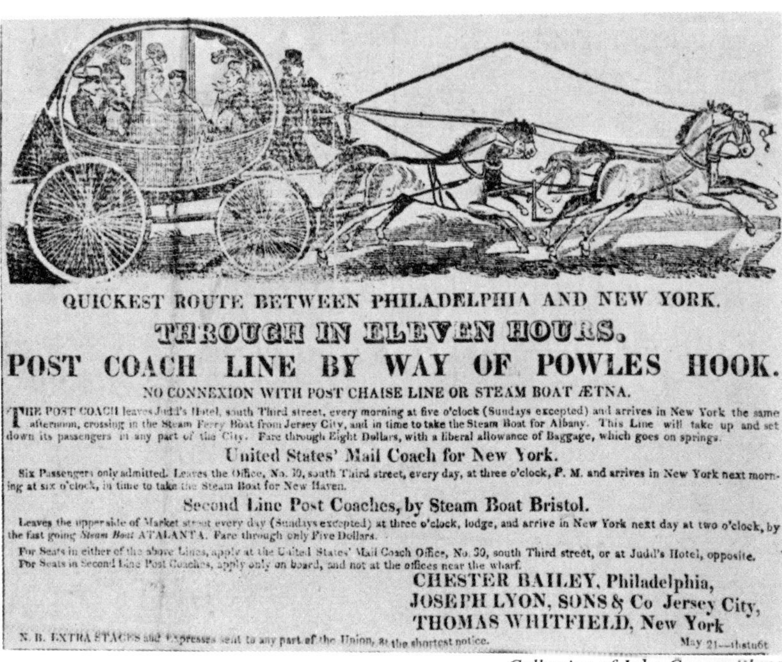

Collection of John Cooper Bland; photograph courtesy of Museum of the City of New York

The advertisement of the Philadelphia–New York coach was published in the *United States Gazette and True American,* Philadelphia, May 28, 1818. The Powles (or Paulus) Hook ferry was for many years one of the most important links between New York and New Jersey. Established in 1764, it ran from the foot of Cortlandt Street to Paulus Hook (Jersey City). In 1812 steam ferryboats were introduced by John C. and Robert L. Stevens.

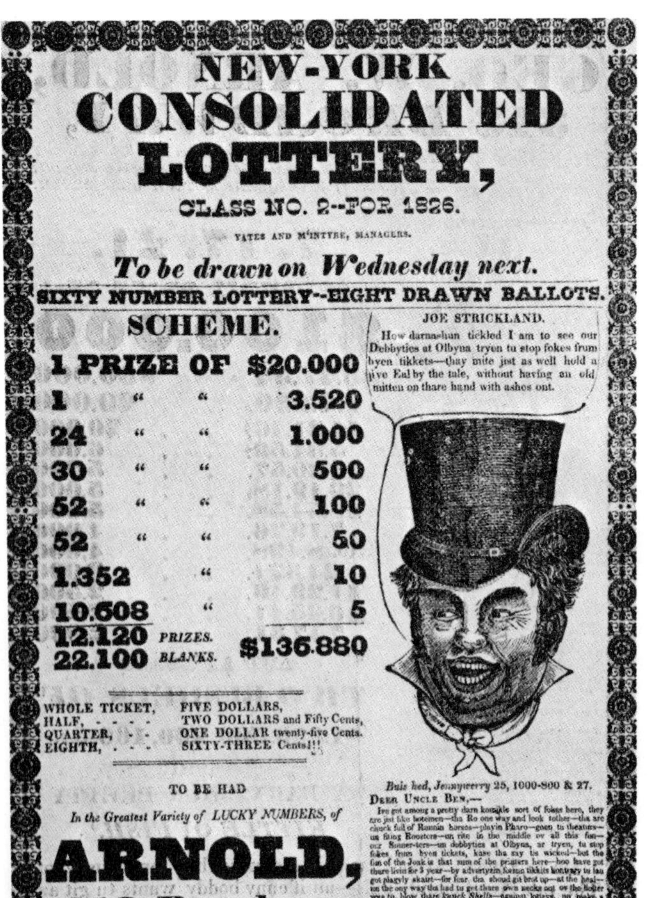

George W. Arnold's advertisement of tickets for the "New-York Consolidated Lottery" of 1826 serves to remind us that lotteries played an important part in New York's development. The Dutch had used them as early as 1655 to raise money for poor relief; in 1746 an official lottery was run off to raise funds for fortifications, and several lotteries were held between 1747 and 1754 to raise funds for establishing King's (Columbia) College. Though lotteries had been forbidden by the new state constitution of 1821, various methods were devised for evading the law until 1833, when they were finally driven underground.

Collection of Edward W. C. Arnold; photograph courtesy of Museum of the City of New York

. . . though engravings were occasionally used, and at least one warehouse-and-shop was devotedly portrayed in a detailed water color.

Collection of Edward W. C. Arnold; photograph courtesy of Museum of the City of New York

John Williams' trade card, advertising his shop at 212 Broadway, northeast corner of Fulton (then Fair) Street, was engraved in 1816, probably by Peter Maverick.

The anonymous water-color drawing (c. 1820) is of Duncan Phyfe's furniture warehouse, store, and workshop at 168–72 Fulton Street, west of Broadway, on the south side of the street opposite St. Paul's churchyard. Both of these locations are shown on page 195 as they appeared thirty years later.

Metropolitan Museum of Art

New York's place as the nation's commercial metropolis was insured by the completion of the Erie Canal in 1825 . . .

Imbert Del. Saml. Maverick Sc.

LANDING OF GEN. LAFAYETTE,
At Castle Garden, New-York, 16th August 1824.

J. Clarence Davies Collection, Museum of the City of New York

GRAND CANAL CELEBRATION IN NEW-YORK, ON FRIDAY NOV. 4.

In order to accommodate all persons desirous of witnessing the grand celebration of the meeting of the waters in New-York, on Friday the 4th instant, the

Steam-Boat Fanny

Will leave the wharf at Norwich, on Wednesday evening at 6 o'clock, and arrive in New-York on Thursday morning.

RETURNING,

Will leave New-York on Friday at sundown, and arrive in Norwich on Saturday morning.

Fare, both to and from, $5.

A year before the Grand Canal Celebration, Castle Garden and the Battery had been the scene of a huge celebration in honor of Lafayette, then on a visit to this country. The view, drawn by Anthony Imbert and engraved by Samuel Maverick, was one of the illustrations for *A Complete History of the Marquis de Lafayette,* by an officer in the late army (New York, 1826). It is a typical example of the engraved illustrations which were common at the time when Imbert himself introduced lithography to New York (see next page).

People came from all parts of the country to see the land and water parades held in New York November 4, 1825, to celebrate the opening of the Erie Canal. This broadside advertisement was issued at Norwich, Connecticut, announcing one of the many excursions which brought visitors to witness the event.

Collection of H. Armour Smith

. . . and the first lithographs produced in New York were pictures of the harbor celebration . . .

Stokes Collection, New York Public Library

The picture above reproduces one section of a long (41½″ × 8½″) lithograph entitled "Grand Canal Celebration. View of the Fleet Preparing to Form in Line" which was folded into Cadwallader D. Colden's *Memoir* of the Canal Celebration (published in 1826, though dated 1825) as one of the illustrations. The picture was drawn by Archibald Robertson and lithographed by Anthony Imbert.

Imbert, as the *Memoir* tells us, was a former French naval officer who had studied painting and drawing while a prisoner in England and was well known as a marine artist (see preceding page). He came to New York in 1824 and soon thereafter established his lithographic press, the first in the city, at 79 Murray Street. (The first American lithographs had been made in Philadelphia in 1819, and Pendleton Brothers in Boston preceded Imbert by at least a couple of years.)

So proud were New Yorkers of Imbert's work that the Common Council in 1827 sent a copy of the *Memoir* to the King of Bavaria, as a tribute of respect to the ruler and the people of the country which was the birthplace of lithography.

The section of the print reproduced here is most of the right-hand half. The small building at the extreme right was the U. S. Revenue Office at Whitehall Slip, Pier 1 on the East River side of the Battery. Left of it is the base of the old "churn" flagstaff, and farther left, Castle Garden, which had been built as a fort in 1808 but had recently been converted into a theater and pleasure resort.

. . . and the floats and other vehicles which paraded through the city in honor of the event.

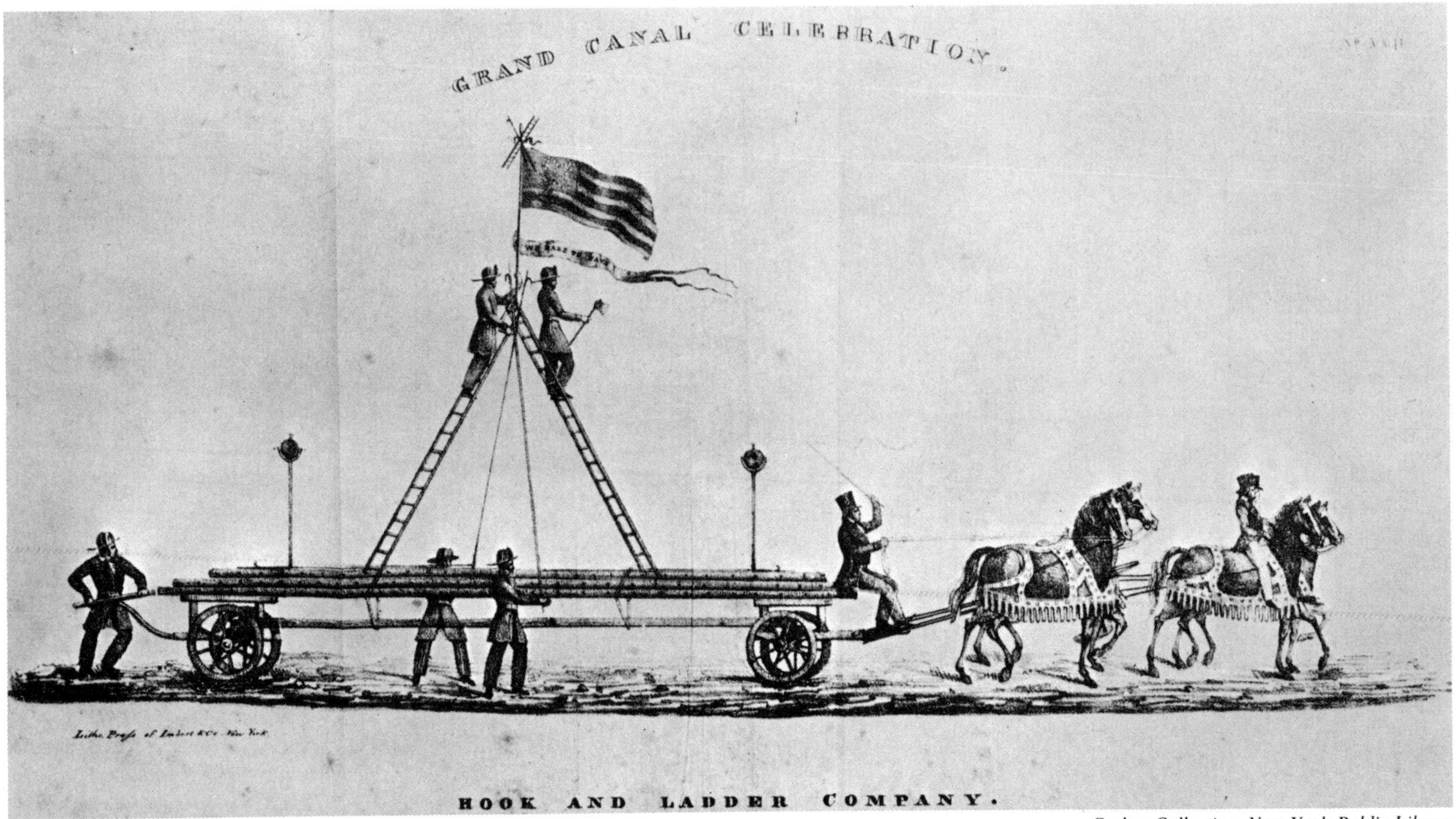

GRAND CANAL CELEBRATION.

HOOK AND LADDER COMPANY.

Stokes Collection, New York Public Library

ABOVE: Lithographed plate No. XXII by Imbert from Colden's *Memoir* of the Grand Canal Celebration. Many civic organizations, and the various trades, were represented in the parade which followed the harbor celebration, and the book contains pictures of the floats and other vehicles fitted up for the occasion. (The motto on the banner floating above the head of the fireman with the ax is "We Raze to Save.") RIGHT: General Solomon van Rensselaer's bill for board for himself and family at the American Hotel (see also page 121) gives an idea of what a visitor to the city could expect to pay for lodging and refreshment at a first-class city hotel in the mid-twenties. The picture of the hotel on the billhead was drawn by A. J. Davis and engraved by O. H. Throop.

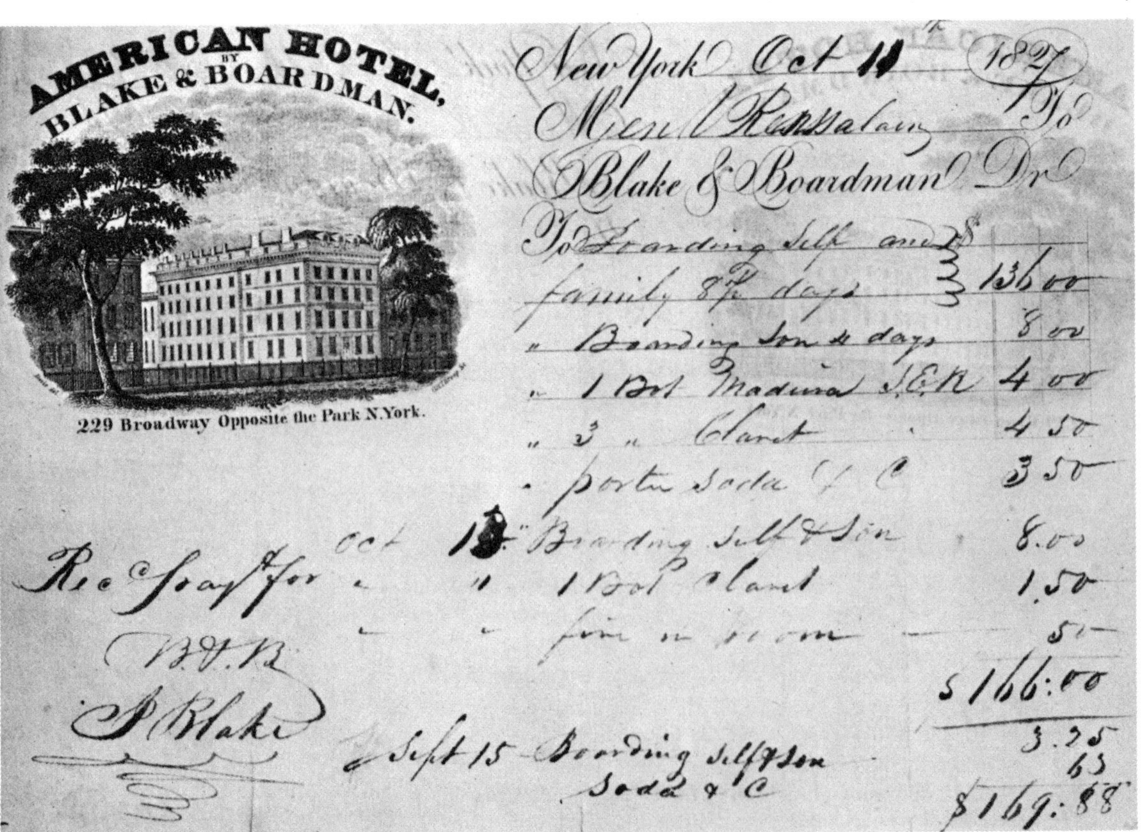

AMERICAN HOTEL,
BY
BLAKE & BOARDMAN.
229 Broadway Opposite the Park N.York.

New York Oct 11 182[illegible]
Mess Rensselaer To
Blake & Boardman Dr

To Boarding Self and family 8½ days		136 00
" Boarding Son 4 days		8 00
" 1 Bot Madeira S.E.K.		4 00
" 3 " Claret		4 50
" porter Soda &c		3 50
Oct 13 " Boarding Self & Son		8.00
" " 1 Bot Claret		1.50
" " fire in room		50
		$166:00
Sept 15 Boarding Self & Son		3.25
Soda &c		63
		$169:88

Rec Payt for
B.V.B.
J. Blake

Collection of Edward W. C. Arnold; photograph courtesy of Museum of the City of New York

Meanwhile, pictures of the city in all mediums dealt increasingly with the city's flourishing commercial life . . .

Both pictures from collection of Edward W. C. Arnold; photographs courtesy of Museum of the City of New York

This view of "South Street from Maiden Lane," drawn and engraved by William J. Bennett about 1828, was one of three prints published by Henry J. Megarey as the first group in a projected series of four entitled *Megarey's Street Views in the City of New-York.* So far as is known, only the first group was published. The other two prints in this group were of "Broadway from the Bowling Green" and "Fulton St. & Market." At left, below, is a detail from Bennett's original water color for this print. Notice the details—the pot, the stick, the cobblestones, and ship's name—which he added in the finished print. (The *Leeds,* a Swallowtail packet, was wrecked later in 1828 in the Thames.) Even after the Erie Canal was opened, New York remained primarily an importing center. But the canal was unquestionably a stimulus to New York's trade. In the year it opened (1825) 500 new mercantile businesses were established in the city, and it was along South Street that the city's commercial life centered. As Mrs. Ann Royall observed in 1826, the activity on Broadway and Wall Street was "only a drop in the bucket compared to that on the wharves or slips" along South Street.

. . . and with the theaters and other amusements . . .

The original Park Theater (page 102) was destroyed by fire in 1820, but a new building was promptly erected, and the theater reopened in 1821. This water color by John Searle shows the interior of the new building in November, 1822, during a performance of *Monsieur Tonson,* a farce by the English dramatist William T. Moncrieffe. Searle made the drawing for William Bayard, and the faces of the people in the audience were all portraits from life. A copy of a key, made by a member of the New-York Historical Society while a number of those represented were still alive, is now owned by the society and identifies eighty-four individuals whose likenesses are included.

New-York Historical Society

William Bayard himself is standing in the first tier of boxes, next to the lady (Miss Ogden) whose shawl hangs over the rail. The artist, Searle, has represented himself in the center front of the orchestra seats, partly turned away from the stage with one eye on the observer. On the stage are Charles Mathews as Monsieur Morbleau and Miss Johnson as Madame Bellegarde.

There was another theater, the Chatham, just up Park Row between Duane and Pearl streets, which opened in 1822. But it was not so fashionable as the Park, and in 1832 was converted into the Second Free Presbyterian Church. The Park Theater burned for the second time in 1848 and was not rebuilt.

Collection of Edward W. C. Arnold; photograph courtesy of Museum of the City of New York

The caption printed beneath this aquatint engraving, published by J. Martin, was as follows:

"MAGNANIMITY OF THE ELEPHANT DISPLAYED IN THE PRESERVATION OF HIS KEEPER J. MARTIN, IN THE BOWERY MENAGERIE IN NEW YORK. Dec. 1826. Two Tigers, male & female breaking the bars of their cage, sprang into the room & seized the Lama & began to devour it: Just at this moment, the keeper J. Martin, entered to feed the animals, with no means of defence but his usual staff, the female tiger now abandon'd the Lama & was in the act of springing on Martin, when the elephant the friend of man, displayed his magnanimity in his rescue, by throwing his trunk round his body & placing him on his back. The Lion at the same time thrust his paw through the grates of his cage & seizing the tiger held him until Martin, by calling, got his friends to his assistance."

The Zoological Institute was on the east side of the Bowery, just north of Bayard Street. P. T. Barnum had a job writing advertisements and publicity for it at one time, before he bought the American Museum.

A few lithographs of the city appeared, as illustrations for books or pamphlets.

FIRST INFANT SCHOOL IN GREEN STREET NEW YORK.

Imbert's Lithography. A. Robertson del.

VIEW FROM THE ROSTRUM

Monitor Nine & Six? Scholars Fifteen! &c.

VIEW FROM THE GALLERY.

Imbert's Lithography A. Robertson del.

The Children Marching & Reciting aloud, "Twice two's Four &c."

Collection of Edward W. C. Arnold; photograph courtesy of Museum of the City of New York

This pair of pictures, drawn by Archibald Robertson and lithographed by Anthony Imbert, was the frontispiece of a pamphlet entitled *The Constitution & By-Laws of the Infant School Society of New York, instituted May 23, 1827* (New York, 1828). The school was located in the basement of the Presbyterian Church on the northwest corner of Canal and Green streets, where it was maintained and supported "by the aid of a few ladies of respectability." In 1827–28 it had from 200 to 400 pupils, all under five years of age. The monitorial system of instruction, so graphically explained by Robertson's drawing, was a variant of the system promoted in England by Joseph Lancaster early in the century.

Because of its cheapness and simplicity (the scholars taught one another to a great extent, and thereby cut down on teachers' salaries) it was early adopted in this country. The Collegiate School of the Dutch Reformed Church (New York's oldest existing educational institution) introduced it as early as 1809, and it was widely used in the city's public schools during the 1830s and 1840s. Lancaster himself came to New York in 1818 and lived here until his death.

Sets of small engraved views, which included interiors of important buildings . . .

Collection of Allen S. Davenport

The pictures on this and the next page are from the so-called Bourne *Views* —a series of nineteen plates (all but one of which contain two pictures) which were published in 1830–31 by George M. Bourne at his shop on Broadway near Franklin Street. Most of the views were drawn by C. W. Burton and printed by J. Neale, but several different engravers made the plates.

The three on this page are reproduced in the same size as the originals.

The one at the top, from Plate 3, was engraved by James Smillie and shows the landing place at the foot of Barclay Street on the Hudson, where the North River Steamboat Line and the Hoboken Ferry had their docks. The building at right housed the office of the Patterson Stage.

Stokes Collection, New York Public Library

The picture at right, from Plate 18, engraved by Hatch and Smillie, shows the original St. Patrick's Cathedral, built 1809–15 from designs by Joseph F. Mangin, at the corner of Mott and Prince streets. The building was rebuilt after a destructive fire in 1869 and still stands.

Stokes Collection, New York Public Library

The picture at left, from Plate 9, engraved by H. Fossette, shows the interior of the Merchants Exchange on Wall Street, designed by M. E. Thompson and built 1825–27. The building was destroyed in the Great Fire of 1835 (see page 150).

. . . as well as scenes in the newer parts of town, were issued by enterprising publishers . . .

Both pictures from Stokes Collection, New York Public Library

The two Bourne views on this page are considerably enlarged from the originals so that the details of the engravings may be more easily seen.

The view at the top is the companion picture to the one of the interior of the Merchants Exchange on the preceding page and was also engraved by Fossette. It was made from Burton's drawing of the Council Chamber at the City Hall. The room, which is on the second floor in the southwest corner of the building, was considerably altered at different times but was restored to something very like its original appearance in 1909, through the generosity of Mrs. Russell Sage.

The view below, from Plate 8, engraved by James Smillie, shows the "Junction of Broadway & the Bowery" at what is now Union Square. (The Bowery is now called Fourth Avenue for several blocks below the square.) The picture is interesting as an illustration of the laborious methods by which the uneven terrain of Manhattan was leveled. A guidebook of 1833 describes the square as having recently been greatly altered and enlarged to include, in addition to the part north of Fourteenth Street, "a large triangle to the east, carved out of the 'Bowery Hill,'" and another large triangle lying west of the present Broadway.

. . . and the first picture book about New York, published in 1831, included engravings of the hotels and theaters . . .

The views on this and the following page, and at the top of page 139, are taken from what may be called the first picture book of New York, Theodore S. Fay's *Views in the City of New-York and its Environs . . . from Accurate, Characteristic, and Picturesque Drawings, Taken from the Objects Themselves . . . with Historical, Topographical and Critical Illustrations* (New York, Peabody & Co., 1831–32). Originally issued in parts, the book contained thirty-eight engraved views and a map. The plates are reproduced here in original size.

Plate 4, reproduced at left, showed the "Residence of Philip Hone, Esq. and American Hotel, Broadway" (see also page 121). It was drawn by J. H. Dakin and engraved by Barnard and Dick. The shop of Peabody & Co., publishers of the book, is between Hone's house and the hotel. The Woolworth Building now occupies this site.

Plate 16, below, bears the title "Park Theater-Park Row. (Tammany Hall in the Distance)," and was drawn and engraved by H. Fossette. The view was made looking up Park Row from the southern tip of City Hall Park. The theater, at right, Fay describes as "one of the homeliest buildings in the city of any note."

The buildings beyond the theater were, in order, the Theater Hotel, Sweeney's Porter House, City Coffee House (formerly Philip G. Rhinelander's residence), Bachelor's Hall (formerly the home of John G. Leake—one of the founders of the Leake and Watts Orphan Asylum), Irish's Porter House, the chemist shop of George Chilton, and Turner's grocery store. Beyond the corner of Beekman Street was the old Brick Presbyterian Church, and in the background, Tammany Hall at Frankfort and Nassau streets (see page 333).

Both pictures from collection of Edward W. C. Arnold; photographs courtesy of Museum of the City of New York

. . . shops and business districts which would be of interest to visitors.

Plate 17 in the Peabody *Views,* drawn by A. J. Davis and engraved by J. Archer, was entitled "Broad Street. (Custom House in the distance.)" The old stepped-gable house next to Joseph Meeks & Sons cabinetmaker's shop is the same building that appeared in the 1787 view of Broad Street (page 86); Fay's text, published in 1832, notes that it had been taken down since the drawing was made, probably in 1830; at which time it was occupied by John Ferris, a cooper. Twenty years later, a writer in *Putnam's Magazine* remembered its destruction without any sorrow. "We never waste a tear," he wrote, "over the death of an old Fogy, especially a Dutch one, which . . . must be admitted to surpass in desolation all the other varieties of conservatism extant." ("New-York Daguerreotyped," *Putnam's,* February, 1853. See also pages 246–47.) The Custom House, at the upper end of Broad Street on Wall Street, occupied a building originally erected as a store on the site of the old Federal Hall.

Both pictures from collection of Edward W. C. Arnold; photographs courtesy of Museum of the City of New York

The picture of "Pearl Street House & Ohio Hotel (Hanover Square in the Distance)" was drawn and engraved by M. Osborne. Fay's text notes that it is "extensively known as the resort of merchants from every part of the Union, especially . . . from Ohio." He also calls attention to the fact that few women appear in the view, and explains "to distant readers" that women seldom if ever go into such crowded business districts as Pearl Street, Wall Street, or South Street.

Many of these pictures were copied and republished in magazines all over the country . . .

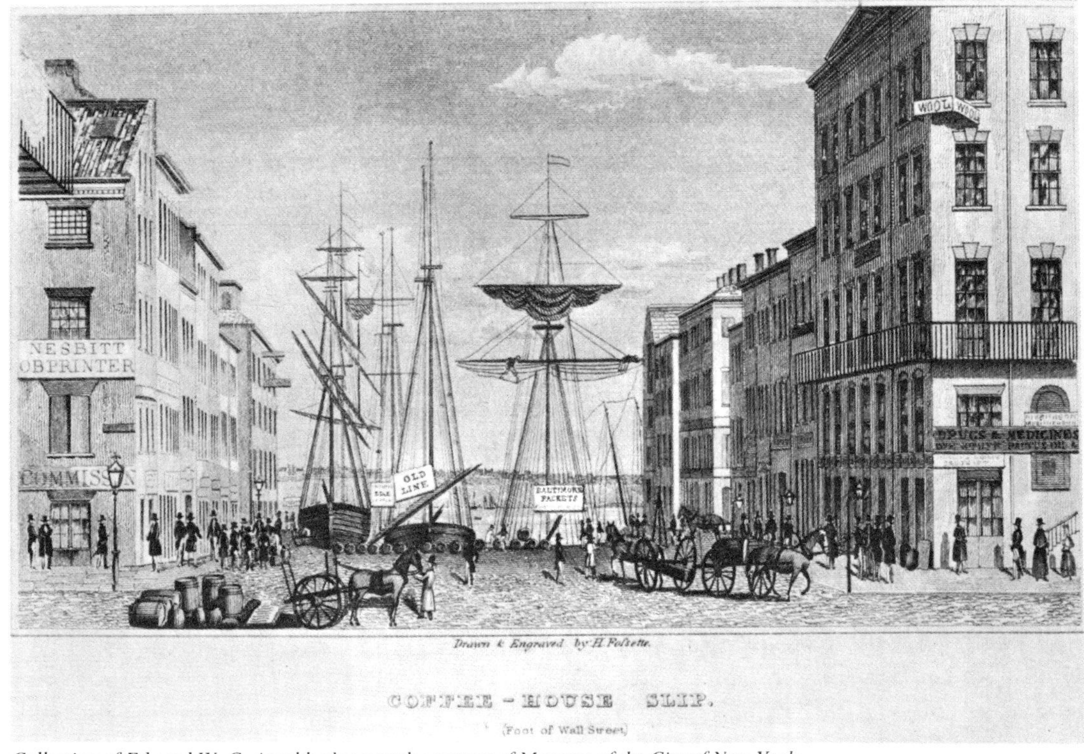

Drawn & Engraved by H. Fossette.

COFFEE-HOUSE SLIP.

(Foot of Wall Street)

Collection of Edward W. C. Arnold; photograph courtesy of Museum of the City of New York

The picture at left of "Coffee-House Slip. (Foot of Wall Street)," drawn and engraved on steel by H. Fossette, was Plate 15 of the Peabody *Views.* It was taken from Water Street, looking down Wall toward the East River, and the five-story building at right had been built in 1805 as the Phoenix Coffee House, to replace the old Merchants' Coffee House (see page 107) which burned down in 1804.

Below is an anonymous wood engraving, "View of Coffee House Slip, New York," from the *American Magazine of Useful Knowledge,* April, 1836—a magazine published in Boston and edited at this time by Nathaniel Hawthorne, a young man who had as yet achieved no reputation as a writer. The text accompanying the picture, almost certainly written by Hawthorne, makes no acknowledgment to Fay or Peabody, but notes that since the sketch was made, New York's Great Fire had swept across this part of the city. "It is a singular truth," he continued, "that the mere shadowy image of a building . . . is likely to have a longer term of existence than the piled brick and mortar of the building. Take a print like this . . . and an edifice like the large one on the right hand corner, and the chances are, that, a century hence, the print will be as good as ever; while the edifice . . . will probably have been torn down to make room for modern improvements, or utterly destroyed by fire. Should posterity know where the proud structure stood, it will be indebted for its knowledge to the woodcut."

Author's collection

View of Coffee House Slip, New York.

. . . and from the late twenties onward people's visual impressions of the city . . .

VIEW OF ST. JOHN'S CHAPEL, FROM THE PARK.
DRAWN AND ENGRAVED FOR
THE NEW-YORK MIRROR.
1829.

Museum of the City of New York

This view of St. John's Chapel, drawn by A. J. Davis and engraved by W. D. Smith, is a steel engraving which was published as the frontispiece of the April 11, 1829, issue of the New York *Mirror.* From 1827 to 1838 the *Mirror* (of which Theodore S. Fay was at one time an editor) published over forty engraved views of New York scenes. St. John's, built in 1803–7, was designed by John McComb, Jr., who also designed Castle Clinton (later Castle Garden and later still the Aquarium), which is now (1953) being restored in Battery Park, and who was the co-designer with Joseph Mangin of the City Hall. It stood on the east side of Varick Street between Beach (now Ericsson) and Laight streets, facing Hudson Square, or St. John's Park as it was usually called. At the time the engraving was made, Hudson Square was one of the loveliest residential districts in the city. By 1867 it had been sold to Commodore Vanderbilt as the site for the New York Central Railroad freight depot. The chapel remained standing until 1918–19, when it was torn down as a belated result of the widening of Varick Street and the building of the West Side subway.

. . . derived increasingly from magazine illustrations . . .

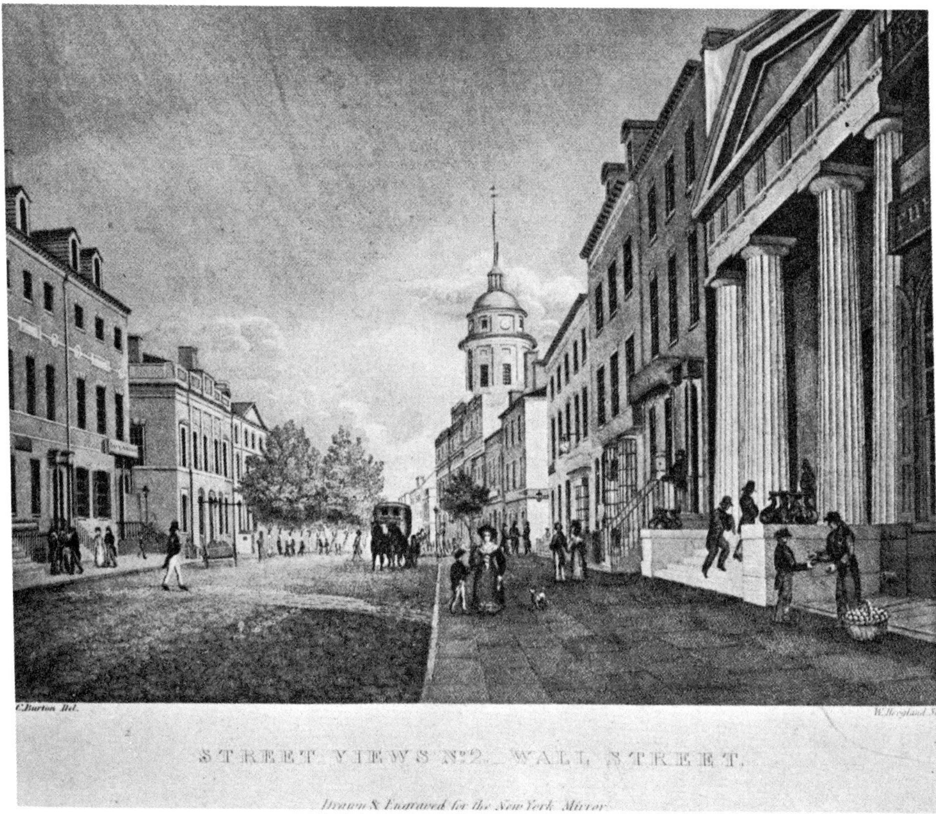

Collection of Allen S. Davenport

Two more steel engravings from the New York *Mirror.* ABOVE: A view of Wall Street drawn by C. Burton and engraved by W. Hoagland, published in 1832. The view was taken from a point east of Broad Street, looking southeast to the Merchants Exchange (with cupola). Banks and insurance offices line the street on both sides. At left, on northwest corner of William Street, was the Bank of America, and left of it the Dry Dock Bank. On the northeast corner of William was the Bank of New York, and beyond it the New York Insurance Co. At extreme right was the Phenix Bank. Down the street, just this side of the Exchange, is the building of the New York *American,* a newspaper published from 1819 to 1845. Most of the intervening buildings were insurance company offices.

J. Clarence Davies Collection, Museum of the City of New York

BELOW: An engraving by James Smillie, from a painting by Robert W. Weir, of the Bloomingdale Asylum, published in the *Mirror* in 1834. Built in 1818–20, the institution was a branch of the New York Hospital, for the care of the insane. The building stood between present Broadway and Amsterdam Avenue just north of 116th Street, where the Low Memorial Library now stands at the center of Columbia University's Campus. Columbia purchased the property in 1892, and the asylum was moved to White Plains, New York, in 1894.

Bloomingdale Village, which lay along the Hudson from about present 100th Street to 110th Street, was still a rural community in the thirties, perhaps the loveliest, as Mrs. Trollope thought, of all those on the upper island.

. . . and book illustrations . . .

Stokes Collection, New York Public Library

This view of Columbia College, drawn by A. J. Davis and engraved by Fenner Sears & Co., was published as one of the illustrations in J. H. Hinton's *The History and Topography of the United States* (London, 1830–32). It is reproduced here in the same size as the original. The college building is at the left, with the college green and yard in front of it. The original part of the building (see page 7 for a view of it in 1790) had been erected in 1756–60, and the wings had been added in 1817–20. The houses beyond the fence, just right of the college, were on the north side of Park Place, running eastward from Church Street to Broadway. The large building at the end of the row was the Park Place Hotel, opened in 1828 on Broadway opposite City Hall Park. The building showing faintly beyond it was Tammany Hall, across the park on Park Row (see page 137).

Columbiana Collection, Columbia University

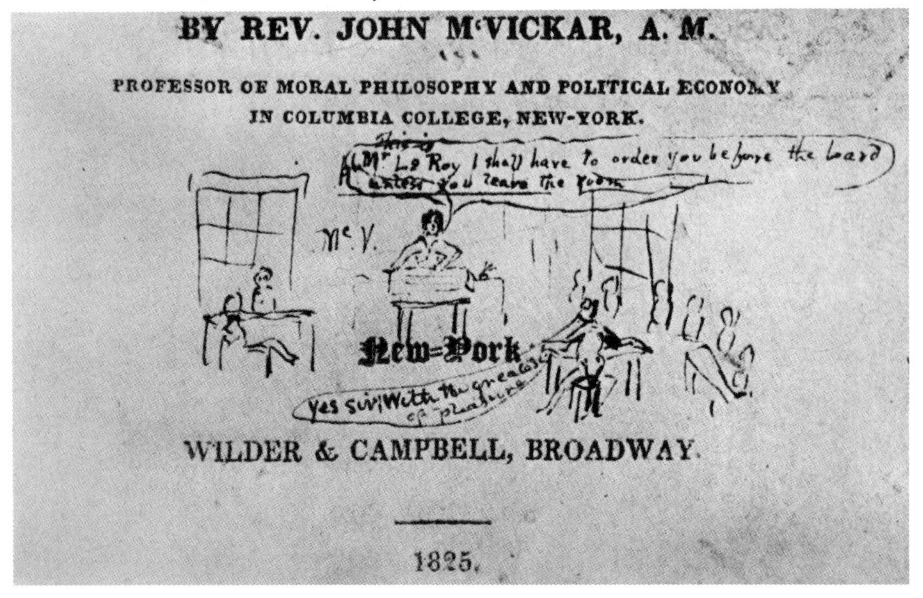

BY REV. JOHN M'VICKAR, A. M.

PROFESSOR OF MORAL PHILOSOPHY AND POLITICAL ECONOMY
IN COLUMBIA COLLEGE, NEW-YORK.

New-York:
WILDER & CAMPBELL, BROADWAY.

1825.

One of the most influential men on the Columbia faculty was the Reverend John McVickar, professor of moral philosophy, who taught everything from grammar and rhetoric to political economy and the evidences of natural and revealed religion. A graduate of Columbia in 1804, and son-in-law of Dr. Samuel Bard, former dean of Columbia's Medical School, McVickar taught at the college for almost fifty years. But, if we may judge from the picture one of his students scrawled on the title page of McVickar's text on *Political Economy,* he had some disciplinary problems in the classroom.

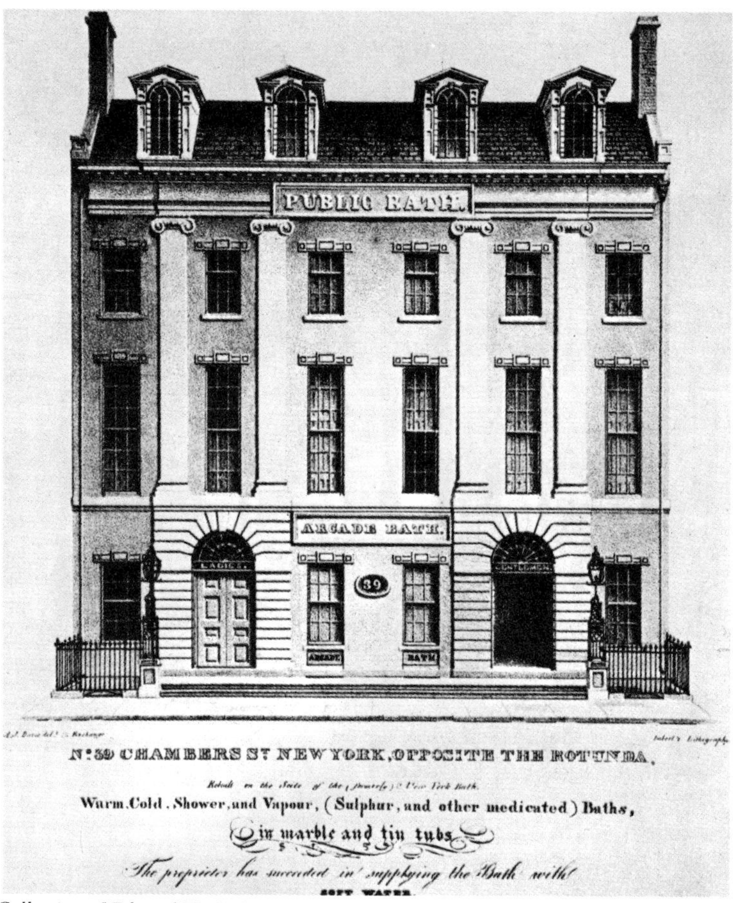

Collection of Edward W. C. Arnold; photograph courtesy of Museum of the City of New York

Two advertisements, both drawn by A. J. Davis and lithographed by Anthony Imbert. The Arcade Bath was a prominent institution in the late twenties and early thirties. The exhibition of the National Academy of Design was held there in 1829, about a year after the print was made. Later Burton's Theater occupied the building.

The Walton house, shown here as it appeared in 1830, had been built in 1752 by William Walton. It stood at No. 326–28 Pearl Street, between Peck Slip and Dover Street, just south of where the Brooklyn Bridge approaches now are. For thirty years it was the handsomest residence in New York, and the lavish entertainments provided by its owner in pre-Revolutionary days were referred to in the British Parliament as proof that the Americans could afford to pay higher taxes. In 1784 it became the first home of the Bank of New York, and after the bank moved to Hanover Square in 1787 it was used as a boardinghouse. An article about the house, published in the New York *Mirror* in 1832, described the portico, "supported by two fluted columns, and surrounded with the armorial bearings of the Walton family, richly carved and ornamented; but like all insignia of nobility on this side of the Atlantic, somewhat the worse for wear."

J. Clarence Davies Collection, Museum of the City of New York

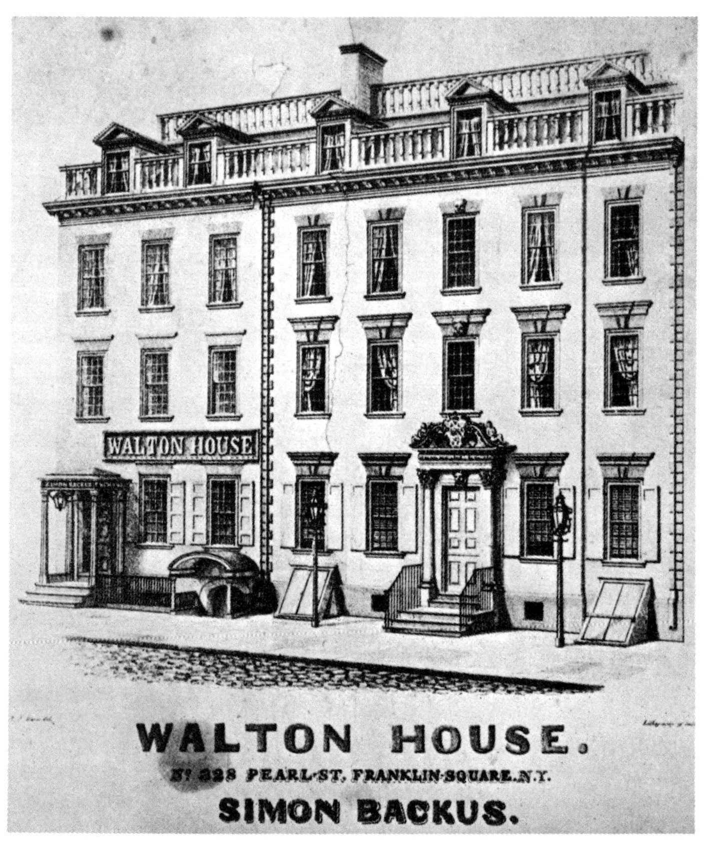

. . . which New York merchants distributed throughout the country.

The North American Hotel (later the New England Hotel), which catered chiefly to Southerners (as the text of the handbill indicates), stood on the northwest corner of Bayard Street and the Bowery. In Lydia Maria Child's *Letters from New York* (New York, 1843) there is the following passage, giving the story of the statue which stood on the roof:

"At the corner of Bayard and Bowery, you will see a hotel, called the North American; and on the top thereof you may spy a wooden image of a lad with ragged knees and elbows. . . . That image commemorates the history of a Yankee boy, by the name of David Reynolds. Some fifty years ago, he came here at the age of twelve or fourteen, without a copper in his pocket. . . . Weary and hungry, he leaned against a tree, where the hotel now stands. . . . While he was trying to devise some honest means to obtain food, a gentleman inquired for a boy to carry his trunk to the wharf, and the Yankee eagerly offered his services. For this job he received twenty-five cents, most of which he spent in purchasing fruit to sell again. He stationed himself by the friendly tree . . . and soon disposed of his little stock to advantage."

NORTH AMERICAN HOTEL

NEW YORK.

---****************---

THIS NEW AND SPLENDID ESTABLISHMENT, SITUATED IN THE MOST PLEASANT AND CENTRAL PART OF THE CITY, IN THE

BOWERY, CORNER OF BAYARD-STREET,

Near the Bowery Theatre, where the Bowery and Wall-street Stages pass hourly.

Offers to gentlemen from the South, and strangers generally, every inducement, as it contains a number of Parlours with Bed-rooms adjoining; single Bed-rooms, &c. The Table wfll be constantly furnished with every luxury of a plentiful New-York market, and the Bar with a choice variety of Wines, and other Liquors, not surpassed by any establishment in the city.

The Proprietor pledges himself to use every exertion to render his House pleasant and agreeable to all those whose pleasure it may be to favor him with their patronage.

PETER B. WALKER.

APRIL, 1832.

W. Applegate, Printer, 257 *Hudson-street, one door above Charlton, New-York.*

Collection of Edward W. C. Arnold; photograph courtesy of Museum of the City of New York

Soon he had a fruit stall under the tree, then a small shop, and then several houses either side. Finally he pulled down the shop and houses and built the hotel. The tree, too, had to be cut down, but "from its beloved trunk he caused his image to be carved, as a memento of his own forlorn beginnings, and his grateful recollections."

Whatever the medium, pictures of New York in the thirties show us a busy town.

Bequest of Mrs. J. Insley Blair, Museum of the City of New York

George Harvey, who painted this water color of "Night-Fall. St. Thomas' Church, Broadway, New York," about 1837, was an English artist who traveled widely in America during the thirties, making pictures which he later used to illustrate travelogues. (He is not to be confused with his more famous contemporary, Sir George Harvey, the Scottish historical painter.)

This was the first St. Thomas' Church, on the northwest corner of Broadway and Houston Street. Built in 1824–26, it was destroyed by fire in 1851, and rebuilt on the same site. In 1870 the church removed to a new building, designed by Richard Upjohn at the present Fifth Avenue and Fifty-third Street site, which burned in 1905 and was replaced in 1916 by the present structure designed by Cram, Goodhue, and Ferguson.

The first house in New York to be lighted by gas was No. 286 Water Street, in 1824. The first streets to have gas lampposts were Beekman, Wall, Fulton, and Cortlandt in 1830.

So great was the interest in business that the characteristic street scenes of the period . . .

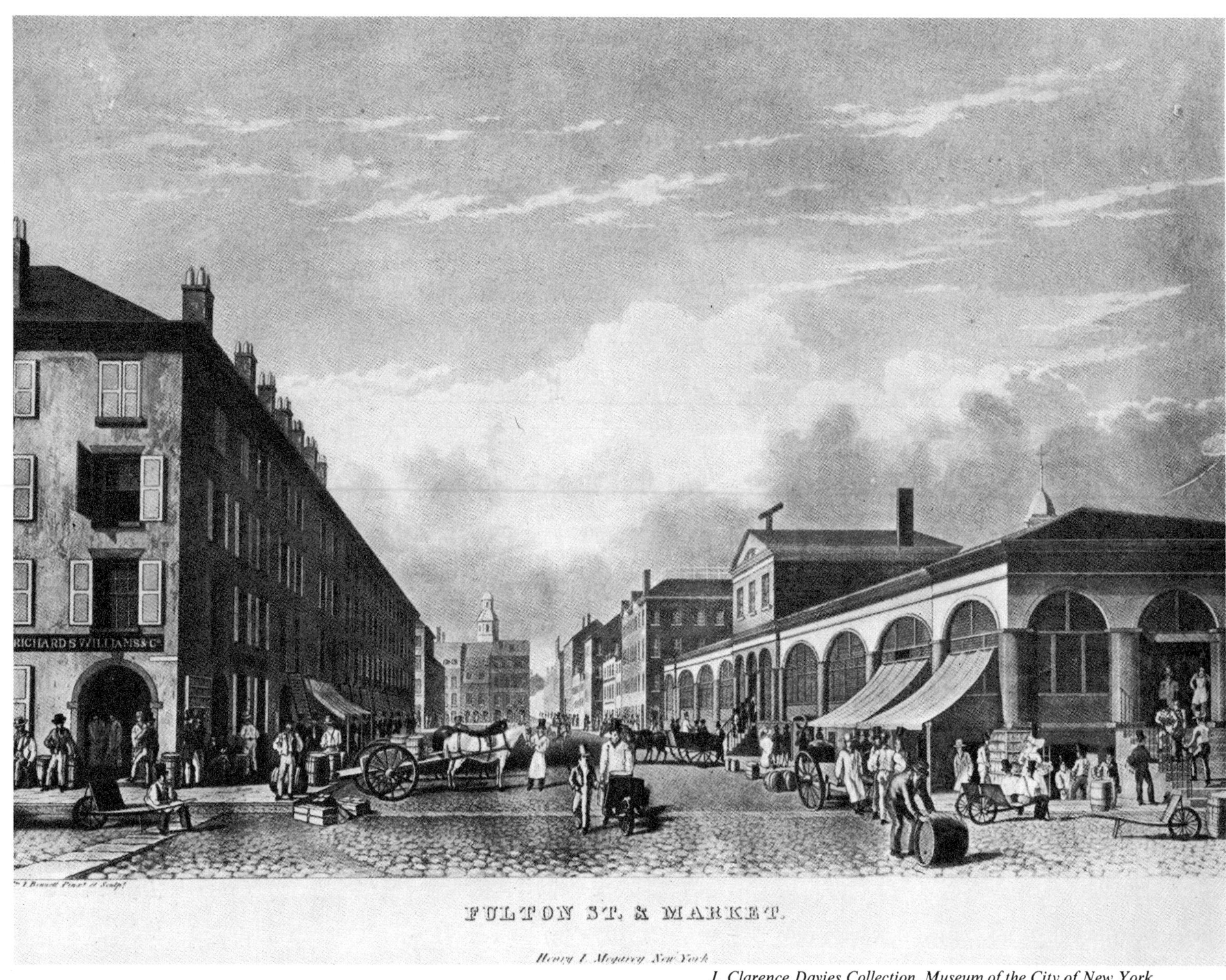

J. Clarence Davies Collection, Museum of the City of New York

This view of Fulton Street and Fulton Market, drawn and engraved by William J. Bennett, was one of the three prints published in *Megarey's Street Views in the City of New-York* (see page 131). The picture was probably drawn in 1834.

Fulton Market, shown at the right, was built in 1821 and remained in use until 1882, when it was replaced by a new building. It stood on the north side of Fulton, between South and Front streets. The tower in the center background is that of the North Dutch Church at the northwest corner of Fulton and William streets.

. . . painstakingly recorded the iconography of commerce as revealed in advertisements and signs.

J. Clarence Davies Collection, Museum of the City of New York

We know, from other evidence, that shop signs were plentiful in the city's streets in the eighteenth century; but it was not until the 1830s that they became important features in the pictures of New York. (Notice, for example, that no legible signs were included in Guy's painting of the Tontine Coffee House, page 107.)

The view of St. Paul's and the Broadway stages, drawn by Hugh Reinagle and lithographed by Pendleton in 1831, typifies the new attitude. At left, on the ground floor of the American Museum, corner of Park Row and Ann Street, is shown Mead's Soda Water Shop, one of the many popular fountains which had been established since the first one was introduced in 1820. Next door was Schuyler's Exchange Lottery Office, soon to be put out of business by the anti-lottery law of 1833.

Stokes Collection, New York Public Library

Most of the vehicles shown are "accommodation" stages, with open sides, which had been introduced by Abraham Brower in 1827. The first omnibus in the city, designed and built by John Stephenson (see pages 366–68), was introduced by Brower early in 1831. These were closed vehicles, with a rear entrance and seats running lengthwise (as in the earlier "sociables"). A Brower omnibus is shown in the center of the picture, just behind the four horses drawing the Lady Clinton stage for Niblo's Garden, but this was undoubtedly one of his older "sociables" relabeled. Omnibus No. 1, which ran from Wall Street to Dry Dock, is shown at left, next to Schuyler's.

LEFT: J. W. Hill's water color of Broadway, looking south from Liberty Street in 1830, should be compared with Holland's view (page 102), looking north from Wall Street along this same section of Broadway.

Since the signs were hard to read in traditional perspective views . . .

Collection of Edward W. C. Arnold; photograph courtesy of Museum of the City of New York

This view of Wall Street from Trinity Church was drawn by Hugh Reinagle and lithographed by Peter Maverick, Jr., in 1834. It is not possible, in this reproduction (slightly less than half the size of the original), to see all the details which are easily visible on the print itself. In the side margins there are detailed profile sketches of the buildings on each side of the street, and at the top a view of Brooklyn as seen from the foot of Wall Street at the East River. The view shows the street just before the steeple of the First Presbyterian Church was destroyed by fire, and about a year before the Great Fire of 1835 which destroyed the Merchants Exchange (with cupola, on right) and most of the other buildings east of Broad Street (continued on page 149).

. . . a blunt head-on perspective was adopted for the new street panoramas (or "pictorial directories") which began to appear.

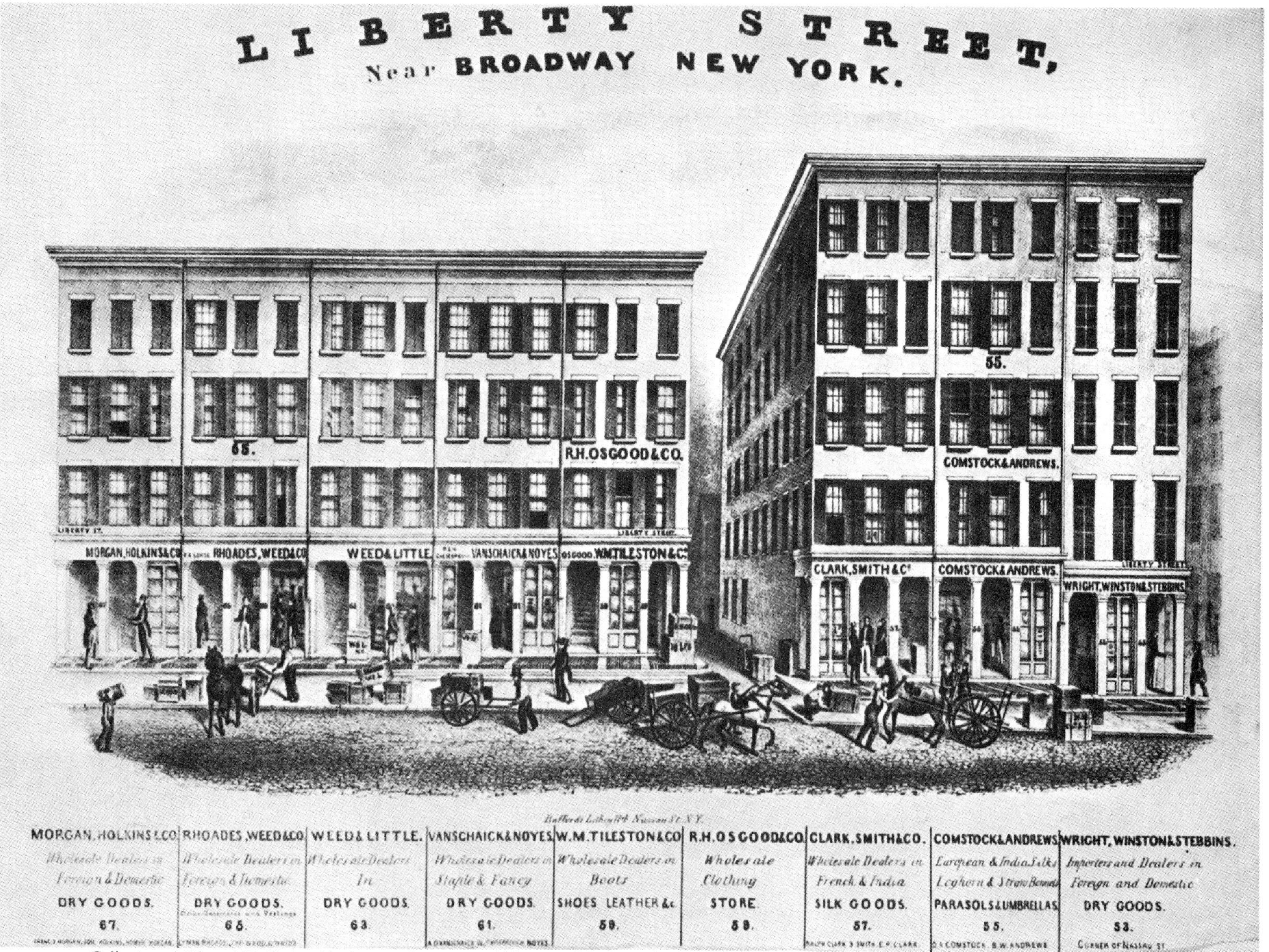

Collection of Edward W. C. Arnold; photograph courtesy of Museum of the City of New York

This lithograph by J. H. Bufford, showing the north side of Liberty Street between Broadway and Nassau Street, was published in 1836 or 1837, and was one of the earliest of the "pictorial directories." For a view of the changes which were soon to befall this part of the city, see page 246. In the late forties and fifties the "pictorial directory" idea was extended and developed in several series of prints which showed the buildings on both sides of the city's principal streets, those on one side at the top of the plate and those on the other, inverted, below. The earliest of these, showing both sides of Broadway from the Battery to Pearl Street, was published in 1848 as *The Illuminated Pictorial Directory of New York.* "Directories" of Maiden Lane, Fulton Street, and Wall Street were published in 1849 and 1850 (see also pages 276–78).

Meanwhile, the popular print makers met a growing demand for pictures of the disasters . . .

Pendleton's lithograph of "the Ruins of Phelps & Peck's Store" shows the ruins of a newly finished six-story brick building on the corner of Fulton and Cliff streets which collapsed on May 4, 1832.

So rapidly were new buildings erected, and so carelessly were they built, that there were a number of such accidents. Shortly after the Phelps & Peck's catastrophe a brick building was blown down in a thundershower, and it was discovered that the walls were only a brick and a half thick at the base and that scarcely any mortar had been used in laying them.

Both pictures from Museum of the City of New York

The aquatint "View of the Ruins After the Great Fire in New York" was engraved by W. J. Bennett from a pastel drawing by Nicolino V. Calyo, and was published by L. P. Clover. The view was made on Exchange Place, looking east. At the left is the ruin of the South Dutch Church, which had been built in 1807 on the site of the original (1692) church. In the center background is the block between William and Hanover streets, running through from Exchange Place to Wall Street, where the Merchants Exchange had stood.

. . . amusements and diversions which enlivened the everyday routine of city life.

Museum of the City of New York

The "Pleasure Railway at Hoboken," here shown in a lithograph made about 1833 by D. W. Kellogg & Co., was one of the attractions at Colonel John Stevens' Elysian Fields resort across the Hudson. Colonel Stevens fixed up a large part of his grounds as a resort in order to stimulate business on his ferry from Manhattan. When Mrs. Trollope visited the place in 1831 she was delighted with it. "It is true," she admitted, "that at Hoboken, as every where else, there are *reposoires,* which as you pass them, blast the sense for a moment, by reeking forth the fumes of whiskey and tobacco. . . . The proprietor of the grounds, however, has contrived with great taste to render these abominations not unpleasing to the eye; there is one in particular, which has quite the air of a Grecian temple. . . ."

Collection of Edward W. C. Arnold; photograph courtesy of Museum of the City of New York

The "Baptising Scene," lithographed by Endicott & Swett, was published by James van Valkenburgh in 1834. The "White Fort" in the background—so called because it was whitewashed—had been built as Fort Gansevoort during the War of 1812. It stood on the Hudson shore at the foot of Gansevoort Street. The baptizing took place somewhere near the foot of Horatio Street.

Prompt publication of a picture of a catastrophe could earn for the printer a national reputation . . .

Awful Conflagration of the Steam Boat

LEXINGTON.

In Long Island Sound, on Monday Eve.g Jan.y 13th 1840: by which melancholy occurrence, over 120 PERSONS PERISHED.

Pub. at Sun Office.

THE LEXINGTON

Left New York, for Stonington, at 3 o'clock on Tuesday afternoon, Jan. 13, 1840. About half past 7 o'clock, when off Eaton's Neck, L. I., the wood-work, casings, &c., about the flues, were discovered to be on fire. An alarm was immediately given, and all efforts to subdue the flames proving unavailing, the pilot headed the boat directly for Long Island shore. When she had got within about two miles of the shore her engine suddenly stopped. In the meantime the life boat and small boats had been got out, but the former was broken to pieces by being struck by one of the wheels, and the latter were swamped by mismanagement in lowering them into the water crowded with passengers. No relief was therefore obtained from either of the boats. All hopes of escape to those on board, except by clinging to such articles of freight as would sustain them, were now cut off. The freight of the Lexington consisted principally of cotton, on which some of the passengers tried to save themselves, but none succeeded except Capt. Hilliard, Mr. Manchester, the pilot, Charles Smith one of the firemen, and a passenger who had been picked up and taken to River Head, and who was so far gone as to be unable to disclose his name. It was believed, however, that he would survive. Capt. H. continued upon his bale of cotton until 11 o'clock, A. M., Tuesday, when he was taken off by a sloop which went out from Southport, having been thus exposed about 15 hours. The same sloop rescued the other two, who were clinging to a fragment of the boat. The bodies of two others, one a colored woman, were likewise, taken from a part of the wreck, on which they had perished from cold. The steamer Statesman on Thursday also picked up one body and thirteen trunks. The bodies of Hempstead the chief engineer, and Sands the head waiter, have also been recovered.

The number of passengers on board is not known with any degree of certainty. It is most probable, however, they numbered about EIGHTY—of whom but two were rescued alive. The boat's company numbered THIRTY, of whom also but two were saved.

The list of passengers subjoined is probably as correct as it will be possible ever to make it.

Passengers Lost with the Lexington,

Mrs. Russell Jarvis, and two children,	New York.
Mr. Fowler,	do
Stephen Waterbury (firm of Mead & Waterbury, 25 Cedar st.)	do
Rev. Doct. Follen, formerly of the Unitarian Church, Chamber st,	Boston.
Thomas James, Tailor, Fulton st.	New York.
John Winslow (firm of D. L. & J. Winslow,)	Providence.
Mrs. Alice Winslow, widow of Henry A. Winslow, who was accompanying the corpse of her husband to Boston for interment,	Providence.
John L. Winslow, (father of the above)	New York.
Charles Bosworth, 37 Frankfort st.,	do
H. C. Craig, firm of Maitland, Kennedy & Co.	do
Robert Shultz,	do
Charles Brackett, clerk with N. Brackett,	do
Charles P. Noyes, clerk, 74½ Pine st,	do
Richard W. Dow, firm of Dow & Co.	Brooklyn.
Charles S. Noyes, clerk with C. B. Babcock,	New York.
Albert E. Harding, firm of Harding & Co.	do
E. B. Patten, 183 Walker st,	do
Mr. McKinney,	do
Hezekiah Lawrence, firm of Kelly & Lawrence,	do
Mr. Bullard,	do
Thomas J. Taylor, firm of James & Taylor,	do

Adolphus S. Harnden, of the Boston and New York Express Package Car Office, having with him about $18,000 in specie, and 70 or $80,000 for brokers in Eastern money.

William Ray, (late of the bark Bahamia)	Kennebunk, Me.
Noah Hickley,	Portland.
N. F. Dyer, (formerly of Braintree)	Pittsburg.
Capt. Eben S. Kimball, (just from Valparaiso)	Salem.
" John D. Carver, barque Brontes,	Plymouth.
" Pierce, mate of do.	Portland.
" John J. Low, agent Boston Ins. Co.	Boston.
" Theophilus Smith,	Dartmouth.
" Benjamin Foster,	Providence.
" Smith,	Dedham.
" Chester Hilliard, (saved)	Norwich.

These Captains had recently returned after several years absence, and were on their way to visit their families at the East.

Wm. A. Green, agent Minot Shoe Co.,	Maine.
Samuel Henry,	Boston.
Charles H. Phelps,	Stonington.
C. W. Woolsey, Sugar Refiner,	East Boston
John Brown, do	do
John Hoyt, (Mail Contractor)	Boston.
Mr. Everett, returning from the burial of a brother who died here last week,	do
Henry J. Finn, Comedian,	do
Charles Eberle, of the Theatre,	do
Royal T. Church,	Baltimore.
Richard Pickett, (clerk with Marquand & Co.)	Newburyport.
John W. Kerle,	Baltimore.
Mr. Walker,	do
Mr. Weston, (firm of Weston & Poindexter) lady and child,	do
John G. Brown, firm of Shall & Brown,	New Orleans.
Master Woodward, son of Charles,	Philadelphia.
J. A. Leach, firm of Leach & Lovejoy,	Boston.
Jesse Comstock,	Providence.
James Walker, seaman,	Cambridgeport.
John Gordon, do	do
Royal Sibley,	Pawtucket.
Nathaniel Hobart,	Boston
H. C. Bradford, (from Kingston, Jam.)	do.
Charles Lee, Esq., son of Gen. Samuel Lee,	Barre, Mass.
John G. Stone,	do
John Lemist, Treas. Boston Leather Co.,	Roxbury.
Jonathan Linfield,	Stoughton, Mass.
Philo Upton,	Egremont, do.
P. Van Cott,	Stonington.
Mr. Stuyvesant,	Boston.
Capt. Mattison,	
Robert Williams,	Cold Spring, N. Y.
Samuel Henry, firm of S. & A. Henry,	Manchester, Eng.
J. Porter Felt, jun.,	Salem.
W. A. Mason,	Gloucester, Mass.
Robert Blake,	Wrentham, do.
A. Green, firm of Green & Allen,	Providence.
Isaac Davis,	Boston.
Mr. Peck,	Southington, Ct.
Thomas White, (firm of Sands & White,)	Boston.
Abraham Howard, firm of Howard & Merry,	do.
P. O. Swain,	
Noah Hinckley,	Portland, Me.
Isaac Davis,	Boston.
John Corey,	Rhode Island.
William Nichols, steward of S. B. Massachusetts.	
Joshua Johnson.	
Robert Blake, Pres. Wrentham Bank,	Wrentham, Mass.
Mr. Bosworth,	Royalton, Vt.
James Smith,	Charlestown, Mass.
Mr. Brooks, comb store,	Boston.
Erastus Coleman, (of the Pavilion)	Do.
John Corey,	Foxbury, Mass.
Mr. Martin and Son,	Manchester, Eng
William H. Wilson, (formerly of Worcester)	Williamsburg.
Thomas Bleeker, carpenter,	Dedham, Mass.
John Brown, colored, 26 Varick street,	New York.
Daniel M'Farlan, mate of brig Clarissa.	
William Nichols, and Joshua Johnson, both colored men,	Providence.

Officers, &c. of the Lexington.

George Childs, Captain.
Edward Thuber, 1st Mate.
David Crowley, 2d do.
Cortland Hempsted, Chief Engineer.
William Quimby, 2d do.
S. Manchester, Pilot, (saved.)
Martin Johnson, Wheelsman.
H. P. Newman, Steward.
R. B. Shultz, Fireman.
Benjamin Cox, do.
Charles Smith, do. (saved.)
Charles Bow, do.
Eight Deck Hands.
Two Wood Passers.
One Boy, Deck Hand.
Joseph Robinson, Cook, (colored.)
Oliver Howell, 2d do. do.
Robert Peters, do. do.
Susan C. Hulcomb, colored Chambermaid.
Jacob Sands, do. Head Waiter.
Seven others, do. Waiters.

SATURDAY MORNING.

We learn this morning, by a gentleman from River Head, that the individual who was saved at that place was David Crowley, of Providence, second mate of the Lexington, his feet frozen. The body of Mr. Stephen Waterbury, and two others floated ashore frozen in the bottom of one of the small boats. The body of a child 4 years old has also floated ashore. The body of C. Hempstead, 1st engineer, has also been recovered, as has also that of Philo Upson, with a life preserver on.

A great quantity of trunks, chests, &c. have floated ashore, and many of them have been rifled. The trunk of the Rev. Mr. Follen has been found in the woods, rifled of everything but papers.

Besides the names already published, we regret to have to add those of John Marshall, glass blower, of this city; and of Mr. Baum, son of the clerk of the Washington Market.

NOON.

The Statesman has just returned with five bodies, and a large number of trunks. The bodies of Mr. Waterbury, Mr. Upson, Mr. Patten, (as supposed) and a little girl about four years of age, are among the number.

Print Room, New York Public Library

. . . and fires and firemen were always popular subjects.

H. Sewell Del
HANINGTON'S DIORAMIC REPRESENTATION OF THE
GREAT FIRE in NEW YORK Dec. 16 ... 17 1835
AMERICAN MUSEUM

J. Clarence Davies Collection, Museum of the City of New York

LEFT: A lithograph, drawn by H. Sewell, advertising a diorama of the Great Fire which was exhibited at the American Museum early in 1836.

BELOW: This lithograph by H. R. Robinson shows one of the great heroes of the old Volunteer Fire Department at a dramatic moment in his career. James Gulick was one of the most popular chief engineers the department ever had. When the Union Market, on Avenue D between Second and Third streets, burned April 4, 1836, Gulick and his men were on hand. But while the fire was raging, Charles G. Hubbs of Engine Co. 13 told Gulick the city's fire and water commissioners were holding a meeting at which they were going to vote to remove him from his office as a result of political pressure. Gulick left the scene, and when the firemen learned what had happened, they left too. "Nor could they be induced to return," as Asa Greene wrote, "until Mr. Gulick, at the instance of the mayor, intreated them to resume their duties, and himself led them back to extinguish the flames."

OPPOSITE: Three days after the steamboat *Lexington,* bound for Stonington, Connecticut, from New York, burned and sank in Long Island Sound, this print was being hawked through the streets of the city. Published as an "Extra" by the New York *Sun,* it is probably the first illustrated extra ever issued. It was a sensational success, and thousands of copies were sent all over the country. New issues of the extra were printed as new information about the disaster reached town. Later copies bore the name of the artist who drew the picture, W. K. Hewitt, and the lithographer whose enterprise made copies available so rapidly: N. Currier of Spruce Street, New York. As a result, Currier overnight achieved a national reputation which laid the foundation of his future business as senior member of the firm of Currier & Ives.

Collection of Harry T. Peters; photograph courtesy of Museum of the City of New York

Politics, too, began to turn up in the prints, especially if firemen were involved . . .

Collection of Edward W. C. Arnold; photograph courtesy of Museum of the City of New York

Like the preceding picture, this was drawn and published by H. R. Robinson, the lithographer, who made a specialty of political cartoons. "The Funeral of Old Tammany" refers to the defeat of the regular Tammany candidates in November, 1836, by the supporters of the deposed chief engineer of the Volunteer Firemen, James Gulick (see preceding page). One of the firemen watching the funeral procession is asking, "Who killed Old Tammany?" and another answers, "James Gulick!" Gulick himself is represented, to the right of the latter fireman, with his initials J. G. on his hat.

. . . since politics was by now a very popular diversion indeed.

AUTHENTIC.
View of the Bar Room, in the Log Cabin, *Broadway, New York.*
Head Quarters of the 14th Ward Tippecanoe Club.

An immoral people cannot long preserve the blessings of free government. This doctrine all parties admit to be true. Mr. CLAY, in his late Nashville speech, and Mr. WEBSTER in his more recent address to the ladies of Richmond, declared in eloquent terms that republican institutions cannot long survive the corruption of popular morals. Such is, *nominally* at least, the general sentiment. But within a year past there has been seen an al- [illegible] in *practice*, of this admitted [illegible] now seem to be the strong conviction of a large portion of active politicians that the people must be corrupted and depraved as fast and as far as possible, in order to effect political reform.

In the above cut we have an illustration of the process adopted by the Hard Cider politicians of New York to accomplish their purposes. It is a picture of their PRIMARY SCHOOL OF POLITICAL MORALITY. The engraving represents the interior of the Whig log cabin on Broadway, in the 14th Ward, in New York city. This Temple of political purity, is of ample dimensions, and its interior divided into two large apartments. Entering from Broadway on the left of the picture, by a door over which should be written the following extract from the "*Log Cabin and Hard Cider Melodies*"—

"In all the States no door stands wider,
Hurrah, Hurrah, Hurrah!
[illegible] you in to drink hard cider,
[illegible] Hurrah, Hurrah!"—[p. 24.]

you first pass around one of those screens which we always find in our Boston drinking shops, erected for the modest and proper purpose of excluding the public gaze from the operations within. Modest virtue always shrinks from public observation. Having circumnavigated the screen, you find yourself at once in an enormous *Bar-room* fitted up in the most attractive manner, decorated with bottles, glasses, decanters and glaring hand-bills innumerable. The hand-bills inform you that here are kept and manufactured for your comfort and *spirit*-ual improvement, a score of delightful beverages;—some of familiar name and nature, and others novel, recently invented and prepared for the special benefit of the politicians of 1840. You may exercise your choice between the old and the new;—between "Hard Cider," "Egg Nogg" and "Irish Whiskey" on one side, and "Tyler Punch," "Harrison Juleps," "North Bend Sherry Cobler," and "Tip and Ty, try it boys!" on the other. Or, if you seek inspiration from something more than the spirit of wine, go to the extreme right, look at the placard "*Harrison Melodies*," and purchase for the gratification of your taste a copy of that charming and chaste publication, from the press of "Weeks, Jordan & Co., Boston: Open the volume to page 68, and you will find how appropriately the work is placed on the shelf of a grog shop; for there it is written—

"Here's a health to Tippecanoe!
Here's a shout to Tippecanoe!
And *he that wont drink* to the pride of North Bend
Is neither a wise one nor true!"

And again on p. 40.

"*Again and again fill your glasses,*
Bid Martin Van Buren adieu,
We'll now please ourselves and the lasses,*
And vote for old Tippecanoe!"

Having admired the *literature*, and drank all you will, of the *liquor-ature*, found in the classic room, contemplate for a moment some of its minor decorations. On the floor there, near the screen, in an empty crockery crate, are a couple of bald eagles,—once the free denizens of the boundless air,—but now "*cabin*-ed, cribbed, confined", with ruffled plumage and drooping wing and faded eye, in this den of abominations, breathing the fumes of alcohol and the odor of cigars, instead of the clear atmosphere of Heaven.—Now cast your eyes upward! Peeping out of a tub among the timbers overhead, you see a Raccoon, (evidently "up the wrong tree,") who appears to be re-enacting the part of the old Cynic Philosopher searching for an honest man. Poor fellow! he had better search elsewhere. The old adage says "there is *truth* in wine:" ("*in vino Veritas*,") but such truth as honest men blush to utter.

*The allusion here is to the ladies of Chillicothe, the donors of the flannel robe after the affair at Sandusky.

Those other hand-bills inform you that several Whig meetings are to be held this evening, at which some new songs are to be sung by vocalists eminent in this novel mode of electioneering. The grim faces pinned and pasted up behind the counter are engraved portraits of "the Hero of Tippecanoe," who is so willing, as the *classic* poet says:—

"To give up to tears, persuasion and prayers,
His Cider, Log-cabin and Coon-skin."—[Melodies, p. 64.]

One [illegible] from the sour look of the veteran, either that his hard cider was producing the cholic, or that the [illegible] him offended his moral sense.

No wonder that he scowls upon the motley congregation who are clustering around the counter, some calling for liquor, some smoking, some noisily arguing, others shouting "hurrah for old *Tipple*-canoe!" and others still singing or chaunting from the "Melodies"

"For fear that we should be thirsty,
I'll tell you what we will do,
We'll fill up the gourd with hard cider,
And drink ——, &c. &c.—[p. 48.]

This is the Ante-room of a much frequented place of political gathering. Through this scene of confusion and intemperance must the Whigs of "Ward 14" approach their audience and reading room, which room you see on the right of the picture. Here is manufactured political enthusiasm. Here the timid gather courage and the brave drink bumpers to the success of their party. Here the young are initiated and the old confirmed in *Tip*-pling habits, and here the supporters of Clay and Webster illustrate the practical value of those moral principles which their eloquent leaders love to eulogise.

Alas, for our country, if her hopes of political safety rest on a foundation like this!

Proceed now through those openings,—a sort of folding doors, at the right, and a few steps place you in the *sanctum-sanctorum* of this strange cabin, surrounded by chairs and tables, and supplied with all the Whig papers of Gotham. Here congregate those faithful followers of "old Tip," who have found their way through the perils of initiation and the Ante-room. Here meet the spirited voter and the inspired stump orator, wandering blacksmiths and patent manufacturers of votes, "cheek by jowl" with all the honest and sober citizens of the Ward, who dare encounter and can escape the filthy perils of the outer passage.

Fellow citizens! Must these things be permitted? Has the country come to this? Shall public opinion sustain a course of electioneering so corrupt and demoralising? Shall a sober man, who loves his country and her institutions, sanction these political orgies? Is the banner of drunkeness to float triumphantly in our streets? Must our elections turn upon such debasing and degrading expedients?

Friends of sobriety, lovers of good order, advocates of temperance,—return to your sober senses, and rescue the country from the dangers which now impend over it! If success is to crown a party which has thus appealed to the appetites of the community, another election will witness a repetition of these measures, and instead of one party, we shall see both striving to corrupt and deprave the people,—stimulating their appetites, ministering to their sensual propensities—for the purpose of procuring their support.

Any attentive observer of the course of events must have seen that within the last year a vast backsliding has taken place from the ranks of the sober and the temperate. The habit of drinking has returned upon hundreds who had become exemplary disciples of sobriety: the moral tone of the community at large is visibly injured: disorder is taking the place of quietness and peace; and we have great reason to be alarmed for the welfare of the people, if these things continue in their present train.

It becomes the honest patriot and the sober man, to pause—to reflect—to ponder well over these startling facts: and by every means in his power—by word and by conduct, to rebuke the wicked in their headlong career, and to teach those who seek to gain the people by corrupting them, that such conduct will not be tolerated in a community like ours, but that any and every party which identifies itself with a deliberate attempt to degrade the character of the American people, will be frowned down by a righteous public indignation.

Collection of Edward W. C. Arnold; photograph courtesy of Museum of the City of New York

This broadside, issued during the presidential campaign of 1840, was an attack on the Whig supporters of William Henry Harrison. The Log Cabin pictured here was the headquarters of the 14th Ward Tippecanoe Club, set up in Broadway near Prince Street. Hone described the dedication ceremonies in his diary, June 16, telling of the "capital speeches by gentlemen of Ohio, Indiana, and Kentucky, among whom was Mr. Ewing . . . whose hand was warm from the recent pressure of Gen. Harrison's. . . . Never did the friends of Mr. Van Buren make so great a mistake as when, by their sneers, they furnished the Whigs those powerful weapons, 'log cabin' and 'hard cider'; they work as the hickory poles did for Jackson."

The people in these prints were not individualized; they were either conventional figures or caricatures borrowed from literature . . .

In both these prints the figures resemble the illustrations in Dickens' immensely popular novels more than the faces and figures one would have encountered in a New York crowd. Indeed, the one at right, lithographed and published by Endicott & Swett, was drawn by someone who humorously signed himself "Hassan Straightshanks" in token of his indebtedness to Cruikshank, the popular English illustrator. It cartoons a parade which really did take place in protest against the militia system, which many people at the time thought should be replaced by a standing army.

Collection of Edward W. C. Arnold; photograph courtesy of Museum of the City of New York

Below is a detail from a line engraving of the "Arrival of the Great Western Steam Ship, off New York on Monday 23rd April 1838." No artist or engraver is named on the print, but one of the characters in the foreground carries a sign advertising the firm of W. & H. Cave of Manchester, England, who were probably the publishers.

Stokes Collection, New York Public Library

. . . and the landscape views of the city were often freighted with romantic literary associations.

August Köllner, who drew this pen and ink sketch, was a German who came to the United States in the late thirties and settled in Philadelphia. During the next twenty years he produced a large number of views of American scenery, and late in life held an exhibition of his work, at which time he added descriptive titles. This one, dated August, 1839, he called "New York Bay, Cooperized," in acknowledgment of the romantic vision of America which he, like so many foreigners (and natives), had derived from James Fenimore Cooper's novels.

Collection of Edward W. C. Arnold; photograph courtesy of Museum of the City of New York

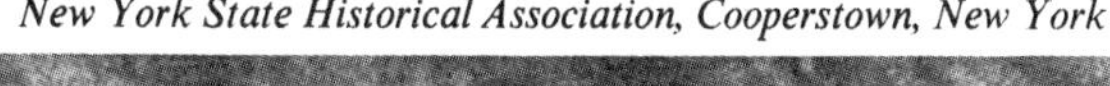

New York State Historical Association, Cooperstown, New York

This "View of New York Harbor from Weehawken" was painted in 1837 by E. C. Coates. Weehawken, where Hamilton had been mortally wounded in his duel with Aaron Burr, was a favorite spot for the painter-poets and poet-painters of the Hudson River School. Coates's painting is a canvas-cousin of Fitz-Greene Halleck's extremely popular lines describing the scene as witnessed by an "enthusiast": "The city bright below; and far away/ Sparkling in golden light, his own romantic bay./ Tall spire, and glittering roof, and battlement,/ And banners floating in the sunny air:/ And white sails o'er the calm blue waters bent,/ Green isle, and circling shore, are blended there/ In wild reality."

But in the typical "views" of the late thirties, the rural images which had dominated the foreground of earlier pictures . . .

J. Clarence Davies Collection, Museum of the City of New York

The picture above is reproduced from an uncolored artist's proof of the print on the facing page.

Museum of the City of New York

The gouache painting of "New York 1837" by Nicolino V. Calyo, at left, provides an interesting contrast with the Coates painting, done in the same year, which is reproduced on the preceding page. Calyo has selected, as his point of view, the East River shore near the Navy Yard in Brooklyn.

. . . were replaced by forms and symbols which, however romanticized they may have been, were those of the urban landscape itself.

Eno Collection, New York Public Library

"New York from Brooklyn Heights" was drawn (and probably colored) by J. W. Hill, engraved by W. J. Bennett, and published by L. P. Clover in 1837.

Taken from the roof of the houses on Columbia Heights, Brooklyn, it pictures the city from Wall Street to Canal Street. The reproduction is only about one quarter of the size of the original, but so precisely was the drawing made that it is quite possible to distinguish most of the important buildings on Manhattan. The domed building at left is the new Merchants Exchange, replacing the one destroyed in the fire of 1835. The large white building left of center is Holt's Hotel on Fulton and Water streets, next to Fulton Market. The church spire farthest to the right is that of St. John's Chapel at Hudson Square.

The street in the lower foreground is Furman Street, which runs along the Brooklyn shore beneath the Heights. Brooklyn had become a city in 1834 (see page 167).

The waterfront, and the shipping in both rivers, received special attention in pictures of the city . . .

Eno Collection, New York Public Library

"New York from Brooklyn" was drawn and engraved by Thomas Hornor between 1834 and 1839, and printed by William Neale. The upper portion is printed in blue ink, and the lower portion, from the Manhattan shore to the Brooklyn docks, in black. The sketchy effect in the foreground contrasts strikingly with the minutely detailed drawing of the city and the distant shore of New Jersey. It has been assumed that Hornor's financial difficulties (revealed in letters he wrote to Dr. John W. Francis and other patrons) may have led him to abandon work on the engraving before it was finished. Yet the ships in the foreground were obviously more interesting to him than the minutely detailed city in the background, and it seems possible that he was intentionally experimenting with less detailed techniques (see also his "unfinished" drawing on page 180).

Stokes Collection, New York Public Library

RIGHT: A detail from a "Panoramic View of New York" drawn and engraved by Robert Havell, the vessels painted by James Pringle, which was published in 1840. The center portion of the print is reproduced here, showing the recently rebuilt Washington Market (just above the bow of the steamboat at left) on West Street between Vesey and Fulton streets, and shad fishermen drawing in their nets.

. . . just as each new vessel to enter the port was welcomed by enthusiastic crowds.

THE BRITISH STEAMER SIRIUS.
The first English Steam Packet which arrived in America, April 22 1838 from London, sent out by the Directors of the British & American Steam Navigation Co of London, consigned to Wadsworth & Smith

Stokes Collection, New York Public Library

This print of "The British Steamer Sirius" was drawn by E. W. Clay and lithographed by H. R. Robinson in 1838. The *Sirius* was the first steamship to reach the United States from a foreign port and the second vessel to cross the Atlantic by steam power alone. (The first was the Dutch ship *Curaçao,* which sailed from Antwerp to the Dutch West Indies in 1827. The American ship *Savannah,* built in New York, had used steam only as auxiliary power when she crossed in 1819.)

The *Sirius* arrived at ten o'clock in the evening, April 22, 1838, followed one day later by the *Great Western* (page 156). The age of steam on the Atlantic had arrived with dramatic suddenness.

One of the most popular prints of the period was really a scene of harbor shipping, though it purported to be a picture of the buildings at Quarantine . . .

The aquatint "View of the New York Quarantine. Staten Island," was drawn and engraved by W. J. Bennett and published by Parker & Co. and Lewis P. Clover in 1833.

Bequest of Mrs. J. Insley Blair, Museum of the City of New York

NEW-YORK QUARANTINE, STATEN ISLAND.
Engraved for Williams' Register, from Parker & Clover's large Picture by Bennett.

This smaller line engraving was copied from Bennett's by S. Stiles & Co. and published as the frontispiece of *Williams' Register* (New York, 1837).

Collection of Allen S. Davenport

. . . and in a similar print which the same artist made a few years later, the buildings have completely disappeared from the title and almost from the picture itself.

J. Clarence Davies Collection, Museum of the City of New York

The aquatint above, entitled "A Brisk Gale, Bay of New York," was made by Bennett six years after the one on the opposite page, in 1839. The Quarantine buildings on Staten Island are hidden by the large vessel in the center. Off to the right, barely discernible, are the buildings of Sailors' Snug Harbor at New Brighton, built in 1832–33, when the institution decided to move from its Manhattan site.

The thirties also discovered the pictorial interest of the shipyards . . .

New York State Historical Association, Cooperstown, New York

In 1833, when James Pringle painted this picture of the Smith and Dimon Shipyard, New York was the leading shipbuilding center in the United States, in spite of stiff competition from Boston and from Bath, Maine. In that year alone, the yards along the East River (where most of them were concentrated) turned out 26 ships and barks, 7 brigs, 36 schooners, and 5 steamboats.

The Smith and Dimon yards were never so large or important as those of W. H. Webb, or Westervelt, or Brown & Bell, but they turned out some important ships. Here, in 1845, was launched the *Rainbow,* the first extreme clipper, and in the following year the *Sea Witch,* which probably broke more speed records than any other American sailing vessel.

OPPOSITE, ABOVE: A water-color drawing made in 1833 by J. W. Hill, of the rotary windmill, or air turbine, which stood at the Hudson shore south of present West Houston Street. BELOW: A water-color drawing (1837) of Browning and Dunham's North River Iron Foundry and locomotive engine shop, foot of North Moore Street at the Hudson. (This is the original drawing for a lithographed advertisement, a copy of which is in the Bella C. Landauer Collection at the New-York Historical Society.)

. . . and of the mills and factories which were turning out the materials and machines . . .

Both pictures from collection of Edward W. C. Arnold; photographs courtesy of Museum of the City of New York

. . . that had already begun to transform the rural landscape of the upper island, beyond the city limits.

Collection of Edward W. C. Arnold; photograph courtesy of Museum of the City of New York

The New York and Harlem Railroad, incorporated in 1831, was the first railroad on Manhattan Island. The line originally commenced at Twenty-third Street and ran up Fourth Avenue, but was later extended south on the Bowery to Prince Street and ultimately down Centre Street to Chambers. By 1834 it had been completed as far north as Yorkville. An account published in that year recorded that horse-drawn cars (built by John Stephenson) ran from Prince Street to Yorkville every half hour, at a fare of 12½ cents. "At Yorkville the company have erected a splendid hotel, which at present is kept by George Nowlan," the writer continued. "It is a spacious two story building . . . having a piazza around both stories . . . commanding a view of the surrounding country, Hell-gate, and the East River, that has no equal on the Island."

Prospect Hall, as it was called, is shown in this gouache by Nicolino V. Calyo, drawn about 1836 when the railroad tunnel under Mount Prospect, from Ninety-second to Ninety-fourth streets, was under construction. The picture shows the blasting operations at the north end of the tunnel. Locomotives were first used on the road in 1839, and by 1842 had been banned below Twenty-third Street.

Those who wanted to escape the crowded and busy city could still find quiet homes up at Manhattanville or over in Brooklyn . . .

J. Clarence Davies Collection, Museum of the City of New York

"Manhattanville, New York," was drawn by J. W. Hill and lithographed by George Endicott in 1834. The village, which lay on the Hudson where the high land dips down at 125th Street, came into existence about 1806. In the 1830s it was still relatively untouched by city concerns. The church at right is St. Mary's.

Collection of Edward W. C. Arnold; photograph courtesy of Museum of the City of New York

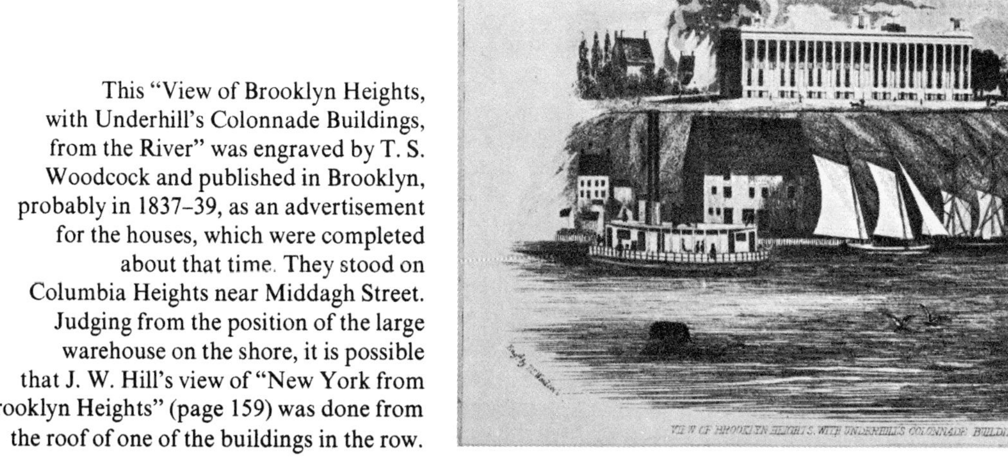

This "View of Brooklyn Heights, with Underhill's Colonnade Buildings, from the River" was engraved by T. S. Woodcock and published in Brooklyn, probably in 1837–39, as an advertisement for the houses, which were completed about that time. They stood on Columbia Heights near Middagh Street. Judging from the position of the large warehouse on the shore, it is possible that J. W. Hill's view of "New York from Brooklyn Heights" (page 159) was done from the roof of one of the buildings in the row.

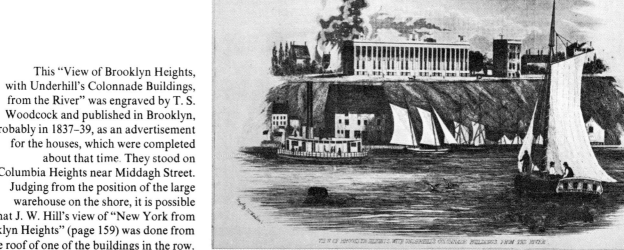

. . . and "self-made" men proudly had pictures made of the palatial homes they built far out of town.

Collection of Edward W. C. Arnold; photograph courtesy of Museum of the City of New York

Arlington House, shown here in a lithograph drawn "from nature and on stone" by J. H. Bufford, stood at No. 209 Clinton Avenue, well beyond the southern limits of the built-up section of Brooklyn. The lithograph, copyrighted in 1839 by the owner of the house, bears a long inscription which informs us that the mansion was "The Seat of James Bennett Esq. M. D. Counsellor at Law, Author of the American System of Practical Book keeping &c. &c. Who is Sole Architect of his own house, and of his own fortune." Further we are informed that the sixteen thirty-foot columns which extended around three sides of the house had "caps invented and the whole designed by the proprietor, which invention entitles him to a new order in Architecture"—called the Columbian Order. The house was later owned by the Halsey family for many years, and in 1880 was acquired by the Academy of the Visitation for use as a girls' school.

In the city itself, local architects occasionally had the chance to design spacious residences on Fifth Avenue . . .

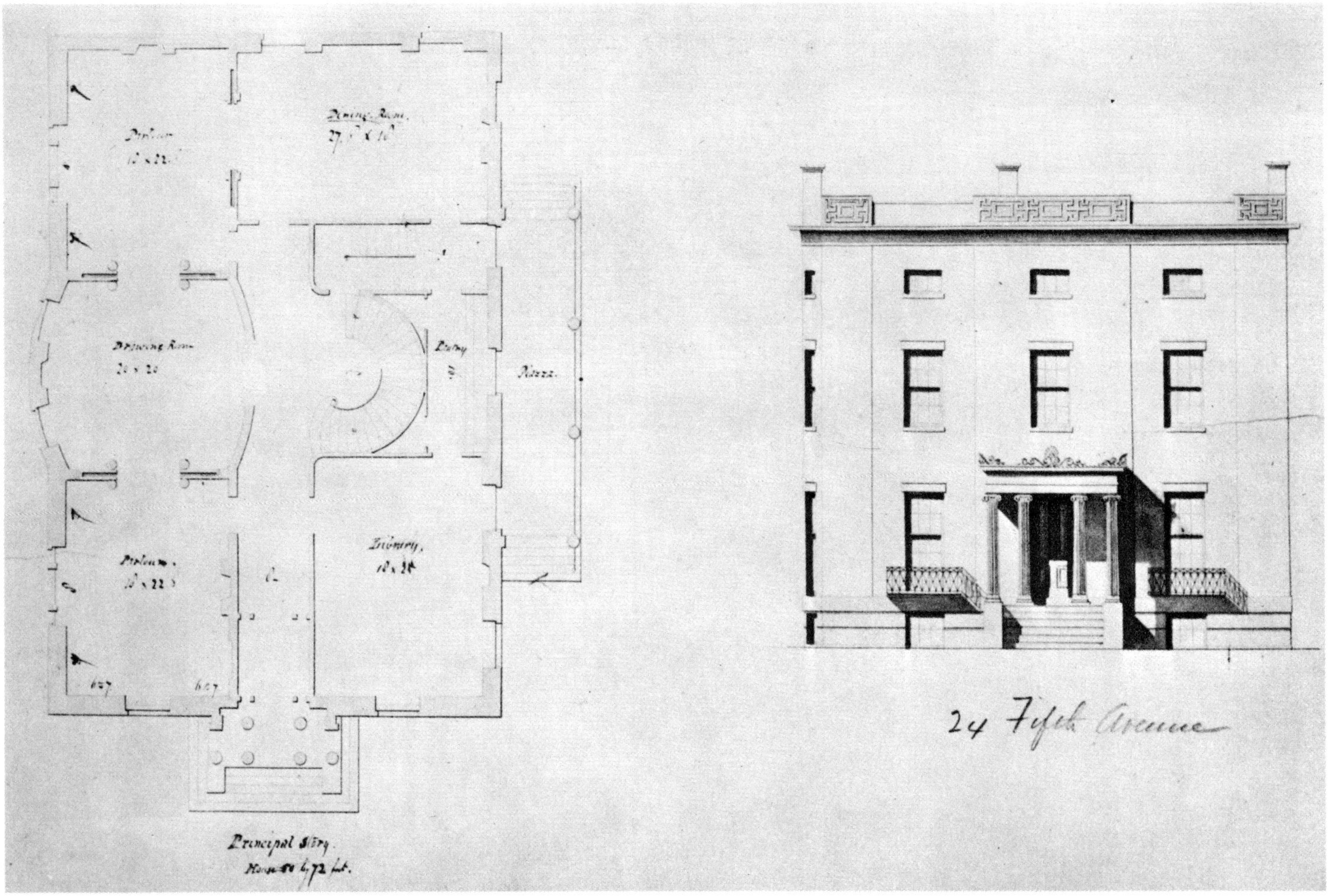

Both pictures from Museum of the City of New York

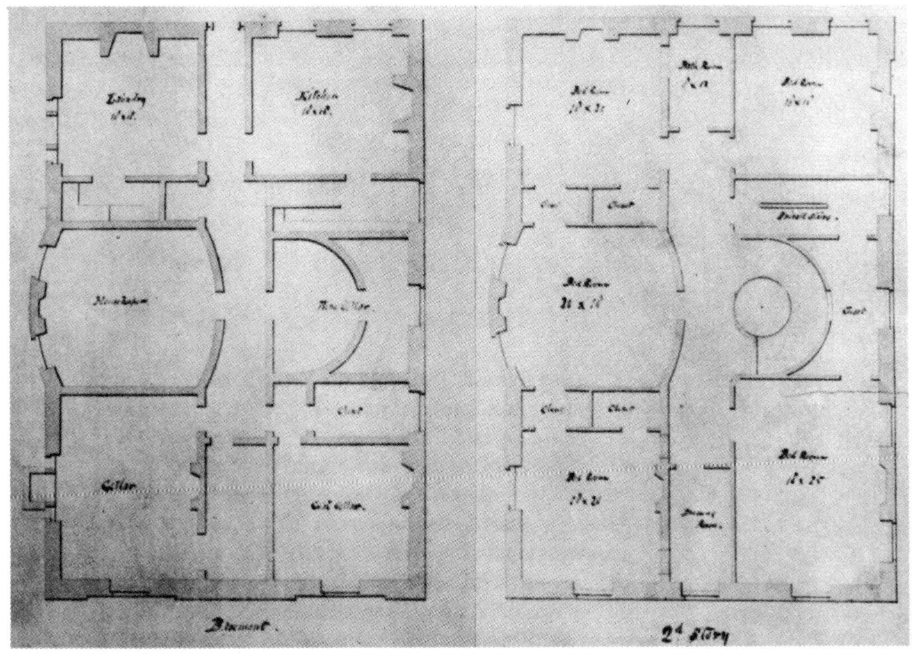

One of the finest free-standing houses in the city was the residence of Henry Brevoort on the northwest corner of Fifth Avenue and Ninth, built in 1834. The architect's plans and front elevation of this house, drawn by A. J. Davis, are here reproduced for the first time.

In 1850 the house was bought by Henry C. de Rham for $57,000, and in 1921 was sold by the De Rham family to George F. Baker, Jr., for $450,000. In 1925 it was torn down to make way for a fifteen-story hotel (see pages 253 and 475).

. . . or on upper Broadway, as the fashionable residential district moved uptown.

J. Clarence Davies Collection, Museum of the City of New York

Water-color drawing by A. S. Hosier of the Ward mansion, on the northeast corner of Broadway and Bond Street, as it appeared about 1835.

Samuel Ward, senior partner of the banking house of Prime, Ward, King & Co. and a trustee of Columbia College, was a patron of the arts as well as a prominent figure in business and social circles. His house contained one of the finest private libraries in the city, and an art gallery where paintings by contemporary American artists hung side by side with those of European masters. (Brooks Brothers' clothing store later occupied this site, before moving to its present location at Madison Avenue and Forty-fourth Street.)

But most of the published prints were of the city's new mansions of commerce and temples of finance.

J. Clarence Davies Collection, Museum of the City of New York

This lithograph of the new Merchants Exchange, designed by Isaiah Rogers, was made and published by William C. Kramp in 1837 from the architect's drawings. The building was begun in 1836, on the site of the one which had been destroyed a year before in the Great Fire, and was completed early in 1842 (see page 22).

Collection of Edward W. C. Arnold; photograph courtesy of Museum of the City of New York

The New Centre Market, at the northeast corner of Centre and Grand streets (where police headquarters was built in 1909), was erected in 1838–39 on the site of an older market, built in 1817. The new building was designed by Thomas Thomas who, with A. J. Davis, Thomas U. Walter, Isaiah Rogers, and others, had established in 1836 the American Institution of Architects (precursor of the present Institute). Contemporary newspaper accounts called it "the first market in this country which may be deemed a complete building."

Smaller temples, devoted to education and the arts, were also pictured . . .

Collection of Edward W. C. Arnold; photograph courtesy of Museum of the City of New York

The Rutgers Female Institute, shown here in an anonymous line engraving, was built in 1838–39 on the east side of Madison Street between Clinton and Montgomery streets. Here, according to the report of the Regents (1840), "solid" studies were blended with "the ornamental branches, as needle work, wax-work, embroidery, drawing and painting." Once a fortnight the young ladies wrote compositions which were "tied in bundles, labelled, and deposited in the library of the institution." Prizes were awarded for the best compositions, and at the 1845 commencement exercises the winning piece, by a Miss Hunter, was read aloud by the chairman of the judges' committee, a young editor of the *Broadway Journal* named Edgar Allan Poe.

The Institute moved, in 1860, to new quarters in the block on Fifth Avenue directly opposite the present New York Public Library building, and in 1883 to 54–58 West Fifty-fifth Street. It later became affiliated with Rutgers University in New Brunswick, N. J.

. . . though education, and "culture" in general, were women's concern more than men's.

Water-color drawing, unsigned, showing Miss Sarah Elizabeth Holden, a New York schoolteacher of the early 1840s, teaching a class with the aid of a phonetic chart.

The high window suggests that Miss Holden's school, like the majority of public schools in New York during the thirties and forties, was in the basement of a church or some other large building. The Public School Society had erected a few well-constructed school buildings, but they were exceptions to the rule of comfortless rooms like those of Primary School No. 24, in the basement of the Universalist Church at Bleecker and Downing streets, where the heating stove smoked so badly in winter that school often had to be dismissed.

BELOW, an unsigned pen and ink drawing, made about 1841, of a Lyceum Lecture by James Pollard Espy, the meteorologist, at Clinton Hall, southwest corner of Nassau and Beekman streets. The New York *Mirror,* February 29, 1840, noted that it was extremely fashionable to attend lectures, and "an army of men of talent, principally from down east, has held the town captive—commanded them nightly and pocketed their dollars." Longfellow, Emerson, Professor Silliman, Charles Francis Adams all drew large crowds.

Both pictures from Museum of the City of New York

In the forties for the first time we begin to get pictures which reflect the social life of New Yorkers. We see them attending receptions . . .

Lent by Miss Clara L. Cheesman to Museum of the City of New York

This silhouette by Augustin Edouart depicts a reception in 1840 at the home of Dr. John C. Cheesman, 473 Broadway (between Grand and Broome streets, on the west side).

Those present were, left to right: Frederick S. Tallmadge; Joseph A. Shelburg; Morton Cheesman; Miss Martha Raphael; Mr. [Ogden?] Hoffman; Mr. Bostwick; Miss Fayetta Raphael; T. M. Cheesman (with violin); Miss A. L. Cheesman (with guitar); Mrs. Cheesman (the hostess); Dr. Ferguson; John M. Smith; Captain Macomber; Dr. Benjamin Raphael; James Greason; Dr. Cheesman; and Russell Isaacs.

The New York *Mirror* for March 21, 1840, commented on the new custom among well-to-do families, "the travelled especially," of getting up weekly "agreeable *soirées* and coteries, where the time imperceptibly glides on over the strains of choicest melody in the intervals of literary conversation."

. . . serenading young ladies, and going to parties . . .

Both pictures from Museum of the City of New York

These two pen and ink drawings are from an album of sketches prepared, apparently, by a young man about town as a sort of illustrated proposal of marriage for the young lady of his choice. The one above is inscribed: "Serenade 12 January 1841. 823 Broadway"; the one below, "Returning from an evening party in Brooklyn."

. . . and we get glimpses of them in the hotels and boardinghouses where more and more of them chose to live.

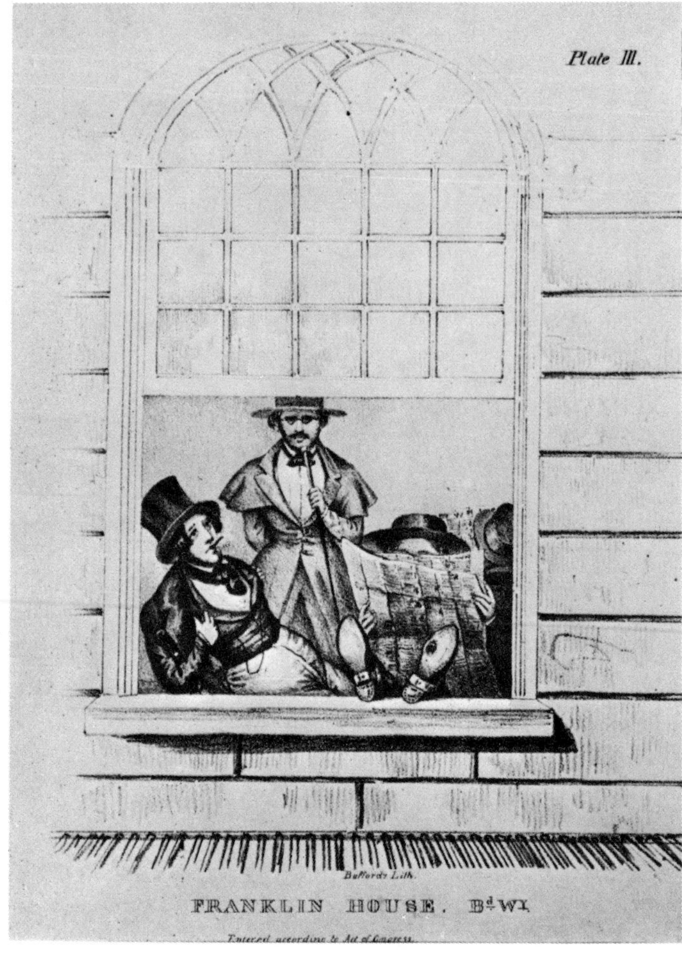

Both of the lithographs on this page were issued by J. H. Bufford about 1840. The Franklin House, corner of Broadway and Dey Street, in whose window the gentlemen are lounging, was one of the most popular hotels in town during the thirties and forties. The "Fashionable Boarding House" might have been anywhere.

Living in hotels and boardinghouses was one of the features of New York life from the thirties on.

Collection of Edward W. C. Arnold; photograph courtesy of Museum of the City of New York

Museum of the City of New York

Mrs. Trollope noted, early in the decade, that "a great number of young married persons board by the year, instead of 'going to housekeeping,'" and the *Mirror* noted, in the fall of 1835, that several of "the most fashionable and wealthy people" in the city had arranged for suites in the Astor House, then being built, as winter residences and had already selected sites on the Hudson for summer villas.

Many observers decried boardinghouse life as a threat to the American home, but the difficulty of getting servants, and the high rents for houses, plus what one English traveler called "the indisposition of young ladies to undertake the responsibilities and troubles of attending to domestic arrangements," all conspired to increase the number of boardinghouses.

But even the pictures of society's belles were quite likely to have commercial overtones.

This 1840 advertisement, lithographed and published by Alfred E. Baker at 8 Wall Street, shows Miss Julia Gardiner (the "Rose" of Long Island) with her escort in front of Bogert & Mecamly's store at 86 Ninth Avenue. Miss Gardiner was the daughter of David Gardiner of Southampton, and was soon to become the wife of the President of the United States. Yet it was not deemed inappropriate to picture her carrying a sign reading, "I'll Purchase at Bogert & Mecamly's No. 86, 9th Ave. Their Goods are Beautiful & Astonishingly Cheap." (Not everyone admired Miss Gardiner. Though Philip Hone called her "a dashing girl of twenty-two" when he recorded her marriage to President Tyler in his diary in 1844, another diarist, George Templeton Strong, noted caustically that "infatuated old John Tyler was married today to one of those large, fleshy Miss Gardiners of Gardiner's Island.")

Museum of the City of New York

Collection of Edward W. C. Arnold; photograph courtesy of Museum of the City of New York

The "New York Belle" whose upper and lower "falsies" are ridiculed in this 1846 lithograph by H. R. Robinson, is shown at left promenading before A. T. Stewart's new store on Broadway between Chambers and Reade streets.

The forties also saw the rise of "comic" pictures . . .

The anonymous "comic" lithograph of "Young America Making his Mark" was probably issued during the late forties, when the phrase "Young America" had become a part of the language as a term for describing the boundless energy and expansive irreverence of the time.

The other lithograph, " 'Vive la France.' Balancier. Both in 'Tow,' " by Alfred E. Baker, is the second in a set of three comics supposed to be a take-off on Edward Dechaux, a prominent art dealer of the forties. Dechaux is represented playing simultaneous games of battledore and shuttlecock with two ladies in his studio, using cupids as "birds."

Both pictures from collection of Edward W. C. Arnold; photographs courtesy of Museum of the City of New York

. . . and sketches of familiar urban types.

Both pictures from author's collection

These engravings, from drawings by F. O. C. Darley, were published in the *United States Magazine and Democratic Review* in the July and November issues, 1843, as illustrations for Joseph C. Neal's "Pennings and Pencillings About Town." Neal was a Philadelphian, not a New Yorker, but the setting of Darley's scenes was more likely New York, where the magazine was published.

Neal's comments on the newsboy (shown here hawking James Gordon Bennett's New York *Herald*) are especially interesting for their emphasis upon the newsboy's role as the typical figure of the nineteenth century, "its walking idea, its symbol, its personification," and as an incarnation of "commercial man, speculating man"—or, alternatively, of "Young America." Tibbs, as Neal calls him, necessarily learns the one great lesson of success. "He looks upon the community as a collective trout—a universal fish which must nibble at his bait, lie in his basket and fill his frying pan. On this maxim, heroes have overrun the world."

Even in panoramic views, the foreground is dominated by people . . .

Stokes Collection, New York Public Library

Like Thomas Hornor's engraved view of "New York from Brooklyn" (page 160), his panoramic wash drawing of New York, looking north from below City Hall Park, is dominated by its foreground—in this case clearly unfinished. It is possible, as suggested by Mr. Stokes and Daniel C. Haskell in *American Historical Prints,* that Hornor abandoned the drawing when he realized that the figures in the foreground were "hopelessly out of scale with the background." In any event, his interest in the costumes and activities of the men, women, and children in the park obviously got him in trouble with perspective, requiring that Park Row (at right) be curved out so that it ran parallel to Broadway (left) instead of running in a straight line diagonally across the picture to meet it (see top of opposite page). The author has been unable to find any explanation for the monumental sculptured groups on the roof of the Park Place Hotel (or Mechanics' Hall Building) at left.

OPPOSITE: The lithograph of the "Croton Water Celebration 1842" was published by J. F. Atwill as a sheet-music title. Looking north along Broadway (left) and Park Row, it depicts the parade to celebrate completion of the Croton Aqueduct, begun in 1837 and finished in July 1842. This was one of the great engineering achievements of the mid-nineteenth century, and it provided New York for the first time with an adequate water supply.

The picture of a street auction in Chatham Square was painted by E. Didier, who exhibited it first at the National Academy of Design in 1843. (W. N. Seymour's hardware store was at No. 4 Chatham Square, near Division Street; H. Kipp's Furniture Warehouse at No. 7 on the corner of East Broadway.)

. . . and street scenes are crowded
with citizens at work
or at play.

J. Clarence Davies Collection, Museum of the City of New York

Museum of the City of New York

Artists who had previously done landscape views of the city . . .

The charming series of water-color drawings on this and the two following pages was made about 1840 by Nicolino V. Calyo, several of whose landscape views have been reproduced earlier in this book (see pages 150, 158, and 166). Charles Brown, the butcher, is shown at his stall, perhaps in the Centre or Fulton Market. The Negro dancer and Negro banjo player remind us that it was in the late thirties and early forties that the minstrel shows, made internationally popular by "Jim Crow" Rice, emerged as a distinctive form of theatrical entertainment. At the depths of the depression of 1837, Philip Hone noted in his diary that up at the Bowery Theater Rice was "made to repeat nightly, almost ad infinitum, his balderdash song." A few nights later, when he dined with Lester Wallack and "Jim Crow" at the Astor House, Hone had to admit that "Rice's negro songs and melodies were exceedingly fine. . . . He is one of the most entertaining men I ever met in company."

All pictures on pages 182 and 183 lent by Mrs. Luke Vincent Lockwood to Museum of the City of New York

Patrick Bryant's oyster stand could have been in any downtown street.
Everywhere you turned there were oyster cellars, oyster houses, and stands like Bryant's where you could stop and enjoy a plate of saddle rocks or blue points.

. . . and sketch them "on the job," as it were.

Both pictures lent by Mrs. Luke Vincent Lockwood to Museum of the City of New York

Two more of Calyo's drawings: a charcoal man and his wagon, and a cab.

Cabs were first introduced in New York in 1840, when Brigham Eaton, of 135 Crosby Street, put three in service in front of the Astor House, late in March. By mid-April there were more than twenty-five in town. According to the *Mirror,* they were "the most convenient things imaginable."

The world's first portrait photograph was taken in New York in 1839, just when the new concern with individual likenesses was appearing in other mediums.

Museum of the City of New York

The daguerreotype reproduced above was almost certainly not, as has been claimed, the first photograph ever made of a human face. It is, however, the earliest one of which copies are known to exist.

It is a portrait of Miss Dorothy Catherine Draper, taken by her brother, Professor John W. Draper of New York University, and sent by him to Sir John Herschel in England in 1840, more than a year before anyone in Europe succeeded in taking a portrait. It may have been taken late in 1839. The original has completely faded, but several photographic copies were made before it had gone. It is reproduced here from an artotype by E. Bierstadt. According to Professor Robert Taft, in *Photography and the American Scene,* Draper's success had probably been anticipated by another New Yorker, Alexander S. Wolcott, by a matter of several months. But no copy of Wolcott's picture is known to exist.

The wash drawing of the razor-strop man was made about 1845 by Ambrose Andrews. It is a portrait of a well-known street character of the period, named Smith, who usually took up his stand on the corner of Wall and Nassau streets.

Collection of Edward W. C. Arnold; photograph courtesy of Museum of the City of New York

And by the mid-forties an artist who set out to make a series of street views . . .

New York. 1846.

Umbrella man.

All pictures on pages 186 and 187 from the collection of Edward W. C. Arnold; photographs courtesy of Museum of the City of New York

. . . first filled his sketchbook with rapid notations of individual faces he noticed as he wandered through the town.

During the late 1840s, August Köllner (see page 157) issued a series of *Views of American Cities,* published by Goupil, Vibert & Co., which included eight of his drawings of New York. (One of these is reproduced on page 196.) In Mr. Arnold's collection there is a sketchbook of "American Vehicles from Nat[ure] by A. Kollner," four pages of which are reproduced here. Apparently, while sketching the New York drays and beer wagons and other characteristic vehicles which might be used in his street scenes, Köllner's eye was frequently caught by faces which he swiftly and vigorously noted in the margins of his page.

Group Three

MID-CENTURY PANORAMA 1845–1855

The so-called Dripps map of New York in 1850 gives a clear idea, even in this greatly reduced reproduction, of the extent to which the city had been built up at mid-century.

Entitled "Map of the City of New York Extending Northward to Fiftieth Street," it was surveyed and drawn by John F. Harrison, lithographed and printed by Kollner, Camp & Co., and published by M. Dripps in 1851.

This and a companion map of Manhattan north of Fiftieth Street were the first published maps to show in detail all the individual lots and buildings in the city.

Stokes Collection, New York Public Library

Even before mid-century the city had expanded
so far uptown that one could
grasp it as a whole only
in a bird's-eye
view . . .

One of the earliest, if not the first, of the bird's-eye views of New York was this lithograph by J. H. Bufford on the cover of the sheet music of "The Carrier Dove, An Admired Ballad sung with great applause at Niblo's Garden by Miss Watson," composed by D. Johnson and published in 1836 or 1837 by Atwill.

Collection of Edward W. C. Arnold; photograph courtesy of Museum of the City of New York

. . . or section by section . . .

The fantastically detailed pen and ink panorama of the city reproduced on this and the three following pages was drawn between 1842 and 1845 by Edward Burckhardt of Bâle, Switzerland, who lived in New York from 1839 to 1870. The drawing was made in eight sections which, when joined together, would provide a circular panorama of the city as seen from the steeple of the North Dutch Church on the northwest corner of Fulton and William streets. As reproduced here, the sections are presented two at a time, first at the top and then at the bottom of this and the following pair of pages.

The pictures on pages 190 and 191 from the New-York Historical Society

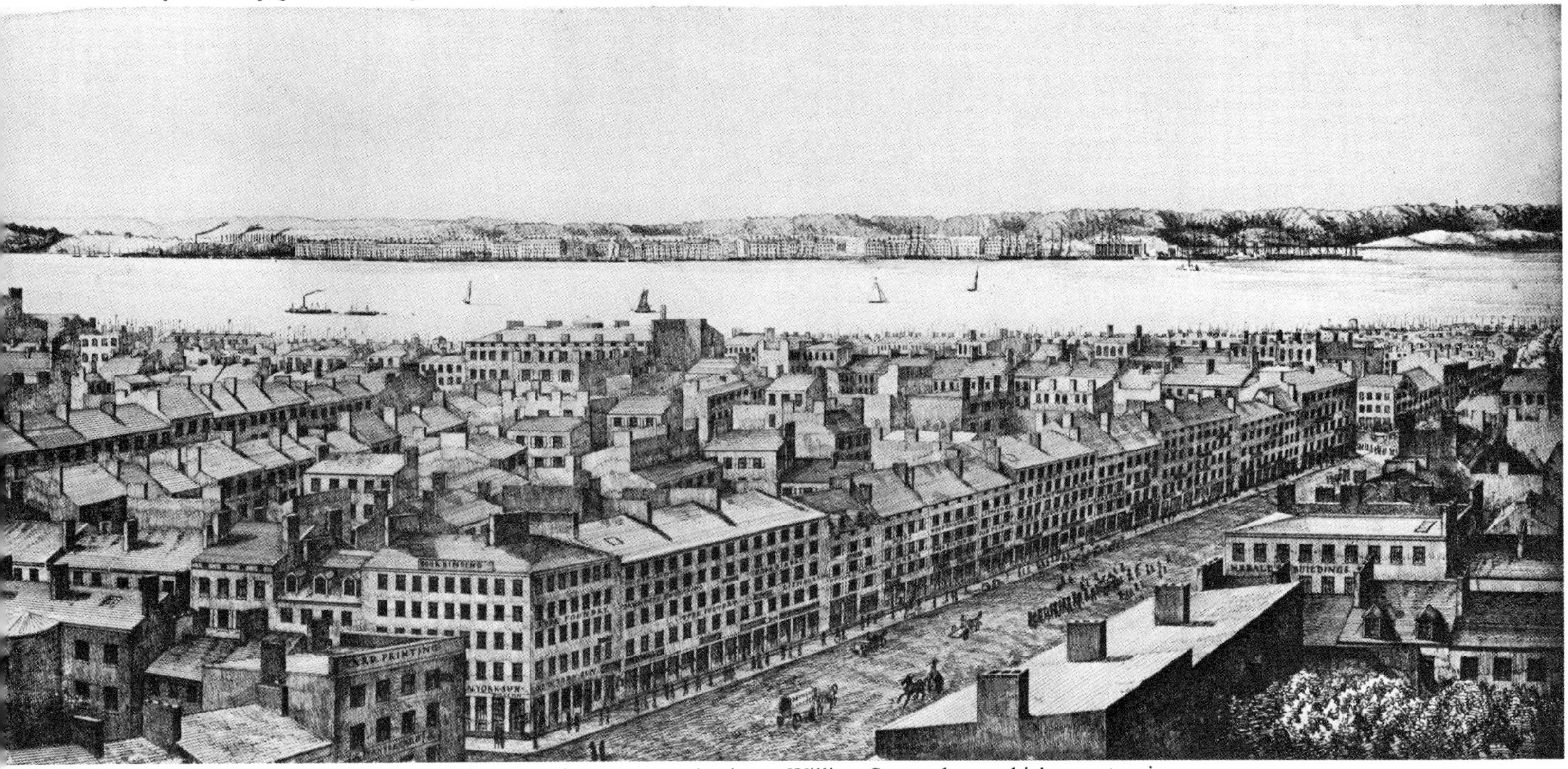

Starting at upper left on the opposite page, the panorama begins at William Street, down which we get a view to the point where it curves eastward south of Wall Street. The belfry in the middle of this first section is that of the Middle Dutch Church at Nassau and Liberty streets, and farther right is the unfinished spire of the third (and present) Trinity Church, which was completed in 1846. Section 2 (above) shows the south side of Fulton Street between Nassau and Broadway. Section 3 (bottom left) shows St. Paul's, at Fulton and Broadway, and Lovejoy's Hotel on Park Row at Beekman Street, this side of City Hall Park. Section 4, looking northwest, includes the steeple of the Brick Church and the City Hall.

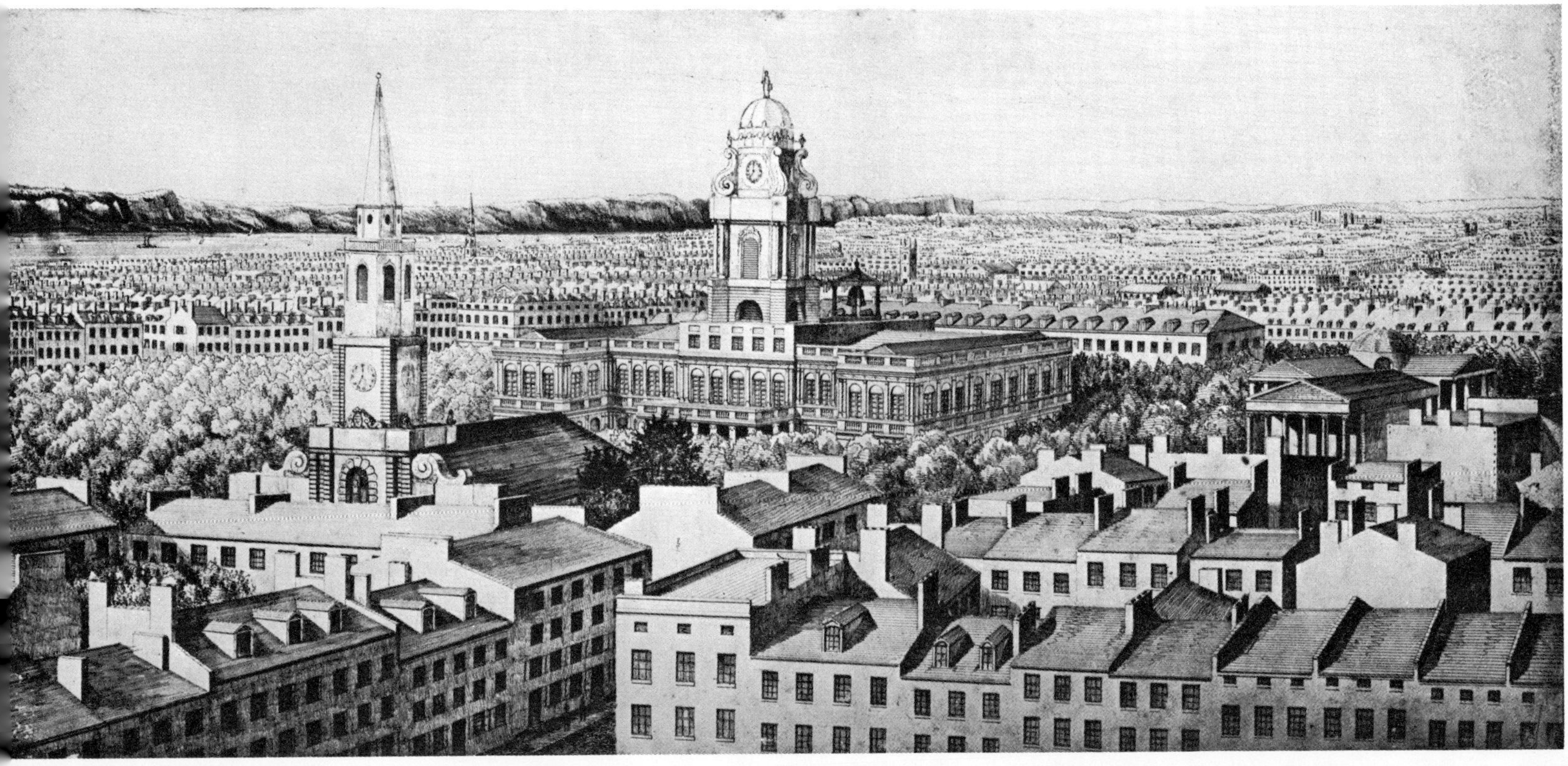

. . . made, as this one was, from one of the steeples which towered . . .

The pictures on pages 192 and 193 from the New-York Historical Society

In Section 5 (above) we are looking northeast up William Street, at left, toward Hell Gate in the distant background. Section 6 (above right) looks eastward toward Peck Slip and, across the East River, the Navy Yard at Wallabout Bay. Section 7 (bottom left) looks southeast down Fulton Street at left and across the East River to Brooklyn Heights (where Underhill's Colonnade Row

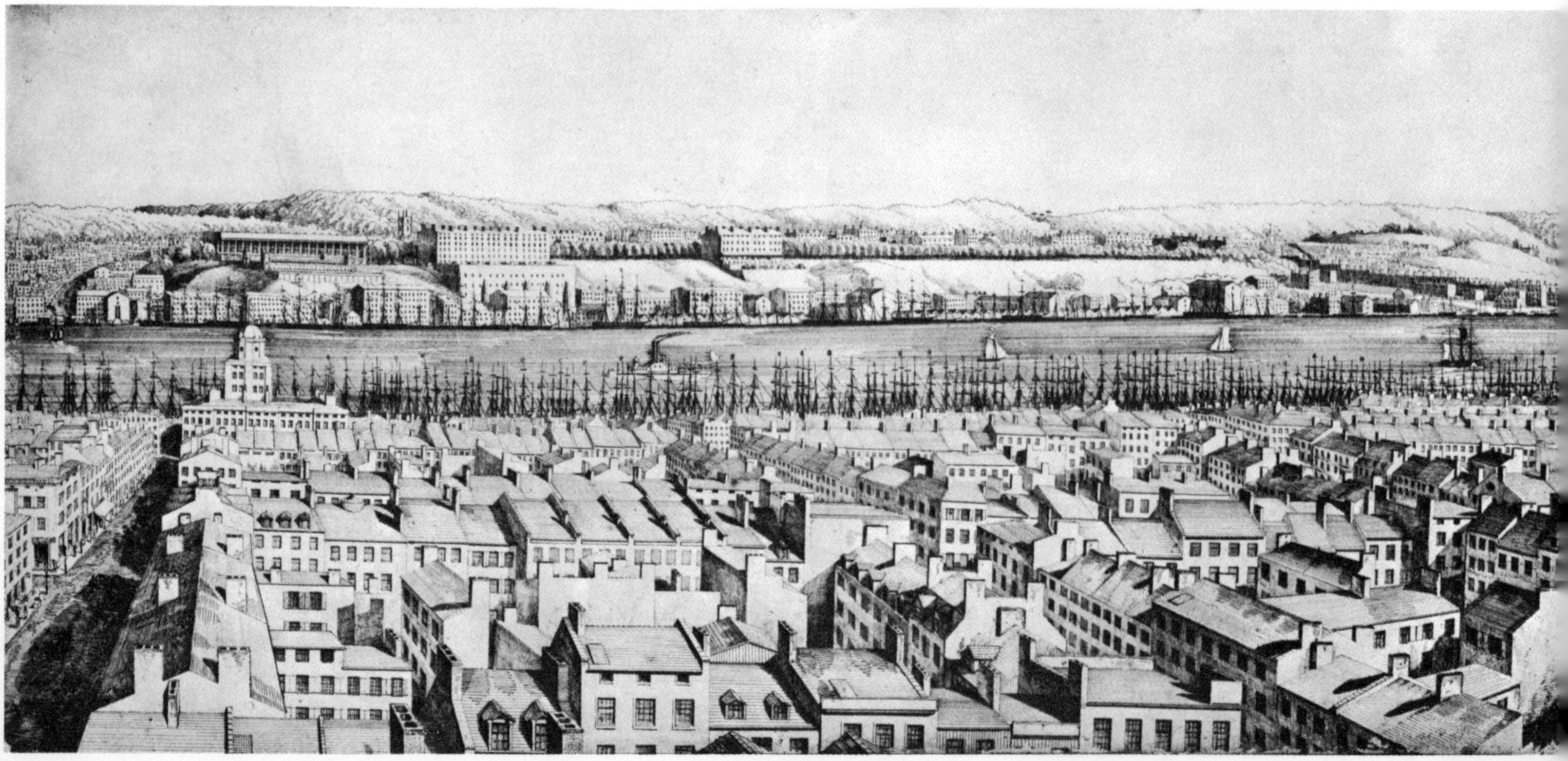

. . . above the usual three- or four-story buildings of the city.

is still a prominent architectural feature). And, finally, Section 8 (below) sweeps across the old part of the city below John Street, in foreground, till it returns to the starting point at William Street. (The large domed building at right is, of course, the new Merchants Exchange on the southeast corner of William and Wall streets. Beyond it, to the left, lies Governor's Island, and in the distance the Narrows.)

Better than any picture, however, was a scale model which reproduced the city in miniature so one could take it in at a glance.

MODEL OF NEW-YORK.

In 1845–46 E. Porter Belden, with the assistance of almost 150 artists, craftsmen, sculptors, and mechanics, designed and built a scale model of the city below Thirty-second Street, with a part of Brooklyn and Governor's Island. The completed model, 20′ × 24′ square, was surmounted by a Gothic canopy nearly 15′ high, ornamented with almost a hundred separate oil paintings of "the leading business establishments and places of note in the city." (One of the artists employed on the canopy was E. C. Coates, whose painting of New York from Weehawken is reproduced on page 157.)

When the model went on exhibition at the Minerva Room (406 Broadway, between Walker and Canal streets), it at once became one of the city's principal sights. Committees of clergymen and teachers endorsed it and the Common Council and the mayor granted it official sanction. The editors of the city's most influential newspapers and magazines, including William Cullen Bryant of the *Post,* jointly issued a circular to editors in other cities, assuring them that it was indeed an accurate representation of the city, and that "the business and commerce of New-York can be better seen by a casual inspection of this model, than by days spent in actually visiting the business localities of the city."

Belden planned to exhibit his model throughout the United States and in Europe. What ultimately happened to it, the author has been unable to discover. Apparently all that survives are these crude woodcuts, from advertisements published in Belden's *New York: Past, Present, and Future* (see page 196).

Both pictures from author's collection

THE MINATURE CITY,
REPRESENTING THE

CITY OF NEW-YORK,
IN CARVED WOOD,
Now being exhibited in different portions of the Union, is a

GREAT WORK OF ART.

It is a perfect *fac-simile* of New-York, representing every street, lane, building, shed, park, fence, tree, and every other object in the city. The district represented includes the whole of New-York, the Harbor, the East and North Rivers, and the greater part of

BROOKLYN,

The following tremendous numbers may astonish the reader, but will be found to be no less correct. There are represented upon

THE MODEL CITY.

Over 200,000 Buildings, including Houses, Stores and Rear-Buildings.
" 2,500,000 Windows and Doors,
" 35,000 Fences and Walls.
" 150,000 Chimneys. 30,000 Trees.
" 20,000 Awnings and Lamp Posts.
" 5,000 Pieces of Shipping.

IT WILL BE BORNE IN MIND THAT THE

MODEL OF NEW YORK

is vastly different from a map or a painting. It is inconceivably superior to any representation upon paper or canvass; each building being a perfect miniature building, and the whole *differing from the actual city only in point of size.*

The average observer, however, found himself plunged into the heart of the city, and had to content himself with seeing the principal sights.

Author's collection

"New York from the steeple of St. Paul's Church, looking East, South, and West," was drawn by J. W. Hill, engraved in aquatint by Henry Papprill, and published in 1849 by H. I. Megarey. In the detail (at left) the roof of St. Paul's is in the left foreground, with Barnum's Museum (currently exhibiting a Balloon Panorama) across Broadway at the corner of Ann Street. Two doors south of Barnum's is the shop of Genin, the Hatter, and south of it, on the northeast corner of Fulton, a cigar store and a clothing store (in the same building John Williams had occupied in 1816; see page 127). Catty-cornered across Broadway, on the southwest corner, is Brady's daguerreotype gallery. At right in the picture above, at Nos. 168–72 Fulton Street, are the "Furniture warerooms & Manufactory" of D. and W. H. Lee, a paint shop, and another furniture warehouse occupying the site of Duncan Phyfe's establishment (also on page 127).

If he had a copy of Belden's guidebook, which was the best available, he probably started off at Barnum's Museum.

Collection of Edward W. C. Arnold; photograph courtesy of Museum of the City of New York

This view of Broadway, from Köllner's series of *Views of American Cities* (see page 187), is a street-level glimpse of the same busy intersection shown in the preceding picture. In addition to Barnum's and St. Paul's it shows the Astor House, designed by Isaiah Rogers and built in 1834–36 on the block between Vesey and Barclay streets where John Jacob Astor's house had been (see page 119). (The guidebook referred to at the top of this page, and quoted on several subsequent pages, is *New York: Past, Present, and Future,* published by G. P. Putnam in 1849. The author was E. Porter Belden, the creator of the "Model of New York" illustrated on page 194. On the whole, it is the most accurate and complete mid-century guide to the city, though its brief prophetic section on "The Future" was as faulty as most guesses about New York's future. If the population went on increasing at its recent rate, he argued, there would be more than two million people living on Manhattan in 1899. "But the island will not furnish adequate room for two millions of inhabitants," he concluded. In 1910 the population of Manhattan alone was 2,331,542. But perhaps he was right about "adequate" room, after all. The borough's population dropped to 1,867,000 in 1930, and has never since climbed as high as two million.)

From there he might have gone to one of the museums or galleries . . .

J. Clarence Davies Collection, Museum of the City of New York

There were, as Belden noted, a number of art galleries in the city. The New York Gallery of the Fine Arts, founded in 1844 by Luman Reed and others, exhibited the works of contemporary American painters, as did the gallery of the American Art Union, 497 Broadway. The Union, founded in 1840 as the Apollo Association, was an organization dedicated to spreading copies of paintings (chiefly engravings) to a wide public somewhat as the book clubs now distribute color reproductions. For five dollars a year you could be a member. With the money taken in, the Union bought pictures and had them engraved for distribution. Then at the end of the year a lottery was held, and the winning members got the original paintings as prizes. It was a highly successful enterprise until the courts stepped in with anti-lottery injunctions in 1850. The 1847 "Distribution of the American Art-Union Prizes" in the Broadway Tabernacle on Worth Street, east of Broadway, is shown in Sarony & Major's lithograph above. The original drawing was made by T. H. Matteson, and it was drawn on stone by Davignon.

. . . or to one of the mechanical and scientific exhibits . . .

Both pictures from Museum of the City of New York

The water-color drawing above, made about 1843 by B. J. Harrison, shows the interior of Niblo's Garden (northeast corner of Broadway and Prince Street) during the annual fair of the American Institute. The Institute was incorporated in 1829 to promote advancements in agriculture, commerce, manufactures, and the arts, and its annual fairs brought exhibitors from all over the Union. It also maintained a library and "repository" which were open to the public.

Niblo's Garden, where the fair was held, burned down in 1846 but was rebuilt in 1849. For many years it was one of the most popular amusement centers in town. It included a theater as well as gardens, and a refreshment pavilion, shown in G. & W. Endicott's lithographed advertisement of Dearborn's Premium Soda Water.

. . . and he certainly should have visited some of the charitable institutions of which the city was justly proud.

Author's collection

The Deaf and Dumb Asylum, established in 1817, had moved into its new building, on the south side of Fiftieth Street between Madison and Fourth (now Park) avenues, in 1829. By 1846 the plant had been enlarged to more than twice its original size, yet it was less than ten years before the growing institution had to move to larger quarters on Washington Heights (west of Fort Washington Avenue at 164th Street, south of the present Columbia-Presbyterian Medical Center). The Fiftieth Street buildings then became the new home of Columbia College, when it moved uptown in 1857.

The view here reproduced (original size) was drawn by F. B. Nichols and engraved by W. Wellstood as one of the illustrations for Belden's book. In the foreground is a locomotive proceeding southward on the Fourth Avenue tracks of the New York and Harlem Railroad. This is one of the earliest pictures of New York showing telegraph poles. A telegraph line from New York to Philadelphia was built in 1845–46. The line ran up Broadway to City Hall, then along the railroad tracks to Harlem, and across the island to Fort Washington where the wires passed under the Hudson (see also page 239).

The Sailors' Home, shown here in a woodcut illustration from Daniel Curry's *New York: A Historical Sketch* (New York, 1853), was maintained at 190 Cherry Street by the American Seamen's Friends Society. Founded in 1841, it was operated as a boardinghouse, and could accommodate about five hundred seamen. The drawing was made by W. Wade, and engraved on wood by J. W. Orr.

Author's collection

THE SAILOR'S HOME.

As for the city's theaters, the guidebook merely noted that "all the great artistes *of Europe" made their first American appearances in New York.*

Belden, in common with many moralists of the time, had little use for plays and playhouses. "We shall be satisfied," he announced, "with leaving unnoticed institutions of this character, except to denounce them as one of the chief causes of the immorality of New York." Belden's position had some justification. C. M. Jenkes's water-color drawing of the Astor Place riot in 1849 recalls the violence and hoodlumism which were sometimes associated with the theater. When the great English actor, W. C. Macready, appeared at the Astor Place Opera House (background of picture), anti-English mobs goaded by the American actor Edwin Forrest (and by the Sixth Ward boss, Isaiah Rynders) rioted in the streets, set the theater on fire, and were not finally dispersed until the Seventh Regiment was called out.

Twenty-three of the rioters were killed and twenty-three injured during three days of violence.

The lithographed cartoon of "The Second Deluge," published by W. Schaus in 1850, is a humorous commentary on the excitement P. T. Barnum succeeded in whipping up for Jenny Lind, the "Swedish Nightingale," when she came to America in 1850. Castle Garden, the "Modern Ark of Noah," was packed at her first concert with 6000 people who had bought seats at auction, one of whom (Genin, the Hatter) paid $225 for his ticket. But, as Barnum was shrewd enough to realize, Jenny was free of the tainted breath of scandal. She had quit opera because the heroines were so often immodest women, and she had refused to sing in Paris!

Both pictures from collection of Edward W. C. Arnold; photographs courtesy of Museum of the City of New York

Beyond that the visitor was simply told to consult the newspaper advertisements, where "the most greedy votary of amusement" could find all he wanted.

Both pictures from collection of Edward W. C. Arnold, courtesy of Museum of the City of New York

Franconi's Hippodrome, on Madison Square at the northwest corner of Broadway and Twenty-third Street, was a short-lived attempt to introduce spectacular pageants, gladiatorial contests, and chariot races to New York audiences. Built in 1853, with brick walls and a wood and canvas roof which apparently spanned the entire enclosure without any pillars to support it, the Hippodrome seated 10,000 people.

Though the opening performance attracted what the *Herald* described as "a dense mass of human beings, exceeding in number any assemblage . . . ever seen inside a building in this city, not excepting even the audiences attracted to the Jenny Lind concerts," the enterprise failed. The building was torn down in 1856 to make way for the Fifth Avenue Hotel, which occupied the site from 1859 to 1909.

Both pictures are from sheet-music covers lithographed and printed by Sarony & Major and published by T. S. Berry in 1853.

Belden urged the stranger to pause now and then and survey "the beautiful specimens of architecture that often meet his gaze. The lofty spires of Trinity . . .

Collection of Edward W. C. Arnold; photograph courtesy of Museum of the City of New York

This anonymous lithograph shows Wall Street, looking west from William Street, in 1856–57. The building at right is the Bank of America, and two doors beyond, at No. 42, is the Merchants' Bank where the Chamber of Commerce (originally established in 1768) met from 1836 to 1858. Across the street, at extreme left, is the Insurance Building, containing the offices of the Sun Mutual Marine Insurance Co., the Commercial Fire Insurance Co., and others.

Belden's guidebook describes Wall Street as the center of New York's "monetary operations," whose transactions "excite the attention of moneyed institutions and men of capital throughout this country and Europe." Here, he wryly observed, "those whose moral principle would shrink from the pursuit of the gambler, often engage in monetary transactions, in a manner and with feelings so nearly allied to those of the latter, as to admit of no favorable comparisons."

*. . . and the symmetry of the Custom House . . .
will alike command
his admiration."*

VIEWS IN NEW-YORK BY ROBERT KERR, ARCHITECT
No. 1
THE CUSTOM HOUSE . WALL STREET

Collection of Edward W. C. Arnold; photograph courtesy of Museum of the City of New York

This view of the Custom House, on Wall Street at the head of Broad Street, was the first in a projected series of lithographed "Views in New York" by Robert Kerr, architect, of 73 Cedar Street. The Custom House (now familiar to everyone as the old Sub-Treasury) was erected in 1842, on the site of Federal Hall, to replace the inadequate building which had previously occupied the site. Designed by Ithiel Town and A. J. Davis, whose architectural partnership produced many fine examples of the Greek Revival, the building was remodeled in 1862 when it became the United States Sub-Treasury. Writing only seven years after it was built, Belden tells us that the Custom House "is too contracted for the immense business transacted within its walls—a business constantly increasing, and which will doubtless require more spacious accommodations long before the present building has lost its reputation as one of the most admired edifices in the country." In 1843 a total of 1808 vessels entered the port of New York, bringing a total of 45,961 passengers, and cargoes on which $11,300,000 of duty was collected. In 1848 a total of 3010 vessels landed 176,671 people, and cargoes on which customs receipts totaled almost $20,000,000.

He would want to see "the ocean steamers, and those aquatic palaces that float on our own waters," Belden thought . . .

J. Clarence Davies Collection, Museum of the City of New York

ABOVE: "New York. Taken from the North west angle of Fort Columbus, Governor's Island," was drawn by F. Catherwood, engraved by Henry Papprill, and published by Henry I. Megarey in 1846. (This view should be compared with the photograph taken from the same spot in 1932; see page 471.)

BELOW: The anonymous painting of the burning of the side-wheeler *Henry Clay,* of which only a portion is reproduced here, records one of the worst steamboat disasters of a period when there were many. The *Henry Clay,* en route from Albany to New York on July 28, 1852, engaged in a race with a rival ship, the *Armenia.* South of Yonkers the *Henry Clay* caught fire from overheated boilers, and was run ashore. Describing the disaster in his diary, George Templeton Strong wrote: "The scene at the wreck yesterday morning was hideous: near thirty bodies exposed along the shore—many children among them. And some enterprising undertakers from Yonkers and New York had sent up their stock of coffins on speculation. 'Looking for deceased friend, sir?' 'Buying a coffin, sir?' 'Only five dollars, sir, and warranted.'"

Collection of Edward W. C. Arnold; photograph courtesy of Museum of the City of New York

. . . and the foundries, "more extensive than the forges of Vulcan," where the ships' engines were built.

Collection of Edward W. C. Arnold; photograph courtesy of Museum of the City of New York

The typical lithographed advertisements of the forties were meticulously detailed and colorful affairs, as informative and as frankly illustrative of the nature of the business as the artists could make them.

This advertisement of the Novelty Iron Works was drawn by J. Penniman and lithographed by Endicott about 1850. The works were at the foot of Twelfth Street on the East River shore, which in those days was on the present line of Avenue D, just east of where the most northerly of the Jacob Riis Houses now stand. (The houses in the right background must have been those along Avenue A, between Fifteenth and Seventeenth streets. See the Dripps map, page 188.)

Stillman and Allen's plant took its name from the first coal-burning river steamer, the *Novelty,* whose boilers and engines had been built here in 1836. The junior partner, Horatio Allen, had built the first American locomotive for actual service on a railroad—the *Best Friend of Charleston*—at the West Point Foundry on Beach Street in 1830. (Cooper's *Tom Thumb* was experimental.)

The Novelty Works in 1850 employed more than a thousand men in its eighteen different departments. They received an average of $1.50 a day, for an eleven-hour day. Besides ships' engines and boilers the plant turned out iron hulls, sugar mills, cotton presses, and other heavy machinery.

"In fine," Belden concluded, "whether he wander along the docks . . .

Museum of the City of New York

The painting above is the final section of a panoramic painting by Samuel B. Waugh, showing the landing of immigrants at the Battery in 1847. The Chinese junk, lying just off Castle Garden, was the *Keying,* said to have been the first Chinese vessel to visit the United States.

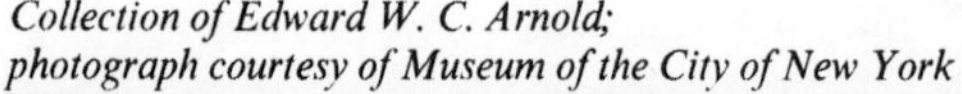

Collection of Edward W. C. Arnold; photograph courtesy of Museum of the City of New York

At left is a lithographed advertisement (1848–49) of J. M. Dunlap's "Hurlgate Ferry Hotel," on the East River at the foot of Eighty-sixth Street. The text below the picture (not reproduced here) promises "An obliging Host, beautiful scenery and cool Summer retreat. Refreshments of the first Quality, with Horses and pleasure Wagons to let, also Boats and Tackle for fishing parties, renders this place second to none in the vicinity of New York." Murphy's stage to and from City Hall ran every fifteen minutes, fare six cents. The building at right is the stable of the Gracie mansion (now the official residence of New York's mayor). The hotel itself was the old Horn's Hook Ferry House.

. . . or perambulate the streets; whether he stand enchanted . . .

J. Clarence Davies Collection, Museum of the City of New York

This lithograph of Chatham Square was published about 1847 by N. Currier. The view was taken from Chatham Street (now Park Row) looking northeast; East Broadway extends into the right background. (The buildings on the far side of the square are the same ones that appear in Didier's painting of the street auction, page 181.) The horse and cart at right are emerging from Oliver Street. "Smith's Anatomical Museum" and Riley's Sign & Shade establishment were at the northeast corner of Division Street and the Bowery, which began at Chatham Square.

The Chatham Square district was New York's "Melting Pot." Writing in 1852, a commentator on the New York scene was fascinated by its variety and color. "Here you see Jew and Gentile, Priest and Levite, as well as all other classes —the old and young of all the nations upon the earth, and all the conditions and hues of the *genus homo*. . . . Chatham-street is a sort of museum or old curiosity shop, and I think Barnum would do well to buy the whole concern, men, women, and goods, and have it in his world of curiosities on the corner of Ann and Broadway." (*Glimpses of New-York City* [Charleston, 1852].)

. . . before the fountains . . . or view from the Battery the expansive bay; he cannot fail to discover objects which fill him with wonder and delight."

Author's collection

The view of the "Park Fountain," one of the illustrations from Belden's book, was drawn by J. B. Forrest and engraved by F. B. Nichols. Belden describes the fountain, near the southern tip of City Hall Park, as the park's most interesting feature. "The jets are so arranged," he wrote, "as to admit of various combinations, which is far more pleasing than a uniformity of the most beautiful figure." The view was made from the Broadway side of the park, looking east, with the steeple of the Brick Church in the background.

Below is a view of the "Bay of New York Taken from the Battery," drawn by J. Bornet, lithographed (and the figures added) by E. Valois, and printed by D. McLellan (1851). Castle Garden is at right, and at left are the Revenue Office and the Staten Island ferry slip, with the ferryboat *Sylph* in dock. In the distance, right of the large tree in the center, is Bedloe's Island, where the Statue of Liberty now stands. The large steamship just left of Castle Garden was the Collins liner *Baltic,* which had just crossed the Atlantic in nine days and eighteen hours, at an average speed of thirteen knots.

Bequest of Mrs. J. Insley Blair, Museum of the City of New York

Belden also suggested Harlem and Manhattanville as objectives for "pleasing excursions" in the upper portion of the island . . .

Museum of the City of New York

Pencil drawing by Mrs. Otis Ormsbee, made about 1843, showing the Red House tavern at Harlem and St. George's Cricket Ground. The Red House, which had formerly been the residence of William McGowan, stood on Third Avenue at about 105th Street.

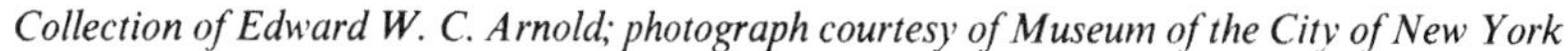

Collection of Edward W. C. Arnold; photograph courtesy of Museum of the City of New York

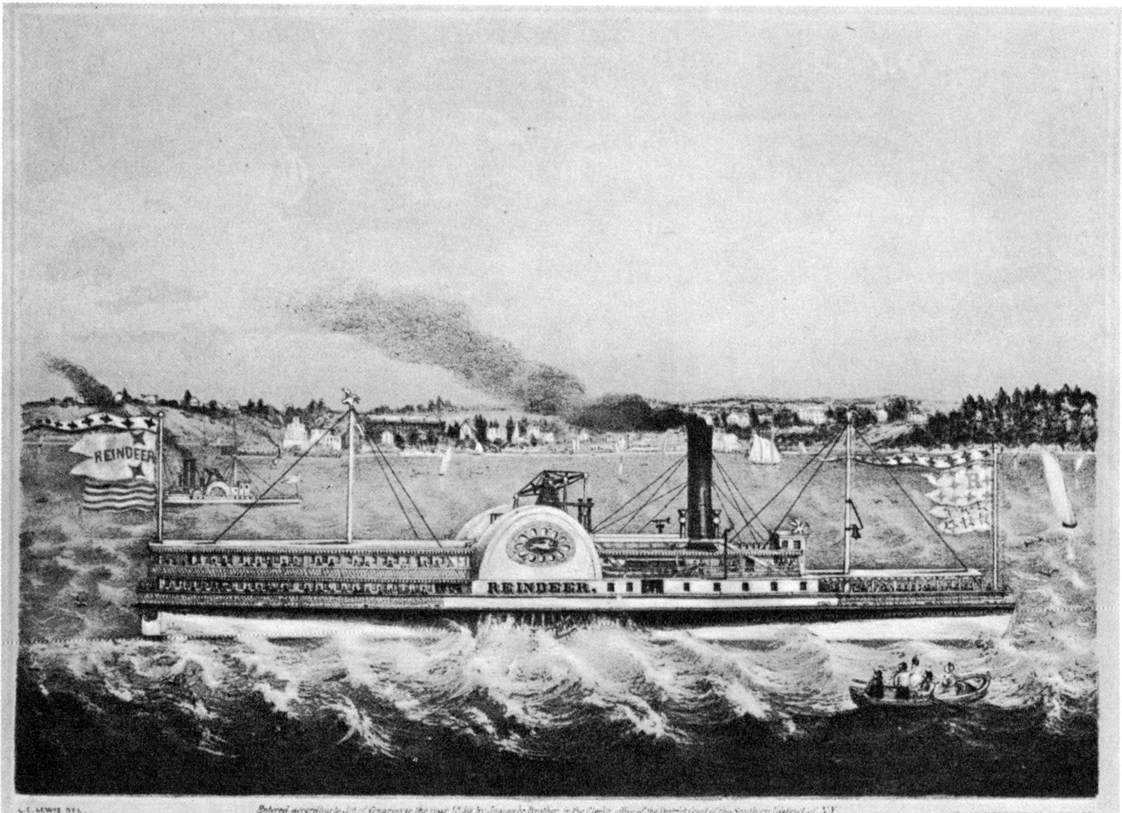

Sheet-music cover of the "Reindeer Polka," drawn by C. E. Lewis, lithographed by C. Currier, and published in 1850 by Horace Waters. Manhattanville, lying north of 125th Street on the Hudson, is in the background. (The *Reindeer,* incidentally, exploded in September, 1852, killing 33 of its 169 passengers.)

. . . where the Croton waterworks "and the lofty aqueduct bridge" were often visited.

J. Clarence Davies Collection, Museum of the City of New York

The "View of the Jet at Harlem River," drawn by F. B. Tower and engraved by W. Bennett, was published as Plate XX of Tower's *Illustrations of the Croton Aqueduct* (New York, 1843). The view was taken from a point on the Harlem about opposite the present Polo Grounds, looking north. The small white blocks in the river by the jet are the foundations of the piers of High Bridge, which was built to carry the aqueduct across the river. The old Roger Morris mansion, at this period occupied by Madame Jumel, is on the heights at left.

A lithograph, drawn by F. F. (Fanny) Palmer and published in 1852 by N. Currier, of bass fishing at Macomb's Dam on the Harlem. Taken from a point somewhat south of the picture above, after High Bridge was completed, this shows Macomb's Dam Bridge (erected 1813) and Robert Macomb's old tollhouse on the Morrisania side of the river. The bridge-dam was demolished in 1858.

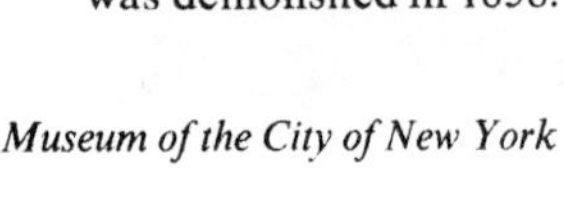

Museum of the City of New York

Brooklyn and Williamsburg, he added, were "not wanting in interest."

Stokes Collection, New York Public Library

The two pictures on this page were both drawn by Edwin Whitefield and issued in his series of "Original Views of North American Cities." Born in England, Whitefield came to this country as a boy and devoted most of his life to creating a pictorial record of important or historically interesting cities, towns, and buildings. The lithograph above, probably published in 1847, shows Brooklyn Heights from the United States Hotel (formerly Holt's) on Fulton Street (see also page 212). The tall spire in center is the Church of the Holy Trinity at Clinton and Montague streets, designed by Minard Lafever. The church was begun in 1844, but not completed until 1847. Brooklyn at this time had a population of about 30,000. Below is Whitefield's "View of Williamsburgh, L. I., from Grand Street" (c. 1852), lithographed by Endicott. Incorporated as a village in 1827, Williamsburg was chartered as a city in 1851, when its population was about 30,000. Curry's guidebook of 1853 describes it as "almost exclusively a city of residences." There were some shipyards and factories, but most of its citizens (who were, according to Curry, chiefly "of the sterling middle class") worked in New York, to which they commuted by ferry.

New-York Historical Society

"The heights of Brooklyn, and its shady streets . . .

Detail of picture at top of preceding page

Stokes Collection, New York Public Library

Though Brooklyn was politically distinct from New York, and by 1850 was a city of almost 100,000, New Yorkers in general thought of it as merely a suburb. As one guidebook condescendingly put it, "Brooklyn, being only an extension of New York city beyond its political limits, is, in all its material characteristics, a portion of that city." The chief link between the two communities was the ferry from Fulton Street in Manhattan to Fulton Street in Brooklyn (shown in this detail from Whitefield's lithograph on page 211).
LEFT: A water-color drawing by William H. Wallace, showing the intersection of Fulton Street and De Kalb Avenue in Brooklyn as seen from the corner of Fulton and Bond streets in 1848.

. . . are the scene of many a pleasing ramble," he noted.

Bequest of Mrs. J. Insley Blair, Museum of the City of New York

Brooklyn's City Hall (now called Borough Hall) had been begun in 1836 but was not finished until 1849. Designed by a local architect named Gamaliel King, it stood on a triangular plot in the intersection of Fulton, Court, and Joralemon streets. The lithograph, above, was drawn by C. Autenrieth and published in 1850 by Henry Hoff in his series of "Views of New York."

Below is an oil painting by H. Boesé showing the stagecoach "Seventy Six," of the Knickerbocker line, passing the home of Jeremiah Johnson, Jr., on Myrtle Avenue. Johnson, who was one of the owners of the stage line, was the son of General Johnson, mayor of Brooklyn 1837–40.

Museum of the City of New York

And finally, Belden urged those who "delight in excursions upon the water" to visit picturesque Staten Island . . .

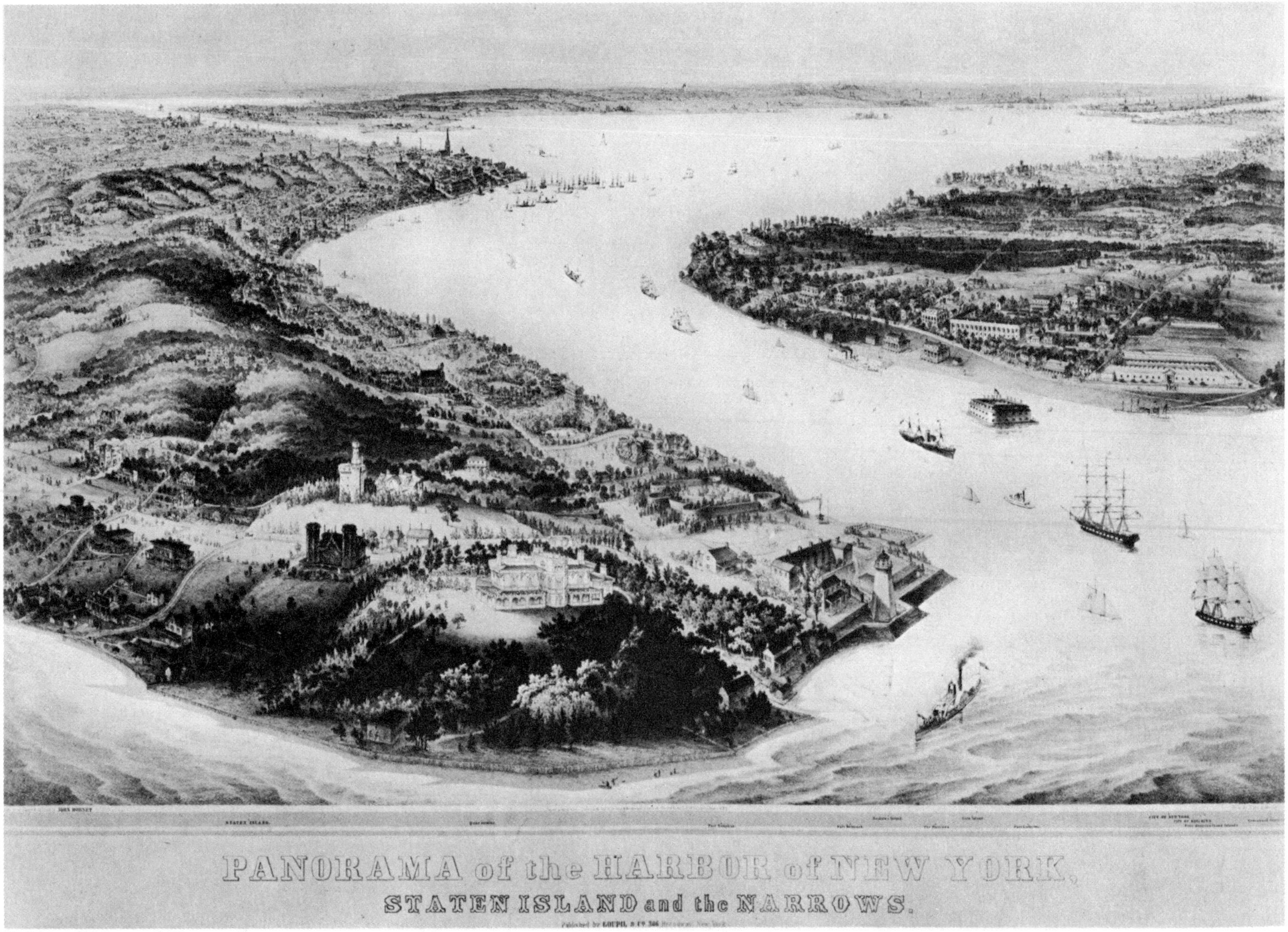

PANORAMA of the HARBOR of NEW YORK,
STATEN ISLAND and the NARROWS.

Division of Prints and Photographs, Library of Congress

ABOVE: "Panorama of the Harbor of New York, Staten Island and the Narrows," drawn by John Bornet, printed by Nagel & Weingartner, published by Goupil & Co., 1854. Fort Hamilton on Long Island at right, Forts Richmond (now Wadsworth) and Tompkins on Staten Island, surrounded by villas and estates. One of these (seen about a half inch from the left margin) appears (RIGHT) in a lithograph drawn by W. R. Miller, published about 1855 by Nathan Lane & Co.: "Summer Residence of J. F. D. Lanier Esq. at Clifton on the South Side of Staten Island."

Collection of Edward W. C. Arnold; photograph courtesy of Museum of the City of New York

. . . where many New Yorkers were building suburban villas in the newly fashionable "Italianate" and "Gothic" styles.

Staten Island Historical Society

The lithograph of "Elliottsville, S. I.," by F. & S. Palmer, was made about 1850. The road in foreground is Richmond Terrace, just east of Bard Avenue (shown running inland at right). The fields at left were part of Sailors' Snug Harbor property. Elliottsville was a real estate development initiated by Samuel Mackenzie Elliott, the great New York oculist who treated Francis Parkman, the poet Lowell, and others.

The architect's drawings for Elliott's own house (center background) are reproduced from William H. Ranlett, *The Architect, a series of Original Designs* (New York, 1847), where it is described as "a villa in a style partaking of the Gothic and Tudor."

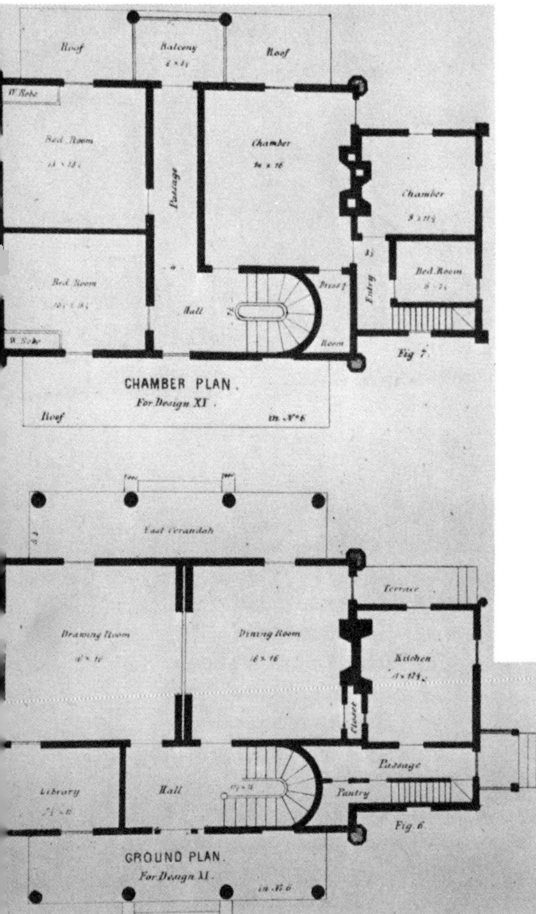

Author's collection

Wherever a mid-century visitor went in the suburbs or outskirts of the city, he would see fine homes in the older Greek Revival tradition . .

"Bloemen Heuvel, The Residence of Mr. J. A. Willink, Flatbush," is a lithograph by G. Hayward, published about 1845. The house was built about 1835, near the intersection of Flatbush and Ocean avenues. It later became a hotel, and was finally torn down about 1910.

Collection of Edward W. C. Arnold; photograph courtesy of Museum of the City of New York

J. Clarence Davies Collection, Museum of the City of New York

W. R. Miller made this water-color drawing of John James Audubon's house on July 4, 1852, about a year after Audubon's death. The house stood between 155th and 156th streets on the shore of the Hudson (see 1916 photograph, page 474).

. . . though the newer and more romantic Gothic forms might turn up anywhere in odd juxtapositions.

J. Clarence Davies Collection, Museum of the City of New York

The "rustic Gothic" pavilion, or summerhouse, on the grounds of Samuel Thomson's "Mount Washington," on Washington Heights, was a sign of the times.

The lithograph, by W. S. Jewett, was published in 1847.

In the city itself a few Gothic town houses had been built . . .

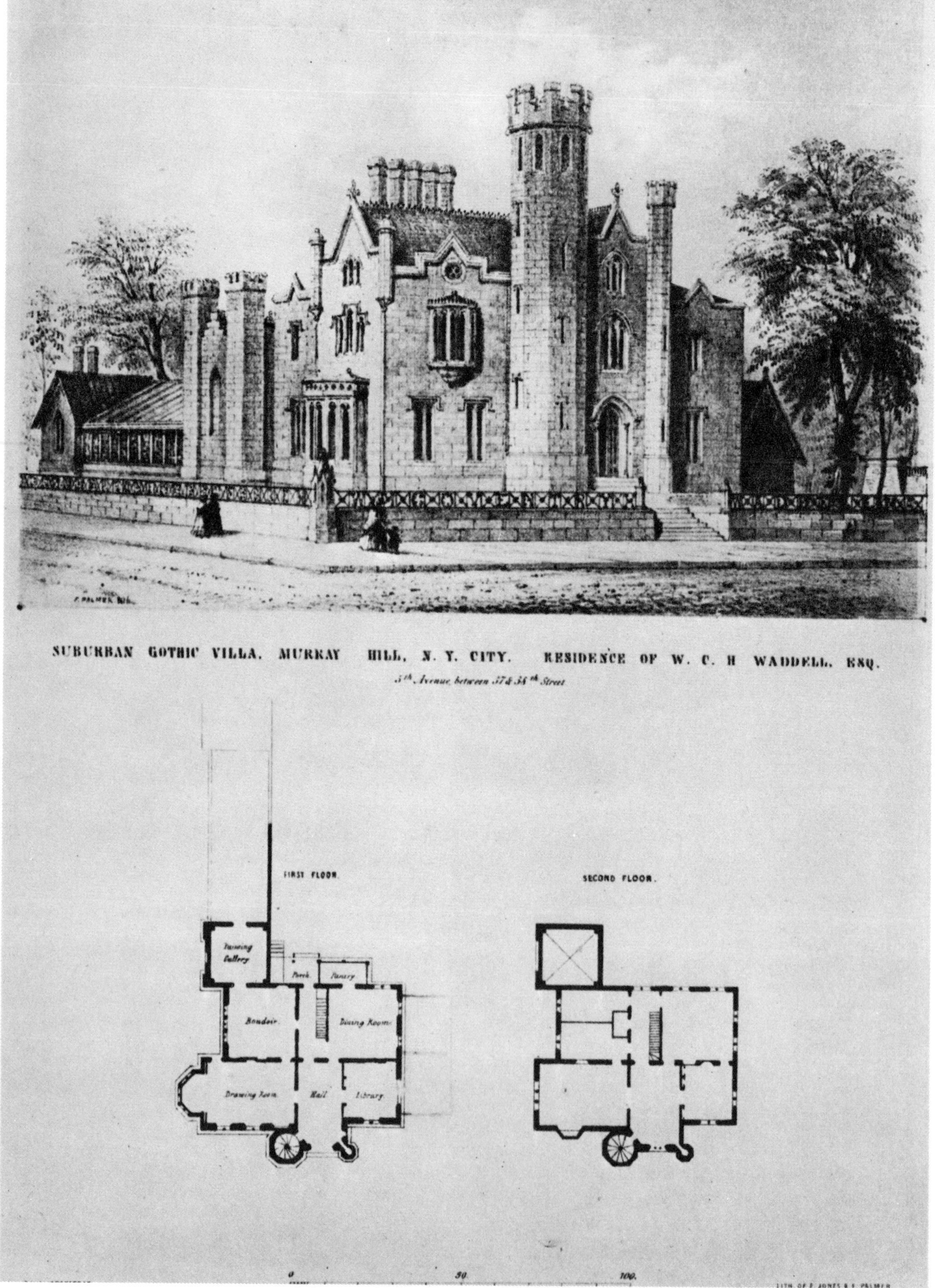

Perspective drawing and plans of a "Suburban Gothic Villa, Murray Hill, N. Y. City. Residence of W. C. H. Waddell," from drawings by the architect A. J. Davis, lithographed by F. Palmer and printed by E. Jones and E. Palmer (1844).

The house stood on the northwest corner of Thirty-seventh Street and Fifth Avenue. (The southwest corner of the old Croton Distributing Reservoir, on the present site of the New York Public Library, can be seen at extreme right.) Worked into the iron fence, as part of the design, the reader can discover the owner's name: W. Coventry Waddell.

The house was torn down in 1857 to make way for the new Brick Presbyterian Church, which occupied the site until it was demolished in 1938.

Collection of Edward W. C. Arnold; photograph courtesy of Museum of the City of New York

. . . but the Greek Revival remained dominant in urban residences . . .

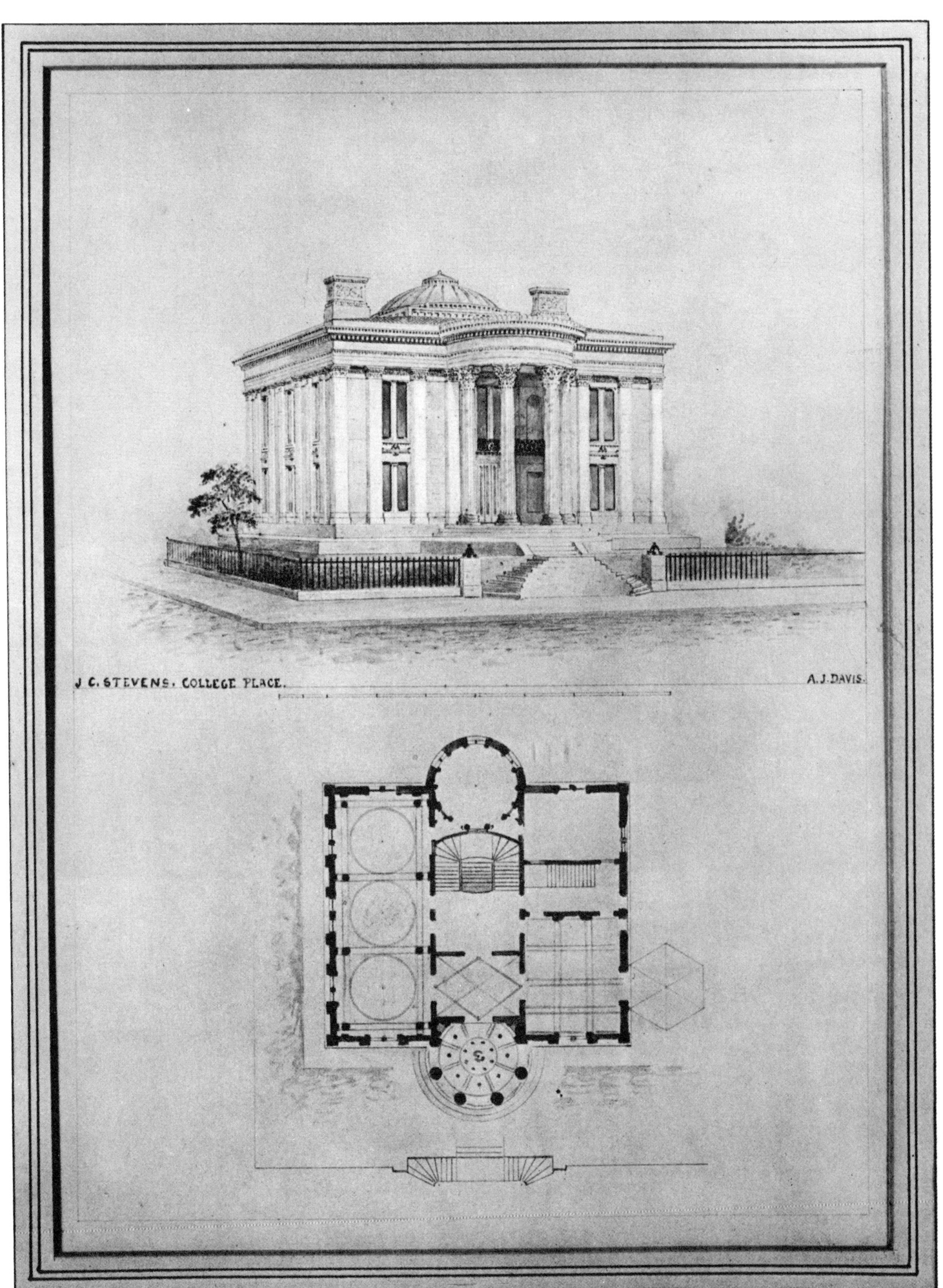

Collection of Edward W. C. Arnold; photograph courtesy of Museum of the City of New York

Perspective drawing and plan of the residence of John Cox Stevens on College Place, by A. J. Davis, about 1849. The house, or "palace" as it was called, stood on property leased from Columbia College, at the southeast corner of Murray Street and College Place (now West Broadway). When excavating for the cellar of the house, in the spring of 1845, two cannon were dug up, presumably those captured from the King's troops by Alexander Hamilton and a group of "Liberty Boys" from the college in August, 1775.

Stevens was a Columbia graduate, a member of the wealthy Hoboken shipbuilding family, first commodore of the New York Yacht Club, and (as ex-Mayor Hone testified) "a mighty good fellow, and most hospitable host."

. . . where well-to-do families lived in increasing comfort, among many new domestic conveniences.

Mrs. William Lathrop Rich, owner; photograph courtesy of Museum of the City of New York

ABOVE: Oil painting by F. Heinrich of Mr. and Mrs. Ernest Fiedler and family in 1850 at their home at 38 Bond Street (north side, east of Broadway).

LEFT: Part of a lithographed advertisement printed by E. Jones in 1845 for Thomas Dusenbury, Plumber, of 269 Water Street. Note the separate curtained compartments for toilet and tub in this elaborate Greek Revival bathroom.

J. Clarence Davies Collection, Museum of the City of New York

Not all New Yorkers were well to do, but the less fortunate were seldom pictured. After all, they could go to California . . .

Bequest of Mrs. J. Insley Blair, Museum of the City of New York

ABOVE: "Steamer Hartford, Capt. Le Fevre, bound for California. Sailed from New York, February 1849," was painted by Joseph B. Smith (whose painting of John Street is reproduced on pages 62–63). The ship is shown leaving its East River pier.

BELOW: Lithographed ship card advertising the clipper *Hurricane,* for California. Built at Hoboken by Isaac C. Smith, the *Hurricane* sailed from New York, under Captain Samuel Very, on December 17, 1851. She was dismasted rounding Cape Horn, but arrived in San Francisco April 15, 1852.

Collection of H. Armour Smith

*. . . and get all the gold they wanted
—or so the papers said.*

Melville Collection, Suffolk Museum, Stony Brook, Long Island

"California News" was painted by William Sidney Mount in 1850.
The scene was the Stony Brook post office, in the Hawkins-Mount house.

But New York itself was Eldorado to thousands of exiles and immigrants from Europe.

Collection of Edward W. C. Arnold; photograph courtesy of Museum of the City of New York

Sheet-music cover, lithographed by Brown & Severin, for the "Reception Polka," published by Wm. Hall & Sons at the time of Louis Kossuth's arrival in New York, December 6, 1851. The scene represents Kossuth being welcomed by crowds in front of the Irving House, on the west side of Broadway at Chambers Street.

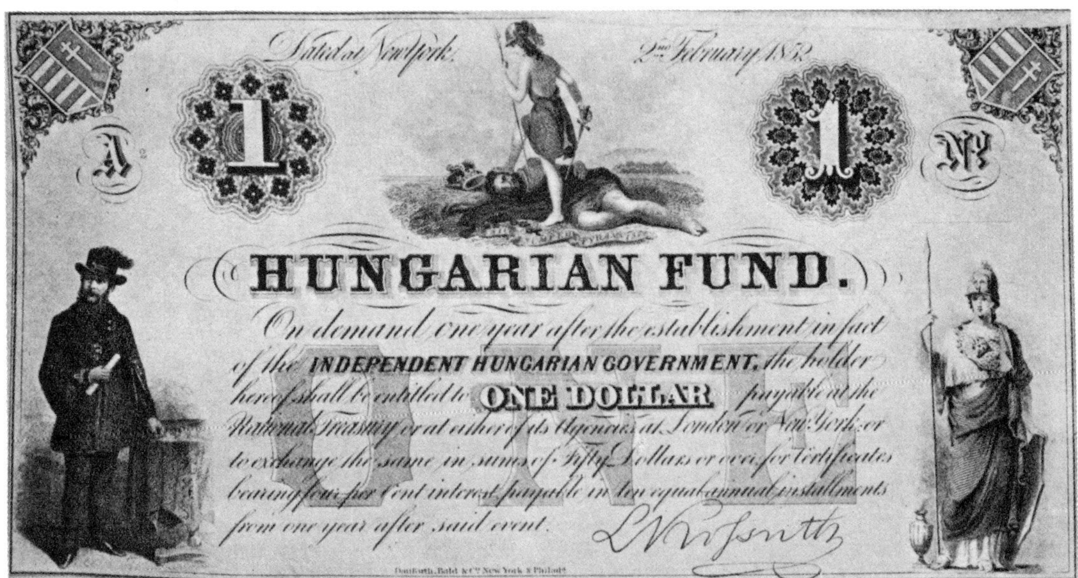

Engraved "Hungarian Fund" certificate, signed by Kossuth, printed by Danforth, Bald & Co., dated February 2, 1852.

Collection of Allen S. Davenport

Though a plain visitor might not be welcomed by a ball at the Astor House, he would see well-dressed crowds in the principal streets . . .

AUTUMN & WINTER FASHIONS FOR 1849 & 1850 BY A. WHEELER Nº 4. COURTLAND ST. NEW YORK.

J. Clarence Davies Collection, Museum of the City of New York

An advertisement of "Autumn & Winter Fashions for 1849 & 1850," lithographed by Sarony & Major for A. Wheeler, No. 4 Cortlandt Street. At the top is a scene in the ballroom of the Astor House, and below a scene in front of the hotel. (St. Paul's churchyard fence at left; City Hall Park at right; Astor House, on west side of Broadway between Vesey and Barclay streets, in center background.)

. . . and could rub elbows with Tammany bigwigs at the Gem Saloon or with substantial German immigrants at a Bowery beer hall.

TEMPERANCE, BUT NO MAINE-LAW.

Both pictures from collection of Edward W. C. Arnold; photographs courtesy of Museum of the City of New York

"Temperance, but no Maine Law," a lithograph drawn and published by A. Fay in 1854, represents the interior of the Gem Saloon, which boasted the largest mirror in the city. The Gem was an "adjunct" of the Broadway Theater, on the west side of Broadway between Pearl and Worth streets. The figures are portraits of Mayor Fernando Wood, James Lawrence, and other celebrities who were opposing the movement for a state prohibition law.

The original water-color drawing, by Fritz Meyer, for a lithograph of the "Interior of the German Winter-Garden, 45 Bowery, New-York," published in 1856. This was one of the most elaborate of the Bowery beer halls, famous for their music and sociability.

And there were also, of course, other places of entertainment —whose interiors were not portrayed.

NEW-YORK By GAS-LIGHT.

Hooking a Victim.

Museum of the City of New York

"New York by Gas-light. Hooking a Victim" was lithographed and published by Serrell & Perkins about 1850. Which "Restaurant" is represented, we do not know, but perhaps it was the one on the corner of Broadway and Canal Street, described in *Glimpses of New-York City* (Charleston, 1852), which had "a sort of secret establishment overhead that I have never rightly understood. You always, day and night, see a set of hacks standing here; *they* understand."

"Sutton's 'Darby & Joan,' 24 Rosevelt Street, New-York," is a woodcut from the *National Police Gazette,* October 18, 1845. In that year the *Gazette* was founded as a crusading paper, supporting the police in their efforts to clean up the city. Robert Sutton, alias Bob the Wheeler, was an ex-boxer who ran this beer joint on the side while engaging in big-time robbery and worse.

Author's collection

A good many New Yorkers, however, took their relaxation as seriously and conscientiously as they took their work.

The "Excursion of the New York Turners (Gymnastic Society)" was drawn by Fr. Venino and lithographed by Dumcke & Keil in 1854. The first German-language newspaper in New York, the *Staats-Zeitung*, had begun publication in 1834 and in 1850 became a daily, so large was the city's German-speaking population.

This advertisement of "Dr. Rich's Institute for Physical Education" was lithographed by Wm. Endicott & Co. about 1850. The Institute, at 159 Crosby Street near Bleecker, was one of the many gymnasiums established during the thirties and forties to counteract the tendency of city life to produce flabby muscles and short wind.

Both pictures from J. Clarence Davies Collection, Museum of the City of New York

City children got their exercise and sport as part of the school curriculum, or in the streets . . .

Museum of the City of New York

Board of Education of the City of New York; photograph courtesy of Museum of the City of New York

ABOVE: The "Institution of Messrs. Abbott, for the Education of Young Ladies, at 412 Houston Street," is here shown in an engraving by W. G. Jackman after a drawing by A. W. Cowles, which served as an illustration for the school's pamphlet catalogue published in 1846. LEFT: A portrait by Thomas Hicks of George T. Trimble, president of the Public School Society. In the background is Public School No. 1, Tryon Row at Park Row (see page 111). BELOW: "City School No. 2, Cor. of North 5th and 5th Streets, Williamsburgh, 1854," was drawn by Jacob S. Woodworth, "aged 13 yrs." (Fifth Street is now Driggs Avenue.) To the left of the school is the Columbian House.

Collection of Edward W. C. Arnold; photograph courtesy of Museum of the City of New York

. . . while young men in the militia drilled earnestly in Washington Square.

Collection of Edward W. C. Arnold; photograph courtesy of Museum of the City of New York

This painting of the Seventh Regiment drilling in Washington Square was made by Major Otto Bötticher in 1851. Another copy belongs to the Seventh Regiment, and there are lithographed prints of it in a number of collections. The principal figures are portraits, painted from daguerreotypes made by Meade Brothers.

In the left background is the University of the City of New York (now New York University) on University Place between Waverly Place and Washington Place. Chartered in 1831, the university commenced classes in 1832. The building was begun in 1833 and finished in 1837. Here Samuel F. B. Morse conducted his experiments with telegraphy, Professor Draper made his first daguerreotypes (see page 185), and Samuel Colt perfected his "peacemaker." The building was demolished in 1894, when the university occupied its new campus on University Heights. To the right of the university is the Reformed Dutch Church, erected 1837–40 and demolished 1895.

The city's growing commercial power depended, of course, upon increasingly rapid and efficient transportation . . .

Bequest of Mrs. J. Insley Blair, Museum of the City of New York

This drawing, of uncertain authorship, shows the passenger station of the Hudson River Railroad, at the intersection of Chambers Street and West Broadway. (The Frederick Hotel was on the northeast corner of those streets.) From this depot, built in 1851, cars were hauled by a "dumb engine" up Hudson Street (into which the tracks are curving in foreground) to Canal, and thence via West Street and Tenth Avenue to the more imposing terminal in the yards between Thirty-first and Thirty-fourth streets where the trains were made up and steam locomotives attached for the run to Greenbush, at that time the end of the line.

. . . and upon what Belden's guidebook called "the rapid transmission of intelligence."

As Belden observed, "To a commercial community, the rapid transmission of intelligence is highly desirable. The Post-Office department, the magnetic telegraph, and the commercial journals afford such mediums to the merchants of New-York."

LEFT: One of a pair of interior views of the post office after it was established in the old Middle Dutch Church building (see page 56), remodeled for the purpose by the architect Martin Thompson. The lithograph by Endicott was issued in 1845, shortly after the remodeling was completed. According to Belden, about 40,000 letters and 120,000 newspapers passed through the office daily in 1849.

J. Clarence Davies Collection, Museum of the City of New York

RIGHT: In the same year that the New York–Philadelphia telegraph line was inaugurated, James Gordon Bennett of the New York *Herald* outsmarted his rivals by chartering a fast vessel to bring news from Europe ahead of regular vessels. N. Currier published the lithograph of his "Extraordinary Express Across the Atlantic. Pilot Boat Wm. J. Romer . . . leaving for England—Feb. 9th 1846."

Museum of the City of New York

Local merchants and manufacturers were in constant contact . . .

New York February 1st. 1847.—

Dear Sir

The time being near when our merchants will be in this city to purchase their spring stock, it is desirable they should know where to select the richest styles & best goods at the <u>very lowest market price</u>. — — With regard to New York, all are aware that every kind of Manufactures & Imports may be bought at a lower price than any city in the Union, and far larger stocks to select from, the difficulty with many of our merchants on their arrival is to know where such houses may be found & therefore make their selection from limited & inferior stocks previously purchased either from the manufacturer or Importer & not unfrequently very dear. Permit me therefore as a wholesale manufacturer of Umbrellas Parasols &c to call your attention to this establishment, which I think you will allow is the most extensive in the United States. It would be useless to go into a detail of the variety of patterns & elegance of styles which I am daily manufacturing & upon which very much depends in order to insure ready sales at a good profit & would respectfully solicit you

Lithographed letterhead of John I. Smith's Fashionable Umbrella & Parasol Manufactory, 232 Pearl Street. This copy of Smith's trade letter, addressed to Mr. Dexter Whitman, Fitzwilliamsville, New Hampshire, was postmarked March 15. (This is the first of four pages of sales talk, including a price list.)

Museum of the City of New York

. . . with customers throughout the United States . . .

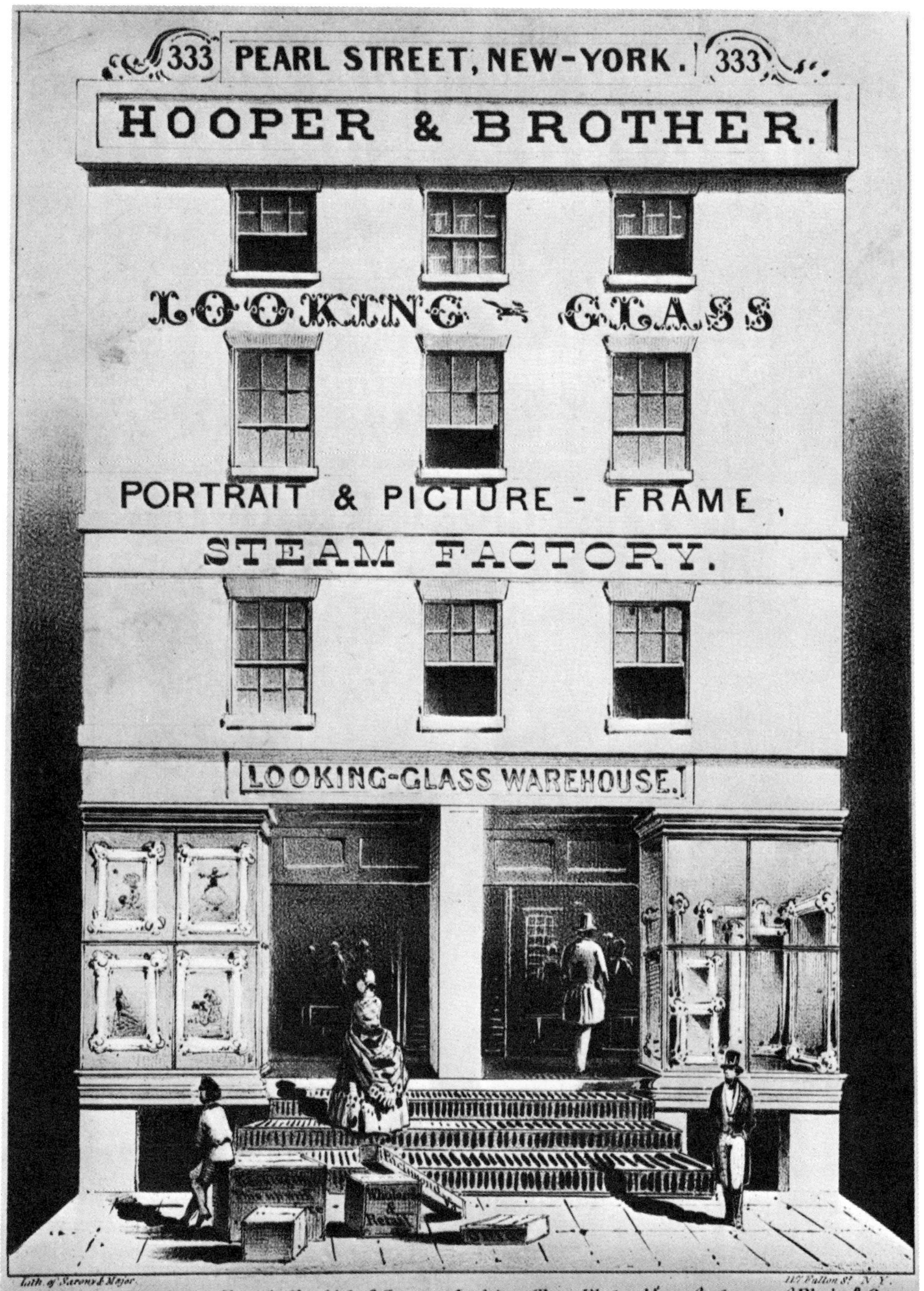

J. Clarence Davies Collection, Museum of the City of New York

Advertisement of Hooper & Brother's picture-frame factory, 333 Pearl Street, lithographed by Sarony & Major about 1849. The packing boxes on the sidewalk are marked "Richmond, Va.," "Ohio," etc.

Belden's guidebook notes that Pearl Street had long been the center of "the importing and jobbing dry goods business, though now that branch of trade has extended into William, Pine, Cedar, Liberty, and other streets."

. . . and the products of all nations were required to stock the city's vast department stores and specialty shops.

Both pictures from collection of Edward W. C. Arnold; photographs courtesy of Museum of the City of New York

S.W. BENEDICT,
WATCH MAKER,
Nº 5 Wall Street,
NEAR TRINITY CHURCH

ABOVE: An artist's proof of Endicott's lithograph of Charles Parsons' drawing of Arnold Constable & Co.'s new store on the northeast corner of Canal and Mercer streets, about 1850–55.

LEFT: Advertisement of S. W. Benedict, Watch Maker, No. 5 Wall Street, engraved by A. Hyatt in 1845. The accompanying text (not reproduced) assures customers that watches imported from T. F. Cooper in England "will be sold as low as if purchased of him in London."

To serve the city's financial institutions, several companies specialized in bank-note engraving . . .

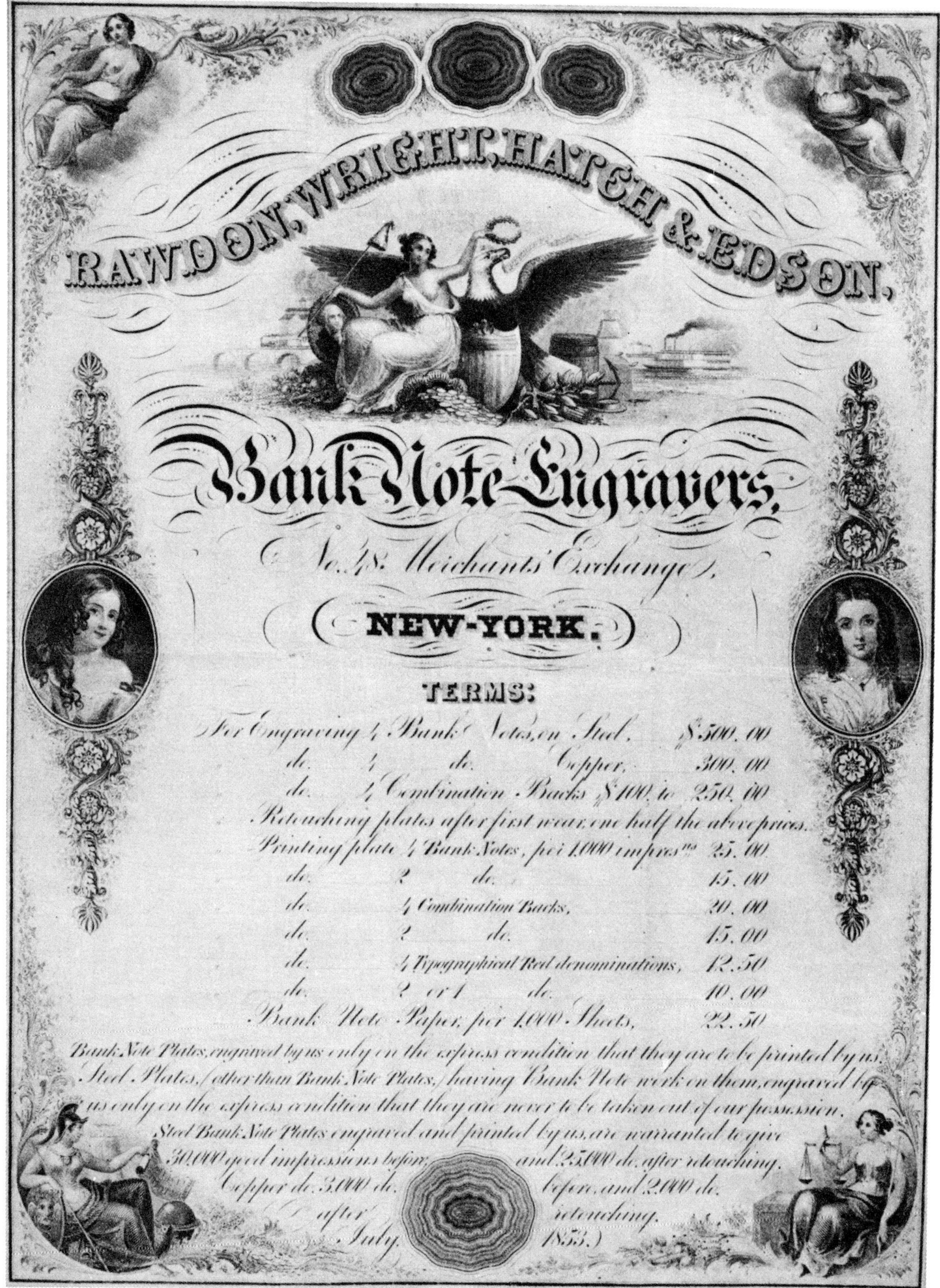

Collection of Allen S. Davenport

Many of the finest engravers worked for the companies which specialized in bank-note work. Freeman Rawdon, Charles C. Wright, and George W. Hatch were all first-rate men, and the company they formed with Edson was one of the most important. This advertisement (and sample) of their work was published in July, 1853, giving prices for various types of engraved plates.

. . . and the metropolitan press made heavy demands on the manufacturers of ink and high-speed presses.

Lithograph by Sarony & Major, advertising Lightbody's Printing Ink Factory on East Sixty-first Street between First and Second avenues. Probably published about 1855.

Collection of Edward W. C. Arnold; photograph courtesy of Museum of the City of New York

J. Clarence Davies Collection, Museum of the City of New York

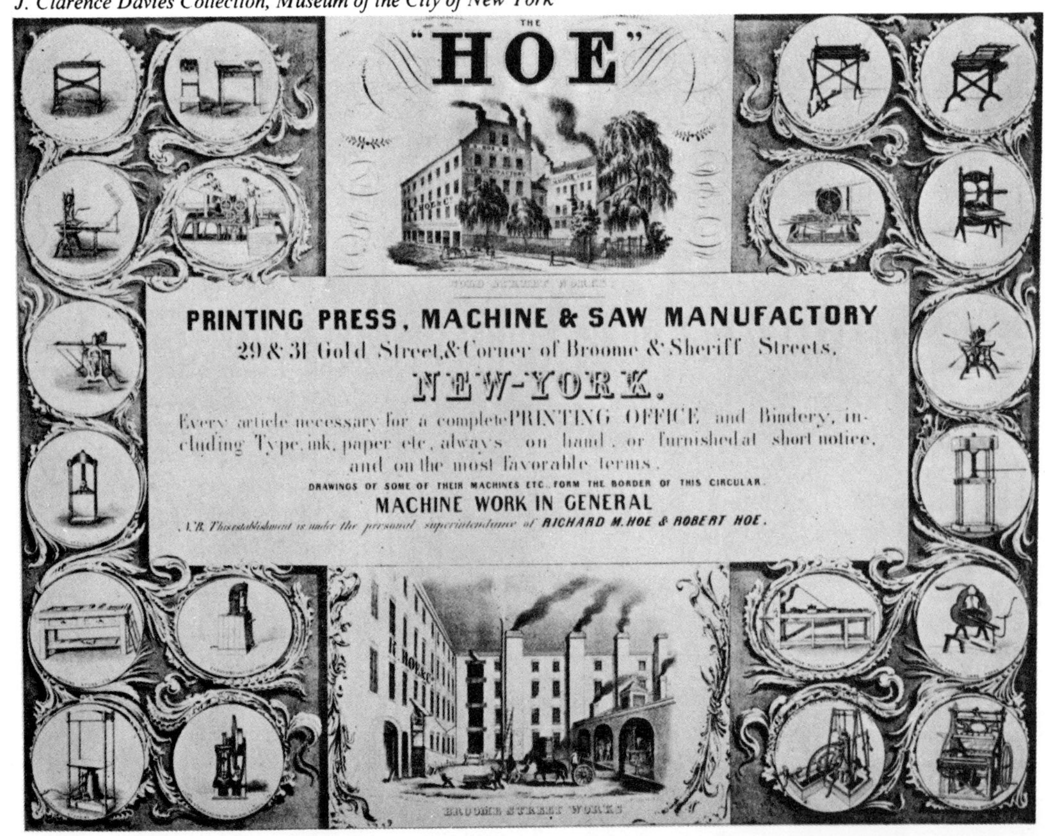

The Hoe cylinder press, here shown with other Hoe machines in an advertisement lithographed by Endicott in 1843, was one of the great nineteenth-century advances in printing. Richard M. Hoe & Co. had two plants at this time, one downtown on Gold Street, and the other (shown at bottom of advertisement) at the corner of Broome and Sheriff streets.

As the city expanded, there was continued demand for building materials . . .

Both pictures from Museum of the City of New York

Portion of a lithograph, by Perkins Lithograph Establishment, advertising the Empire Stone Dressing Co., and showing their plant on the East River shore just north of Bellevue Hospital, between Twenty-eighth and Thirtieth streets in 1851.

Advertisement of F. Basham, manufacturer of architectural ornaments in plaster, cement, and scagliola. Lithograph by E. Jones (1844).

Notice that in addition to making "mouldings, consols, centre flowers, rosettes, capitols" and other ornaments, Mr. Basham also offered "Busts taken from the LIVING or DEAD on the shortest notice!" Observe also the amount of "Gothic" ornament available (see page 238).

. . . and for the services of some of the country's ablest architects.

Lithograph by Ackerman of the interior of Grace Church, northeast corner of Broadway and Tenth Street, published in 1849. Designed by James Renwick, who later designed St. Patrick's Cathedral, this was one of the masterpieces of the Gothic Revival in New York. Like other churches of the period, however, its vaulting was of lath and plaster, not stone (and may have been decorated with ornaments made at Basham's shop, page 237). Grace Church in the fifties was probably the most fashionable in town, and its sexton, Mr. Brown, was for years society's arbiter of who should and should not be invited to balls and parties.

A water-color drawing, made in 1846 by Mrs. A. W. Palmer, of the frame building set up in Trinity churchyard as a working studio for Richard Upjohn, the architect. Here Upjohn drew up the plans for every detail of the present Trinity Church. Here, too, the wood and stone carving was done and the glass for the windows designed and leaded.

Both pictures from collection of Edward W. C. Arnold; photographs courtesy of Museum of the City of New York

But it was only in bird's-eye perspective that one could fully appreciate the fine buildings towering here and there above the crowded streets.

This "Birds-Eye View of Trinity Church, New York," was drawn and lithographed by John Forsyth and E. W. Mimee in 1847, after Upjohn's work was completed.

(Notice the telegraph pole on the northeast corner of Broadway and Wall Street. See page 199.)

J. Clarence Davies Collection, Museum of the City of New York

Birds-Eye View of TRINITY CHURCH, NEW-YORK.

And it was only in broad, panoramic views, after all, that one could grasp the mid-century metropolis . . .

Collection of Edward W. C. Arnold; photograph courtesy of Museum of the City of New York

This bird's-eye view of New York from the southwest was lithographed about 1852 by K. Th. Westermann and published in Germany by Franz Wentzel.

The view is interesting, despite its distortions of perspective, for the sense it gives that one is looking at a miniature model of the city—such as Belden's must have been (page 194). Note also that the city's chief "sights"—Castle Garden, Trinity, the Custom House, the Merchants Exchange, City Hall, Broadway, and Brooklyn Heights—are exaggeratedly prominent.

. . . as more than an incongruous assortment of guidebook "sights" and "places of interest."

J. Clarence Davies Collection, Museum of the City of New York

This bird's-eye view of New York, looking south from above Union Square, was drawn and lithographed by C. Bachmann and published by John Bachmann in 1849. (A later state of the print was published by Williams & Stevens.)

Union Square, which had been a raw gash in the landscape eighteen years before (see page 136), was by this time one of the finest residential districts in town. Belden's guidebook speaks of the "splendid private mansions, some of which are of costly magnificence," which surround the square. At center left, two blocks east of the Bowery, is St. Mark's Church, built 1795–99 on the site of Stuyvesant's Bouwerie Chapel. Just south of the square, on Broadway at Tenth, is Grace Church (the tall white steeple left of center). At the right is tree-lined Fifth Avenue, leading south to Washington Square as it was at the time described in Henry James's novel.

A writer in *Putnam's Magazine,* February, 1853, objected to a copy of the print because it gave no idea of the city's size. In it, he said, the city "has the appearance of some large trading town, like Poughkeepsie, or Troy, on the Hudson, rather than of such a great metropolis as it really is." Out-of-town readers were reminded that Broadway and the Bowery were not, in reality, "so thinly populated that one can distinguish the gentlemen . . . who, in the print, perambulate at leisure through the middle of the street."

Group Four

DOCUMENTS OF CHANGE 1855–1870

J. Clarence Davies Collection, Museum of the City of New York

OPPOSITE: The New York Crystal Palace, shown here in a lithograph drawn by F. F. Palmer and published by N. Currier in 1853, was an iron and glass exhibition building erected in 1852 for America's first World's Fair, held in the city the following year. It stood on the present site of Bryant Park, east of Sixth Avenue (foreground) between Forty-first Street (right) and Forty-second Street. A corner of the Croton Distributing Reservoir, on the site now occupied by the New York Public Library, may be seen at the right.

The first large iron and glass structure in America—inspired of course by the London Crystal Palace of 1851—the building was designed by George Carstenson and Charles Geldemeister. Reputedly fireproof, wood and other combustible materials used in the interior caught fire in 1858 and the building almost instantly collapsed. The broadside at right tells the rest of the story.

The tall tower at the left of the Currier lithograph is the Latting Observatory, a tower of timber braced with iron which was built by Waring Latting at the time of the fair. A steam elevator carried paying customers to the first and second landings where there were telescopes for viewing the panorama of the city and surrounding country. The observatory burned down in 1856.

CRYSTAL PALACE

RELICS!

Mrs. RICHARDSON, of New York, (who was one of the unfortunate persons burnt out by the fire that destroyed the Crystal Palace,) by permission of the MAYOR OF NEW YORK, and of JOHN H. WHITE, Esq., Crystal Palace Receiver, obtained a number of curiosities very valuable for a cabinet, produced by the melting of the Building, and articles on exhibition, which she now offers to visitors at the FAIR, AT PALACE GARDEN, as interesting souvenirs of all that remains of the finest building ever erected in America—a building made entirely of glass and iron, except the floors—and supposed to be almost wholly free from danger of fire; yet, it was utterly destroyed on the 5th of October, 1858, in fifteen minutes' time. The evidence of the immense heat will be seen in the articles now offered for sale, as well worthy the attention of the curious.

An interesting memorial of the great Crystal Palace Exhibition, is found in Mrs. RICHARDSON'S collection of Relics, which is on exhibition in the 2d floor. They consist of vitrified masses of glass, metals, &c., showing the intense heat which prevailed in the building at the time of its destruction.—THE SUN, Oct. 11.

Wynkoop, Hallenbeck & Thomas, Printers, 113 Fulton Street, N. Y.

Museum of the City of New York

The late forties and early fifties witnessed the introduction of iron buildings and elevators . . .

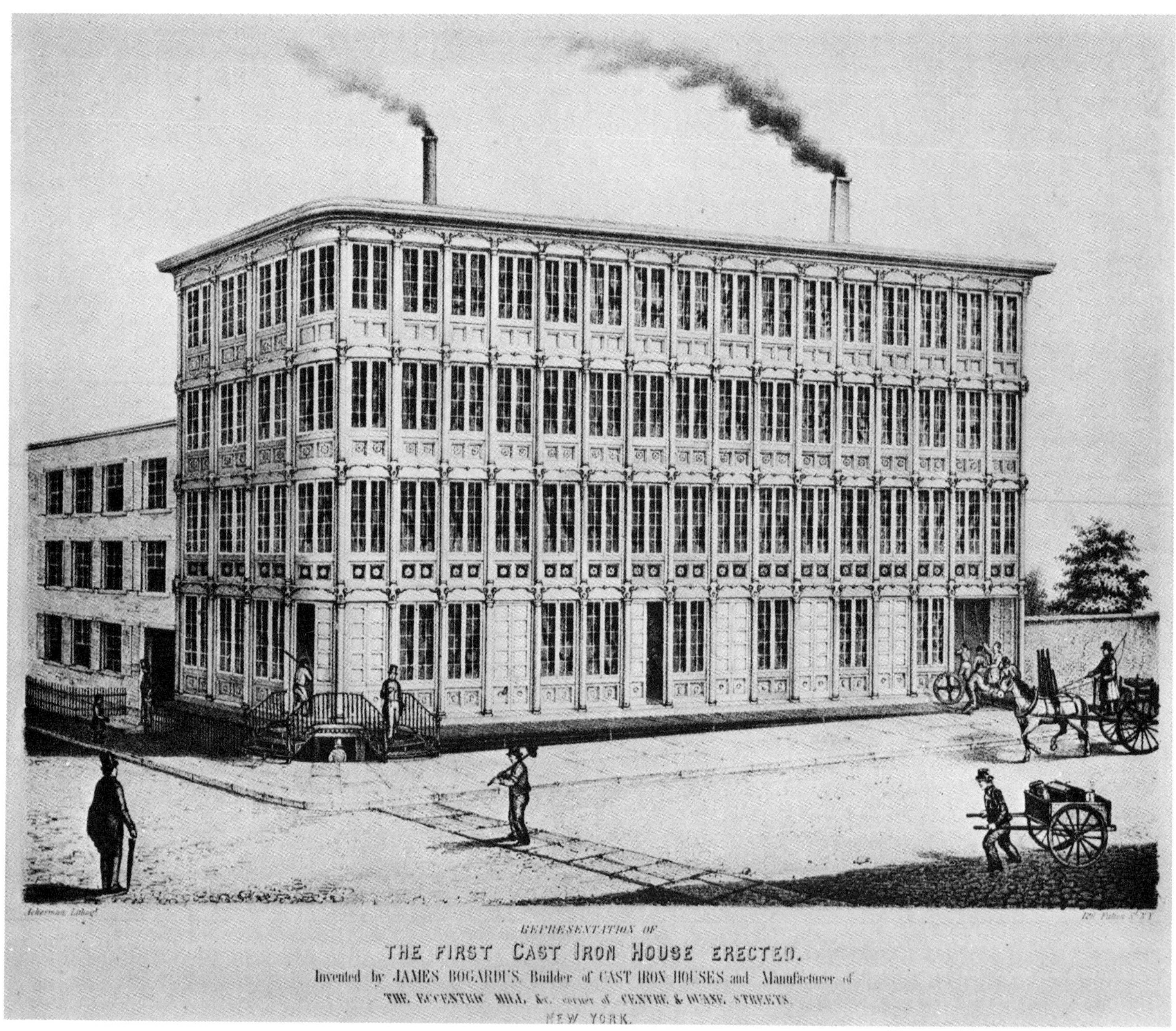
THE FIRST CAST IRON HOUSE ERECTED.
Invented by JAMES BOGARDUS, Builder of CAST IRON HOUSES and Manufacturer of
NEW YORK.

Museum of the City of New York

This lithograph by Ackerman, published in 1848 or 1849, is entitled "Representation of The First Cast Iron House Erected. Invented by James Bogardus, Builder of Cast Iron Houses and Manufacturer of the Eccentric Mill &c. corner of Centre & Duane Streets, New York." Bogardus was the pioneer of iron architecture in America, and this building—despite its irrelevant decorative details—is the direct ancestor of such modern steel and glass skyscrapers as Lever House and the United Nations buildings.

Though this was the first of his buildings to be started, another, on the northwest corner of Washington and Murray streets, was apparently the first to be completed. According to the New York *Evening Post,* May 3, 1849, the new building "lately put up by Edgar H. Lang" at the latter site was the only one of its kind in the world "excepting that in Centre Street, which now stands unfinished." The Centre Street building was taken down in 1859, when Duane Street was widened, but the other—the first iron building to be completed—still stands (see page 493).

. . . two developments which would ultimately transform the city.

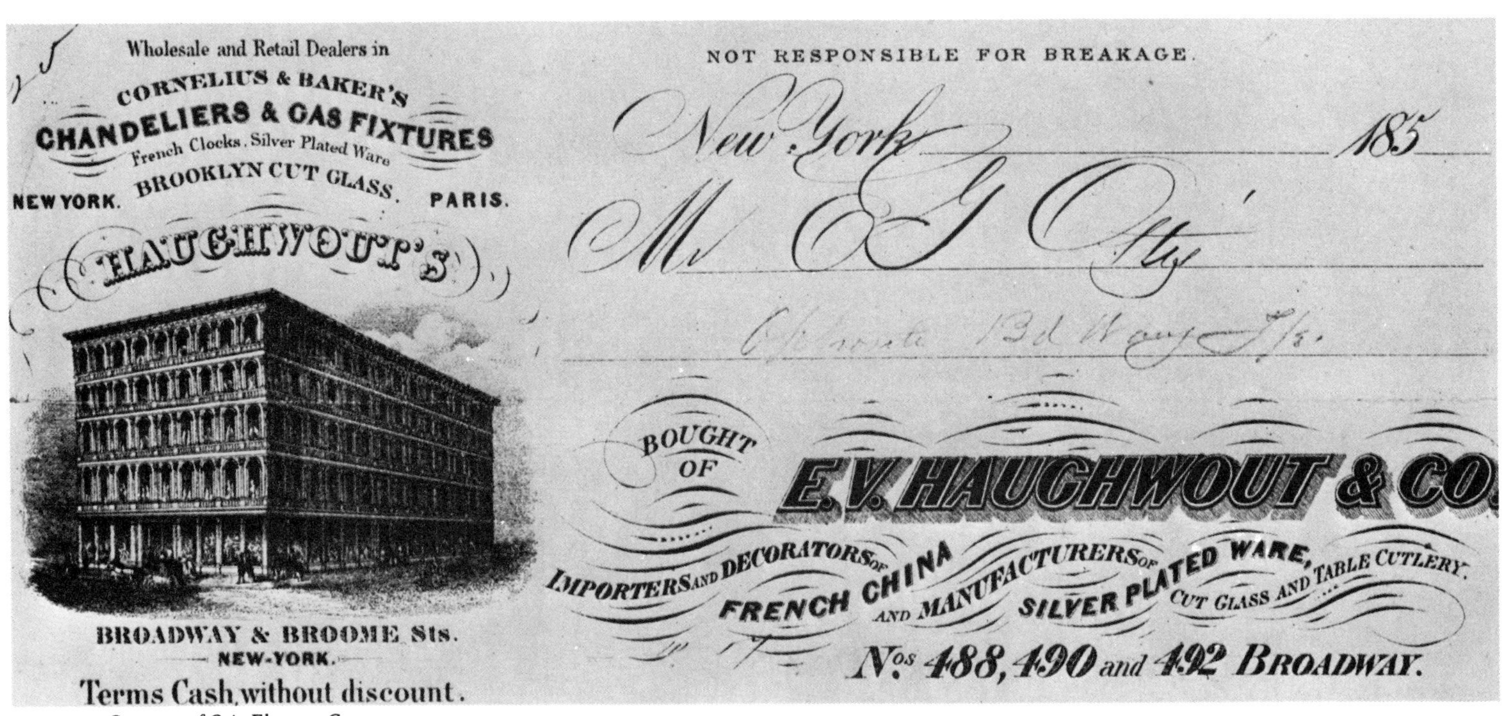

Courtesy of Otis Elevator Company

Author's collection

Though passenger elevators had been used earlier (see, for example, page 243), the first one to be equipped with automatic safety devices—and hence the first truly practicable one—was designed by Elisha Graves Otis and installed in E. V. Haughwout's new store on the northeast corner of Broadway and Broome Street in 1857. (The elevator in the Fifth Avenue Hotel, often referred to as the first, was not installed until two years later.) Haughwout's lithographed billhead, above, made out to Otis himself, contains a view of the store (see also page 248).

One of the early New York firms to manufacture iron buildings was J. B. & W. W. Cornell's Iron Works, on the west side of Centre Street between White and Walker. Their advertisement, engraved on wood by J. W. Orr, was published in David Bigelow's *History of Prominent Mercantile and Manufacturing Firms* (Boston, 1857).

It was an age of accelerated change, and the desire for an accurate record of "progress and improvements" . . .

Liberty-street, in process of re-building, 1852.

Author's collection

This wood engraving, like those on the following page, is an illustration from a series of unsigned articles entitled "New York Daguerreotyped" which was published in *Putnam's Magazine,* starting in February, 1853. The emphasis throughout the series is on the rapidity with which the city is growing "in spite of the mean and unsuitable docks and markets, the filthy streets, the farce of a half-fledged and inefficient police, and the miserably bad government, generally, of an unprincipled common-council." The illustrations, according to a footnote, are "engravings from Daguerreotypes . . . made expressly for this purpose."

The first of these, drawn by C. E. Döpler and engraved by J. W. Orr, shows "Liberty-street, in process of rebuilding, 1852." The old brick buildings have been torn down, to be replaced by others faced with white marble, and the whole street—in the course of a single year—was "completely metamorphosed."

. . . led to considerable dissatisfaction with available pictorial techniques . . .

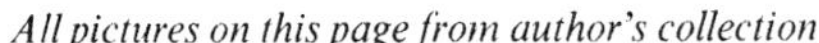
View of Dey st. from Greenwich st., looking towards Broadway.

LEFT AND RIGHT: Two illustrations from "New York Daguerreotyped," *Putnam's*, April, 1853. "Dey Street, which, but a short time since, was exclusively occupied by private dwellings and boarding houses, has been entirely torn down," *Putnam's* noted, "and rebuilt for the accommodation of drygoods dealers." Illustration drawn by Wells, engraved on wood by Richardson-Cox.

The Russ pavement (right) was composed of blocks of granite, set on a bed of crushed stone and cement. An experimental block of Broadway, from Chambers to Reade Street, was laid in July, 1846, and the entire street below Chambers was paved between 1848 and 1852. The picture engraved by J. W. Orr shows the paving being extended north of Reade Street.

BELOW: Two illustrations from a later article in the series, *Putnam's*, March, 1854. Of London Terrace (left), shown in the picture drawn by J. Wilson and engraved by Richardson-Cox, the author observed: "It has a more imposing effect in the engraving than the reality warrants, the houses being of moderate dimensions." The same could have been said of the picture (by the same craftsmen) of the row of Gothic houses on Twentieth Street at Sixth Avenue.

Laying the Russ Pavement in Broadway, corner of Reade-street.

All pictures on this page from author's collection

London Terrace, West Twenty-third-street.

Block in Twentieth-street corner Sixth Avenue.

. . . a dissatisfaction which clearly had some justification.

In the first article of *Putnam's* series on New York architecture (see pages 246–47), the author made what he called "a concentrated apology" for the illustrations, and in subsequent issues he frequently notes their deficiencies: "too small adequately to represent the variety of styles and decorations"; or "Our artist has done no sort of justice to anything but the size of the building."

The two pictures on this page illustrate the problem which *Putnam's* and other magazines faced. Above is an anonymous wood engraving of Haughwout's store on the northeast corner of Broadway and Broome Street, made in 1857 or 1858, when the building was new (see page 245). Below is a recent photograph of the building (taken in August, 1952). Except in minor respects, the building is unchanged (even the clock above the Broadway entrance is still there). Yet how different the building looks! Curiously enough, it looks taller in the modern photograph, though its five stories must have seemed very high in the fifties.

Both pictures courtesy of Otis Elevator Company

Photographs were common enough in the fifties so that photographic realism became a standard by which to judge other pictorial mediums. Early in the decade . . .

Museum of the City of New York

The photographs on this and the following two pages were made by Victor Prevost, a French artist who came to New York in 1848 and set up as a photographer in 1853. His photographs were made on waxed paper negatives, more than forty of which are preserved in the New-York Historical Society. The picture above, looking north from the Battery in 1853 (when it was being enlarged), is sometimes referred to as "the first outdoor photograph ever made in New York." Certainly it is one of the earliest that have come down to us, but there were earlier ones. In fact the first daguerreotype ever taken in America, according to Professor Robert Taft, was an outdoor scene in New York. On September 27, 1839 (five months and seven days after the New York *Observer* published a letter from Samuel F. B. Morse in Paris, describing Daguerre's successful experiments), an Englishman named D. W. Seager exhibited at Chilton's, on Broadway, a daguerreotype view of St. Paul's Chapel "and the surrounding shrubbery and houses, with a corner of the Astor House." By 1850 there were seventy-one daguerreotype galleries in New York, employing 127 operators, but most of their business was "likenesses." (One of them, A. J. Beals, advertised: "Families waited upon in or out of the city to take Likenesses of sick or deceased persons, at moderate prices.")

. . . photographers began documenting the city with an accuracy of detail which had hitherto been impossible . . .

New-York Historical Society

This photograph, taken by Prevost in 1853 or 1854, shows the house built in 1835 by Dr. Valentine Mott as his summer residence. It stood just north of present West Ninety-third Street on a site which is now in the middle of Broadway. In 1868 when the Boulevard (as upper Broadway was then called) was opened, the house was moved to the northwest corner of Ninety-third Street. By 1897 it had been demolished, and in 1901 the Evangelical Church of the Advent was built on the site.

Dr. Mott, one of the great physicians and surgeons of the period, loved by rich and poor, lived here for three months or so every summer, driving daily in his well-known gig to his office downtown and to his work at Bellevue Hospital.

. . . and which encouraged an interest in subjects whose pictorial value had not hitherto been apparent.

New-York Historical Society

Prevost made this photograph at the New York Crystal Palace in 1854. Machinery exhibits were among the most popular features of the World's Fair, and this steam engine—called the Southern Belle—was one of the most elaborate on exhibition. It was made by the Winter Iron Works in Montgomery, Alabama. Handsome as it was, it did not unduly impress the practical mechanic who reviewed the exhibitions for Greeley's *Tribune.* It was, he said, "true to the name *belle* —very showy, and (at present) very useless. No shop would ever dream of making or buying such an engine for use. It would keep one man busy the whole time to keep it bright and clean."

Among Prevost's negatives there are pictures of many buildings in the city, including a marble-cutting establishment and W. & J. Sloane's carpet warehouse as well as churches and fine houses.

One of New York's early photographic amateurs was an ex-president of Columbia College . . .

Nathaniel Fish Moore, a graduate of Columbia in the class of 1802 (during the presidency of his uncle, Benjamin Moore), served as president of the college from 1842 to 1849. After his resignation he went abroad, where he became interested in photography during a visit to the London Crystal Palace exhibition in 1851. (Three of the five medals for daguerreotypes at the exhibition were won, incidentally, by Americans.) On his return to New York he became an enthusiastic amateur, employing the recently invented wet-plate process which had been developed by Frederick Scott Archer in England.

ABOVE: Moore's photograph of Columbia College, looking northwest from the entrance to the college grounds at Church Street and Park Place, was made in 1854 and presented by Moore to Dr. W. H. Walter, the college organist, who later presented it to the college library.

BELOW: A photograph taken by Moore about 1855 from the roof or an upper window of one of the houses which stood on the west side of Hudson Street, facing St. John's Park. Looking northwest toward the Hudson River, it shows the back yards (and laundry lines) of the houses on the south side of Laight Street between Hudson and Greenwich streets.

. . . who took pictures not only of familiar scenes and the homes of his friends . . .

All pictures on pages 252 and 253 from the Columbiana Collection, Columbia University

ABOVE: Moore's photograph, probably taken about 1855, of the house built originally for Henry Brevoort, Jr., and owned at this time by Henry C. de Rham (see page 169). Mr. de Rham is standing at the top of the steps, and his wife at the open window at left.

BELOW: Chelsea House, the residence of Moore's cousin, Clement Clarke Moore—professor of Greek and Oriental literature at the General Theological Seminary and author of *'Twas the night before Christmas.* The house had been built in 1777 by Clement Moore's grandmother, the widow of Captain Thomas Clarke, and a story had been added by the Moores about 1825. It stood just south of Twenty-third Street, between present Ninth and Tenth avenues. The original London Terrace row (see page 247) was built across the street on the north side of Twenty-third, where the present huge apartments of the same name now stand.

. . . but also of people he knew and loved.

Columbiana Collection, Columbia University

It has not been possible to identify with certainty the subject of this portrait, one of Moore's finest photographs. Mr. Arthur Sheehan suggests the man is probably Pierre Toussaint, a leading hairdresser in New York from 1787 to 1853. A letter from Moore to Toussaint is preserved in the New York Public Library.

Many other photographers were also at work in the city, taking pictures of well-known and little-known citizens . . .

Both pictures from Museum of the City of New York

Harry Howard, one of the most famous of New York's Volunteer Firemen, is here shown in a portrait by "J. Gurney, Photographist." The photograph is inscribed to "Seamen, Lichtenstein, Esq. with the Chief's Compliments, October, 1858"—just a year after Howard became chief engineer. Shortly afterward, he was struck down by an attack of paralysis on his way to a fire in Grand Street. Twenty years later, when he was a kind of pensioner in the city's Department of Public Works, George W. Sheldon asked him upon what part of his life as a fireman he looked back with most satisfaction. "Upon none of it," he replied, quickly and emphatically. "See this arm of mine [paralyzed and stiff]. . . . That's what I got for being a fireman. What can compensate me for that?"

Not knowing who his parents were, Howard had grown up in the old Lower East Side neighborhoods where the Volunteers were everyone's heroes. Some of the Volunteers made out better than Howard, including William M. Tweed of the Americus 6 engine company. Under Boss Tweed's leadership, Tammany Hall later adopted as its emblem the tiger which had decorated the Americus engine. The original tiger decoration, on the front panel of the engine, is here shown in a photograph made for this book by John Harvey Heffren. It was painted in 1851 by Joseph H. Johnson, an artist who was a charter member of the company.

. . . and making a pictorial record of the uptown migration of institutions . . .

RIGHT: A print by H. H. Snelling from a negative by L. E. Walker, showing the old Columbia College building in the winter of 1856–57, just before the college moved uptown to its new quarters on Fiftieth Street (see pages 199 and 413). Taken from about the same place as Moore's 1854 picture (page 252), this shows Park Place being cut through the old campus.

BELOW: An enlargement of a carte-de-visite photograph, taken by an unidentified photographer, about 1860, showing St. Patrick's Cathedral under construction. The picture was made from the corner of Madison Avenue and Fiftieth Street, just north of Columbia's new campus, looking northwest toward the houses on Fifty-first and Fifty-second streets, west of Fifth Avenue.

New-York Historical Society

Museum of the City of New York

. . . and residences as the city expanded northward.

Museum of the City of New York

An unattributed photograph of the double residences at 714 and 716 Broadway, opposite Washington Place, about 1860. Ex-Mayor Hone had occupied No. 716 (at left) in 1836 and 1837, in the interim between leaving his old house at 235 Broadway and moving into his new one at No. 1 Great Jones Street. Hone described it as "a fine house, delightfully situated," for which he paid $1600 a year rent. By 1860 the neighborhood had run down considerably.

An unattributed photograph of the residence at No. 4 West Fifty-fourth Street, looking south. The un-built-up blocks behind the house and garden belonged to Columbia, and were a part of the property originally included in the Elgin Botanic Gardens (see page 102). Rockefeller Center now occupies the site. In the left background are the derricks being used in constructing St. Patrick's (see opposite page). The house later became the residence of John D. Rockefeller, who bought the property from Collis P. Huntington in 1885. The garden of the Museum of Modern Art now occupies the site.

Courtesy of Rockefeller Center, Inc.

By the end of the fifties the camera could even catch people in motion, given bright enough light . . .

Museum of the City of New York

An unattributed photograph of people skating in Central Park during the winter of 1859-60. The shanties and houses in the background are on the south side of Fifty-ninth Street, between Fifth and Seventh avenues, now the site of the Plaza, St. Moritz, Essex House, and other hotels.

. . . though the average outdoor photograph was better if there weren't many people in it, and if those few stood still.

Museum of the City of New York

Most photographs of the city's streets in this period were taken on Sunday, when few people were about. The long exposures required with early equipment produced blurred and ghostly images of moving figures (see top of page 257). There are even "ghosts" on the sidewalk corner in this otherwise remarkably clear photograph, taken about 1860, of Bruce's New-York Type-Foundry, corner of City Hall Place (left background) and Chambers Street. The tracks in the foreground are on Centre Street.

For pictures of people doing things, especially indoors . . .

Author's collection

. . . the fifties and sixties were still dependent upon older techniques . . .

Author's collection

ABOVE: A woodcut made by Alexander Anderson in New York about 1800, printed from the original block, as an example of the crude work formerly done, in an article about wood engraving in David Bigelow's *History of Prominent Mercantile and Manufacturing Firms* (1857).

Author's collection

RIGHT: A wood engraving by J. W. Orr, from a drawing by J. M. Lenan, to illustrate *The Old Brewery and the New Mission House at the Five Points,* by Ladies of the Mission (New York, 1854). According to the article on engraving in Bigelow's book, Orr's establishment was the most up to date and extensive in the city.

Museum of the City of New York

OLD APPLE WOMAN AT STEWART'S.

RIGHT: There were old beggars as well as young in the city. "The Old Apple Woman at Stewart's" is here portrayed in a wood engraving from *Cries of the Metropolis: or, Humble Life in New York,* published by George A. Tuttle & Co. (Rutland, Vermont, 1857). For years she had had her chair at the door of A. T. Stewart's old store, but was timid about setting up by his new marble dry-goods palace until Mr. Stewart himself very kindly had her chair moved up there.

OPPOSITE: A page from *An Abridged Specimen of Printing Types made at Bruce's New-York Type-Foundry* (New York, 1869), showing some of the "electrotyped ornaments" which were available for billheads and advertisements. These electrotypes, made from wood engravings, show "typical" store and shop interiors of the fifties. The same catalogue contained a later series, copyrighted by Bruce in 1861.

For book and magazine illustrations, wood engraving was really the only practicable method of reproducing pictures, since it was the only form of engraving which could be printed by a regular printing press simultaneously with ordinary type and on the same sheet. The engraving at right, by Loomis-Annin, was the frontispiece of J. S. Gibbons' *The Banks of New York . . . and the Panic of 1857* (New York, 1858). It is indicative of the spirit of the time that a serious (and still highly interesting) book on the workings of the banking system had as its frontispiece a portrait, not of a bank president, but of "A Veteran Specie Clerk" —James Corkery of the Bank for Savings, who had, according to Gibbons, outlived "three presidents, two cashiers, and several successive companies of clerks."

The water-color sketch, below, was made in 1859 by William Gross of 48 First Avenue, who bought his milk from Henry Keim, shown here with his daughters, Caroline (left) and Teresa Kate, driving his milk wagon. The Keims lived at 87 Delancey Street from 1859 to 1867.

Author's collection

Museum of the City of New York

For pictures of dramatic crises in the life of the city . . .

Museum of the City of New York

This painting of "Wall Street, half past 2 o'clock, Oct. 13, 1857," represents the scene just after the banks in the city suspended specie payments during the financial panic which preceded the depression of that year. It was painted by James H. Cafferty and Charles G. Rosenberg, and finished early in 1858. Many prominent Wall Street characters of the time are portrayed, and are identified in the *Bulletin* of the Museum of the City of New York for May, 1940.

To relieve the suffering which resulted from the widespread unemployment during the subsequent depression, the city initiated a program of public works, including an intensification of the work already begun at Central Park.

. . . or of the manners and customs of the period . . .

MANNERS AND CUSTOMS OF ye GREAT REPUBLICANS.
FROM A SKETCH ON THE WALLS OF THE ATRIUM OF THE "ASTOR DOMUS", SHEWING THE MEN OF MARK IN CONCLAVE IN THE ASTOR Corridor
From the Collection of Sir Pilfer Sing Sing – Sydney, S.A.

. . . the artist's brush and pencil were still indispensable.

Pictures on pages 264 and 265 from collection of Edward W. C. Arnold; photographs courtesy of Museum of the City of New York

The series of drawings on this and the preceding page was made in 1857 by J. M'Nevin. The drawings themselves were patterned after Richard Doyle's famous series on the "Manners and Customs of the English," which had been published in *Punch* in 1849. But the specific scenes, and the particular objects of satirical comment, were typically New York.

On the opposite page we see the merchants (and loafers) who gathered daily in the corridor of the Astor House, and the crowds bursting off the ferry from Brooklyn.

A wood engraving of the caricature of a woman's rights convention (above) was published in *Harper's Weekly* in 1859.

*To meet the increasing demand for copies of such pictures—
a demand reflected in the rise
of the illustrated
weeklies . . .*

Author's collection

One of the most significant trends in journalism during the 1850s was the rise of the illustrated magazines, especially the weeklies. Up in Boston, *Gleason's Pictorial Drawing Room Companion* was started in 1851; in New York, *Frank Leslie's Illustrated Newspaper* (1855) was soon rivaled by *Harper's Weekly* (1857) and the New York *Illustrated News* (1859).

To meet the increasing demand for illustrations, the craft of wood engraving developed very rapidly. The pictures were either drawn directly upon, or transferred to, blocks of boxwood. Skilled engravers then cut away all the wooden surface not covered by lines of the drawing, and the printing was done from the resulting block or from electrotype plates made from it.

Large pictures required several blocks of the specially prepared boxwood, bolted together, as shown in the photograph (above) of an original block made for *Harper's Weekly* in 1879. (The surface of the block was dusted with chalk, before this photograph was made, in order to heighten the contrast between the cut-away portions and those which took ink.)

. . . the technique of wood engraving was rapidly improved and its capabilities greatly extended.

"THE GERMAN BAND."—J. G. BROWN.

Author's collection

The illustration above, published in *Harper's Weekly,* April 26, 1879, was printed from the boxwood block shown on the opposite page. Though later than the other pictures in this group, it is reproduced here as a typical sample of the technique of illustration in the period from 1850 to 1890.

This particular engraving was made from a painting by J. G. Brown called "The German Band," which was shown at the annual exhibition of the National Academy of Design in 1879.

In an article accompanying the picture, the *Weekly* describes Brown as "a *genre* painter of fine talents, whose pictures always possess a pleasing quality that makes them popular. . . . The painting from which our engraving is made is a faithful study from the streets of New York. The German bands are becoming a feature here, and there can be no doubt in the minds of our citizens that if we are to be compelled to listen to music whether we will or no, at almost any hour of the day or evening, the brass band is a great improvement on the Italian hand-organ."

The engravings for the weeklies were, at first, often hastily executed from crude drawings . . .

76 GLEASON'S PICTORIAL DRAWING ROOM COMPANION.

THE YACHT AMERICA.

Our artist has given us a scene here, representing the launch of the yacht America, designed to compete with the English yachts, on a sailing match off the English coast. She is owned by a party of gentlemen, whose names are not known to us, and was built by William H. Brown. The America will go to England. and race with the yacht club there. If she beats them, she is to be paid for by the club; if she is beaten, she is then to be given up to them as a forfeit.

The yacht's length is 96 feet; breadth, 23 feet 6 inches; depth, 9 feet 3 inches. Her frame is composed of hackmatac, chestnut, locust, oak and cedar, secured by diagonal iron braces, 3 feet apart, $3\frac{1}{2}$ inches by $\frac{3}{8}$ inch, bolted through each frame. Her cabin is 21 feet long, and has two state-rooms, one on each side, 8 feet long.

Yachting has, for a long time, been a favorite diversion of noblemen and gentlemen on the continent of Europe, and some excellent specimens of nautical skill have been produced in foreign countries. We predict the day is not very remote, when this species of maritime craft constructed by Yankee energy and talent, shall fully rival those of any other nation in the world, and even, as in other exhibitions of naval architecture, surpass th m.

New York Public Library

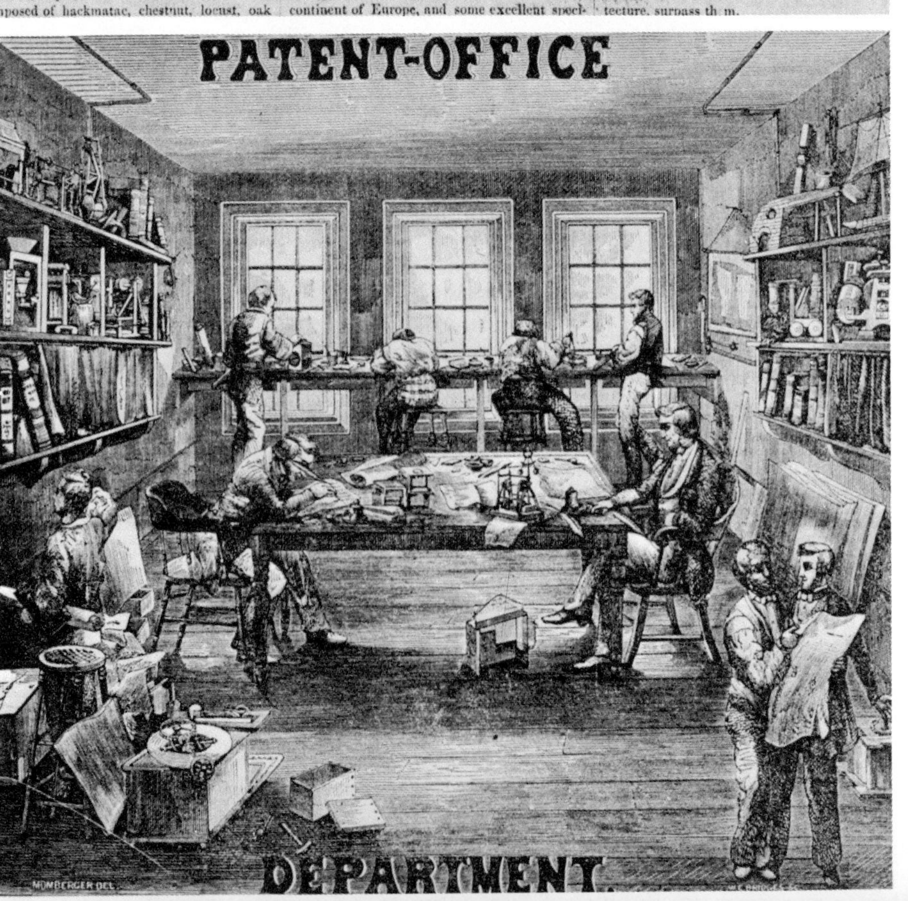

ABOVE: The illustrated article on "The Yacht America," reproduced here about two thirds of original size, was published in *Gleason's Pictorial,* May 31, 1851. The *America* was designed by George Steers and built at Brown's shipyard at the foot of Eleventh and Twelfth streets on the East River (just south of the Novelty Iron Works, at whose slip a steamboat is shown in the background). The article's prophecy that American yachts would soon surpass all others was promptly fulfilled by the *America* herself, when she won the international regatta at Cowes on August 22 and brought home the trophy which has ever since borne her name, the America's Cup.

BELOW: An engraving published in the *Scientific American,* September 20, 1851, showing the magazine's Patent Office Department at their offices, 128 Fulton Street. The picture was drawn by Momberger and engraved by W. E. Bridges.

Author's collection

. . . but from the beginning, journalistic illustration attempted to be both specific and vivid.

NEW YORK BOOK TRADE SALES.
BROTHER AND CO. SALES-ROOM, PARK PLACE, NEW YORK.

New York Public Library

This anonymous wood engraving of the "Interior of Bangs Brother & Co. Sales-Room, Park Place, New York," was published in *Frank Leslie's Illustrated Newspaper,* April 5, 1856. It was one of two illustrations for an article on "New York Book Trade Sales."

Bangs' auction room had for many years enjoyed almost a monopoly of the book-distributing trade. Twice a year booksellers from all over the country came to the city to purchase their stock from the books offered by more than a hundred publishing houses at Bangs' auctions. According to the article accompanying the picture, "Harper & Brother have at one sale disposed of books to the amount of seventy-five thousand dollars." (James Harper, wearing glasses, is shown in profile just below the auctioneer.)
The article also described a rival auction, just established, whose rooms on Broadway were run by Leavitt, Delisser & Co.

The pictorial journalism of the fifties and sixties provided . . .

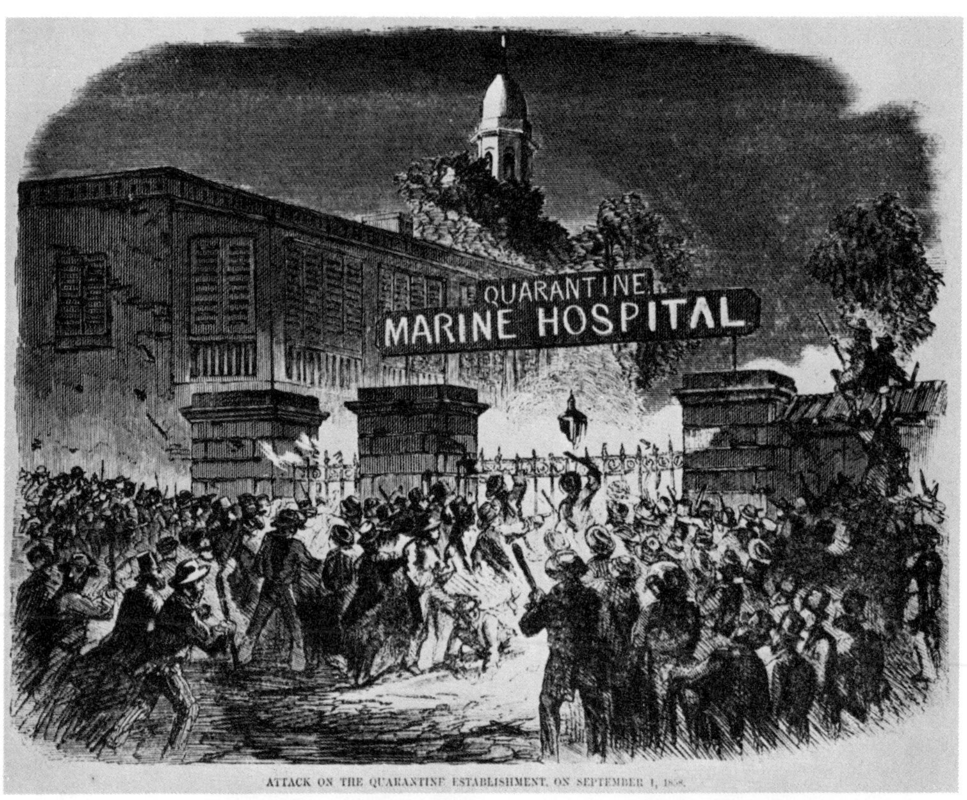

ATTACK ON THE QUARANTINE ESTABLISHMENT, ON SEPTEMBER 1, 1858.

Both pictures from author's collection

THE BLOOD STAINS IN THE PASSAGE.

The picture of the "Attack on the Quarantine Establishment" appeared in *Harper's Weekly*, September 11, 1858. "For years," said the accompanying text, "the existence of a quarantine on Staten Island has been a grave injury to the city and to the island; breeding pestilence on the latter . . . and occasioning every year yellow fever panics which inflicted severe injury on the trade of the port." A commission, appointed by the governor, had done nothing about removing the source of trouble, and the Staten Islanders took matters into their own hands. On September 1, at nine o'clock in the evening, a large party, "disguised and armed," attacked the hospital from two sides, removed the patients, and set the buildings on fire.

"The Blood Stain in the Passage" is typical of the purely utilitarian illustrations accompanying news stories in the weeklies. It was one of several pictures dealing with a murder committed in Willis' gambling house at 581 Broadway, the details of which were described in *Harper's Weekly*, October 30, 1858. Willis' faro rooms were on the second floor of a building just across the street from the fashionable Metropolitan Hotel.

. . . the first visual record of aspects of city life which pictures had previously ignored.

Pictures on this page from author's collection

"Painful as it may be to dwell upon such scenes," said the editorial in the February 11, 1860, issue of the New York *Illustrated News*, "they must not be blinked by society. . . . Let the public look at these plague-spots—this dark back-ground of our civilization—and devise measures to remove it, if such a thing be possible."

Thus the pictures on this and the following page were introduced. The scenes were sketched at "Dutch Hill"—the region along the East River between Thirty-eighth and Forty-fourth streets, including the present sites of Tudor City and the United Nations. Here, in a village of filthy shanties, lived New York's "pioneers," the immigrant laborers who moved ahead of the advancing urban frontier, leveling hills, filling up valleys, and grading the avenues and streets. To "look this evil full in the face," the magazine sent a reporter and an artist to interview the Thomas Glennan family (upper right), Mrs. Hassett (center left), John Bradley and his wife (below), and other residents of the district.

BACKGROUNDS OF CIVILIZATION.—Interior of Mr. John Bradley's Cottage. His Family and Fellow-Lodgers.

While some of the "artist correspondents" were making the first fumbling attempts to record the visual reality of urban poverty . . .

The second in the *Illustrated News'* series of articles on "The Background of our Civilization" dealt with the Five Points district (February 18, 1860). Strictly speaking, the Five Points was originally the multiple intersection of Orange (now Baxter), Cross (now Park), and Anthony (now Worth) streets, but by 1840 the name was applied to the whole slum region thereabouts, just southeast of where the Collect Pond had once been (see page 118).

Above, right, is a "View of Cow Bay," an alley off Worth Street. Below, the "Ball-Room of Mr. Pete Williams, deceased, at present conducted by Mr. Pritties," in a Baxter Street basement. Juba, billed as "the greatest jig dancer that the exhibition boards have ever known," got his start here when Pete Williams ran the place.

Official reports as early as 1834 had called attention to the horrible conditions in the city's tenements, and various civic associations had grappled with the problem. But it was still true, as the *Illustrated News* said, that few New Yorkers outside of the slums had any idea what they were like. It was to be six years yet before the first tenement-house legislation was passed.

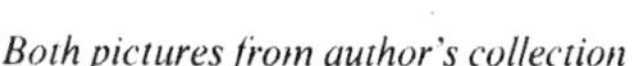

Both pictures from author's collection

. . . others developed their own distinctively fresh techniques
for capturing the grace and "style"
of social life . . .

Author's collection

Winslow Homer's drawing of the "Great Fair Given at the City Assembly Rooms" was published as a two-page wood engraving in *Harper's Weekly,* December 28, 1861.

"This fair was got up," said the *Weekly,* "by the Ladies of New York, without distinction of sect, for the relief of the poor, especially that part of them left destitute by the war. It proved a complete success. The array of beauty and fashion which gathered round the tables has never been surpassed, and the proceeds will prove a handsome fund. . . ."

. . . but the majority of artist-reporters were simply assigned . . .

GRAND BASE BALL MATCH FOR THE CHAMPIONSHIP, BETWEEN THE EXCELSIOR AND ATLANTIC CL

"Once make Cricket and Base Ball and Quoits and Foot Ball and the rest of them national pastimes, and there will be little room left for big crimes to grow among us," said the New York *Illustrated News* of August 4, 1860. Hence, they were glad to show a picture of the championship baseball game between the Atlantics and the Excelsiors, played on July 19 at the latter's club grounds in south Brooklyn—from a sketch by "our own artist," J. H. Gouter. The Excelsiors won, 23-4, before a crowd of at least 12,000 people.

The picture of "The Grand Trotting Match between Flora Temple and George M. Patchen" at the Union course on Long Island, on June 6, 1860, was published in the *News,* June 16, with a document signed by the three judges of the race certifying "that the Artist of the New York *Illustrated News* was the only one present on the Judges' stand who took a sketch of the trot." Competition between the weeklies was getting severe, and many pictures were faked. But the public wanted *authentic* pictures.

. . . to the routine coverage of sports and other news events.

...OOKLYN, AT THE EXCELSIOR CLUB GROUNDS, SOUTH BROOKLYN, ON THURSDAY, JULY 19.—FROM A SKETCH MADE BY OUR OWN ARTIST.

Both pictures from author's collection

THE GRAND TROTTING MATCH BETWEEN FLORA TEMPLE AND GEORGE M. PATCHEN, ON WEDNESDAY, JUNE 6, ON THE UNION COURSE, L. I., FLORA TEMPLE BEING THE WINNER IN THREE STRAIGHT HEATS.
TIME—2:21—2:21—2:21 1-2.—FROM A SKETCH TAKEN BY OUR OWN ARTIST FROM THE JUDGES' STAND.—(SEE CERTIFICATE ON FIRST PAGE.)

Meanwhile, pictures in all mediums continued to emphasize the city's commercial progress . . .

Collection of Edward W. C. Arnold; photograph courtesy of Museum of the City of New York

This line engraving by Doty & Bergen provided a "pictorial directory" of the stores on Park Row about 1854. The old Park Theater had burned down in 1848, and John Jacob Astor had thereafter erected the row of five brownstone-front stores here shown (for an earlier picture of this site, see page 137).

. . . and the splendor and hustle of Broadway, with its busy retail shops and magnificent hotels.

Museum of the City of New York

This lithograph by F. Heppenheimer, showing the "St. Nicholas-Hotel, Broadway, N. Y.," was published in 1855 by W. Stephenson & Co. as one of a series of street views. The St. Nicholas, on the west side of Broadway between Broome and Spring streets, was opened in 1853. An English M.P. who visited it in the following year was overwhelmed by its splendors (as was everyone who described it). "Every chimney-piece and table slab is of marble," he wrote; "every carpet is of velvet pile; chair covers and curtains are made of silk or satin damask; the looking-glasses are set in frames worthy of Windsor Castle; and the embroidery on the mosquito nettings itself might be exhibited to royalty. . . . The St. Nicholas contains 1000 beds, and its white marble front forms one of the greatest ornaments of Broadway. The profits of this establishment during 1854 were reported to be 53,600 dollars. . . ." (W. E. Baxter, *America and the Americans* [London, 1855].)

(For an interior view of Phalon's establishment, just right of the hotel's main entrance, see page 281.)

In formerly fashionable residential districts, dwellings were being crowded out by shops and warehouses, or converted into stores . . .

Collection of Edward W. C. Arnold; photograph courtesy of Museum of the City of New York

This is a detail from the right-hand end of another of W. Stephenson & Co.'s series of street views: a lithograph by F. Heppenheimer entitled "View of Broadway, New York, from Exchange Alley to Morris Street. West Side," published in 1855. The small converted residence at 53 Broadway contained a variety of offices, including those of the Greenwood Cemetery in Brooklyn, the American Mining Co., and the New York-Havre Steamship Line, as well as the law offices of Theodore Sedgwick (soon to become U. S. District Attorney) and the studio of George Platt, interior decorator (see next page). The basement of the house at right was a barbershop, called Harding's Hair Dressing & Shaving Rooms. To the left is Fisher & Robinson's lace-importing firm. The sandwich man in the foreground advertises Shermans Radical Cure Trusses.

. . . while new and more elegant residences, with interiors designed by professional decorators . . .

Courtesy of George Platt Lynes

One of the earliest professional interior designers in this country was George Platt, who came to New York from England in the late forties. From his studio at 53 Broadway (see opposite) came designs for furniture as well as charmingly executed designs for the entire furnishing and decoration of residences. His water-color drawing (somewhat torn) of the interior of his own house, about 1850, is reproduced above. (The table in the foreground, of his own design, is still in use in the New York home of Platt's great-grandson, Mr. Russell Lynes.)

Author's collection

The pictures at left, engraved by J. W. Orr, are illustrations of a chair, a fire screen, and an ottoman designed by Platt "in the Louis XIV style," reproduced from A. J. Downing's *The Architecture of Country Houses* (New York, 1851), in which Platt is referred to as "at present the most popular interior decorator in the country."

. . . were being built uptown on the newly laid-out avenues and fashionable squares.

New York Public Library

Author's collection

The above illustration of "A Parlor View in a New York Dwelling House," drawn by A. Kimbel and engraved by N. Orr, was published in *Gleason's Pictorial,* November 11, 1854. It represents, we are told, the interior of "a magnificent mansion up town, where one of the most eminent of our merchants has surrounded himself and family with all the elegancies and luxuries to which years of successful enterprise entitle him." Farther along in the article it turns out that all the furniture in the room was made by "the French house of Bembe & Kimbel," 56 Walker Street, New York, and that Mr. Kimbel's "unique styles appear to be American modifications of those now in vogue abroad." LEFT: An illustration by C. E. Döpler, engraved by J. W. Orr, for one of Jacob Abbott's storybooks, *John True.* The author's instructions to the illustrator called for "A corner in a handsome breakfast room in the Fifth Avenue. A small table neatly set for luncheon near a large bow window. Rich furniture partly or wholly shown. Handsome curtains to the window. . . ." (See Jacob Abbott, *The Harper Establishment; or How the Story Books are Made* [New York, 1855], pages 108-10.)

The interiors of commercial establishments were also increasingly elaborate . . .

293

The above Engraving represents the interior of the most splendid establishment of its kind in the City of New-York—in the Union—probably in the world. Its decorations and furniture cost upwards of $16,000, a larger sum than was ever before expended upon any Hair Dressing Establishment since time began. The Fresco work of the ceiling, by De Lamano, is a brilliant triumph of a brilliant Art. One side of the Apartment is walled with $5,000 worth of mirrors. The washstand, with its statuary, costs $1,500. The marble floor $1,500. The magnificent shaving chairs $100 each, 15 in number, and the silver toilet services about $2,500. All luxury and comfort that taste, skill and money could crowd within the space, has been accomplished, and

PHALON'S

HAIR DRESSING ESTABLISHMENT,

IN THE ST. NICHOLAS HOTEL, NEW-YORK,

Is as great a lion in its way as the palace of St. Mark in Venice. The Baths, on the lower floor, were fitted up at an expense of $5,000, and are the finest in the city.

J. Clarence Davies Collection, Museum of the City of New York

A wood engraving by W. Roberts, showing the interior of Phalon's hairdressing establishment in the St. Nicholas Hotel (see page 277). This advertisement was probably published in 1853, about the time the hotel opened, but it has not been possible to determine where it appeared.

. . . as the weeklies delighted in showing (no doubt for a fee) . . .

MESSRS. C. B. HATCH & CO.'S GENTLEMENS' FURNISHING STORE, No. 403 BROADWAY, NEW YORK.

Both pictures from author's collection

MARBLE REFECTORIES OF NEW YORK.—THE NEWLY-OPENED BAR-ROOM OF MESSRS. THOMAS BROS., CORNER OF BROADWAY AND WASHINGTON PLACE. See page 341.

Both of these illustrations appeared in the New York *Illustrated News.* The one above, in the issue of July 28, 1860, shows the interior of C. B. Hatch & Co.'s gentlemen's furnishing store, 403 Broadway.

That below, of the "newly opened Bar-Room of Messrs Thomas Bros., Corner of Broadway and Washington Place," in the issue of October 6, 1860. Both were accompanied by highly flattering articles about the establishments and their proprietors.

. . . and some of the great new department-store buildings were among the city's most imposing structures.

LORD & TAYLOR
DRY - GOODS,
461, 463, 465 & 467, BROADWAY, (COR. GRAND ST.) NEW YORK.

Collection of Edward W. C. Arnold; photograph courtesy of Museum of the City of New York

Lord & Taylor, which had commenced business down on Catherine Street in 1826, moved into this new building on the northwest corner of Broadway and Grand Street in 1859. Designed by Griffith Thomas, the building is here shown in a lithograph by Henry Lawrence, published in 1860. An article in the New York *Times,* August 29, 1859, described the building as "more like an Italian palace than a place for the sale of broadcloth.

"Its extravagant ornamentation," the *Times* went on, "would be regarded as a fault by persons of more moderate taste than New Yorkers. . . . A most notable ornament in the building is the huge gas chandelier that lights up the staircase. It was made by Tiffany at a cost of $500, and is original and unique of its kind."

So rapidly did the city change in the fifties that an evident nostalgia began to appear in pictures of the older parts of it.

Lith of Sarony, Major & Knapp, 449 Broadway N.Y.
for D.T. Valentine's Manual, 1863
OLD STOREHOUSES COR. PEARL & CHATHAM ST. 1861.

Both pictures from author's collection

The illustrations on this page are both from lithographs by Sarony, Major & Knapp in David T. Valentine's *Manual of the Common Council* for 1863, and are typical of the views of the contemporary city which appear in the *Manuals* of the late fifties and early sixties.

The *Manuals*, which Valentine edited from 1842 to 1866, are a storehouse of pictures. Some of those purporting to show the city in the seventeenth and eighteenth centuries are reasonably good lithographic copies of engravings or drawings made contemporaneously with the scene; but some are mere fabrications. The most useful pictures in the lot, from the point of view of this book, are those which show the city as Valentine and his contemporaries knew it.

The one reproduced above shows the northeast corner of Pearl and Chatham streets as it was in 1861.

The one below is a view up Baxter Street from the corner of Hester Street, with the Centre Market (see page 171) in the distance. The large building on the southwest corner of Baxter and Grand streets is Odd Fellows Hall.

Lith of Sarony, Major & Knapp, 449 Broadway N.Y.
for D.T. Valentine's Manual, 1863
VIEW OF BAXTER (LATE ORANGE ST) BETW. HESTER & GRAND ST. 1861.

But the telegraph wires running past the old markets,
and the "express" wagons
all over town . . .

ABOVE: The wash drawing by L. Oram shows Fulton Market in 1860, from the corner of Beekman and Front streets, with the masts of the shipping along the East River in the background.
BELOW: A wood engraving by Purcell & Dutton advertising Studley's Express, about 1860. The building in the background is the New York & New Haven Railroad depot, erected in 1857 on the north half of the block between Twenty-sixth and Twenty-seventh streets, west of Fourth Avenue. Just south of this passenger station, on the same block, was the depot of the New York & Harlem Railroad. In effect, as I. N. Phelps Stokes pointed out, "these two stations, side by side, formed the nucleus of the Union Station idea in the United States."

Both pictures from J. Clarence Davies Collection, Museum of the City of New York

. . . were the true symbols of the city's undaunted confidence in the beneficence of change and exchange.

J. Clarence Davies Collection, Museum of the City of New York

This engaging lithograph, drawn "from nature" and published by Otto Botticher, depicts the "Turn Out of the Employees of the American Express Company cor: Hudson, Jay & Staple Streets, New York City June 21, 1858."

The express business in America had been originated less than twenty years before, by a Yankee named William F. Harnden who maintained a regular express service between New York and Boston, with connections in Albany, Philadelphia, and other cities. By 1850 there were many rival express companies, three of which were merged in that year to form the American Express Co. The president of the company was Henry Wells; its secretary, William G. Fargo; and its superintendent, John Butterfield. An offshoot of this company was Wells, Fargo & Co., established in New York in 1852 "to forward Gold Dust, Bullion, Specie, Packages, Parcels & Freight of all kinds, to and from New York and San Francisco . . . and all the principal towns of California and Oregon."

The Botticher lithograph shows one of the company's wagons emerging from Duane Street (the trees are in a small, triangular park) and turning north on Hudson Street along the tracks of the New York Central and Hudson River Railroad. The man holding the reins is Henry Wells himself.

Seen in bird's-eye perspective, New York at the beginning of the eighteen-sixties was literally on top of the world.

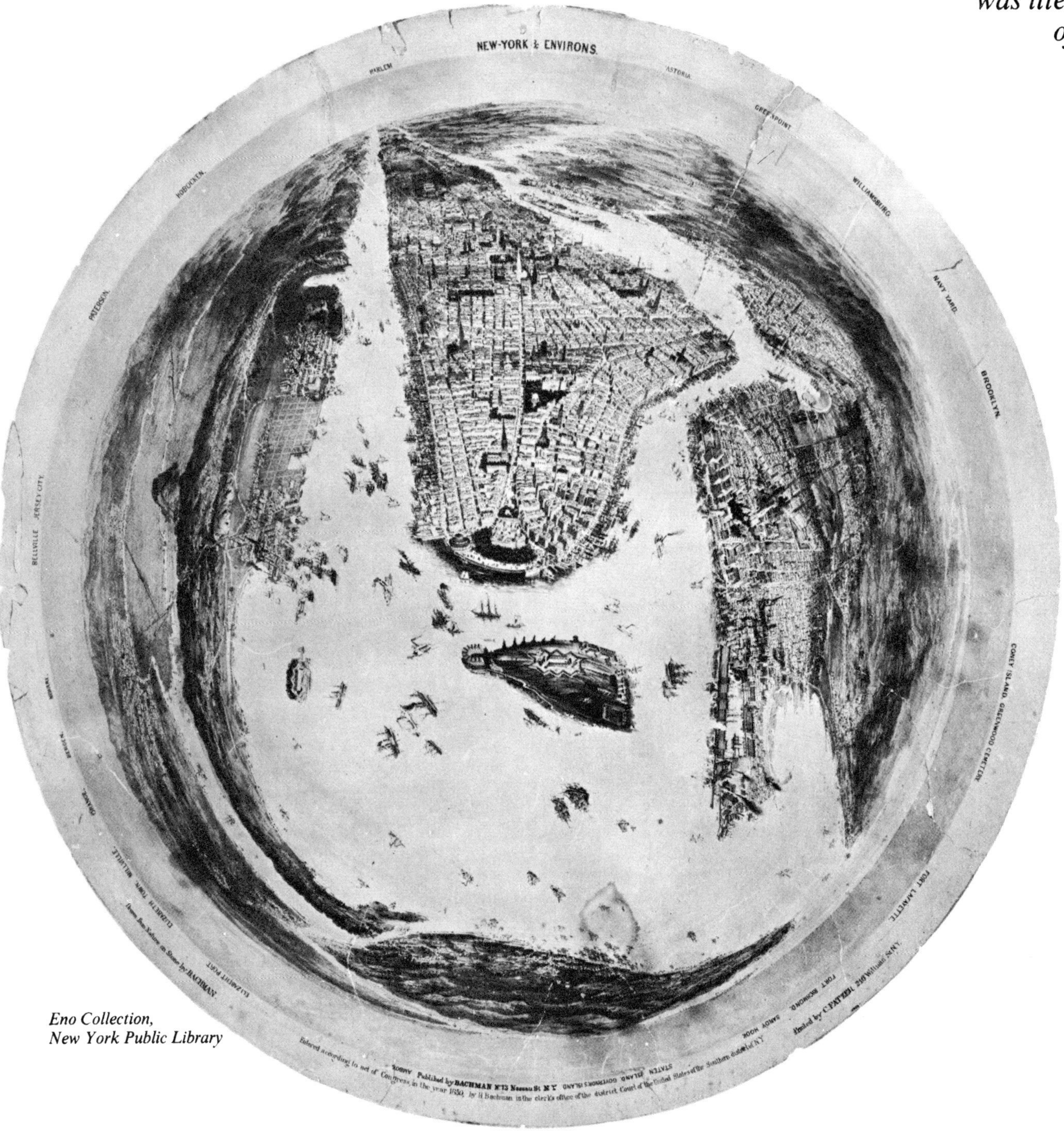

Eno Collection,
New York Public Library

This extraordinary panorama of "New York & Environs" was drawn "from Nature on Stone" by (John) Bachman and published in 1859. Its ingenious perspective suggests an enthusiastic, if somewhat exaggerated, conception of the city's global consequence on the eve of the Civil War. It is perhaps worth noting that within a year or so the city's mayor, Fernando Wood, officially proposed that New York secede from the Union and set up on its own.

Manhattan lay dense and compact at the center . . .

Stokes Collection, New York Public Library

A detail from a lithograph "Panorama of New York and Vicinity" drawn and published by John Bachman (1866). In left foreground a baseball game is in progress at the Elysian Fields, in Hoboken, where the earliest recorded baseball games were played. (The New York Knickerbockers, organized in 1845, was the first regular baseball club.) The large house in right foreground is the Stevens Castle, still standing.

J. Clarence Davies Collection, Museum of the City of New York

A lithograph by Endicott & Co., about 1861, of "Erie Railway Company's Steam Ferry Boat 'Pavonia,' Plying between Chambers St. and Long Dock, Jersey City."

. . . of a group of tributary and suburban communities.

J. Clarence Davies Collection, Museum of the City of New York

This Currier & Ives lithograph of "New York Bay from Bay Ridge, L.I.," drawn by Fanny F. Palmer, provides an interesting contrast with earlier views (see especially pages 99, 106, 158 and 159). The foreground here is dominated by the trim lawn and graveled drive of a suburban villa, rather than the rural surroundings of a country seat or the warehouses and factories of the urban waterfront. New York itself (at far right) is only the largest of several clusters of spires and masts in the background and is no more prominent in the printed caption than Communipaw, Jersey City, or Hoboken.

In some respects these neighboring places were really a part of the city . . .

Both pictures from J. Clarence Davies Collection, Museum of the City of New York

ABOVE: "Union Pond, Williamsburgh, L. I.," shown here in a lithograph by Thomas & Eno, was opened as a skating rink in the winter of 1862-63, and many New Yorkers came over on the Grand Street ferry to enjoy it. (If Winslow Homer did not draw the original of this print, the artist had certainly learned to see with Homer's eyes. See page 273.)

Williamsburg had become a part of the city of Brooklyn in 1855.

BELOW: This "View of Astoria, L.I., from the New York Side" (1862) is another Currier & Ives lithograph from a drawing by Fanny F. Palmer. The village of Astoria, originally known as Hallett's Cove, was incorporated in 1839. It remained a distinctive village until the post-Civil War period, and did not become a part of New York City until 1898.

The view was probably made from a point on the Manhattan shore near Eighty-eighth Street (see page 293).

. . . though many of them still retained their distinctive character as separate towns and villages.

HISTORICAL
MORRISANIA.
(VILLAGE.)
1861.

1. Chauncey Smith
2. Nicholas McGraw.
3. William H. Morris,
4. Miller & Kimpton, Coal and Lumber Yard
5. Joseph S. Ives,
6. Stewart & Blauvelt, Sash and Blind M'f'rs.
7. McGraw or Morrisania Hall,
8. Judge Silas D. Gifford,
9. Joseph Ives,
10. Baptist Church,
11. James L. Parshall,
12. Austin Carr,
13. A. Rice,
14. John S. Lyons Coal and Wood Yard,
15. J. Anderson,
16. St. Augustine,
17. J. B. Ayers,
18. F. Cordes,
19. Andrew Attendorph,
20., 21. J. Webb,
22. R. H. Elton,
23. Charles Snyder
24. A. Folmar,
25. Wm. R. Collins,
26. T. Wicks,
27. Chas. L. Georgi,
28. Oliver Tilden Shop,
29. C. L. Georgi's Old Homestead,
30. Geo. Hand,
31. Caspar Market,
32. Old Mill Brook.

J. Clarence Davies Collection, Museum of the City of New York

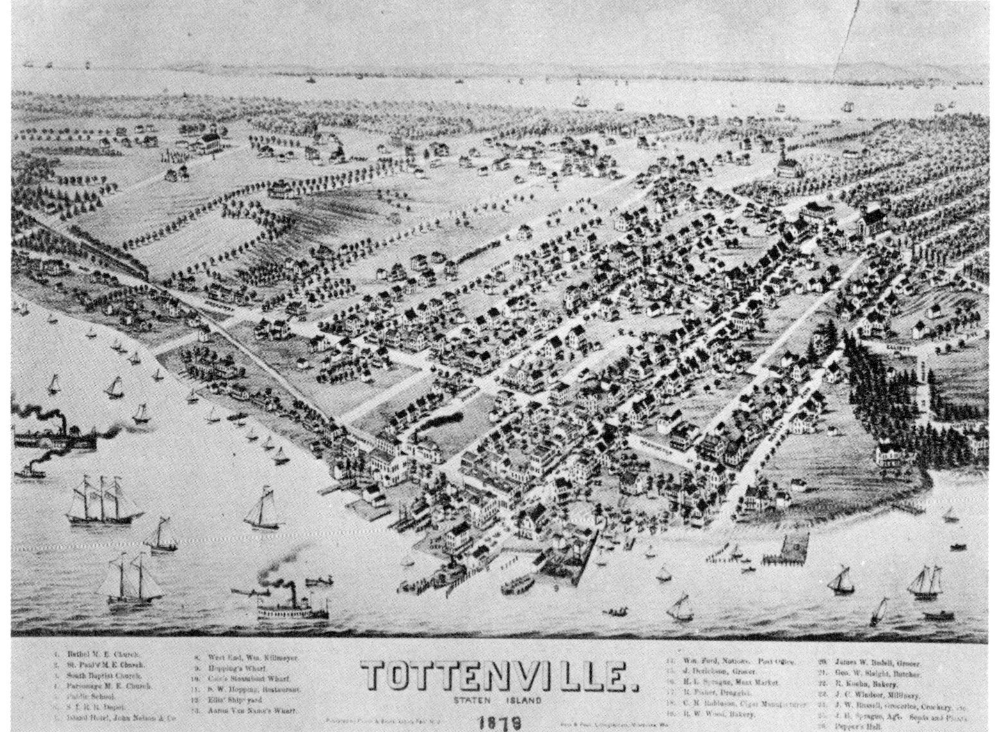

ABOVE: An anonymous lithograph of "Historical Morrisania. (Village.) 1861." Crossing the foreground is the Boston Road. The horse and wagon are going west on present 169th Street. The spire in the center of the view is St. Augustine's Catholic Church at the corner of Franklin Avenue and Jefferson Street.

LEFT: "Tottenville. Staten Island" was lithographed in Milwaukee by Beck & Pauli and published by Fowler & Evans of Asbury Park, New Jersey. The view represents the village as it would be seen from above the Arthur Kill, looking southeast toward Raritan Bay and the Atlantic Highlands in the distance. The ferry at the foot of Totten Street crossed the Kill to Perth Amboy, New Jersey.

Staten Island Historical Society

Far beyond the city limits, New Yorkers were erecting spacious suburban villas . . .

Both pictures from Museum of the City of New York

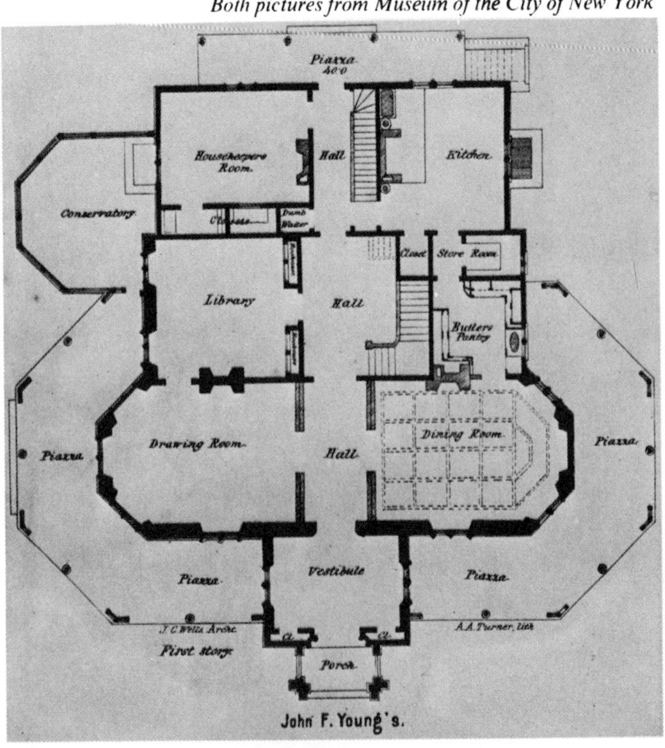

These photolithographs by A. A. Turner, showing the exterior and the plan of the first floor of the residence of John F. Young at Fordham Village, were published in 1860 by D. Appleton & Co. as two of the plates in *Villas on the Hudson. A Collection of Photo-Lithographs of Thirty-One Country Residences.*

Five years earlier W. E. Baxter had observed that suburban villas were "starting up like mushrooms on spots which five years ago were part of the dense and tangled forest; and the value of property everywhere, but especially along the various lines of railroad, has increased in a ratio almost incredible. Small fortunes have been made by owners of real estate at Yonkers, and other places on the Hudson River." (*America and the Americans* [London, 1855].)

. . . quite unlike the older "country estates" which still survived on upper Manhattan.

Thomas F. Healy Collection

These two lithographs by George Hayward both appeared in Valentine's *Manuals of the Common Council.* The one above shows the "Residence of Isaac Dyckman, Kingsbridge, N.Y.," as it was in 1861 (the year it was published). Originally built in 1748, and rebuilt in 1783, the house still stands at 204th Street and Broadway.

J. Clarence Davies Collection, Museum of the City of New York

The lithograph at right, drawn and published in 1864, shows "J. Jacob Astor's Former Residence 88th St. near East River," where Washington Irving had lived in 1835 and 1836 while he was writing *Astoria,* an account of the Far West fur trade in which Astor made his fortune. The house was built about 1802 and was demolished five years after this picture was published. The lawns stretched down to the shore opposite Astoria on the Long Island side (see page 290).

Uptown, beyond Fiftieth Street, where farms and shanties dotted the landscape . . .

J. Clarence Davies Collection, Museum of the City of New York

This view of the junction of Broadway (at left) and Eighth Avenue —now Columbus Circle—is George Hayward's original drawing for a lithograph published in Valentine's *Manual* in 1862.

The drawing is dated October 17, 1861. The houses behind the long wooden building in foreground stood just about where the Fisk Building now stands.

. . . a large tract of land had been set aside as a park . . .

J. Clarence Davies Collection, Museum of the City of New York

Plans for Central Park had been proposed, by A. J. Downing and others, as early as 1850, but the property was not purchased until 1856. By that time it was a scrubby and disorganized tract of rocky land, dotted with a few gaunt farms and a number of squatters' shanties, at the center of which were the receiving reservoirs of the Croton water system.

Work on the park began in 1857, as part of the city's program of work relief for the unemployed during that depression year. Under the leadership of Andrew H. Green, the commissioners had selected Frederick Law Olmsted and Calvert Vaux as designers for the park (see next page), and the work of clearing and grading and planting progressed rapidly. By the mid-sixties an enthusiastic New Yorker congratulated the commissioners: "On a bare, unsightly, and disgusting spot, they have created an area of beauty, charming as the Garden of the Lord."

The bird's-eye view of "Central Park. (Winter)" was drawn by John Bachman, lithographed by J. Bien, and published by Edmund Foerster & Co. in 1865.

. . . in order to rescue it and restore its natural beauty before it,
like everything else on the island,
should be leveled
and built up.

NO. 5.
FROM POINT E.

PRESENT OUTLINES.

EFFECT PROPOSED.

Lent by the Department of Parks, City of New York, to the Museum of the City of New York

This is a page from the prize-winning "Greensward" plan for Central Park, submitted by Frederick Law Olmsted and Calvert Vaux in 1857. At the top of each page is a small reproduction of their original landscape plan.

Below this is a photograph of some part of the property, taken from a point indicated on the little map by a letter of the alphabet. Then at the bottom of the page there is a miniature oil painting of the scene as it will look when the plan has been carried out.

Point E, on the page reproduced here, was just south of the Old Reservoir (the double rectangle in the center of the map), about on a line with Seventy-eighth Street, and an arrow indicates that the photograph was taken looking southwest toward Seventy-second Street where a lake was to be built, as shown in the painting of the "Effect Proposed."

When the Civil War broke out, the city suddenly was filled with soldiers.

New York State Historical Association, Cooperstown, New York

Author's collection

CAMP ON THE BATTERY, NEW YORK CITY.

ABOVE: An oil painting by an unknown (and apparently untrained) artist of "Zouaves at Astor House, New York City," about 1861. It was probably intended to represent Colonel Elmer Ellsworth's Fire-Brigade Zouaves, enlisted from the ranks of the Volunteer Fire Department. George Templeton Strong noted in his diary, April 29, 1861, that he had seen them that afternoon marching down Chatham Street on their march to the embarkation dock. "At the Astor House, they halted and received a flag. . . . These young fellows march badly, but they will fight hard if judiciously handled." (*The Diary of George Templeton Strong*, ed. by Nevins and Thomas [New York, 1952].)

LEFT: An anonymous wood engraving, "Camp on the Battery, New York City," from *Harper's Weekly*, May 11, 1861. About 2500 men were encamped here, waiting to be shipped to the front. Other pictures in this issue of the *Weekly* showed the temporary barracks in City Hall Park and the departure of the 13th (Brooklyn) Regiment and Colonel Corcoran's 69th (Irish) Regiment.

In the first flush of martial enthusiasm, merchants and their clerks left their ledgers to don handsome uniforms . . .

This and the lithograph on the opposite page belong to a series of military cartoons drawn by Draner (Renard), printed by Lemercier, and published in Paris by Daziaro.

The one on this page bears the title: "Etats-Unis. 1862. 7th Regt of New York."

Collection of Edward W. C. Arnold; photograph courtesy of Museum of the City of New York

. . . and the Bowery "Bhoys" joined the Fire Brigade Zouaves.

Collection of Edward W. C. Arnold; photograph courtesy of Museum of the City of New York

Another in the series of military cartoons by Draner, published in Paris (see opposite page). This one is captioned "Etats-Unis. 1865—New-York Fire-Brigade Zouaves" (see page 297).

Colonel Ellsworth's ex-firemen, incidentally, had a chance to show their abilities almost at once. Shortly after they arrived in Washington, Willard's Hotel was threatened by a fire in an adjoining building. According to the New York *Times* correspondent, Ellsworth ordered 100 of his men, then quartered in the House of Representatives wing of the Capitol, to help. "The order was followed by nearly the whole regiment jumping from the windows of the Capitol and scaling the fences. They could not enter the engine houses, and broke down the doors, taking out the machines, and reached the spot before the city firemen were awake. . . . They formed pyramids on each other's shoulders, climbing into the windows, scaling lightning rods, and succeeded in two hours in saving the whole structure. Willard treated them handsomely. . . ." (New York *Times,* May 10, 1861.)

But when it turned out to be a real war, enlistments fell off, despite handsome bounties . . .

RECRUITING FOR THE WAR—SCENE AT THE RECRUITING TENTS IN THE PARK, NEW YORK.

New York Public Library

An anonymous wood engraving, "Recruiting for the War," from *Frank Leslie's Illustrated Newspaper,* March 19, 1864. The recruiting station was in City Hall Park.

. . . and when the draft was introduced, thousands of New Yorkers rioted in protest.

CHARGE OF THE POLICE ON THE RIOTERS AT THE "TRIBUNE" OFFICE.

All pictures from author's collection

Three anonymous wood engravings from *Harper's Weekly,* August 1, 1863, illustrating the draft riots which occurred in New York July 13-16. The rioting started as a protest by the poorer citizens against a draft law which favored those who could afford to pay $300 for a substitute, but it soon turned into a general insurrection against the established order. For four days blood-maddened mobs from the dives and tenements roamed the city almost at will, burning, looting, and killing. Estimated totals: more than 1200 people killed and about 8000 injured; 18 Negroes hanged, plus 5 drowned and more than 70 others missing; more than 100 buildings burned, including the provost marshal's office, the Colored Orphan Asylum, an armory, and many dwellings and stores.

SACKING BROOKS'S CLOTHING STORE.

HANGING A NEGRO IN CLARKSON STREET.

Throughout the war, parading soldiers were a familiar sight in the streets . . .

Collection of Edward W. C. Arnold; photograph courtesy of Museum of the City of New York

This lithograph by Endicott & Co. of "Printing-House Square" was published by Baker & Godwin about 1864. The open space at the intersection of Park Row (right) and Nassau Street acquired its name about 1860 from the presence of so many newspaper and publishing offices in the neighborhood. The most conspicuous landmark was the New York *Times* building, erected in 1857–58 on the former site of the Brick Presbyterian Church between Park Row and Nassau. To the left of it, across Nassau, on the southeast corner of Spruce Street, was Currier & Ives' shop. North of Spruce, in the New York *Tribune* building, were the offices of Baker & Godwin (publishers of the print) and Joy, Coe & Co.'s advertising agency.

South of the *Times* building, on Park Row at Beekman, were the offices of the *World* and the *Scientific American* (whose Patent Office department is illustrated on page 268).

The horsecars were those of the Third Avenue Railroad, running up Park Row from Broadway (right background, at St. Paul's Chapel) to Third Avenue and thence to the Harlem River. There were five other street railways in town by 1860, and sixteen omnibus lines.

. . . and New Yorkers did their full share in caring for the sick and wounded.

Author's collection

This lithograph by Major & Knapp, from Valentine's *Manual* of 1864, shows the hospital on the fourth floor of the Soldiers' Depot at 50-52 Howard Street. This depot was set up with New York State funds.

Early in 1861 various groups met in the city to form relief organizations (see page 305). Out of their combined efforts and those of similar organizations in other cities came the United States Sanitary Commission, whose volunteer workers cared for the sick and wounded, staffed battlefield hospitals, and provided medicines and surgical dressings and other supplies. Frederick Law Olmsted, the designer and superintendent of Central Park, was general secretary of the commission, and Henry W. Bellows, pastor of All Souls Unitarian Church, was its president. Other New Yorkers, including Professor Wolcott Gibbs of the College of the City of New York and George Templeton Strong, served the commission throughout the war.

Private houses and other buildings were taken over by the army for offices and recruiting stations . . .

New-York Historical Society

These houses on State Street, facing Battery Park, were all occupied by army offices when the photograph was taken in 1864. No. 16, at right, was a recruiting station; No. 17, the office of the chief quartermaster; No. 18 the office of the assistant quartermaster. The sign on No. 19 is illegible.

. . . and citizen volunteers worked hard and long to help relieve suffering on the distant battlefields.

The "Women's Central Association of Relief," formed in April, 1861, had its headquarters at Cooper Union. These photographs were taken in July, 1865.

The boxes of medical supplies on the sidewalk are addressed to U. S. Sanitary Commission offices in Beaufort, South Carolina; Newbern, North Carolina; Washington, D.C.; and New Orleans.

The women working in the office are identified, on the back of the original photograph, as: left to right, Mrs. William B. Rice, Miss [Louisa Lee?] Schuyler, Mrs. [William Preston?] Griffin, Mrs. [T. M.] d'Oremieulx [sister of Wolcott Gibbs], and Miss Collins.

Both pictures from Museum of the City of New York

Meanwhile, as the photographs of the period show it, life went on much as usual.

Museum of the City of New York

Photograph of a party at the summer home of Mr. and Mrs. George R. Satterlee, Grimes Hill, Stapleton, Staten Island, in 1863. The couple playing chess are Mrs. Edward Oothout (on whose hair some very bad photographic retouching has been done) and Joseph H. Choate. (Photographer unidentified.)

In the suburbs and in the city there was time to relax occasionally . . .

Both pictures from Museum of the City of New York

These photographs of the interior and exterior of C. A. Marsh's drugstore, on the corner of Third Avenue and 125th Street in Harlem, are reproduced from stereoscopic views made in 1865.

. . . but business, after a brief setback, boomed as never before.

The photograph above shows the west side of Hudson Street, between Chambers and Reade, in the summer of 1865. The picture of Coger's Ship Joiner's establishment, at 480 Water Street, was probably taken about 1863.

Both pictures from New-York Historical Society

Neither Union victories nor Lincoln's funeral sidetracked the drive for trade.

WORKING MODEL OF A PETROLEUM WELL.
WITH ENGINE DERRICK & TRUCK.
DRAWN BY TWENTY POWERFUL HORSES.
Furnished by WED W. CLARKE & Co., Central Petroleum Exchange 10 Pine Street, NEW YORK CITY.
Being a leading feature in the Great National Procession in honour of victories gained by our American Armies and Navy, and in commemoration of the Reinauguration of President Lincoln, March 4th 1865.

New-York Historical Society

"Oil is King Now, not Cotton," proclaimed a sign on this float which took part in the grand triumphal parade in New York, March 6, 1865. The photograph was taken looking south on Fifth Avenue from Thirteenth Street, with the First Presbyterian Church in background at Eleventh Street. The petroleum float was one of many provided by the city's business firms, "whose chief object in participating in the festival," as *Harper's Weekly* bluntly put it, "was the opportunity to advertise their wares."

Collection of Edward W. C. Arnold; photograph courtesy of Museum of the City of New York

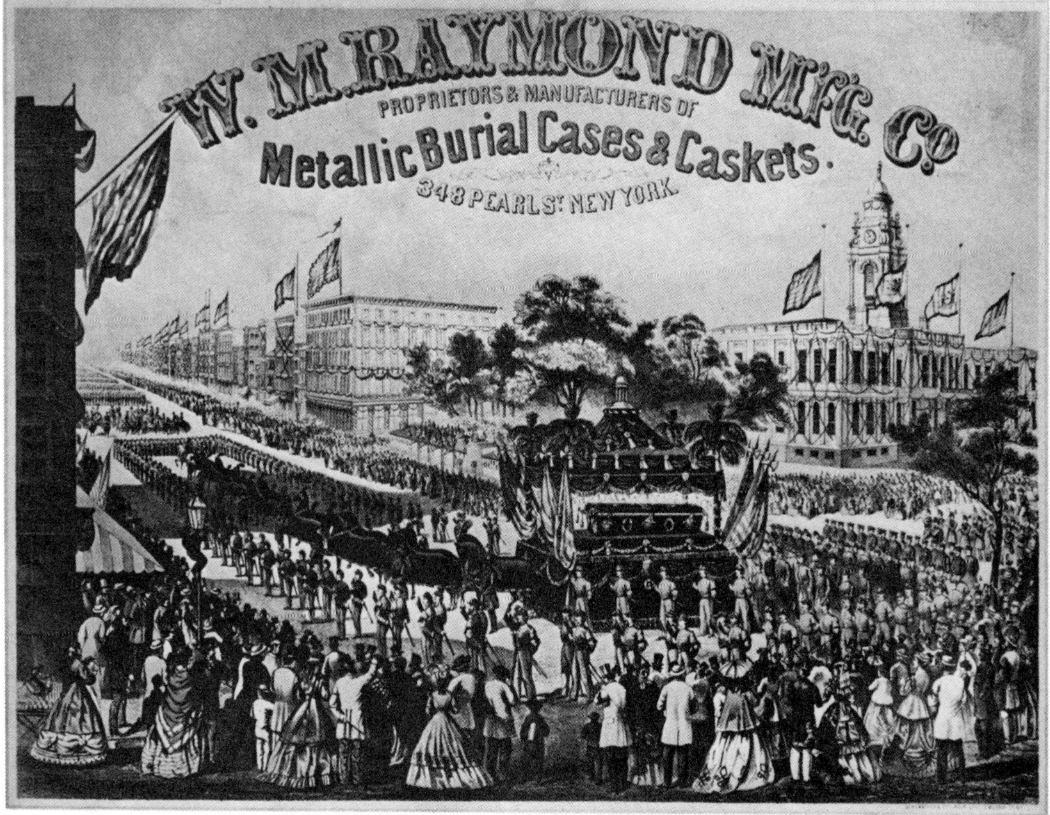

This lithograph by Schumacher & Ettlinger was issued as an advertisement by one of the city's largest coffin manufacturers. It shows President Lincoln's funeral procession, April 25, 1865, moving from the City Hall, where the body had lain in state, up Broadway on its way to the Hudson River Railroad Depot.

Home from the battlefields, Brady the photographer found Broadway even busier than before, and other photographers . . .

The photograph at right, of Broadway north from Spring Street, was taken in 1867 by Mathew B. Brady (whose prewar daguerreotype gallery is shown on page 195).

The photograph of Wall Street, below, was taken by an unidentified photographer, in 1864, from the steps of the Sub-Treasury at the head of Broad Street, looking eastward. The colonnaded building at left is the second Merchants Exchange, which had been converted for use as the Custom House in 1863.

Museum of the City of New York

New York Stock Exchange; photograph courtesy of Museum of the City of New York

. . . hurried to record old landmarks before they were destroyed . . .

Both pictures from New-York Historical Society

The photographs on this page were taken by Rockwood in the winter of 1866–67, just before St. John's Park was torn up to make way for Commodore Vanderbilt's Hudson River Railroad freight depot. In the picture at left we are looking east across the park to St. John's Chapel on Varick Street, between Beach and Laight streets (see page 140).

The picture below was taken from the corner of Beach Street, looking north on Hudson Street along the railroad's tracks.

. . . as faster transportation, and the grading of new streets, quickened the uptown march of progress.

This anonymous photograph, taken in 1869, shows the West Side and Yonkers Patent Railway Co.'s elevated line where it curved out of Greenwich Street (left background) into Ninth Avenue. The delivery wagons at right are on Gansevoort Street, and the hydrant is on the corner of Little West Twelfth Street.

This was an extension of the experimental elevated line built by Charles T. Harvey in 1867-68. Its cars were propelled by a cable which passed around huge pulleys like the one shown here, enclosed in a wooden cover. In 1871 the line was taken over by the New York Elevated Railroad Co., which introduced steam locomotives.

New-York Historical Society

In this anonymous photograph we are looking northwest from the corner of Madison Avenue and Fifty-fifth Street in 1870. The white building at left is Mrs. Mary Mason Jones's "Marble Row" residence, later owned by Mrs. Paran Stevens, on the northeast corner of Fifth Avenue and Fifty-seventh. The shanties just this side of the Northwest Reformed Dutch Church (whose tower is still under construction) are on the present site of the modern office building at 575 Madison Avenue.

J. Clarence Davies Collection, Museum of the City of New York

It was in these years that the city's photographers began turning out the novel, three-dimensional stereoscopic pictures . . .

Collection of H. Armour Smith

ABOVE: Stereoscopic photograph published by D. Appleton & Co. about 1865, showing booths in Appleton's bookstore, at 346 Broadway, where stereoscopes (both floor models and hand models) and stereoscopic views were for sale.

BELOW: Stereoscopic view of South Ferry, about 1867.

Museum of the City of New York

. . . in which so much of the changing scene was preserved.

Collection of H. Armour Smith

New-York Historical Society

ABOVE: Stereoscopic view of the old New York Post Office, in the former Middle Dutch Church, taken by G. E. Woodward. The post office occupied this building from 1844 to 1875, when it moved to new quarters in a building at the foot of City Hall Park (see page 401).

RIGHT: One panel of a stereoscopic view taken about 1873 by Anthony, showing the Third Avenue Railway carbarns on the east side of Third between Sixty-fifth and Sixty-sixth streets.

BELOW: Stereoscopic view, probably by Anthony, showing the Loew footbridge across Broadway at Fulton Street in 1867 (photograph taken from St. Paul's churchyard, looking southeast). The bridge was built in 1866 at the instigation of Genin, the hatter, and other merchants who found that Broadway traffic discouraged customers from crossing Broadway to their shops. It was torn down in 1868 on protest from Knox, the hatter, and other merchants on *his* side of Broadway, who claimed that it darkened their stores and wasn't very successful anyway.

Collection of H. Armour Smith

Photography was the rage, and everybody was ready to pose at a moment's notice.

Brown Brothers

A group posing for an unidentified photographer on the Loew bridge (see opposite page). St. Paul's Chapel is in the background. Probably taken in 1866.

A family group on the back porch of 436 West Twenty-second Street about 1875. This house, built about 1825, was for a number of years the home of Edwin Forrest, the actor. At the time of the photograph it was owned by the Drummond family. The young man in light trousers is Dr. I. W. Drummond.

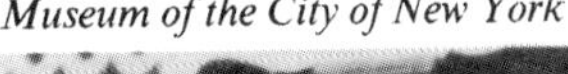

Museum of the City of New York

When just anybody could be immortalized in a tintype for twenty-five cents, wood engravings in books and magazines got by only if they were "from a photograph."

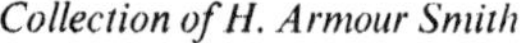

Collection of H. Armour Smith

THE CURBSTONE SINGERS.

(From photograph of group by Gurney.)

Author's collection

CAPTAIN JAMES PRICE.—[PHOTOGRAPHED BY ROCKWOOD.]

ABOVE LEFT: The tintype shown here in its original size, with the original embossed mount, bears on the reverse a printed label reading: "Alden's Premium Pictures, Taken in Barnum's Museum, New York City. Branch rooms, summer season, at Saratoga Springs." It was probably taken about 1870 in Barnum's third museum, on Fourteenth Street.

ABOVE RIGHT: A wood engraving by N. Orr & Co., drawn by W. M. Cary "from photograph of group by Gurney," entitled "The Curbstone Singers." This was one of the illustrations in *The Mysteries and Miseries of the Great Metropolis,* by "A.P.," the Amateur Vagabond (New York, D. Appleton & Co., 1874).

LEFT: A wood engraving of "Captain James Price.—[Photographed by Rockwood.]" from Jacob Abbott's article, "The Ocean Steamer," in *Harper's Magazine,* July, 1870. Price was captain of the Atlantic passenger liner *Minnesota.*

Author's collection

Even the high-priced portrait painters had to work for a kind of photographic realism.

Metropolitan Museum of Art

When Eastman Johnson painted this group portrait of the Alfrederick Smith Hatch family in 1871 he received $1000 a head for every Hatch, including the newborn baby.

The Hatch residence, on Park Avenue at Thirty-seventh Street, was typical of the modern, well-to-do city house of the period. Mr. Hatch, seated right at the desk, was a member of the New York Stock Exchange and served as its president in 1883–84. His father, Dr. Horace Hatch, is shown reading a paper at left, just behind Mrs. Ruggles, the mother of Mrs. Hatch (at the fireplace).

In the midst of all the changes and "improvements" a few artists . . .

New-York Historical Society

Both drawings from Museum of the City of New York

. . . explored the charm of the city's vanishing past . . .

Author's collection

Dry-point etching of "The Old Beach House Cor. Cedar & Greenwich St" by Henry Farrer, 1874 (reproduced same size as original).

Farrer came to New York from England in 1861, at the age of seventeen, and soon took up marine and landscape painting in water color. His etchings of the city, which he began to produce in the seventies, were among his most popular works.

OPPOSITE: The pen and ink drawings reproduced on the facing page were made by Eliza Greatorex, a former governess, widow of an eminent organist, and first woman to become an associate of the National Academy of Design. Her sketches of old landmarks and houses were later etched by H. Thatcher and published in a volume entitled *Old New York from the Battery to Bloomingdale* with text by M. Despard (New York, G. P. Putnam, 1875). The one above, dated 1856, shows the old pear tree, planted by Peter Stuyvesant in 1644, which stood at the corner of Third Avenue and East Thirteenth Street until it was finally removed in 1867. The panel from a stereoscopic photograph by Anthony also shows the venerable tree, as it was about 1865. The drawing below, dated 1867, is of Bloomingdale Village. The Reformed Church, demolished two years later, stood on the old Bloomingdale Road (now Broadway) at about Sixty-eighth Street.

. . . but the dominant note of prosperous activity was set . . .

ABOVE: "Along the Docks, New York City," was drawn by A. R. Waud and published as a double-page wood engraving in *Harper's Weekly,* September 4, 1869. The view shows the docks along West Street, looking north from Rector. The side-wheeler *Stonington* (upper left) was originally one of Daniel Drew's vessels. Jubilee Jim Fisk, Jr., made his first New York appearance as negotiator of the purchase of this and other ships by a Boston firm.

RIGHT: Another in *Harper's Weekly's* series of pictures "Along the Docks of New York," from the issue of February 11, 1871. Drawn by G. Reynolds (whose signature is reversed in the engraving), it shows a coffee stand at 82 Cortlandt Street, just around the corner from West Street.

Both pictures from New York Public Library

. . . by the journalistic wood engravings in the illustrated weeklies.

BROADWAY, FEBRUARY, 1868.—[DRAWN BY W. S. L. JEWETT.]

Both pictures from author's collection

"Broadway, February, 1868," drawn by W. S. L. Jewett, was published in *Harper's Weekly,* February 15, 1868. The journalistic, "reportorial" quality of the illustration is amusingly confirmed by the picture below, which appeared in the *Weekly* five weeks later (March 21).

ARREST OF PLACARD-BEARERS.—[SKETCHED BY R. WEIR.]

Here, in a wood engraving from a sketch by R. Weir, we see the arrest of a group of men who, as the accompanying story tells us, had been "employed by a certain class of advertisers to carry their placards about the streets," obstructing the sidewalks and becoming a public nuisance. At the head of the group is the fellow with a stuffed glove on his cap who had appeared in Jewett's earlier drawing, to the right of the old gentleman with the flowing beard.

Uptown and downtown, East Side and West Side, the magazines' roving artist correspondents . . .

THE MORNING WALK—YOUNG LADIES' SCHOOL PROMENADING THE AVENUE.—DRAWN BY WINSLOW HOMER.—[SEE PAGE 202.]

Both pictures from author's collection

Winslow Homer's drawing of "The Morning Walk—Young Ladies School Promenading the Avenue" was published in *Harper's Weekly,* March 28, 1868. The text informs us that "these young and beautiful representatives" of one of the city's well-known and fashionable boarding schools are taking their daily after-breakfast walk along Fifth Avenue at Madison Square, "under the lead of the teacher." The contrasting pictures of hot-weather refreshments "In Broadway" and "In the Bowery" were drawn by Thomas Hogan and published in the *Weekly,* August 15 ,1868. "Every citizen of New York will recognize instantly the accuracy of the picture," the *Weekly* said, and "nothing could more clearly convey to the minds of the thousands of distant readers, who are always wishing to know more about New York, the vast difference between the two great streets, and the two great classes of the metropolis."

IN BROADWAY.

IN THE BOWERY.

. . . sketched characteristic scenes of life in the city's streets . . .

SCENE IN PRINTING-HOUSE SQUARE, NEW YORK CITY.—Sketched by Stanley Fox.

Both pictures from author's collection

This "Scene in Printing House Square," from *Harper's Weekly,* July 25, 1868, was sketched by Stanley Fox, one of the regular staff of the magazine's artist correspondents. "Immediately in front of the *Times* and *Tribune* offices," the accompanying text reported, "there are to be found on all days and almost at all hours, a motley congregation of street peddlars, auctioneers, etc., and their customers."

DUMPING GROUND AT THE FOOT OF BEACH STREET, NEW YORK CITY.—[Sketched by Stanley Fox.]

LEFT: Fox's drawing of the "Dumping Ground at the Foot of Beach Street," from the *Weekly,* September 29, 1866, was described in the text as "a faithful picture representing an everyday scene at any of the great dumping grounds of the city. These nondescripts whom our artist has portrayed digging so busily and eagerly at this heap of rubbish live upon the refuse of respectable folk." The bones, coals, and rags they collected were sold for a "meagre pittance" which was promptly spent, the article reported, "for a little bread and as much bad whiskey as can be bought."

. . . *in the foundries and shipyards.*

CASTING OF THE ENORMOUS CYLINDER FOR MARINE ENGINE AT THE ETNA WORKS, NEW YORK CITY

P.M.S.S.C.
GREAT REPUBLIC
LAUNCH OF THE SEA STEAMER "GREAT REPUBLIC."—SKETCHED BY CHARLES PARSONS.

ABOVE: A. R. Waud's picture of the "Casting of the Enormous Cylinder for Marine Engine at the Etna Works" appeared in *Harper's Weekly,* March 3, 1866.

LEFT: Charles Parsons' sketch of the "Launch of the Sea Steamer 'Great Republic'" was the front-page illustration of the *Weekly* of November 24, 1866. The ship was built for the Pacific Mail Steamship Co. by Henry Steers at his shipyard in Greenpoint, across the river in Brooklyn. The *Great Republic* was the largest wooden merchant ship ever built up to that time. Her engines were built at the Novelty Iron Works.

Both pictures from author's collection

The city's "age of iron" had come, bringing with it potentialities for new urban forms . . .

Museum of the City of New York

One of the largest manufacturers of iron buildings in the fifties and sixties was D. D. Badger & Co., whose Architectural Iron Works on the southwest corner of Avenue C and Fourteenth Street (just south of present Stuyvesant Town) are shown above in a lithograph by Sarony, Major & Knapp. The lithograph was one of the illustrations in a catalogue of the firm, printed by Baker & Godwin (New York, 1865).

The anonymous lithograph at right, of about the same period, shows some of the Renaissance and Gothic forms into which their architectural iron was cast and wrought (see page 244 for the designs popular in iron construction a decade earlier). Badger's plant was taken over in the seventies by Hotchkiss, Field & Co.

Collection of Edward W. C. Arnold; photograph courtesy of Museum of the City of New York

. . . which were as yet barely discernible amid the confusion of images borrowed from the past.

Collection of Edward W. C. Arnold; photograph courtesy of the Museum of the City of New York

"The front of the building is wholly constructed of iron and glass, and is singularly imposing, somewhat resembling the entrance to a large gothic cathedral." Thus begins a contemporary magazine's description of the Grover & Baker Sewing Machine Co.'s new building at 495 Broadway, just north of Broome Street, shown here in a lithograph by Thomas & Eno, probably made in 1860—the year the building was completed.

For the city still liked to see itself,
part of the time at least,
as a quiet place of
churches and
schools . . .

Collection of Edward W. C. Arnold; photograph courtesy of Museum of the City of New York

The Church of the Transfiguration, now known to most New Yorkers as "The Little Church Around the Corner," is here shown in a lithograph from a painting by William D. Taillefer, about 1865. The church was erected in 1856 on the north side of Twenty-ninth Street, east of Fifth Avenue, and still stands.

This lithograph by F. Ratellier, from a drawing by Camille Dryer, shows Manhattan College (center) and the Church of the Annunciation on the west side of Broadway at 131st Street about 1867.

Founded as an academy in 1849, by the Catholic order of Brothers of the Christian Schools, the college occupied this site in Manhattanville from 1853 to 1923, when it moved to Spuyten Duyvil Parkway and 242nd Street in the Bronx. The original Academy of the Holy Infancy was incorporated as a college in 1863.

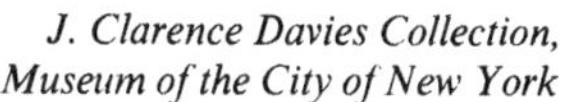

J. Clarence Davies Collection,
Museum of the City of New York

. . . where elegance and refinement were delightfully secure, and where even the harsh—and apparently inevitable—contrasts . . .

THE GRAND DRIVE, CENTRAL PARK N.Y.

Both pictures from J. Clarence Davies Collection, Museum of the City of New York

ABOVE: A Currier & Ives lithograph of "The Grand Drive, Central Park, New York," published in 1869.

RIGHT: The original pencil drawing, attributed to Thomas Worth, for the lithograph. The penciled notes at the bottom of the drawing instruct the lithographer to omit the figures on horseback "as this path only for pedestrians" and suggest the substitution of "Gents walking here also children."

. . . of poverty and wealth in the "iron age" could be softened by the glow of sentiment.

J. Clarence Davies Collection, Museum of the City of New York

"New Year's Eve," a lithograph drawn by F. Fuchs and published by Kimmel & Forster about 1865. The toy store was at the corner of Broadway and Canal Street.

Author's collection

Group Five

THE CITY IN MOTION 1870–1890

EIGHTEEN MILES AROUND NEW YORK.

In studying this Pictorial Map the spectator is supposed to be stationed somewhere in mid-air above Fort Hamilton, at the outlet of the Narrows, from which convenient height he can cast his eye over all the country lying within a radius of eighteen miles around New York. In the centre he will see the great metropolis, with its busy marts and wharves, its splendid Park, and the surrounding islands. On the right, the city of Brooklyn, and the towns lying eastward as far as Jamaica and Hempstead, and northward as far as New Rochelle, with the railroads that make them suburbs of New York, and the islands and headlands of the Sound. On the left he will see Staten Island, with its picturesque villas, Jersey City, Newark, and all the pleasant suburban villages and towns of New Jersey as far south as Perth Amboy, westward to West Orange, and northward to Caldwell and Paterson. Following the course of the Hudson, he will see all the towns and places of interest on its banks between New York and Yonkers, which can be reached either by railroad or by the various lines of steamboats that, during the spring, summer, and autumn months, enliven the surface of that river. Some of the most pleasant excursions that can be made are connected with places of picturesque or historic interest along these shores.

The map illustrates the growth of New York, and indicates what would have been the territorial extent of the metropolis of the Western World but for its cramped position between two wide and deep rivers. The surrounding cities and villages on each side in reality belong to New York, with which they are connected by means of transit so rapid that the merchant or broker doing business in the lower part of the town can reach his house in Orange, Elizabeth, College Point, Jamaica, or Hempstead in less time than the street cars or stages would take him to the region of Central Park. The completion of the Brooklyn Bridge will make the transit still more rapid and convenient on that side of the town, and at some future day a tunnel under the Hudson may do the same for the other.

"New York from a Balloon. Pictorial Map of New York and Vicinity, Showing the Suburban Towns, and Railroad and Water Communications," was published as a supplement to *Harper's Weekly,* May 6, 1871. In it, as the caption says, the spectator is supposed to be stationed somewhere in mid-air above Fort Hamilton, where he can see "what would have been the territorial extent of the metropolis of the Western World but for its cramped position between two wide and deep rivers."

New York's consolidation with Brooklyn was twenty-seven years away, and it would be three years yet before the city's boundaries were extended for the first time beyond the limits of Manhattan Island, by the annexation of Kingsbridge, West Farms, and Morrisania in what is now the Bronx. But as the map suggests, it was increasingly obvious that "the surrounding cities and villages on each side in reality belong to New York, with which they are connected by means of transit so rapid that the merchant or broker doing business in the lower part of the town can reach his house in Orange, Elizabeth, College Point, Jamaica, or Hempstead in less time than the street cars or stages would take him to the region of Central Park."

Incidentally, though Nadar in France had actually taken photographs from a balloon as early as 1858, this is of course a purely suppositious view. In that connection it is interesting to observe the exaggerated height of the church steeples.

Starting from an expansive over-all view of the thriving metropolis, the pictorial journalism of the eighteen-seventies . . .

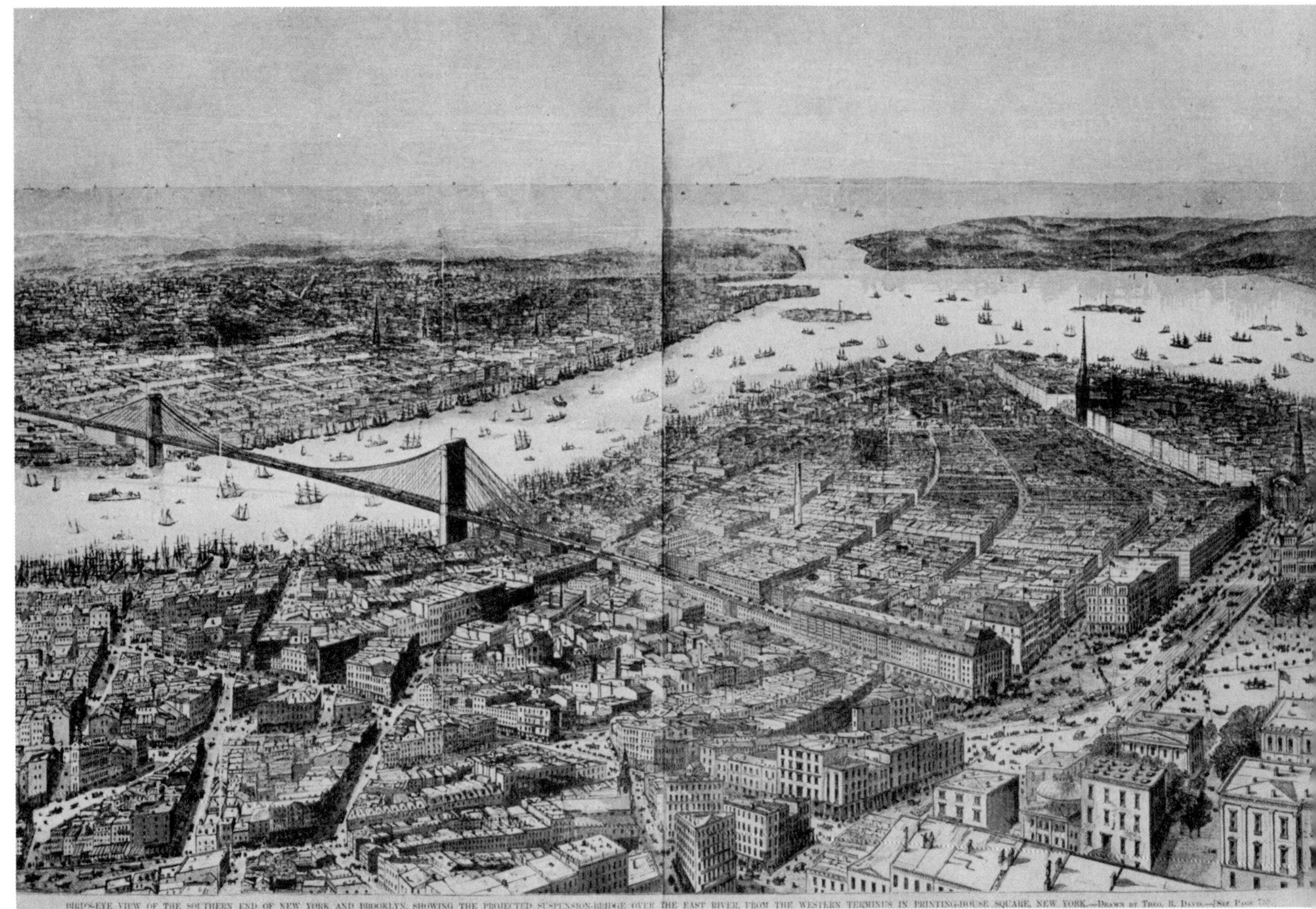

BIRD'S-EYE VIEW OF THE SOUTHERN END OF NEW YORK AND BROOKLYN, SHOWING THE PROJECTED SUSPENSION-BRIDGE OVER THE EAST RIVER, FROM THE WESTERN TERMINUS IN PRINTING-HOUSE SQUARE, NEW YORK.—Drawn by Theo. R. Davis.

Author's collection

In his "Bird's-Eye View of the Southern End of New York and Brooklyn," published in *Harper's Weekly,* November 19, 1870, Theodore R. Davis drew a completed Brooklyn Bridge though work on the first of its two towers had scarcely begun (see page 338) and the bridge would not be finished for thirteen years. The point was, of course, that in the expansive optimism of the period any over-all view of the metropolitan area required the bridge to exist. And since one was imagining what the city looked like from the air, why not imagine it as it was sure to be?

The supposed point of view is somewhere above the present intersection of Worth and Lafayette streets, looking southwest. Duane Street runs from center foreground past St. Andrew's Catholic Church (corner of Cardinal Place) to the intersection of Chambers Street and Chatham Street (now Park Row). Left of Duane and almost parallel is Baxter, and between them the slums of the Five Points region. In the right foreground is the eastern end of the scandalous County Court House built by the Tweed Ring, and beyond it a part of City Hall. The tall Shot Tower, right of mid-center, was on the north side of Beekman, between Cliff and Gold streets.

. . . moves down into the heart of the city and shows us how it works. We are taken inside a newspaper's plant . . .

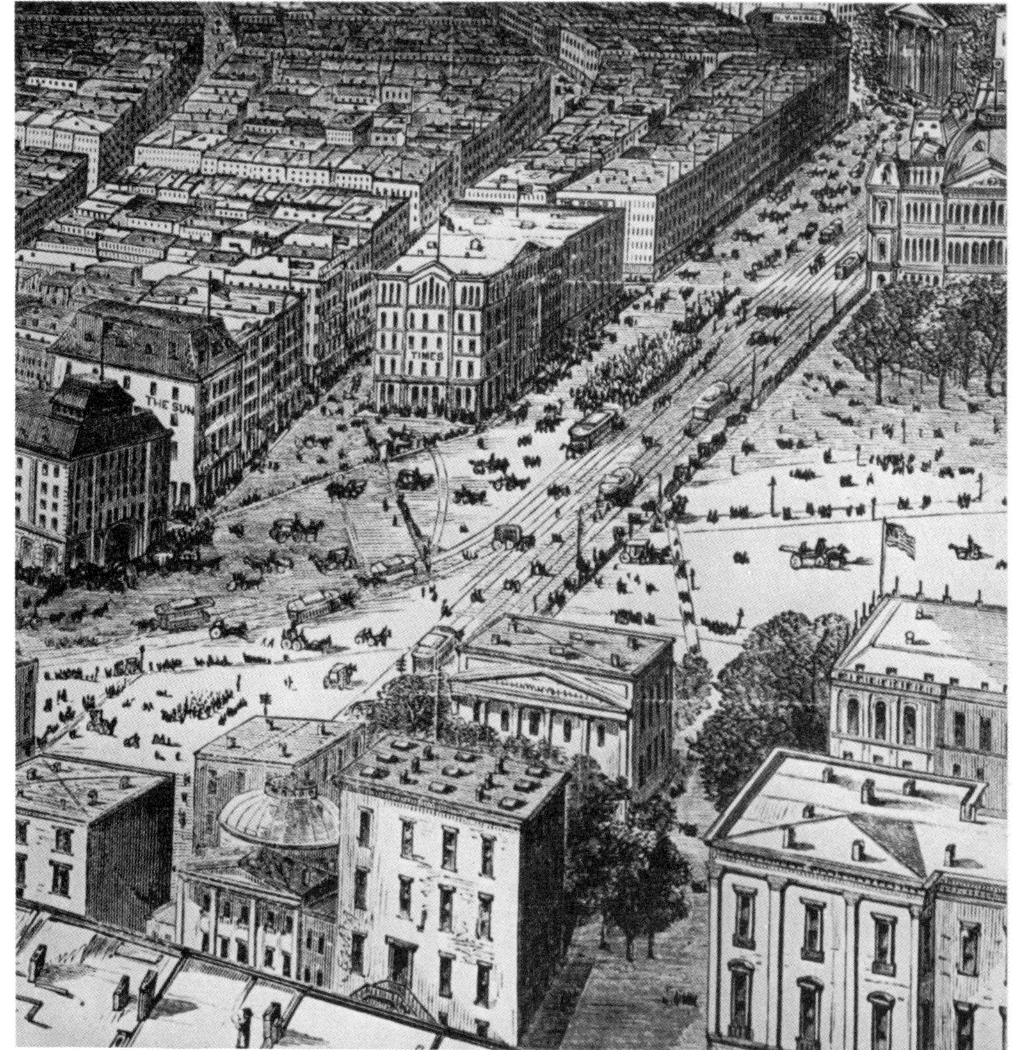

All pictures from author's collection

LEFT: An enlarged detail of the lower right corner of the large view on page 332, showing Printing House Square, with offices of the *Sun, Tribune, Times,* and *World* (see page 302).

In 1868 the New York *Sun* moved into the old Tammany Hall building at the corner of Park Row and Frankfort Street (see page 137), which had been enlarged and modernized the previous year. The illustrations below, and those on the following page, are from an eight-page "institutional" advertisement called "The New York Sun; its Rise, Progress, Character, and Condition," written by Oliver Dyer and published in the back advertising pages of *Harper's Magazine,* March, 1870. "When one enters the first floor corner door of the spacious and elegant edifice . . . he finds himself in the Publication Office," Dyer wrote, ". . . presenting an animated spectacle which is fairly represented in the picture of the scene." The wood engravings were made by the N. Orr Co.

THE SUN BUILDING.

PUBLICATION OFFICE.

. . . and see the editors, compositors, and pressmen turning out their "daily photograph of the whole world's doings."

EDITORIAL ROOMS.—PREPARING "COPY."

All pictures from author's collection

Step by step the *Sun's* advertisement described, in picture and text, the process of publishing a metropolitan daily. In the cuts reproduced here we see the office of the managing editor (who served also as city editor) on the third floor; the composing room on the top floor; and the press room in the basement. The three Bullock presses were the foreman's pride and joy—"just as snug and tidy as a woman," he told Dyer, as he laid his hand affectionately on one of them, "and a deal easier to manage."

This use of a sequence of pictures to illustrate a process is an early example of a technique which was rapidly developed during the seventies. Interest in the journalistic use of pictures went hand in hand with an increasing sense of the importance of the pictorial quality in journalism itself. In Charles A. Dana's statement of the *Sun's* policy, shortly after he acquired control of the thirty-five-year-old paper in 1868, he had said: "It will study condensation, clearness, point, and will endeavor to present *its daily photograph of the whole world's doings* in the most luminous and lively manner." [Author's italics.]

COMPOSING ROOM.—SETTING UP THE NEWS.

PRESS ROOM.—PRINTING OFF THE EDITION.

Or we visit one of the great commercial exchanges . . .

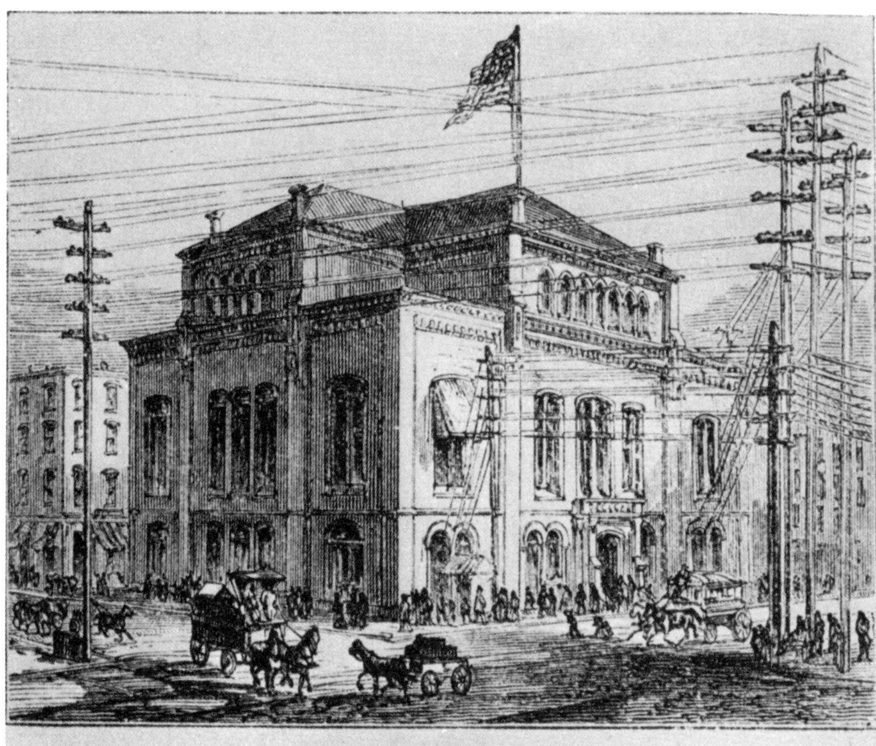

CORN AND PRODUCE EXCHANGE BUILDING.

Both pictures from author's collection

These pictures were among the illustrations for an article on "The Corn and Produce Exchange" in *Harper's Magazine,* September, 1877. The building stood on Whitehall Street, between Pearl and Water streets, where the U. S. Army building now stands. Along with the Iron Exchange, the Cotton Exchange, and the Barge Office, it was one of the great centers of the city's exporting business. (In 1882 the exchange moved to the building it now occupies, farther up Whitehall Street at Bowling Green.)

The picture below shows the brokers and shippers examining samples of the flour, grain, and other produce offered for sale, while others are bidding for carload lots.

PRODUCE EXCHANGE.

. . . and follow step by step the various processes . . .

LOADING FROM A FLOATING ELEVATOR.

BETWEEN DECKS—RECEIVING CARGO.

These pictures of a floating grain elevator loading a ship in New York Harbor were among the illustrations for an article by Ernest Ingersoll on "The Lading of a Ship," *Harper's Magazine,* September, 1877.

In the upper picture the elevator is transferring wheat from an Erie Canal barge to an oceangoing freighter. At left, men on the freighter bag the wheat for stowing below decks.

Both pictures from author's collection

. . . involved in handling the city's domestic and foreign commerce.

LEFT: "A Scene at the Atlantic Docks, Brooklyn," drawn by Reynolds and engraved by Richardson, was published in *Appleton's Journal,* April 1, 1871.

BELOW: The stereoscopic photograph "Looking Along the Docks, from Fulton Market, showing floating Grain Elevators," was made by E. & H. T. Anthony about 1870.

Fascination with the pictorial values of such industrial forms is a notable feature of the pictures of the seventies. But the fascination is a curious mixture of admiration and dread. The text accompanying the wood engraving from *Appleton's,* for example, tells us that the site of the Atlantic Docks, once a desolate swamp, is now "beautiful, for ships and cargoes can never be otherwise," and the elevator itself is delighted in for its "slanting roof and bulging sides . . . ancient and Dutch like, with a breadth of Amsterdam in its general appearance." Yet the subsequent description of loading operations emphasizes the "diabolical" quality of the vast machines, their "metallic grind" and ceaseless jarring, in "a great struggle, a battle, a fight rather with a nightmare than with an enemy in the open field."

Author's collection

Museum of the City of New York

We see how the great engineering achievements of the time are carried out . . .

THE BROOKLYN PIER—GENERAL VIEW OF FOUNDATION.

ABOVE: A "general view" of the construction work on the foundation of the Brooklyn pier of the Brooklyn Bridge, from *Harper's Weekly,* December 17, 1870.

Both pictures from author's collectio

BELOW: A "sectional view," from the same issue, showing what was going on below the surface. In both views we are looking west across the river toward Manhattan, with Trinity Church just left of the left-hand derrick mast.

FOUNDATION LINE
SECTIONAL VIEW OF FOUNDATION, SHOWING CAISSON AND MASON-WORK.

The two smallest shafts in the sectional view were supply shafts through which cement, gravel, and sand would be passed, after the excavation was complete, to fill the entire space. The medium-sized shafts were the air shafts through which laborers descended from the large cylindrical air locks into the working pit. The large excavating shafts at the sides were filled with water which acted as a gauge, indicating the amount of air pressure being maintained by the pumps in the caisson where the men were working.

. . . and we are shown what is happening to the children of the city's poor.

All pictures from author's collection

ABOVE: Two illustrations from an article on "The Little Laborers of New York" by Charles Loring Brace, *Harper's Magazine,* August, 1873. More than 100,000 minor children were employed in factories in and around the city. The Children's Aid Society maintained night schools "where boys and girls who labor all day can acquire a little education at night." There were already, Brace noted, more than 60,000 New Yorkers who could neither read nor write and child labor threatened to "swell this ignorant throng."

BELOW: Two illustrations from an article by B. K. Peirce on the "New York House of Refuge," *Appleton's Journal,* March 18, 1871. Both were drawn by Cary and engraved by J. Filmer. The institution was a model one, for its time, and people came from all over the world to study its methods of rehabilitating juvenile delinquents. But only 700 boys and girls were under its hospitable roof in 1871, while an estimated 10,000 were "adrift in the streets"—destitute, begging, and prowling in gangs.

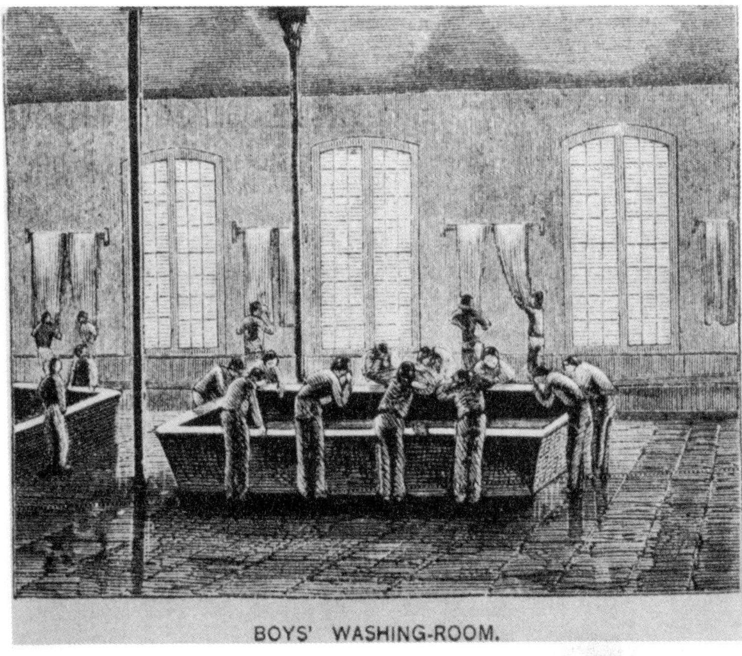

We go backstage at the theater to see how a play is put on . . .

RIGHT: A wood engraving from a photograph by Rockwood of Edwin Booth's new theater at the corner of Sixth Avenue and Twenty-third Street, from *Harper's Weekly*, January 9, 1869. Designed by Renwick and Sands, this was the most elaborate theater yet built in the city, and was equipped with the latest "machinery." But the theater was not a successful venture, and in 1883 it was converted into stores.

BELOW: Two illustrations, drawn by A. C. Warren and engraved by J. Filmer, for O. B. Bunce's article, "Behind, Below, and Above the Scenes [at Booth's]," *Appleton's Journal*, May 28, 1870.

BOOTH'S NEW THEATRE, TWENTY-THIRD STREET AND SIXTH AVENUE, NEW YORK.—PHOTOGRAPHED BY ROCKWOOD.—[SEE PAGE 21.]

FLY-GALLERY.

All pictures from author's collection

THE STAGE—SETTING THE SCENES.

. . . and climb a fire tower with the watchman on duty guarding the city against disaster.

This full-page spread of pictures of the "Watch-Tower, Corner of Spring and Varick Streets, New York," was drawn by Winslow Homer for *Harper's Weekly,* February 28, 1874.

The tower, built for the city in 1853 by James Bogardus, was the second iron structure of the sort. The first, uptown at Thirty-third Street, had been erected in 1851 after several wooden towers had burned.

Thomas F. Healy Collection; photograph courtesy of Museum of the City of New York

Everything was grist to the journalist illustrator's mill: people in the city's markets and restaurants . . .

Jules Tavernier's drawing of "Washington Market, New York—Thanksgiving Time," engraved by Lagarde, was published in *Harper's Weekly's* Supplement, November 30, 1872. Though the market was nothing but a collection "of low, straggling sheds, divided into irregular lanes and stalls, where order is impossible and cleanliness nearly so," it was nevertheless, as the text indicated, the "chief center whence New York, Brooklyn, and Jersey City draw their market supplies."

BELOW: C. S. Reinhart's drawing of "The Lunch Counter" is reproduced from a wood engraving in *Harper's Weekly*, September 27, 1873.

Both pictures from author's collection

. . . in the fashionable stores and parks, or scrabbling for a handout to keep themselves alive.

New York Public Library

LEFT: Wood engraving from a drawing by Hyde, published in *Frank Leslie's Illustrated Newspaper*, January 11, 1873, showing "Ladies Ascending in the Elevator" at Lord & Taylor's new store, Broadway and Twentieth Street, on opening day.

BELOW LEFT: C. S. Reinhart's "Scene in Union Square" was one of the illustrations for William H. Rideing's "Life on Broadway," *Harper's Magazine*, January, 1878.

BELOW RIGHT: A wood engraving from a sketch by C. A. Keetels, entitled "Helping the Poor—Gratuitous Distribution of Coal by the City—Scene in Cherry Street," published in *Harper's Weekly*, March 10, 1877.

Author's collection

Author's collection

With increasing mobility, both physical and social, went a relaxation of older standards of propriety and morality . . .

Author's collection

E. A. Abbey's drawing of "The Summer Exodus—Leaving by Steamboat" is reproduced from a wood engraving in *Harper's Weekly,* August 24, 1872. It was increasingly fashionable to go away for the summer, though the *Weekly* had reservations about life away from city comforts. "The poetry of country life exists, indeed, chiefly in the imagination," it said, "except where there is sufficient wealth to ingraft city convenience upon the rural retreat."

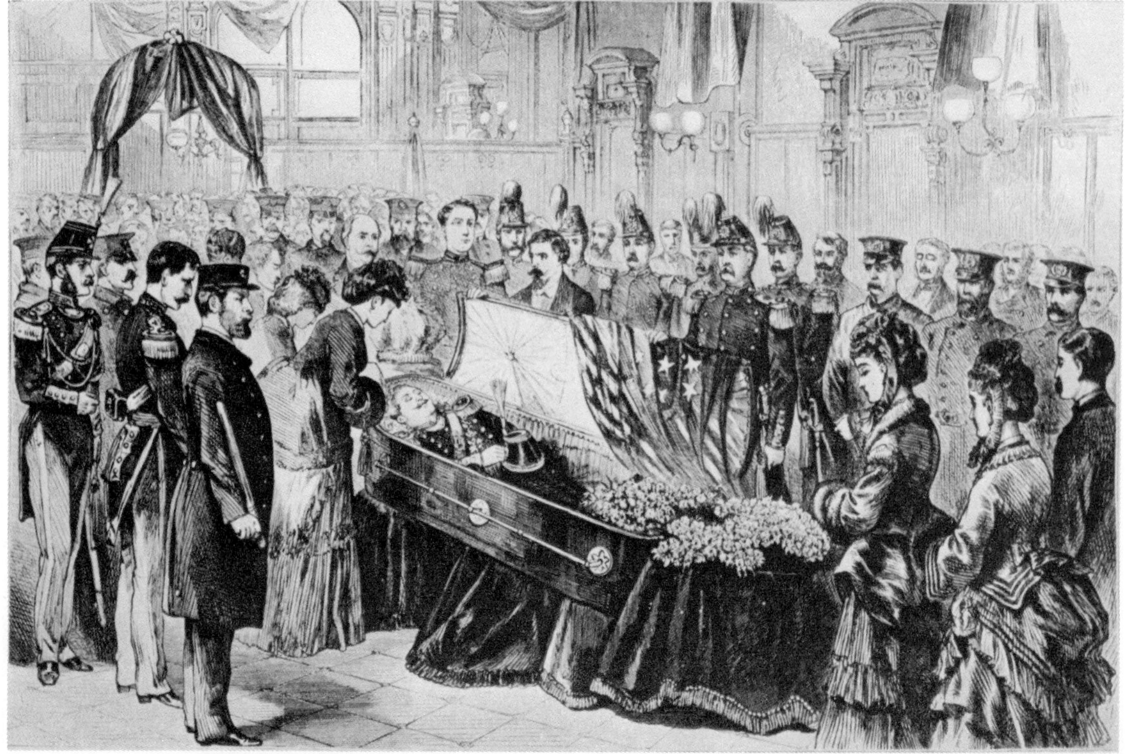

A country boy who enjoyed urban conveniences to the free-spending limit was Colonel Jim Fisk, Jr., shown here in his coffin after having been shot by Edward Stokes. The picture, which was published in *Frank Leslie's Illustrated Newspaper,* January 27, 1872, shows Fisk lying in state in the Erie Railroad's offices in the Grand Opera House, Eighth Avenue and Twenty-third Street.

New York Public Library

. . . and city life, from a distance at least, looked increasingly exciting.

LEFT: A wood engraving from the *National Police Gazette,* July 26, 1879, illustrating a "moral" tale about a young lady-killer who "was taken in and done for, like the veriest countryman, by a brace of sharp damsels and their male accomplice."

BELOW: "Inside Harry Hill's Dance-House" was one of the illustrations in Matthew Hale Smith's *Sunshine and Shadow in New York* (Hartford, 1868)—one of a numerous crop of books purporting to give the real, behind-the-scenes dope on the city's virtues and (more to the point) vices. Hill's place, on Houston Street near Broadway, was for many years one of the best publicized concert saloons in New York. As Smith described it, it was "a reputable vile house," where "the élite of the women of the town" mixed with judges, lawyers, merchants, politicians, doctors, and other professional men.

Both pictures from author's collection

It was during the seventies that the florid and tantalizing imagery of "the wicked city" was fixed in the popular mind . . .

THE HUSBAND

THE WIFE.

MARRIED LIFE IN NEW YORK

George Ellington's book on *The Women of New York* (New York, 1870), from which both of these pictures are reproduced, was one of many publications which exploited the glamorous aspects of the city's wickedness. "In it," Ellington's preface announces (and you can almost hear the lips smack), "the women of the Metropolis are boldly and truthfully unveiled." The "exposures" are made, of course, in the interests of reform, and in hopes that the women of the city "may yet become as celebrated for their virtues as those of rural districts throughout the land."

The married women of the city are responsible, we are told, "for an immense amount of the wickedness done in Gotham." As for the female models, with their "particularly beautiful limbs" and "busts of unusual magnificence," there are hints of all sorts of scandals about "the delicate relations in which they stand to their artistic employers."

THE ARTIST'S STUDIO.

Both pictures from Museum of the City of New York

. . . not, as a matter of fact, without some justification.

Collection of Edward W. C. Arnold; photograph courtesy of Museum of the City of New York

J. Clarence Davies Collection, Museum of the City of New York

The lithograph above, drawn by L. Geissler and printed by the Eno Lith. Co., is from the sheet-music cover of the "Marche D'Aika Amazonian" published in 1868 by Dodworth & Son. The picture represents a scene in "The White Fawn," a musical spectacle produced at Niblo's Garden that season. Even the rather sedate George Templeton Strong went to see this "most showy, and least draped, specimen of what may be called the *Feminine-Femoral* School of Dramatic Art," which drew as bitter denunciations from the pulpit—and as large and enthusiastic audiences—as its predecessor, "The Black Crook," of two seasons before.

The photolithograph of "Fifth Avenue four years after Madame Restell's death" was published in *Puck,* the humorous weekly, April 17, 1878. (There was a German-language edition of *Puck,* as well as the regular English edition, and it was the former from which this copy of the cartoon is taken.) Madame Restell was a notorious abortionist who grew wealthy serving—and blackmailing—some of the city's "best families." When Anthony Comstock, the famous vice crusader, finally succeeded in having her arrested in 1878, she committed suicide.

Walt Whitman had some reason for his assertion in *Democratic Vistas* (1871) that beneath "the glow and grandeur" on the surface, New York's social life was pervaded with "flippancy and vulgarity, low cunning, infidelity . . . everywhere an abnormal libidinousness, unhealthy forms . . . the capacity for good motherhood deceasing or deceas'd."

But the city was not so wicked as it sometimes looked . . .

A. T. Stewart's Frauen-Hotel, oder: Wohlthun trägt Zinsen.

J. Clarence Davies Collection, Museum of the City of New York

The cartoon above, a photolithograph from *Puck's* German-language edition, refers to the hotel for working women which A. T. Stewart began shortly before his death as a philanthropic attempt to provide decent homes for "respectable females." Stewart's executor opened the hotel, on the west side of Park Avenue between Thirty-second and Thirty-third streets, in April, 1878. But the rules imposed on lodgers were so severe, and the prices so high, that the "philanthropic" scheme failed after two months. The executor reopened the building as the Park Avenue Hotel, which it remained until torn down in 1927 to make way for the 2 Park Avenue office building.

Author's collection

The wood engraving at right, from *Harper's Magazine,* April, 1871, was one of the illustrations for W. O. Stoddard's article on "The Bowery, Saturday Night." It shows the interior of the Atlantic Garden, one of the most celebrated of the Bowery beer gardens, on the night of September 10, 1870, when the German clientele was celebrating the Battle of Sedan. Even on this occasion, Stoddard says, nobody got drunk; and on ordinary nights the crowd was "so quiet over its beer and wine as to seem almost stupid."

. . . and many of its citizens were doing their best to make it a decenter place in which to live.

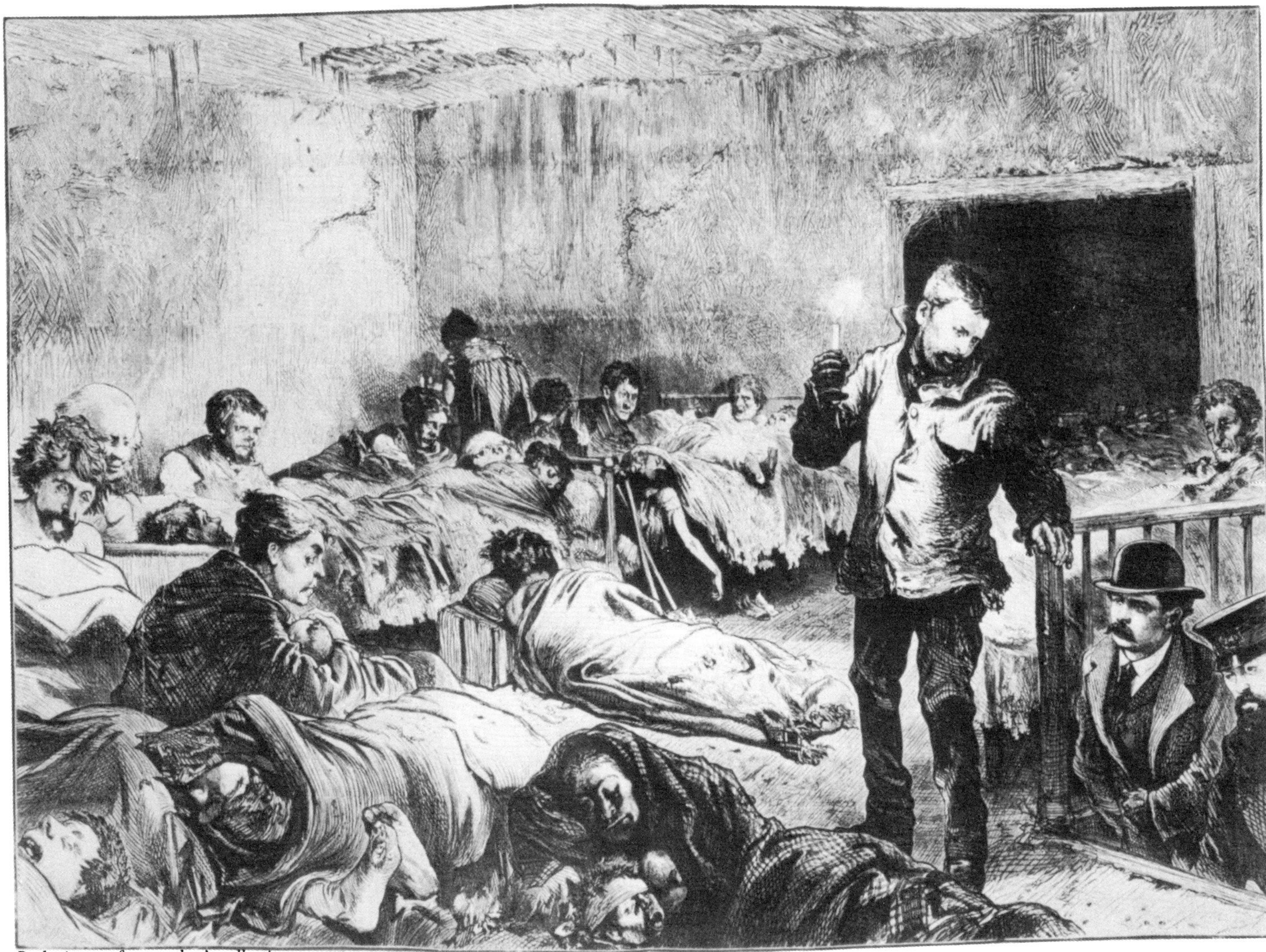

Both pictures from author's collection

GENERAL VIEW OF BUILDINGS — IN COURSE OF ERECTION ON 71ST & 72ND STS. & 1ST AVE. N.Y. — FOR THE IMPROVED DWELLINGS ASSOCIATION

Concern with "how the other half lives" became general in the seventies, and the phrase itself was used as the subtitle of a series of illustrated articles on "Our Homeless Poor" which was published in *Frank Leslie's Illustrated Newspaper* in 1872 (eighteen years before Jacob Riis used it as the title of his famous book). The wood engraving above, drawn "from life" by Matt Morgan, appeared in the issue of March 9, and was entitled "A Midnight Visit to one of the Cheap Lodging Houses in Water Street."

The first law regulating tenement houses had been passed in 1867, and a second law, with stronger provisions, was passed in 1879. The Improved Dwellings Association, one of several early organizations devoted to finding practical solutions for the problem, built the model tenement shown at left in 1880. Designed by Vaux and Radford, whose perspective drawing of the building is here reproduced, the houses are still standing on First Avenue, north of Seventy-first Street (see page 483).

The symbolic achievement of the period was the Brooklyn Bridge, from whose towers . . .

Author's collection

The wood engraving at right is one of W. P. Snyder's illustrations for W. C. Conant's article on "The Brooklyn Bridge," *Harper's Magazine,* May, 1883. It shows Mr. E. F. Farrington, one of Washington Roebling's chief aides, making the test trip across the East River on the first loop of cable to be strung between the two towers, August 25, 1876.

To the accompaniment of booming cannon, shrieking steam whistles, and shouts of applause from the spectators he was swept across the river, "to all appearances self-propelled," and then swept back again. Round trip: twenty-two minutes.

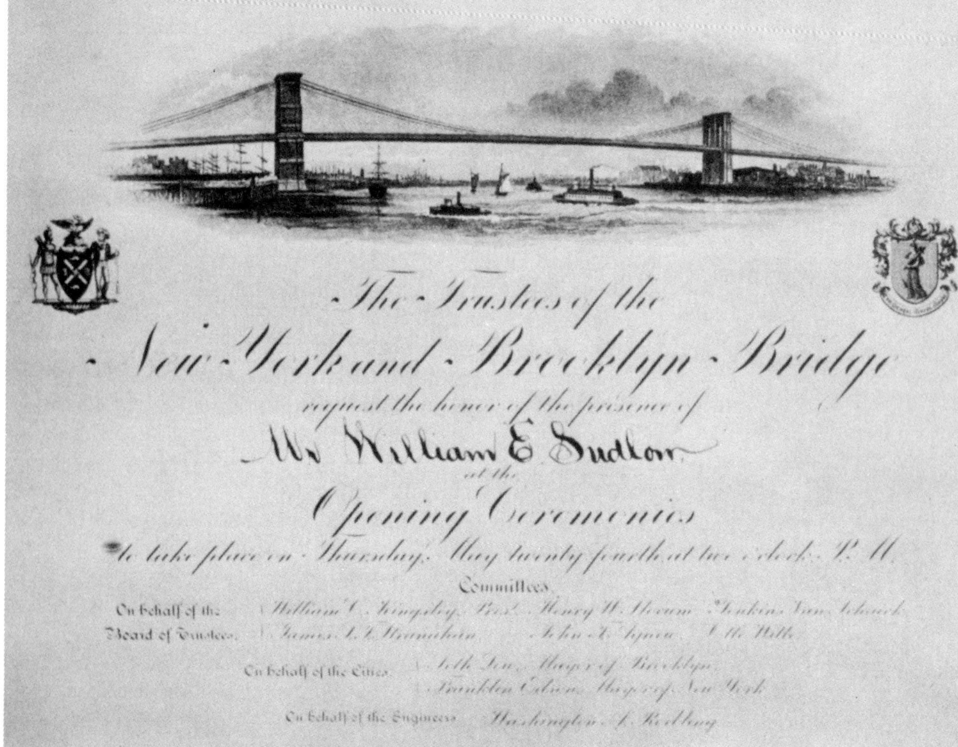

The Trustees of the
New York and Brooklyn Bridge
request the honor of the presence of
Mr William E Sudlow
at the
Opening Ceremonies
to take place on Thursday, May twenty fourth at two o'clock P. M.

Committees.

On behalf of the Board of Trustees. William C. Kingsley, Pres. Henry W. Slocum Jenkins Van Schaick
James S. T. Stranahan John T. Agnew Otto Witte

On behalf of the Cities. Seth Low, Mayor of Brooklyn.
Franklin Edson, Mayor of New York

On behalf of the Engineers Washington A. Roebling

The bridge was formally opened to traffic May 24, 1883, with appropriate ceremonies.

Collection of Allen S. Davenport

. . . one could almost get the bird's-eye views of the city which people had so often imagined.

Museum of the City of New York

Brooklyn Museum

One of the most remarkable photographic panoramas of the city (above) was taken from the Brooklyn tower of the bridge early in 1876 by J. H. Beals. Taken on five separate negatives, which fit together with astonishing precision, the panorama is over seven feet long and shows the city from the Battery to Rutgers Street. Beals also took a fifteen-plate panorama of the city from a Jersey City hotel at about this same period.

LEFT: George B. Brainerd's photograph of Brooklyn from the bridge tower was made about the same time. In it we are looking down on the intersection of Front, Dock, and James streets (shown in Guy's painting of Front Street, page 108, a half century earlier). The foundation of the approach to the bridge is just right of center, in the bed of James Street. At right, Fulton Street enters the picture just above the middle and then curves south at its intersection with Main Street.

RIGHT: An anonymous photograph of lower New York from the Manhattan tower of the bridge, taken about 1879.

Brown Brothers

It was a time when everyone was going someplace . . .

Both pictures from J. Clarence Davies Collection, Museum of the City of New Yor

A pair of chromolithograph cartoons by William Bruns, published in 1882: "Are you Going Far?—Not Far . . . Only to this Car! Ta! Ta!"

BELOW: Timetable card of the steamer *City of Richmond* (1881), lithographed by Meyer, Merkel, & Ottman. Long Branch had been a popular summer resort for many years, and had attracted increasing numbers after President Grant built his "summer White House" there in 1870.

Collection of H. Armour Smit

EXPRESS BOAT

NEW YORK AND LONG BRANCH.

THREE DAILY TRIPS. DIRECT TO THE OCEAN PIER.

City of Richmond

LEAVE NEW YORK, PIER 3 N.R.
5.00 & 11.00 A.M. 3.45 P.M.
SUNDAYS FOOT WEST 20TH ST. 8.30 A.M. 1.30 P.M.
PIER 3 N.R. 9.00 A.M. 2.00 P.M.

THE ENTIRELY NEW & FAST STEAMER,
City of Richmond.

LEAVE LONG BRANCH OCEAN PIER.
7.45 A.M. 1.15 & 6.15 P.M.
SUNDAYS 11.30 A.M. & 5.00 P.M.

. . . or arriving from somewhere . . .

INSPECTION OF CABIN PASSENGERS' BAGGAGE ON THE DOCK.

Author's collection

LANDING IMMIGRANTS AT CASTLE GARDEN.

Author's collection

The wood engravings above were among the illustrations for an article on "The New York Custom-House," by R. Wheatley, *Harper's Magazine,* June, 1884. The "Inspection of Cabin Passengers' Baggage on the Dock," drawn by W. A. Rogers and engraved by Pettit, shows passengers from the Cunard liner *Servia.* The other, "Landing Immigrants at Castle Garden," was drawn by Schell & Hogan and engraved by W. R. Brighton. During the five years 1880–84 almost 2,000,000 alien immigrants arrived at New York. Though many of them stayed in the metropolitan area (of the city's 1,209,561 people in 1880, the census counted only 727,000 as native), thousands went west. The cash value of railroad tickets sold to immigrants at the Castle Garden Depot in 1881 was more than $5,000,000.

LEFT: A photograph taken in 1888 by Breading G. Way, showing an excursion boat leaving her pier near the foot of Montague Street in Brooklyn. The crowds on the waterfront and the flags suggest some special celebration.

Brooklyn Museum

. . . or just enjoying motion for its own sake.

"Summer Diversions at the Seaside.—A Coasting Party at Coney Island—'More Scared than Hurt'" is a wood engraving "from a Sketch by a Staff Artist" which was published in *Frank Leslie's Illustrated Newspaper,* July 24, 1886. This first of all roller coasters had been built in 1884 by Lamarcus A. Thompson, a Sunday school teacher from Elkhart, Indiana, and was an immediate success. Within a few years Thompson and rival manufacturers were making improved models for amusement parks all over the United States and Europe.

New York Public Library

Members of the Kings County Wheelmen in front of their clubhouse at 1255 Bedford Avenue (between Fulton and Herkimer streets) in Brooklyn, 1889. (Photographer unidentified.)

New-York Historical Society

Everything was in transit,
it sometimes
seemed.

New-York Historical Society

ABOVE: Unattributed photograph of the temporary railroad trestle between 100th and 116th streets, built by McIntire Bros. about 1874 for use while the Fourth (now Park) Avenue improvement was under construction.
BELOW: Two photographs of the Brighton Beach Hotel being moved back 1500 feet from the waterfront at Coney Island in 1890. The picture at right was taken by Breading G. Way; the other is unidentified.

New-York Historical Society

Brooklyn Museum

In striking contrast with the air of planted solidity which was achieved in the architecture of the time . . .

J. Clarence Davies Collection, Museum of the City of New York

Courtesy of the New York Telephone Company

The Grand Union Hotel, like the Grand Central Depot, was typical of the massive-mansard architectural taste of the early seventies. (The wood engraving, from a drawing by L. Oram, was published about 1885.) The St. Denis, at the corner of Broadway and Eleventh Street (shown here in a lithograph by Armstrong & Co., about 1875), and the Hotel Martin (shown in a lithograph by J. Vitou & Cie, published in France) were of an earlier period. It was in the second-floor corner "parlor room" of the St. Denis, on the evening of May 11, 1877, that Alexander Graham Bell introduced his "speaking telephone" to a New York audience, gathered at the invitation of President F. A. P. Barnard of Columbia.

Museum of the City of New York

Collection of Edward W. C. Arnold; photograph courtesy of Museum of the City of New York

. . . was the aerial lightness of the disorderly web of wires . . .

New-York Historical Society

Three months after Bell's first New York demonstration of his telephone (see previous page) there were five instruments in service in the city, and the first New York telephone directory—listing 252 subscribers—was published the following year. The Bell Company opened the first exchange, at 82 Nassau Street, in March, 1879.

By 1880, when this lithograph by J. J. Fogerty was published, the confusion of telegraph and telephone wires in the business district had become a prominent feature in pictures of the city streets. This view shows Broadway, looking north from Cortlandt Street (left) and Maiden Lane (right). The Western Union building on the northwest corner of Dey Street had been built in 1872–75.

. . . that soon stretched, even more delicate than the cables of the bridge, through the city's streets.

Brown Brothers

Brown Brothers

UPPER LEFT: Fifth Avenue, looking north from Forty-second Street, about 1880. On the right, northeast corner of Forty-third Street, is Temple Emanu-El, erected in 1868 from designs by Leopold Eidlitz. Note the single telephone wire at left. UPPER RIGHT: Looking north on Fifth Avenue from Madison Square, about 1884. Notice the line of telegraph poles by-passing Fifth and running up Broadway. The Statue of Liberty's arm and torch had been set up in Madison Square after being exhibited at the Centennial in Philadelphia (compare later view on page 406). LOWER LEFT: Broad Street, looking south from Wall Street, in 1885. The square tower is that of the new Produce Exchange (see page 335). The Drexel Building, headquarters of J. P. Morgan, is on corner at left, and the Stock Exchange at right. LOWER RIGHT: The southwest corner of Fulton Street and Broadway in 1888 (see page 195 for a view of this neighborhood forty years earlier).

J. Clarence Davies Collection, Museum of the City of New York

Brown Brothers

It was the preoccupation with rapid transit during the seventies and eighties . . .

Author's collection

To many New Yorkers the poles and wires were hideous symbols of changes they did not like. This sketch by Johnston shows the old mansion at the corner of Bridge and State streets, erected about 1804 by Archibald Gracie (whose country estate on the East River at Eighty-eighth Street is now the mayor's official residence). It was one of a series of drawings by members of the newly founded Architectural League, published as illustrations for Richard Grant White's "Old New York and its Houses" in the *Century Magazine*, October, 1883. "Look at it," wrote White, "and see if, in all New York, beyond the regions of trade, there is one [modern] house of which the outside shows such promise of gentle breeding within. Then look upon the poles which the artist, with hardy faithfulness . . . has preserved in this view, and see in this offensive incongruity one illustration of the spirit which seized upon New York some forty years ago, and left it a vast assemblage of engines of rapacity and architectural horrors." (For another illustration from White's article, see page 374.)

BELOW: "Pen Sketches of Rapid Transit," a photolithograph by Leggo Bros. & Co. from a drawing by Gustave Dieterich, was published in 1875 to illustrate some of the many types of elevated railroads which had been proposed by various inventors and promoters. All the buildings except the "Scientific American Patent Office" (upper right) have signs advertising that they are "To Let" or that the tenant has "Removed."

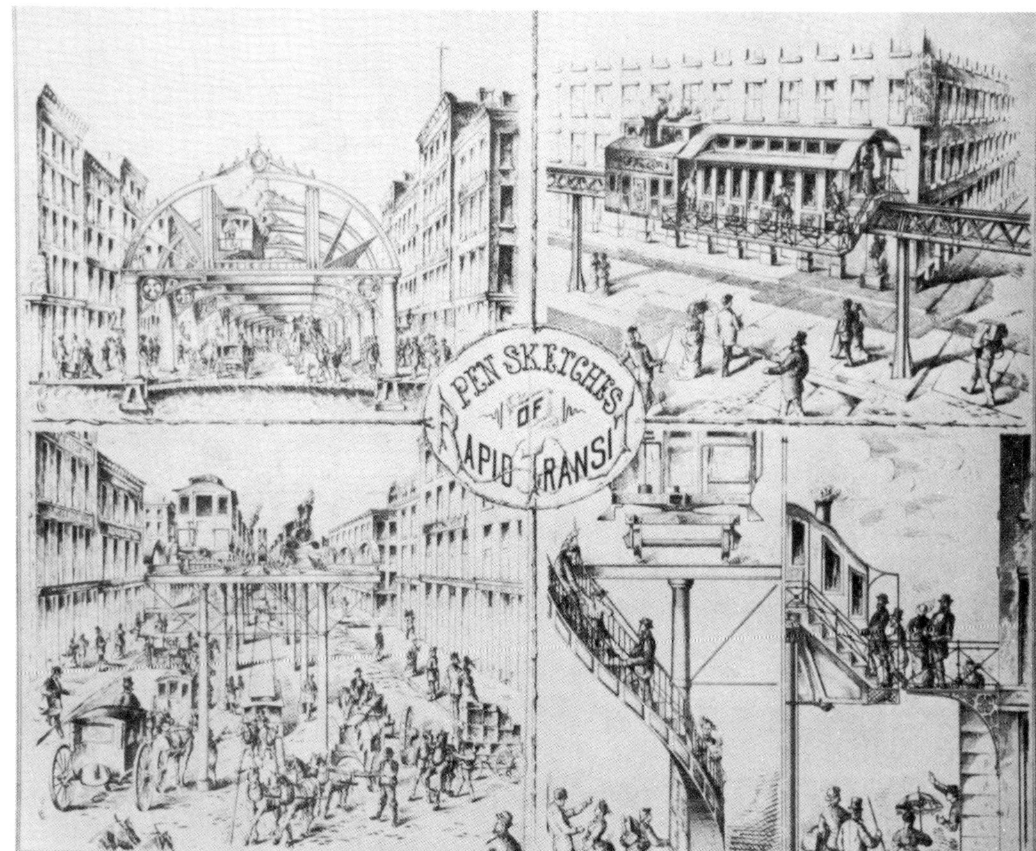

A sample of the monorail design, upper right, was actually built on the Centennial grounds in Philadelphia in 1876, but was never adopted by any city transit system.

Collection of Edward W. C. Arnold; photograph courtesy of Museum of the City of New York

. . . which produced the first of the new structural forms to capture the visual imagination of the city's artists and photographers . . .

RIGHT: Foundations for elevated line in the Annexed District (the Bronx) in 1884. The view looks north on the right of way cutting through the blocks between Alexander and Willis avenues, with 143rd Street crossing the middle of the photograph.

New-York Historical Society

J. Clarence Davies Collection, Museum of the City of New York

LEFT: Construction of the El at Ninth Avenue and Forty-second Street, about 1875–76.
BELOW LEFT: Building the El on Columbus Avenue (then Ninth) in 1878. The view looks northeast from about Ninety-seventh Street toward Central Park. The houses at left are on the block between Columbus Avenue and Central Park West, Ninety-eighth to Ninety-ninth streets.
BELOW RIGHT: Engine house of the El. (This was probably taken at the depot on East Ninety-eighth Street, between Third and Fourth avenues about 1880.)

New-York Historical Society

New-York Historical Society

. . . who were fascinated by the El's apparently insubstantial skeleton and its flamboyant curves.

Author's collection

Charles Graham's 1898 drawing of the El curve at 110th Street was published in E. Idell Zeisloft's *The New Metropolis* (New York, 1899).

The photograph below, taken about 1879 from an upper window of 73 Pearl Street, shows the famous snake curve of the El tracks at Coenties Slip.

New-York Historical Society

Other equally flamboyant curves also fascinated them, of course, and many pictures . . .

SHOOTING AT THE ELEVATED.

A PARTY OF NEW YORK GIRLS ENJOY A LITTLE AFTER-DINNER PISTOL PRACTICE AT THE TRAINS THAT RUSH BY THE WINDOWS OF THEIR HOTEL.

Culver Service

THREE SHEETS IN THE WIND.

A GALLANT MEMBER OF THE NEW YORK YACHT CLUB HAS A PICNIC ALL OF HIS OWN IN THE PRIVATE PARLORS OF THAT "SWAGGER" INSTITUTION.

Culver Service

"Shooting at the Elevated," showing the gay New York girls enjoying "a little after-dinner pistol practice at the trains that rush by the windows of their hotel," is a wood engraving from the *Police Gazette,* December 23, 1882. The other *Gazette* picture, "Three Sheets in the Wind," was published in the issue of July 10, 1886, and purports to show a "gallant" member of the New York Yacht Club having "a picnic all his own in the private parlors of that 'swagger' institution."

Author's collection

ALLEN'S DANCE HOUSE.

The picture of "Allen's Dance House," right, is from *New York by Sunlight and Gaslight* (New York, 1882), written by a journalist named James D. McCabe who ground out a half dozen or more books which were intended, as this one was, to be "a faithful and graphic picture" of the city. John Allen's Water Street dive was really pretty old stuff by 1880. Allen had been known in the sixties as "The Wickedest Man in New York," in spite of the fact that he had been a student at Union Theological Seminary and kept copies of the Bible in the upstairs rooms where his "girls" took their clients. In 1868 some of the city's most eminent clergymen got a lot of publicity by announcing they had converted him—but it turned out that they had merely rented his place for some revival meetings.

. . . of the seventies and eighties show the city as a gay place, of theaters and concert halls . . .

UNION SQUARE IN MIDSUMMER.

Museum of the City of New York

The lithograph of "Union Square in Midsummer," drawn by Maerz and printed by the Courier Lith. Co., was issued as a supplement to the New York *Mirror,* August 12, 1882. The offices of the *Mirror* (later called the *Dramatic Mirror*) are shown just right of the Union Square Hotel. Union Square was still a great theatrical center (as the pictures of actors and actresses around the border of the print suggest), though the "Rialto," as it was called, along Broadway from Madison Square to Forty-second Street was already superseding it. The stretch of sidewalk along Fourteenth Street in front of the Morton House and the Union Square Theater (at right) was still known as the "Slave Market" because of the actors who hung around there in summer looking for jobs.

The Metropolitan Concert Hall, shown here in a lithograph by Hopcraft & Co., was built on the southwest corner of Broadway and Forty-first Street in 1880. A failure as a concert hall, in spite of Rudolph Aronson's orchestra and the roof garden, it was converted into a theater in 1881. By 1884 it was a skating rink, and in 1887 it was demolished to make way for the Broadway Theater.

Collection of Edward W. C. Arnold; photograph courtesy of Museum of the City of New York

*. . . and elegant bars,
where there was always
some new sensation
to experience . . .*

The Hoffman House Bar, shown below in a lithographed advertisement of Hoffman House Bouquet Cigars (about 1883), was one of the gayest and most splendid in the city. On Broadway, opposite Madison Square, it was for many years the haunt of prominent actors and wealthy businessmen, and everyone had heard about (if he hadn't been in to see) Bouguereau's scandalous painting of a nude surrounded by satyrs which hung above the bar. Among the figures in the lithograph one can easily recognize Grover Cleveland and Chauncey Depew in the center foreground. Just over Cleveland's right shoulder is "Buffalo Bill" Cody. Behind Depew, approaching the cigar counter, is Tony Pastor—the music-hall impresario who "discovered" Lillian Russell and a host of other stars. The man just selecting a cigar is Nat Goodwin, the comedian who at one time or another was married to many of the charmers of the period, including Maxine Elliott.

The broadside at right announces a bullfight which was put on July 31, 1880, at the Central Park Arena, on the corner of Sixth (now Lenox) Avenue and 116th Street. According to the New York *Herald,* 3000 people attended the opening performance.

Bella C. Landauer Collection, New-York Historical Society

CENTRAL PARK
BULL-FIGHT
ARENA.
Cor 116th St. & Sixth Ave.
Between the Two Stations of the Third and Sixth Avenue Elevated Railroads.

The Celebrated (Toreros) Spanish Bull-Fighters will give
3 GRAND BULL-FIGHT
PERFORMANCES ONLY.
On SAT. JULY 31st.
WED. AUGUST 3d and SAT. AUGUST 6th.

Three Grand Bull-Fights will be given by a first-class company of Spanish Bull-fighters under the direction of the famous Spanish

Espada—Angel Valdemoro.

This professional has been very successful in all his performances, and was one of the three chiefs who took part in the bull-fights, given on the accession to the throne of Spain of the present King Alfonso XII. He was also leader in the Royal Bull-fights which took place at the marriage of said King.

All the artists are among the most celebrated and applauded in all the Spanish cities, and they will play most difficult and risky feats with the bulls, avoiding the rage of the animals by their great skill and intelligence with the aid of the CAPAS.

They will perform all the feats used in Spain, except that of the lances of the PICADORES, without committing ANY CRUELTY TO THE ANIMALS. The spectacle will be very exciting and extremely agreeable for the ladies and other persons who will go to these performances.

NO IRON will be used, causing any injury to the animals; only taking capas in the entertainment—the bull, the man with the cloak and BANDERILLAS, and the ESPADA or swordsman, without any iron.

A Large Arena has been built at great expense, expressly to accommodate 10,000 people, enabling the manager to accommodate the audience and give to the performance the required splendor.

SIX WILD TEXAS BULLS!!

Will perform. In case of one not being wild enough, it will be replaced by another

The bulls will be from Texas, as the fights in Havana have shown their excellent qualities for this amusement.

Tickets for Sale now at the following places: 49 Seventh Ave.; Express Co., 940 Broadway; and at Love & Alden, 207 Broadway, Cor. Fulton Street, N. Y.

The sale of Tickets will commence Tuesday 27th inst. at the above places

As THREE performances ONLY will take place at present, the sale of Tickets will be open at the said offices for any of the three performances as the demand will be so great that it will be impossible to accommodate all at the first performance.

General Admission $1.50. Seats in Amphitheatre 50c.
Seats on First and Second Rows $1. Private Box [6 chairs] $12.
Children Under 8 Years Half-Price.
Doors Open at 3. Performance to Commence at 5 P. M.
A First-Class Band has been engaged for the occasion.

ANGEL FERNANDEZ,

Museum of the City of New York

. . . and where even sober businessmen liked to blow off steam occasionally.

CHRISTMAS CARNIVAL IN THE NEW YORK STOCK EXCHANGE.

Author's collection

New York Public Library

Harry Wolf's drawing of the "Christmas Carnival in the New York Stock Exchange" was one of the illustrations for an article by R. Wheatley, published in *Harper's Magazine,* November, 1885. Occasionally, the article tells us, "the nervous force necessarily expended [by the stockbrokers] in rapid reasoning and quick decision" is directed into other channels. "At the Christmas season it luxuriates in the blowing of tin horns and bugles, smashing of broker hats, pelting with blown bladders, wet towels, and surreptitious snow-balls . . ." and so on. As a rule, we are told, stockbrokers are "a self-indulgent, genial, expansive, and generous class of fellow citizens. They dine well, dress well, bubble over with animal spirits, bear bravely the reverses of fortune, and enjoy robust health." A couple of pages later we get what may have been the explanation of their high spirits. "Failures in business," Wheatley ingenuously says, "are not so common with brokers as with their clients."

The illustration at right, from *Frank Leslie's Illustrated Newspaper,* October 27, 1888, is probably the first picture of a New York ticker-tape celebration. It shows a political parade in Wall Street during the Harrison-Cleveland campaign, and "the veritable blizzard of white 'tape'" from the windows of the Stock Exchange (at left) is described as one of the novelties of the occasion.

Yet New York took work seriously, and one of the city's leading manufacturers hired a photographer . . .

All pictures from Museum of the City of New York

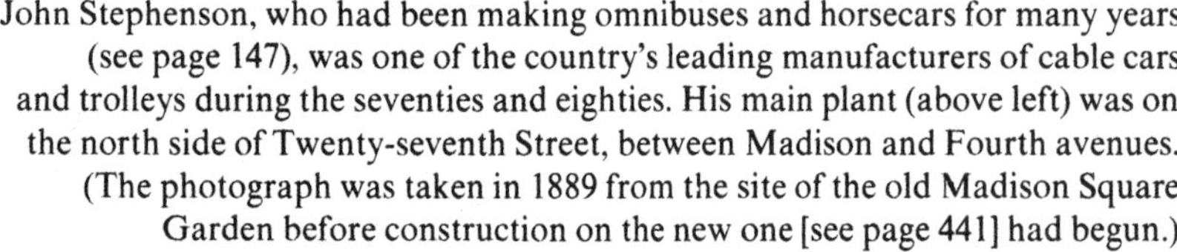

John Stephenson, who had been making omnibuses and horsecars for many years (see page 147), was one of the country's leading manufacturers of cable cars and trolleys during the seventies and eighties. His main plant (above left) was on the north side of Twenty-seventh Street, between Madison and Fourth avenues. (The photograph was taken in 1889 from the site of the old Madison Square Garden before construction on the new one [see page 441] had begun.)

For data on the other pictures, see the following page.

. . . to make pictures not only of every vehicle he turned out but also of the plant where the work was done . . .

On the opposite page, top right, is one of the Broadway stagecoaches designed and built by Stephenson in the sixties. The large picture, lower left, is a horsecar of the seventies, the interior of which is shown at center right. The other interior, at the bottom of the page, is that of one of the extra-fare "Special" cars, which operated on a fixed schedule, morning and night, to serve well-to-do commuters.

On this page are four pictures of the interior of the factory, probably taken about 1889. ABOVE LEFT: the woodworking shop; CENTER LEFT: the body shop; LOWER LEFT: the forge in the machine shop; and LOWER RIGHT: the metalworking shop where the car trucks were assembled.

All pictures from Museum of the City of New York

. . . thus providing one of the earliest and most complete series of documentary industrial photographs.

Stephenson shipped cars to customers all over the world. The horsecars below were bound for India, China (the "Company of the Iron Road Horse-car," presumably at Shanghai), and Amsterdam, Holland. Later he manufactured trolley cars, and his company made the first cars for the subway that opened in 1904.

Above photographs from Museum of the City of New York

Like many of the men who created great American industries, Stephenson was always at home with the machines and tools of his business, and from 1851 to 1874 he lived right next door to his factory, at 47 East Twenty-seventh Street (shown in photograph at right). The portrait photograph, by Naegeli, was probably taken about 1880.

Both pictures lent by Mrs. Harry A. Thompson to Museum of the City of New York

Other citizens called upon the photographers for detailed camera records of their homes, and at least one family . . .

All pictures from Museum of the City of New York

James Lancaster Morgan's house (left) at 7 Pierrepont Street, Brooklyn, was built in 1870. Sometime about 1880 Mr. and Mrs. Morgan had the photographer B. J. Smith take a complete set of pictures of the interior.

Below at left is the entrance hall. Through the curtained double door at left is the parlor (see next page), and at the rear, through another curtained door, are the stairs leading to the second story. Mrs. Morgan's bedroom is shown below at right.

. . . over on Brooklyn Heights had a new set of photographs taken every time the house was redecorated . . .

Both pictures from Museum of the City of New York

The photograph at the top of this page shows the Morgans' front parlor in the early 1880s. The door at right leads to the front hall (see previous page). Through the double door in the background we get a glimpse of the dining room, into which we move in the photograph below.

On the opposite page are photographs of these same rooms taken in 1888 and in 1891 or '92. After Mrs. Morgan's death in 1885, her husband gave the house to his son and daughter-in-law, Mr. and Mrs. James L. Morgan, Jr.

—which was frequently, so quickly did fashions change in those days.

All pictures from Museum of the City of New York

These photographs of their first and second ventures in redecorating and refurnishing their home, taken together with the earlier pictures made for the senior Morgans, provide one of the most detailed records now available of the cycles of fashionable taste in the last third of the nineteenth century. Note, for example, what happens to the mantelpieces in both rooms; or follow the fortunes of the "occasional" chair in the left background of the earliest photograph of the living room, by the door to the dining room.

The leaders of fashion, of course, were the very rich, whose ostentatious patronage of the arts . . .

The art gallery in the William Astor house on the southwest corner of Fifth Avenue and Thirty-fourth Street was one of the most famous rooms in the city. Here Mrs. Astor, with the ritualistic assistance of Ward McAllister, held her annual ball; it was the physical capacity of this room which limited those on the list of invited guests—and therefore those who were really "in" society—to the fabled and fabulous Four Hundred.

New-York Historical Society

BELOW: Across Thirty-fourth Street, on the northwest corner of Fifth Avenue, stood the marble mansion which Alexander T. Stewart had built for himself in the late sixties, and in which his widow still lived when these photographs were taken in the mid-eighties. At left we are looking down the grand hall toward the art gallery. At right is Mrs. Stewart's bedroom.

Brown Brothers

Brown Brothers

. . . conspired with the developing taste for expensive and showy splendor to produce . . .

Museum of the City of New York

This picture of the library in J. Pierpont Morgan's house, northeast corner of Madison Avenue and Thirty-sixth Street, is reproduced from a photogravure in *Artistic Houses, Being a Series of Interior Views of the Most Beautiful and Celebrated Homes in the United States, with a Description of the Art Treasures Contained therein* (New York, D. Appleton & Co., 1883). Morgan's house was the first private residence in the city to be lighted by electricity, and the wall and ceiling fixtures with their naked bulbs, to say nothing of the desk lamp and "bridge lamp" with their untidy cords, can be clearly seen in the picture.

The Studio Building at 51–55 West Tenth Street, designed by Richard Morris Hunt, was the first building in the city designed specifically for artists' studios. Frederick E. Church, J. F. Kensett, and Albert Bierstadt were early tenants.

Ware Memorial Library, Columbia University

. . . an aesthetic debauch which was soon reflected in architecture.

The illustrations at right and lower left, drawn by C. Piton from photographs by Rockwood, are from an article on "Recent Building in New York" by Montgomery Schuyler in *Harper's Magazine,* September, 1883. LOWER LEFT: Two houses on Madison Avenue, the one at left designed by G. E. Harney and the other by McKim, Mead & White. RIGHT: Entrances of two houses at the corner of Fifth Avenue and Sixty-seventh Street, designed by Lamb & Rich. Schuyler, who was one of the best architectural critics we have ever had, was especially severe in his strictures on Lamb & Rich's "fortuitous aggregation of unrelated parts," with its decorative details "fished from the slums of the Rococo."

The sketch at lower right, of an old mantel in the Gracie house on State Street, was drawn by Cass Gilbert—then a young member of the Architectural League—as one of the illustrations for Richard Grant White's article on "Old New York and its Houses," *Century Magazine,* October, 1883 (see page 359).

All pictures from author's collection

Meanwhile amateur and professional photographers, using improved cameras which could take instantaneous pictures . . .

Author's collection

A major change in ways of looking at the city was brought about by the introduction during the eighties of portable cameras capable of taking instantaneous pictures. In an article on "Modern Amateur Photography" in *Harper's Magazine,* January, 1889, F. C. Beach described a number of these cameras, and his piece was illustrated with several half-tone reproductions of photographs —including the one at left, taken by Charles Simpson, showing an amateur "Operating a Detective Camera." These light and portable cameras (the most famous of which was Eastman's Kodak, introduced in 1888) had become "very popular and numerous," he wrote, and were particularly useful "when photographing in crowded streets or when one is travelling." (See page 392 for data on the first use of half-tone illustrations from photographs.)

The photograph below, showing an amateur with his detective camera at the zoo in Central Park, was taken about 1885 by George B. Brainerd.

Brooklyn Museum

. . . were able to catch unposed scenes of the life and activity in the city's streets . . .

All pictures from Brooklyn Museum

These photographs, made in and around Brooklyn by George B. Brainerd in the mid-eighties, are typical of the pictures made with the new instantaneous cameras. UPPER LEFT: The Soap Fat Man. UPPER RIGHT: An old sailor displaying a glass-encased model of a clipper ship on Fulton Street. LOWER LEFT: A letter carrier at Christmastime. LOWER RIGHT: A longshoreman on the Brooklyn waterfront.

It is worth remembering that these pictures were made in the years immediately preceding the publication of Eadweard Muybridge's photographic studies of *Animal Locomotion* (1887), at a time when many people—including the painter Thomas Eakins—were experimenting with rapid sequences of exposures which revealed the patterns of movement. As early as 1863 Oliver Wendell Holmes had written for the *Atlantic Monthly* an essay on walking, basing his observations upon the walking figures he had observed in instantaneous stereoscopic views of Paris and New York.

. . . and to capture fleeting and often strikingly beautiful patterns of motion and form.

Both pictures from Brooklyn Museum

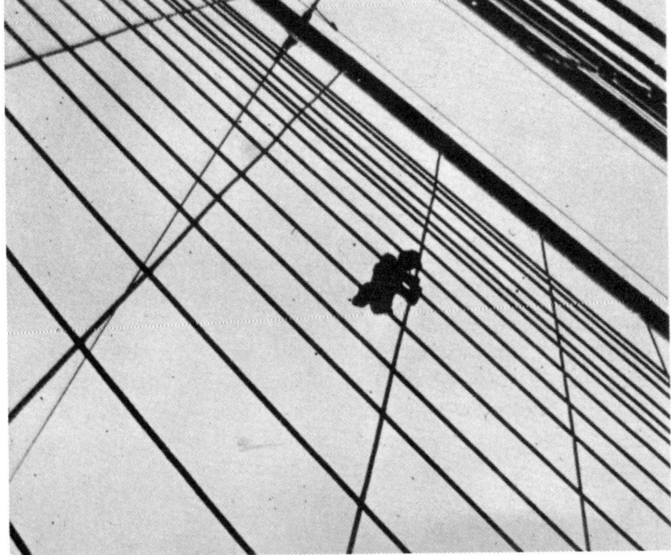

The photograph above, probably made at Coney Island, was taken in 1888 by Breading G. Way. The one below, of a painter at work on the cables of the Brooklyn Bridge, was made in 1885 by George B. Brainerd.

Collection of T. Anthony Caruso

This photograph of the first women medical students at Bellevue Hospital was taken about 1888. Unfortunately the photographer has not been certainly identified, but the author recently discovered a reference, in the preface to a book published in 1892, to a Mr. O. G. Mason, "at present and for the past twenty-five years official photographer at Bellevue Hospital" (see page 387 for further details). Perhaps, therefore, this is Mason's work. In any event, it deserves a place in the history of American photography comparable to that held in painting by Thomas Eakins' "The Gross Clinic" (1875) and "The Agnew Clinic" (1889).

. . . and no matter what the occasion, they were on hand . . .

Author's collection

The photograph of "Lawn Tennis at Prospect Park," taken by Gubelman, is reproduced from a contact print mounted on cardboard and bound into the *Twenty-Fifth Annual Report of the Brooklyn Park Commissioners* (1886) as one of several illustrations. Until the half-tone process of printing from photographs was developed (see page 392) such individually mounted prints were frequently used in books for which there was a limited market. But it was an expensive procedure and not practicable for commercial publication. Tennis, which had been introduced to America by some Staten Islanders in the late seventies, had become so popular by 1885 that the park commissioners had laid out two hundred courts for free use by the more than four hundred tennis clubs then active in Brooklyn alone.

The photographs below were both taken after the great blizzard of 1888. The one at left, by an unidentified photographer, was taken at the corner of Broadway and Twelfth Street, looking south toward A. T. Stewart's store at Tenth (now John Wanamaker's). A law had been passed in 1884 requiring all telegraph, telephone, and electric wires to be removed from the streets, and the first underground conduits were laid in 1886. But the wreckage after the blizzard hastened the work, and most of the poles were taken down in the next few years. The other picture was taken in Brooklyn by Breading G. Way.

J. Clarence Davies Collection, Museum of the City of New York

Brooklyn Museum

LEFT: A photograph of the funeral procession of General Grant, August 8, 1885. The picture was taken from the wall of the old distributing reservoir (on the present site of the Public Library), looking south on Fifth Avenue. The monstrous building on the northeast corner of Thirty-ninth Street was the Union League Club, designed by Peabody & Stearns and decorated throughout by John La Farge and Louis Tiffany. BELOW: One panel of a stereoscopic view by L. G. Strand showing the Labor Day Parade in Union Square (turning west off Fourth Avenue into Seventeenth Street) in 1887. The tobacco workers, whose float is seen in the foreground, had need of their "Fortitude Association." A man and wife rolling cigars seventeen hours a day in a sweatshop could earn a maximum of fifteen or sixteen dollars in a seven-day week.

Museum of the City of New York

Both pictures from J. Clarence Davies Collection, Museum of the City of New York

RIGHT: An unattributed photograph of the explosion on October 10, 1885, when Flood Rock was blasted out of Hell Gate Channel in the East River, thus removing a major hazard to navigation.

The camera's chief contribution to men's awareness of the city during the eighties was, however, to make familiar—and believable—the reality of urban poverty.

Brown Brothers

This photograph of Hester Street, looking west from Clinton Street toward the Bowery (with the El structure in left background), was taken about 1888. Popularly known as the Pig-Market, this stretch of the street was the principal shopping center of the most crowded slum district in the city: the Tenth Ward, known to the health officers as the "typhus ward" and to the Bureau of Vital Statistics as the "suicide ward."

Into these tenements human beings were packed more densely than anywhere else in the world—London's worst slums and the rabbit warrens of China and India not excepted. The Tenth Ward in 1890 averaged 522 people per acre, as opposed to an average of 114 per acre for Manhattan as a whole and 60 per acre for the entire city.

It was true, of course, as Jacob Riis admitted, that New York's tenements had less of the slum look than those of other cities. Some of them even had brownstone fronts! But as Riis also said, "To get at the pregnant facts of tenement-house life one must look beneath the surface," and that is what he and other reporters, armed with cameras, proceeded to do.

Although there was still no practical way to reproduce photographs directly . . .

On February 12, 1888, the New York *Sun* ran the story reproduced at right, headlined: "Flashes from the Slums. Pictures Taken in Dark Places by the Lighting Process. Some of the Results of a Journey Through the City with an Instantaneous Camera—The Poor, the Idle, and the Vicious." The article explains how Jacob Riis, a police reporter, and three other members of the Society of Amateur Photographers—Dr. Henry G. Piffard, Richard Hoe Lawrence, and Dr. John T. Nagle—had gone about taking pictures from which Riis could make lantern slides to illustrate his lectures on "The Other Half: How It Lives and Dies in New York." The pen drawing at the bottom of the middle column was the *Sun's* version of the photograph below, showing a "growler gang" at their headquarters under the pier at the Jackson Street dump (now Corlaer's Hook Park). These were members of the "Short Tail Gang," long famous along the East River waterfront.

Jacob A. Riis Collection, Museum of the City of New York

10 THE SUN, SUND.

FLASHES FROM THE SLUMS.

PICTURES TAKEN IN DARK PLACES BY THE LIGHTNING PROCESS.

Some of the Results of a Journey Through the City with an Instantaneous Camera—The Poor, the Idle, and the Vicious.

OH, COME OFF.

BURGLAR BILLY

A Thrilling Adventure.

BY

POLICE CAPT. EDW'D CASSIDY

Of the Eldridge Street Station.

BEAUTY UNDER WATER.

New York Public Library

. . . in newspapers or magazines, it was a reporter's camera record of life in the tenements . . .

The pen and ink sketch at left, drawn from the photograph below, was published in the *Evening Sun*, May 25, 1895, as one of the illustrations for an article headlined: "Goodby to the Bend—Getting Ready to Raze the Old Mulberry Street Slum." The photograph was one of a number Riis had taken about 1887 or 1888 while he was campaigning for a cleanup in "the Bend"—a campaign which finally resulted in the city's demolishing the whole block of tenements bounded by Bayard, Mulberry, Park, and Baxter streets and creating Columbus Park on the site.

Both pictures from Jacob A. Riis Collection, Museum of the City of New York

. . . which first gave the public a picture, so "real" that it could not be ignored . . .

Three of Riis's photographs made in the late 1880s. BELOW: Making neckties in a Division Street tenement. The bulk of sweatshop work was done in tenements, rather than in factories, because they were beyond the reach of laws regulating factory labor. RIGHT: A rear tenement in Roosevelt Street.

All pictures from Jacob A. Riis Collection, Museum of the City of New York

RIGHT: A "Black and Tan" stale-beer dive in Thompson Street—one of the foul cellar dives, often run by a political leader of the district, which Riis described as the meeting places of "all the law-breakers and all the human wrecks within reach."

. . . of the idiot and degraded face of hopeless poverty which was bred in the city's slums.

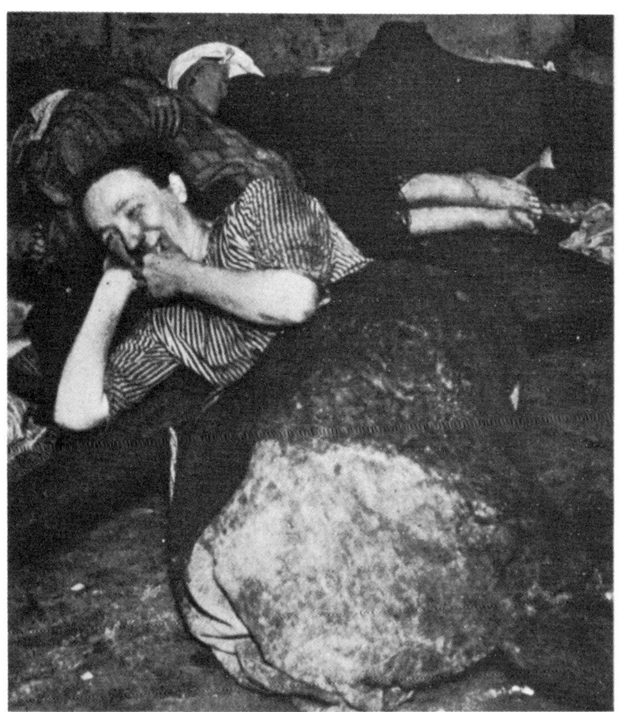

The photograph at left, taken by Riis about 1890, shows some of the homeless derelicts who were allowed to sleep in the police station at 18 Eldridge Street. BELOW: A photograph from which Kenyon Cox made a pen and ink drawing which was used as an illustration in Riis's book, *How the Other Half Lives* (New York, Scribner, 1890, page 69). Riis describes the scene, photographed by flashlight in 1888: "In a room not thirteen feet either way slept twelve men and women, two or three in bunks set in a sort of alcove, the rest on the floor. A kerosene lamp burned dimly in the fearful atmosphere, probably to guide other and later arrivals to their 'beds,' for it was only just past midnight." This was one of the hundreds of unlicensed lodging houses—in this case in a Bayard Street tenement—which provided shelter for "Five Cents a Spot."

Both pictures from Jacob A. Riis Collection, Museum of the City of New York

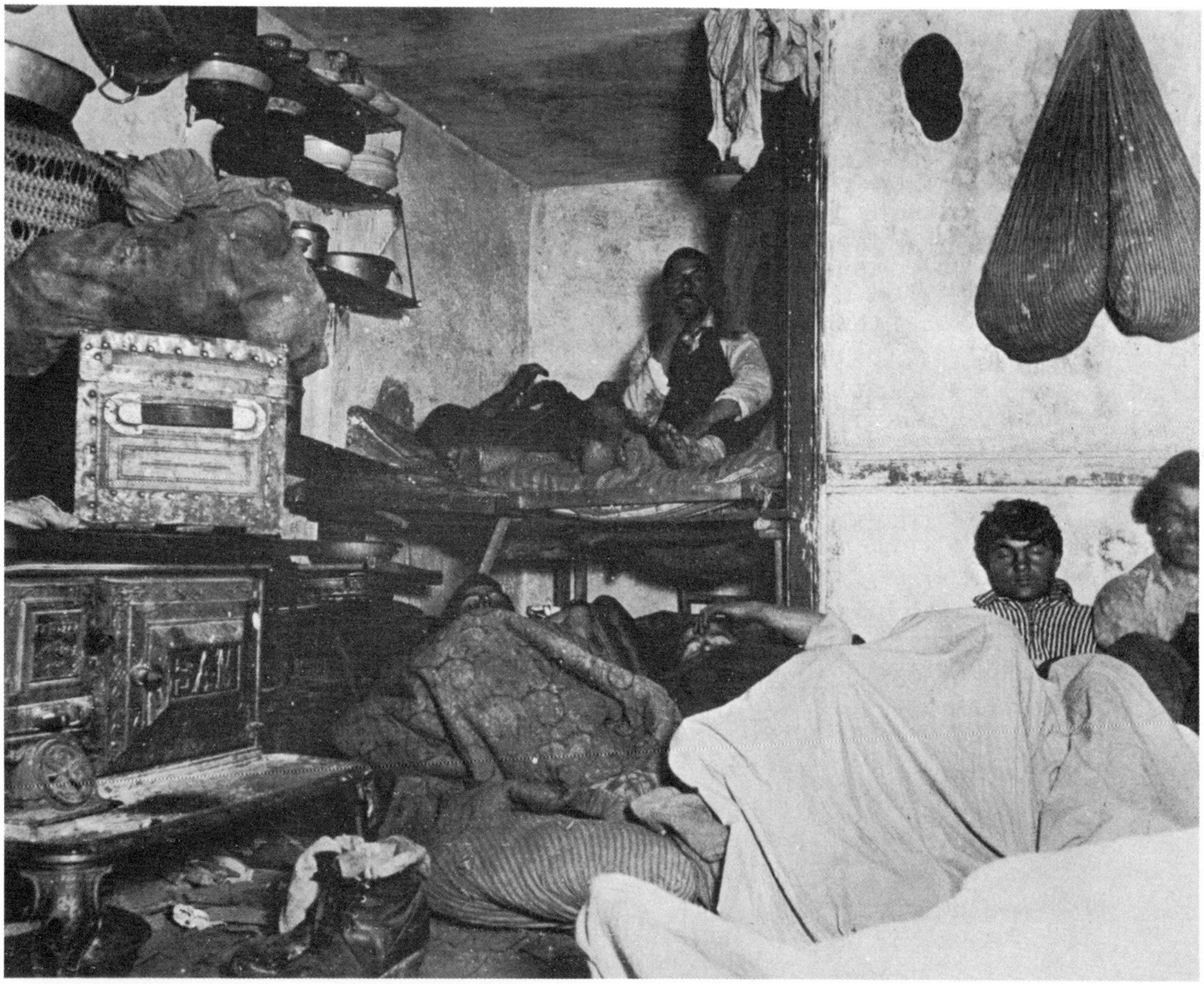

The pictures taken by Jacob Riis and others were used over and over again . . .

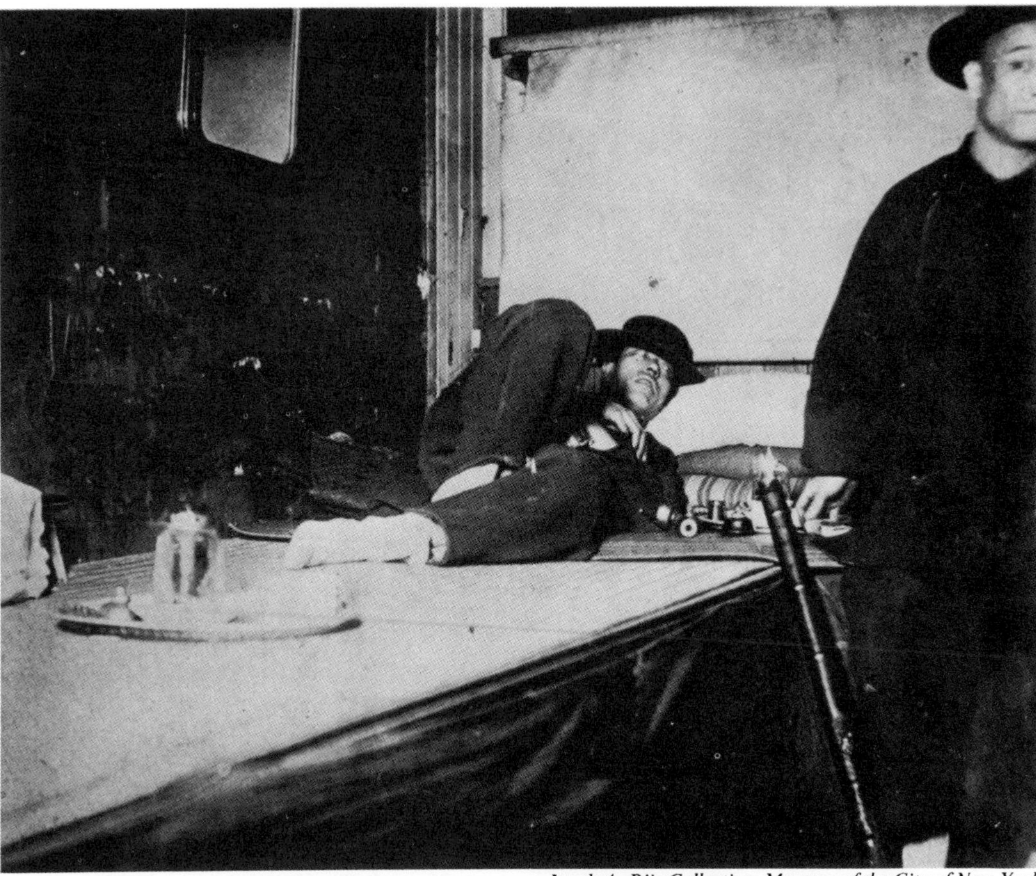

Jacob A. Riis Collection, Museum of the City of New York

The photograph at right, showing an opium smoker in a Mott Street fan-tan den, was used as the basis for illustrations in at least two books, as well as for one of Riis's lantern slides. Below, at left, is the drawing signed "Kenyon Cox—1889—after photograph" which was published in Riis's own *How the Other Half Lives* (page 98). The other, drawn by R. T. Sperry, was one of the illustrations in *Darkness and Daylight; or Lights and Shadows of New York Life,* written by Mrs. Helen Campbell, Thomas W. Knox, and Inspector Thomas Byrnes, and published at Hartford, Connecticut, in 1892, by A. D. Worthington.

The publisher's preface to the latter book gives interesting evidence of the importance which was attached to photographic realism in the illustrations. "The old method of employing artists of quick talent to seize the general outline of a scene, and [later] enlarge the hasty sketch and reproduce the details from memory, was open to serious objection," he wrote. Therefore, all the illustrations in this book are drawn from photographs. "In no instance have artists been allowed to exercise their imaginations by drawing pictures of impossible scenes, or exaggerating what is already bad enough. . . . Exactly as the reader sees these pictures, just so were the scenes presented to the camera's merciless and unfailing eye. . . . Nothing is lacking but the actual *movement* of the persons represented."

Both pictures from author's collection

IN A CHINESE JOINT.

. . . to illustrate books and articles and lectures which tried to tell the truth about "how the other half lives" in New York.

Many of the photographs used in *Darkness and Daylight* (see previous page) were made, the publisher tells us, "by flashlight, without the aid of which much of the life herein shown so truthfully could not have been presented at all." Most of the full-page illustrations, such as the one above of "Supperless and Homeless Street Boys Sleeping out at Night," were "facsimiles" of flashlight photographs taken by "Mr. O. G. Mason (at present and for the past twenty-five years official photographer at Bellevue Hospital)" to whom the publisher pays special tribute. "Always ready for emergencies, possessing ability and facilities to meet them, he was in every way the right man in the right place." Among the other photographers whose work was included were Riis, E. Warrin, Jr., and Frederick Vilmar, one of whom probably took the picture from which R. T. Sperry made the drawing at left, showing a group of prostitutes at the Florence Night Mission, 29 Bleecker Street. A footnote in the text tells us that the girl hiding her face (at right), who went by the name of "Shakespeare," had since been found murdered in a cheap lodging house on Water Street.

Both pictures from author's collection

Meanwhile the city authorities were doing their best to keep things under control.

Author's collection

The picture of a policeman reporting at a station house with a foundling, picked up in an alley, was another of the illustrations based on a photograph by O. G. Mason for *Darkness and Daylight* (see page 387). Every year, according to the text by Thomas W. Knox, more than 200 foundlings and another 100 or more dead infants were picked up by the police. Homeless and lost children, like the little girl in Riis's photograph below, were turned over to Matron Webb at police headquarters.

Jacob A. Riis Collection, Museum of the City of New York

There were official uses of photography, as well as journalistic, of course. The rogues' gallery was a well-established institution by the mid-eighties. The picture below, "Photographing a Prisoner for the Rogues Gallery at Police Headquarters," was one of the illustrations in *Darkness and Daylight.*

Author's collection

But the problem went much deeper than temporary assistance or law enforcement . . .

Museum of the City of New York

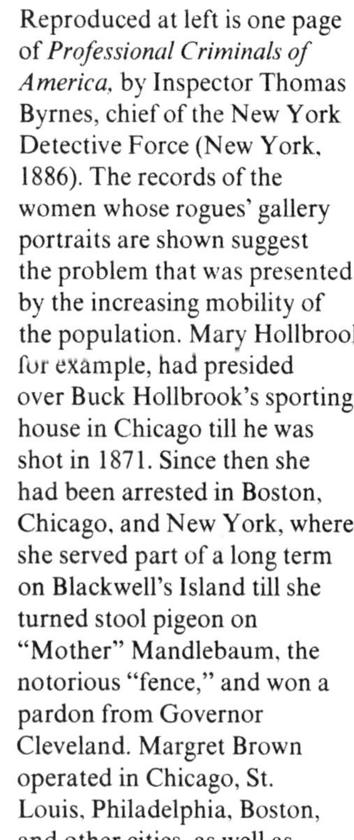

Reproduced at left is one page of *Professional Criminals of America,* by Inspector Thomas Byrnes, chief of the New York Detective Force (New York, 1886). The records of the women whose rogues' gallery portraits are shown suggest the problem that was presented by the increasing mobility of the population. Mary Hollbrook, for example, had presided over Buck Hollbrook's sporting house in Chicago till he was shot in 1871. Since then she had been arrested in Boston, Chicago, and New York, where she served part of a long term on Blackwell's Island till she turned stool pigeon on "Mother" Mandlebaum, the notorious "fence," and won a pardon from Governor Cleveland. Margret Brown operated in Chicago, St. Louis, Philadelphia, Boston, and other cities, as well as in New York.

BELOW: A vignette from *Darkness and Daylight* (see page 386). "As to clubbing," Knox was told by an old police officer, "there is no doubt that some of the men lose their temper sooner than others do."

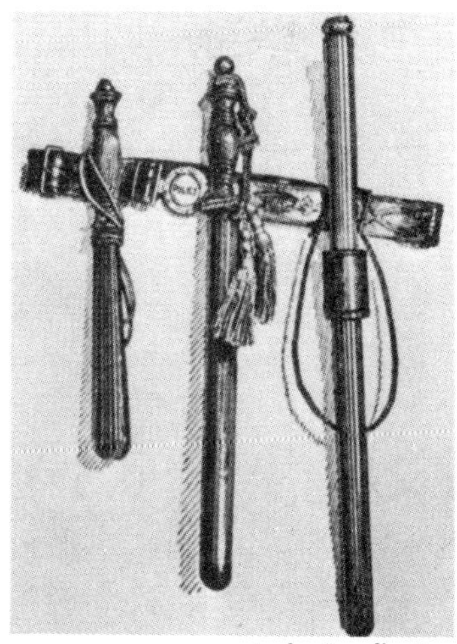

Author's collection

. . . and not even the most devoted charity could more than scratch the surface of urban misery.

All pictures from Jacob A. Riis Collection, Museum of the City of New York

Three more photographs taken by Riis during the late 1880s.

ABOVE LEFT: A scene at the Female Almshouse on Blackwell's Island.

ABOVE RIGHT: Sister Irene at the New York Foundling Asylum, which she had started in 1869 down on Twelfth Street, but which now occupied a large building on Lexington Avenue, between Sixty-eighth and Sixty-ninth streets.

RIGHT: Prayer time at the Five Points House of Industry, 155 Worth Street.

Group Six

TRANSIT TO THE GREATER CITY 1890–1910

"New York and Brooklyn Bridge," published in 1889 by the Albertype Co.

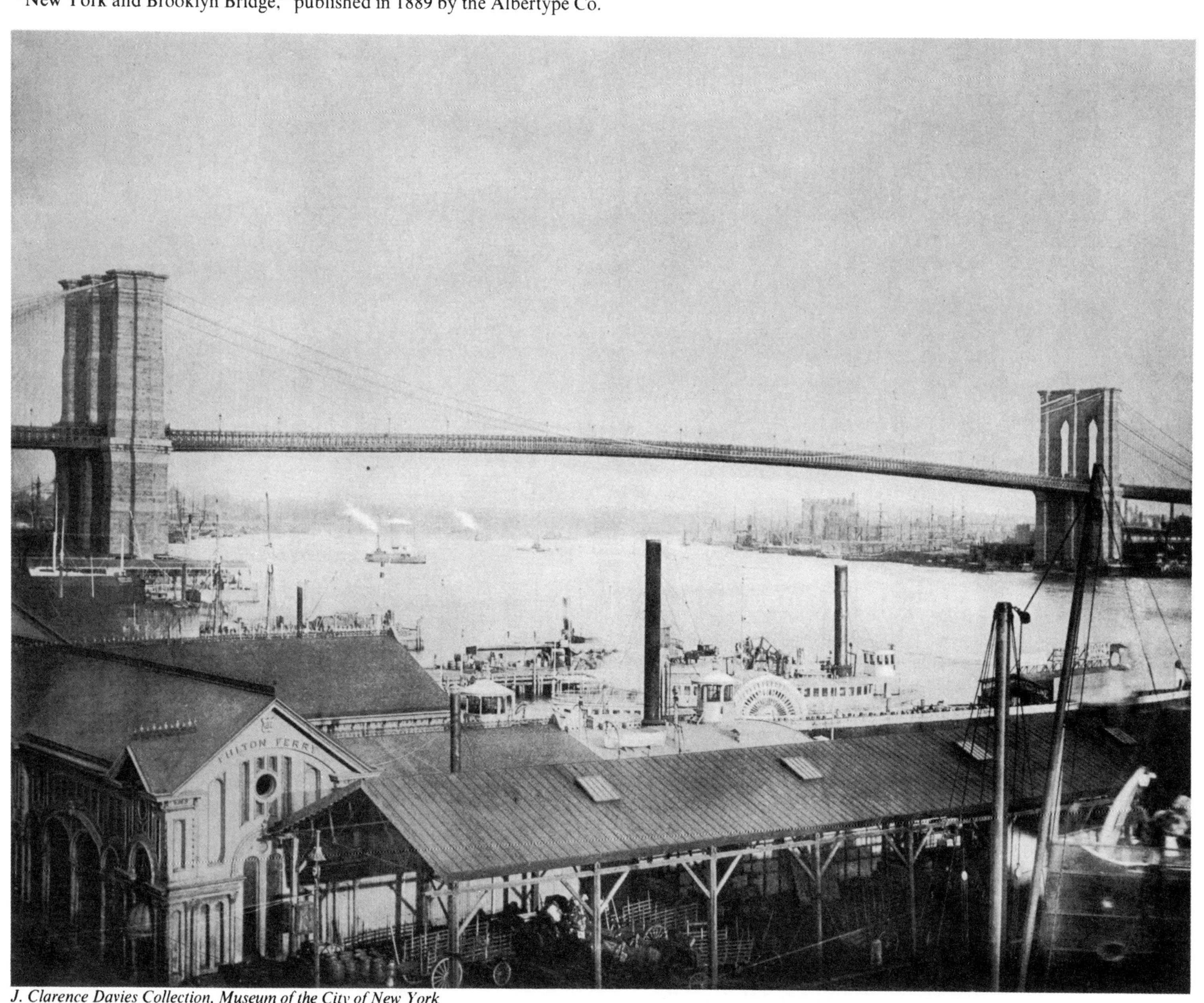

J. Clarence Davies Collection, Museum of the City of New York

By the time that practical methods had been developed for reproducing photographs on the printed page . . .

A SCENE IN SHANTYTOWN, NEW YORK.
REPRODUCTION DIRECT FROM NATURE.

New York Public Library

Author's collection

AN OLD NEW YORK BROOM MAN.
From an instantaneous photograph.

The development of the half-tone plate, in the 1880s, provided the first practical method of reproducing photographs directly on the printed page, without having to make a drawing from the photograph first. It is noteworthy that the first photograph reproduced in a daily newspaper was a picture made on the "urban frontier"—Henry J. Newton's "A Scene in Shantytown, New York." The half-tone plate was made by Stephen Henry Horgan, and it was published in the New York *Daily Graphic,* the world's first illustrated daily, March 4, 1880.

It was a decade or more before the method had been sufficiently perfected to be generally adopted by newspapers, but magazines used it with increasing frequency during the eighties. The illustration at right, reproduced here twice its original size, is from F. C. Beach's article on "Modern Amateur Photography," *Harper's Magazine,* 1889.

. . . the city was entering its most violent era of expansion.

J. Clarence Davies Collection, Museum of the City of New York

Shantytowns were everywhere on the frontiers of the expanding city. As Thomas A. Janvier put it, early in the nineties, what was going on in the upper island had been going on in the lower half for more than two hundred years: "Constantly the line of substantial buildings is advancing northward, and . . . the old constantly is displaced by or is obscured by the new." But Janvier was not being conventionally nostalgic. "It is the beginning of the conquest that is interesting," he continued, "the period during which the houses of brick and stone are coming into a straggling existence on the lines of the City Plan [see page 110], but while yet many of the little wooden houses still stand at hopeless odds with the new thoroughfares, to testify to the lines of country roads which have disappeared beneath a gridironing of city streets."

The shanties in the photograph above were on "Carnegie Hill," Fifth Avenue at Ninety-first, about 1898, and were soon afterward torn down to make way for the Andrew Carnegie mansion (which is now the headquarters of Columbia University's New York School of Social Work). BELOW LEFT: Photograph made about 1898 in Brooklyn, looking west from Franklin Street toward the Brooklyn Museum, with Eastern Parkway at right. BELOW RIGHT: Looking north along Eighth Avenue (now Central Park West) toward the American Museum of Natural History about 1890; Seventy-fifth Street in foreground.

J. Clarence Davies Collection, Museum of the City of New York

Brown Brothers

The metropolis was almost literally exploding, upward as well as outward, and by the mid-nineties . . .

It was during the nineties that the upward thrust of the skyline first became a theme in pictures of the city. The first use of the word "skyline" in a picture title seems to have been in Hearst's New York *Journal,* May 3, 1896, which included as a pictorial supplement a panoramic drawing of "The Skyline of New York" by Charles Graham. Almost two years earlier, however, *Harper's Weekly* had published in its issue for August 11, 1894, a pair of panoramic views entitled "The Age of Skyscrapers—Tall Buildings in the Business District of New York City."

One of these was a photograph taken from Brooklyn. The other, reproduced at right above, was a "View from the North River," drawn by G. W. Peters, which is—so far as the author has been able to discover—the earliest picture reflecting a consciousness of the skyline as a symbol of the city's increasing power and prestige. At the right, just north of the Battery, is the Washington Building, erected in 1882 by Cyrus W. Field at No. 1 Broadway—which was sometimes called "the first skyscraper" and had been for several years the tallest office building in the world. The square tower with cupola and flagpole, a little to the right of Trinity's steeple, is the Manhattan Life Insurance building at 66 Broadway, which had just been completed and was the first building in the city to rise higher than the cross on top of Trinity. The domed skyscraper near the left end is the Pulitzer (New York *World*) Building, opposite City Hall on Park Row.

The picture below is one of a pair drawn by Fred Pansing for *Harper's Weekly,* March 20, 1897, jointly titled "New York Skyscrapers—The Effective Change Wrought by these Buildings on the City's Appearance within a few Years." One picture showed the city as it had looked in 1881, while this one depicted "The Sky-line of Buildings Below Chambers Street in 1897."

Actually, as the two pictures reproduced here clearly show, the skyline had changed enormously in less than three years. Trinity's steeple is now outtopped by many buildings, and the Manhattan Life tower has itself been outstripped by the twin towers of the Park Row (or Syndicate) Building, erected in 1897–98 on the site of the historic Park Theater (see page 103).

In an article on "The Sky-line of New York" in this same issue of the *Weekly,* Montgomery Schuyler concludes that, although few of the individual skyscrapers have much merit as architecture, "it is in the aggregation that the immense impressiveness lies. It is not an architectural vision," he insists, "but it does, most tremendously, 'look like business.'"

. . . Manhattan's skyline was becoming the most dramatic visual symbol . . .

Both pictures from author's collection

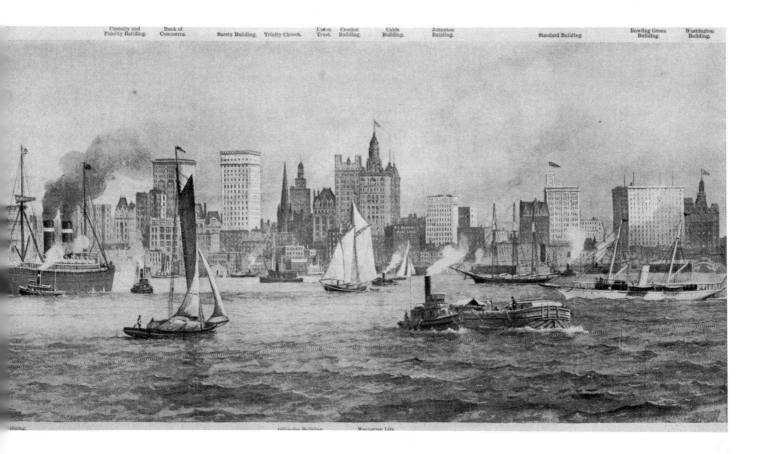

Mariner's Museum, Newport News, Virginia

Museum of the City of New York

ABOVE: The picture of the Fall River Line's steamer *Priscilla* was drawn by Fred Pansing for a lithographed advertisement published about 1897. The building just behind Pier 18 is the American Tract Society building at the corner of Nassau and Spruce streets, and left of it is the *World* building. The square tower at right is the American Surety Co.'s 306-foot structure at the corner of Broadway and Pine, and at extreme right the Manhattan Life building.

LEFT: The first steel-skeleton building in New York was the Tower Building at 50 Broadway, designed by Bradford L. Gilbert. Construction began on June 27, 1888, and the building was completed September 27, 1889, four years after Jenney's pioneering Home Insurance Co. building in Chicago. So wary were New Yorkers of a building whose walls were supported by the metal frame, rather than vice versa, that Gilbert had to reassure them by occupying the topmost offices himself. But by 1894 *Harper's Weekly* noted that people were no longer startled by the skyscrapers. "We are getting to be more accustomed to the lofty structures, and so conventional ideas, born of what we are accustomed to look at, are being gradually modified."

OPPOSITE: Photograph of "St. Paul and Park Row Buildings, New York. Two Tallest Buildings in the World," copyright 1901 by the Detroit Photographic Co. The view was taken looking northeast from a building at the corner of John and William streets. The mansard dome of the post office in City Hall Park shows at right, and the steeple of St. Paul's Chapel at left.

*By 1900 the race for taller and taller skyscrapers was on,
and before the twentieth century
was a decade old . . .*

Library of Congress, Division of Prints and Photographs

. . . men had visions of a towered and canyoned city only a little more fantastic . . .

"King's Dream of New York," drawn by Harry M. Pettit, was published in *King's Views of New York 1908–1909*, published in 1908 by Moses King. In it we are supposed to be looking up Broadway, from Exchange Place or thereabouts, as it would be in the future. The scale of the imagined future is suggested by Trinity Church (at lower left, just inside the margin) and by the 612-foot Singer Building (just right of and beyond Trinity), designed by Ernest Flagg, which had recently been completed at the northwest corner of Liberty Street as "the tallest building in the world" —a title it held for eighteen months. Note the tower in the center from which a dirigible-balloon for Japan has just cast off —an idea which was still around when the mooring mast was stuck on top of the Empire State Building twenty years later.

Both pictures from author's collection

The advertisement of the Electro-Light Engraving Co., dramatically associating height with commercial leadership, was published in the *Catalogue of the Twenty-Third Annual Exhibition of the Architectural League of New York* (1908). The building, incidentally, was the home of Scott & Bowne, manufacturers of Scott's Emulsion, at the southeast corner of Rose and Pearl streets.

. . . than the reality which had already been achieved.

brary of Congress, Division of Prints and Photographs

The photograph at left, copyright 1905 by the Detroit Photographic Co., was taken looking south on Nassau Street from just above Ann Street. The white building on the right is the Bennett Building, between Ann and Fulton streets (which also is shown quite prominently in the photograph on page 397).

Brown Brothers

The photograph at right was taken about 1905, looking north on Broad Street toward the Sub-Treasury from below Exchange Place. The brokers of the Curb Exchange (which has recently renamed itself the American Stock Exchange in a humorless effort to rid itself of its history) are seen milling around the curb in the foreground. The Stock Exchange proper is, of course, the pedimented temple at left, erected in 1903 from designs by George B. Post to replace its less impressive predecessor (see pages 86 and 138).

In the mid-nineties the spire of Trinity still dominated the financial district . . .

BELOW: Looking north up Broadway from Bowling Green about 1896 (the year in which the statue of Abraham de Peyster was erected). For a later view of this same region, see page 473.

RIGHT: Looking west on Wall Street about 1895.

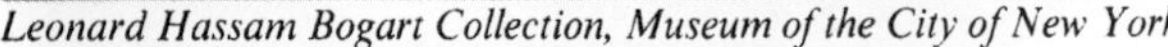

Leonard Hassam Bogart Collection, Museum of the City of New York

Brown Brothers

Library of Congress, Division of Prints and Photographs

LEFT: This curious photograph was one of the illustrations for an article in the English monthly, *Pearson's Magazine,* in 1907. The accompanying text made quite a fuss over it, describing it as "the first successful attempt to catch in the camera the great gambling scene on the floor of the New York Stock Exchange." Because of the "extraordinary precautions" taken to prevent photographers from showing the public what goes on in Wall Street, the article continues, the picture was made "through the empty sleeve of a coat used to conceal the camera from the sharp eyes of the Stock Exchange Guards."

. . . and the municipal center was still stifled by outmoded ideals of urban magnificence. The various city departments . . .

J. Clarence Davies Collection, Museum of the City of New York

LEFT: The post office at the southern end of City Hall Park, built in 1875, was already completely inadequate —besides being staggeringly ugly. The photograph, copyright 1894 by J. S. Johnston, was taken looking north up Broadway (at left) and Park Row (right). At the left is the Astor House.

BELOW LEFT: Police and reporters at the scene after the collapse of the Taylor Building, 68–74 Park Place, August 22, 1891. Sixty people were killed in the disaster.

BELOW RIGHT: "Sidewalk superintendents" at a fire in 1898, from a photograph by Raoul Froger-Doudement.

New-York Historical Society

Brooklyn Museum

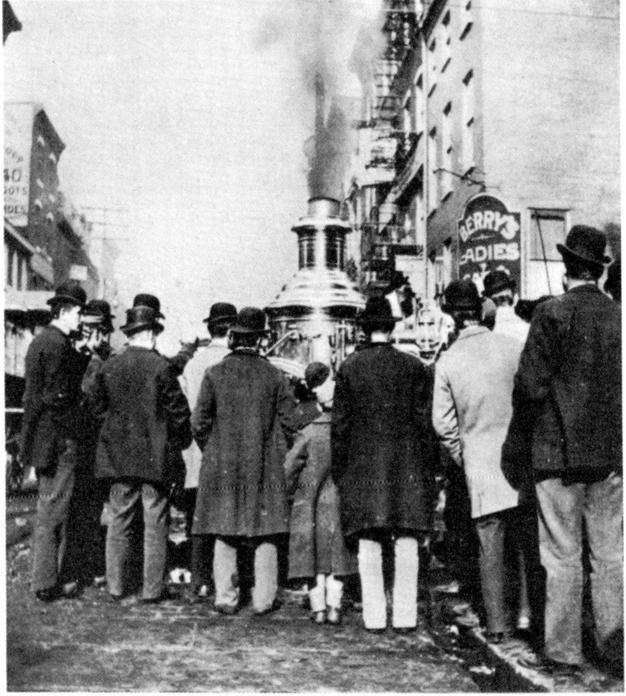

. . . were faced with mounting problems of sanitation and health . . .

RIGHT: When Tammany was temporarily ousted from City Hall in 1894, Mayor William L. Strong's reform administration inherited a terrible mess. The street cleaning department, under Colonel George E. Waring, began trying to clean up conditions like those shown in Riis's photograph of Varick Street.

BELOW: Two photographs by Byron showing snow removal after a blizzard in 1899. At left, men shoveling snow into carts in what is now Times Square. At right, dumping the carts from piers into the river.

Jacob A. Riis Collection, Museum of the City of New York

Both pictures from J. Clarence Davies Collection, Museum of the City of New York

. . . and it required heroic efforts to clean up . . .

Library of Congress, Division of Prints and Photographs

LEFT: An undated photograph, by the George Grantham Bain News Service, of the Pure Food Laboratory in New York, probably made about 1905.

BELOW LEFT: A photograph of Gansevoort Market, on West Street between Gansevoort and Little West Twelfth, about 1890. This was a "farmers' market," where wagonloads of produce from farms in Jersey, Westchester, and Long Island were brought for sale direct to the consumer.

BELOW RIGHT: A 1906 photograph by Byron showing the interior of August Siltz's poultry market, 267 Washington Street (northeast corner of Murray Street).

J. Clarence Davies Collection, Museum of the City of New York

Byron Collection, Museum of the City of New York

. . . even part of the mess which had resulted from years of civic irresponsibility.

Jacob A. Riis Collection, Museum of the City of New York

This photograph from the Riis Collection shows the site of what is now William H. Seward Park as it looked in 1898, after the slums had been demolished on the blocks between Hester Street (at left) and Division Street (crossing from center right to meet Hester Street in left background). The large building with awnings at the corner of East Broadway and Jefferson Street (right) is the headquarters of the Educational Alliance, organized in 1889 by various Jewish groups to provide recreation and education for the slum dwellers of the neighborhood. At the extreme right is Henry Street, where Lillian Wald had established the famous Henry Street Settlement in 1893.

(For a view of this neighborhood a century earlier, see page 96.)

With improved transit facilities, the business district continued to spread farther and farther uptown . . .

Both pictures from J. Clarence Davies Collection, Museum of the City of New York

Cable cars, which had been recommended by the rapid transit commissioners as early as 1884, were introduced on the Broadway and Third Avenue lines in 1891.

In the photograph at left, taken by J. S. Johnston in 1895, we are looking north along the Bowery from Grand Street.

The photograph at right, taken in 1891, shows the repaving of Broadway at Union Square after the cable track had been laid. This section of the track soon became known as "Dead Man's Curve" because of the number of accidents which resulted from the way the cable whipped the cars around the corners (see page 17). Even before the cables had been installed on these routes, however, experiments with electric cars had been made on the Sixth Avenue line, and by 1900 most of the city's transit system was electrified.

. . . surging past Madison Square, up Broadway and Sixth Avenue . . .

Brown Brothers

In this 1898 photograph we are looking north from Madison Square along Fifth Avenue (center) and Broadway (at left). It was a sign of the times that in this year Delmonico's, which had for many years catered to fashionable New Yorkers at their restaurant on the corner of Fifth Avenue and Twenty-sixth Street, opposite the north end of the square, moved uptown to even grander quarters at Forty-fourth Street. The old Fifth Avenue Hotel (left foreground), which had been built in 1859 on the former site of Franconi's Hippodrome (see page 201), was still the favorite meeting place of New York's Republican leaders, including Tom Platt and young Theodore Roosevelt; but it was no longer a center of fashion (see earlier view, page 358).

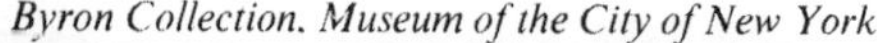

Byron Collection. Museum of the City of New York

This photograph, taken by Byron in 1897, shows the crowds at the bargain counter in Siegel Cooper's huge store on the east side of Sixth Avenue between Eighteenth and Nineteenth streets.

. . . to a new center of business and entertainment at Herald Square.

Culver Service

Herald Square, at the intersection of Broadway (left) and Sixth Avenue, is shown here in a photograph made about 1900. The New York *Herald* building, designed for James Gordon Bennett by McKim, Mead & White and erected in 1893, was one of the city's architectural wonders, with its Venetian arcade and the row of bronze owls around the cornice who winked their electric eyes at night to tell the time. On the roof above the main entrance can be seen the famous clock (now on a pedestal at the north end of the square) with the bronze figures, nicknamed Stuff and Guff, who struck the hours.

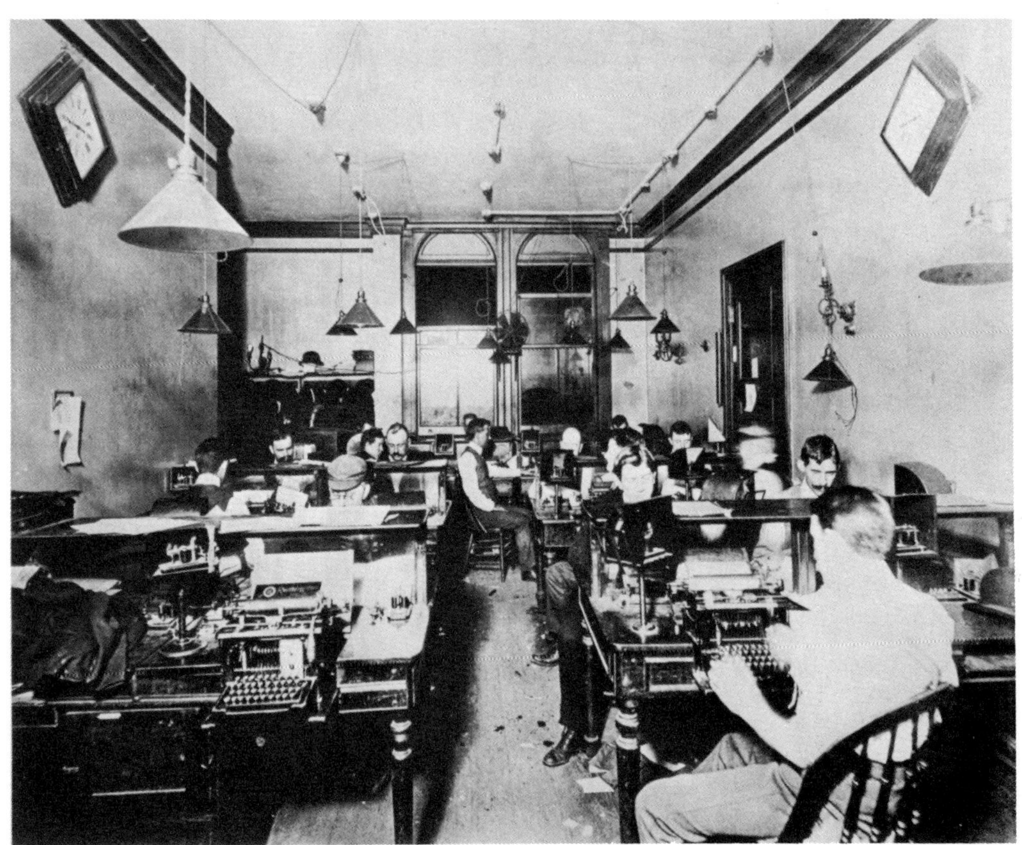

The photograph at right, of the *Herald's* telegraph department, was taken about 1905 by George Grantham Bain.

Library of Congress, Division of Prints and Photographs

By 1900 the "Great White Way" . . .

BELOW: A picture post card of "Herald Square, N.Y.," at night, published about 1905. RIGHT: A photograph by Alfred Hewitt, entitled "In the Heart of Manhattan," which was published in *Harper's Magazine,* February, 1907, as one of the illustrations for Edward S. Martin's article on "Manhattan Lights." The view was taken looking north from Times Square. Rector's restaurant is at right, and the New York Theater a block farther up. An electric sign at the corner of Forty-fourth Street points around the corner to the Hudson Theater where Shaw's *Man and Superman* was playing.

Author's collection

Museum of the City of New York

BELOW LEFT: A photograph taken by Byron in 1904, showing the north side of Forty-fourth Street between Broadway and Sixth Avenue, and the Hudson Theater, where Ethel Barrymore was starring in *Cousin Kate.* BELOW RIGHT: The office of the New York *Dramatic Mirror,* on Broadway at Fortieth Street, photographed by Byron in 1898. The magazine had moved uptown from its Union Square offices (see page 363) in order to be near the new center of the city's theatrical and entertainment business.

Both pictures from Byron Collection, Museum of the City of New York

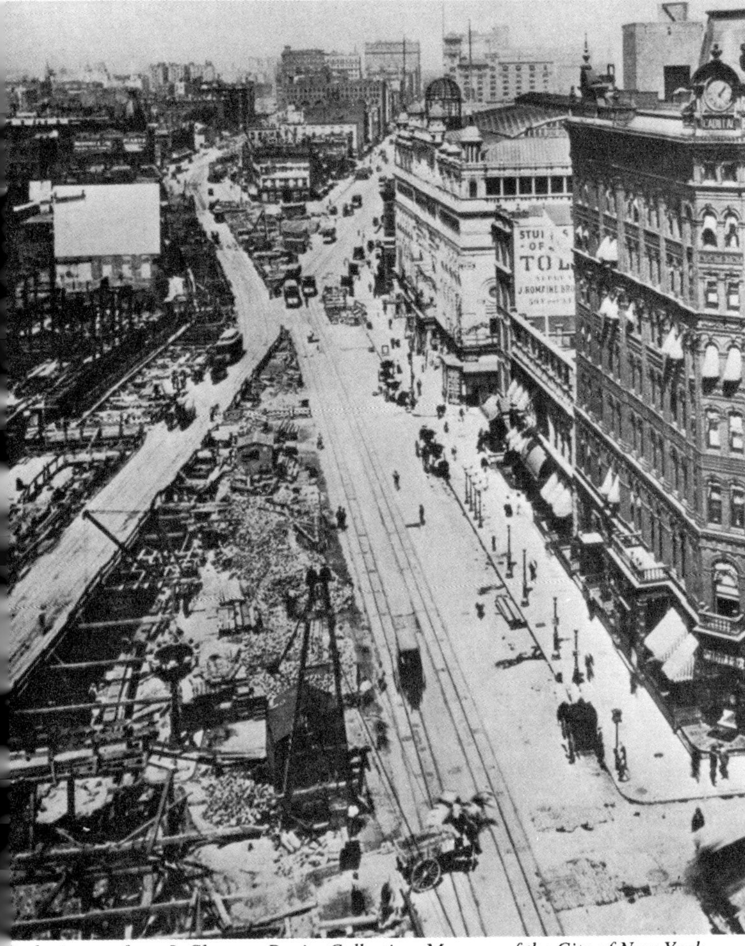

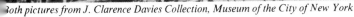

Both pictures from J. Clarence Davies Collection, Museum of the City of New York

Museum of the City of New York

The two photographs above show construction on the *Times* building. The one at left was taken in 1902 from below Forty-third Street, looking north across the triangular plot between Broadway (right) and Seventh Avenue (left) where excavation had begun for the new skyscraper's foundations. On the corner of Forty-third and Broadway is the Hotel Cadillac, and beyond it Rector's. Between Forty-fourth and Forty-fifth are the Criterion and New York theaters, occupying the vast entertainment palace originally built by Oscar Hammerstein as the Olympia Music Hall, comprising a theater, concert hall, roof garden, oriental café, and other features.

The other photograph was taken by Byron in 1904, looking south along Broadway from Forty-fourth Street. The steel frame of the *Times* tower is already being covered with its sheath of terra cotta and pink granite. Designed by Eidlitz & Mackenzie, the building soon became one of the city's most famous landmarks—as witness the "humorous" post card at right, drawn by Charles Rose.

Though a few old families hung on at the southern end of Fifth Avenue . . .

RIGHT: A photograph taken in 1889 by Paul C. Oscanyan, looking north on Fifth Avenue from Washington Square. The arch was a temporary wooden structure, designed by Stanford White and erected by private subscription as part of the celebration of the centennial of Washington's inauguration. It was later removed, and the permanent arch, also designed by White, was erected in the square in 1890–92.

BELOW: A photograph of the group on top of the new Washington Memorial Arch, April 5, 1892, for the ceremony when the last block of marble was put in place. The man in high hat and striped pants, holding the mallet, is William Rhinelander Stewart, head of the committee which had raised the funds for the memorial. Just behind the mallet is Stanford White, the architect, and on Mr. Stewart's left, also wearing a silk hat, is Richard Watson Gilder, the poet-editor of the *Century Magazine* and secretary of the committee.

Museum of the City of New York

New-York Historical Society

. . . the leaders of fashion had moved uptown, abandoning the lower avenue . . .

LEFT: This view of "A Fire on Fifth Avenue," drawn by G. A. Travers, is reproduced from a chromolithograph in Zeisloft's *The New Metropolis.* It depicts the burning of the Hanover Apartment Hotel, southeast corner of Fifth Avenue and Fifteenth Street, in 1898. In the picture we are looking east along Fifteenth Street toward Union Square. Below, at left, are two of the most famous private residences of an earlier day: the William B. Astor house on the southwest corner of Fifth Avenue and Thirty-fourth, and the A. T. Stewart mansion on the northwest corner (see also page 372).

uthor's collection

Below, at right, is a photograph taken by Byron in 1898, looking north on Fifth Avenue from Sixty-fifth Street. In the foreground is the huge château, designed by Richard Morris Hunt, to which Mrs. Astor removed from the Thirty-fourth Street house.

Culver Service

Byron Collection, Museum of the City of New York

. . . to be taken over by expensive shops and apartments and luxurious hotels.

Brown Brothers

J. Clarence Davies Collection, Museum of the City of New York

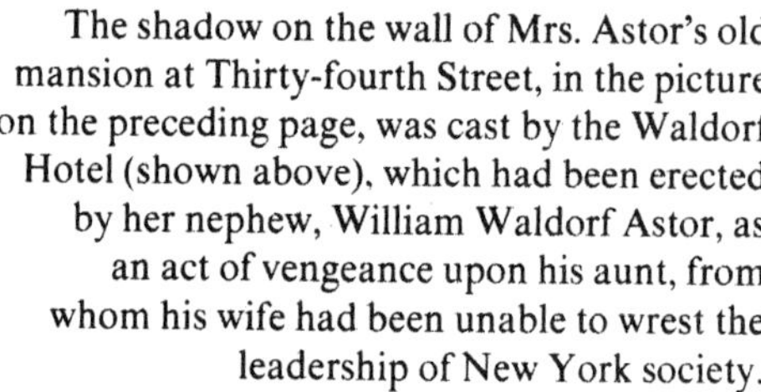

The shadow on the wall of Mrs. Astor's old mansion at Thirty-fourth Street, in the picture on the preceding page, was cast by the Waldorf Hotel (shown above), which had been erected by her nephew, William Waldorf Astor, as an act of vengeance upon his aunt, from whom his wife had been unable to wrest the leadership of New York society.

Less than a year after it was completed, in 1893, Mrs. Astor capitulated and hired Hunt to build her the new house uptown. In 1897 her son erected the Astoria on the old site, and the combined hotels were operated as a unit to the profit of both the rival branches of the family. The picture above at right was taken in 1898. The shop next to the Stewart mansion was the Fifth Avenue Art Galleries, and next to it, at the southwest corner of Thirty-fifth, was the New York Club. Below, at right, the main office of the Waldorf-Astoria in 1902.

Library of Congress, Division of Prints and Photographs

Upper Madison Avenue, which had been way out of town when Columbia moved there forty years before, was solidly built up . . .

Culver Service

LEFT: Looking north on Madison Avenue from Forty-first Street, about 1900. The church at the corner of Forty-fourth is St. Bartholomew's, where the Canadian Pacific Building now stands.

BELOW: A bird's-eye view, drawn by Kyes and Woodbury, of Columbia College, looking northwest from Forty-ninth Street and Lexington Avenue (see page 256). The picture was published in *Harper's Weekly*, November 3, 1894, as an illustration to accompany an article by Brander Matthews on "Columbia College: The Development of a Great University."

Under the leadership of President Seth Low, Columbia's undergraduate and graduate schools were rapidly expanding, and the Madison Avenue site was already badly overcrowded. Before Matthews' article appeared in print the trustees had acquired the property on Morningside Heights to which the university was soon to move (see page 415).

Author's collection

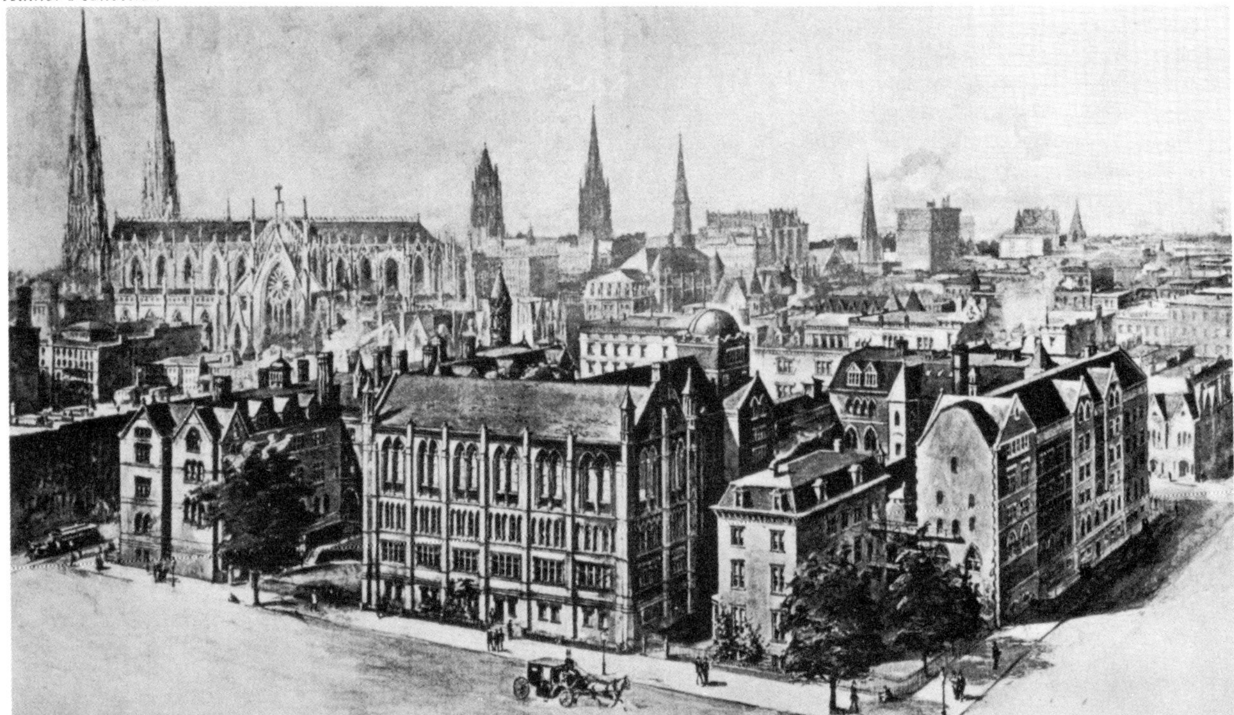

. . . and the gridiron blocks beyond Harlem were filling up with chunks of speculative row-houses.

New-York Historical Society

ABOVE: The photograph above was taken about 1882 from a point near the southeast corner of Sixth (now Lenox) Avenue and West 133rd street, looking northeast. The row of houses in the background is on the north side of West 134th, just west of Fifth Avenue. By 1898 all the vacant lots had been covered.

RIGHT: Looking northwest from the roof of a building on the east side of Broadway, between 120th and 122nd streets, toward Grant's Tomb on Riverside Drive about 1901. The old building in the foreground is the College Tavern, long a favorite haunt of Columbia students. It stood on the double block now occupied by the buildings of the Union Theological Seminary. The houses on the southeast corner of 122nd Street and the Drive stood on the present site of the Riverside Church.

Columbiana Collection, Columbia University

Far up on the west side a "New Acropolis" was rising on Morningside Heights, to be a center of the city's cultural life . . .

Byron Collection, Museum of the City of New York

LEFT: This photograph of the Cathedral of St. John the Divine under construction was taken by Byron in 1904. The site for the cathedral had been acquired in 1887, when the trustees bought the old Leake and Watts Orphan Asylum property west of Amsterdam Avenue between 110th and 113th streets. Work on the building, designed by Heims and La Farge, began in 1892. The first service, in the crypt beneath the choir, was held in 1899. The building at left, used as the Synod House, was one of the old asylum buildings. Beyond the buttresses of the arch can be seen St. Luke's Hospital, on Amsterdam between 113th and 114th streets.

BELOW: A photograph taken by Ambrose Fowler, October 24, 1896, showing the new Columbia University buildings under construction on the former site of the Bloomingdale Asylum (see page 141). At the extreme left is one of the asylum buildings, which was used for many years as the Faculty Club, and to the right of the Low Memorial Library (center) is another of the asylum buildings, which is still in use as Alumni House. Behind and to the right of it are Schermerhorn and Fayerweather halls, under construction. The building across Amsterdam, at extreme right, is an apartment house on the present site of the Casa Italiana. The old building this side of the library stands in the midst of the former asylum gardens, between 114th Street (in foreground) and 116th.

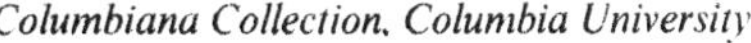

Columbiana Collection, Columbia University

. . . and only at the northern limits of Manhattan was anything left of the island's original wooded charm.

Both pictures from Museum of the City of New Yor

ABOVE: Looking north up the Hudson from the top of Grant's Tomb about 1903, showing the Claremont Inn and the Riverside Drive viaduct at Manhattanville, with Washington Heights in the background. Claremont had been built in the late eighteenth century and occupied by George Pollock, a wealthy merchant, as his country seat. Before the Civil War it had been converted for use as a restaurant and inn, and it was for many years a popular objective for all-day excursions from the city. The building was finally torn down in 1952, and a playground was laid out on the site. (See page 76 for a view of this same region in Revolutionary days.)

RIGHT: A photograph by William Henry Jackson, the famous photographer of the West, taken in 1890. The view was made from a point on the east shore of Manhattan above 182nd Street, looking south along the Harlem River to the Washington Bridge and High Bridge.

Parts of the boroughs which were consolidated with Manhattan in 1898 to form Greater New York were still distinctly rural . . .

Staten Island Historical Society

ABOVE: A panoramic photograph of the annual fair of the Richmond County Agricultural Society, Staten Island, taken in 1905 by A. Loeffler. The General Berry Housing Project now occupies this site.

Courtesy of Flatbush Reformed Church

LEFT: Looking south on Flatbush Avenue, Brooklyn, from near present corner of Martense Street, about 1885. The Flatbush Reformed Dutch Church was erected in 1796 on the site of two earlier church buildings. One of the oldest churches in the city, whose bell has tolled the death of every President of the United States, it still stands at the now busy intersection of Flatbush and Church avenues.

LEFT: The Lott farm in Flatlands, Brooklyn, about 1905.

New-York Historical Society

. . . but the surveyors had already been through the woods and farms . . .

New-York Historical Society

J. Clarence Davies Collection, Museum of the City of New York

ABOVE: Boating on the Bronx River at West Farms in 1887. Bolton's bleaching mill, in the background, stood on the east bank, just above the Boston Road in what is now Bronx Park (see also page 125).

BELOW: Surveyors at work in the Annexed District of the Bronx about 1890.

All pictures from J. Clarence Davies Collection, Museum of the City of New York

ABOVE LEFT: The drafting room at the Bronx headquarters of the Topographical Bureau, Board of Public Improvements, in 1891. Seated fourth from the left is Louis Risse, chief engineer of the Board. Standing behind him in the corner is J. Clarence Davies, who later made a fortune in Bronx real estate (see page 420).

ABOVE RIGHT: Chief Engineer Louis Risse at his desk in 1892, holding the plans which had been drawn up in his office for the Grand Concourse.

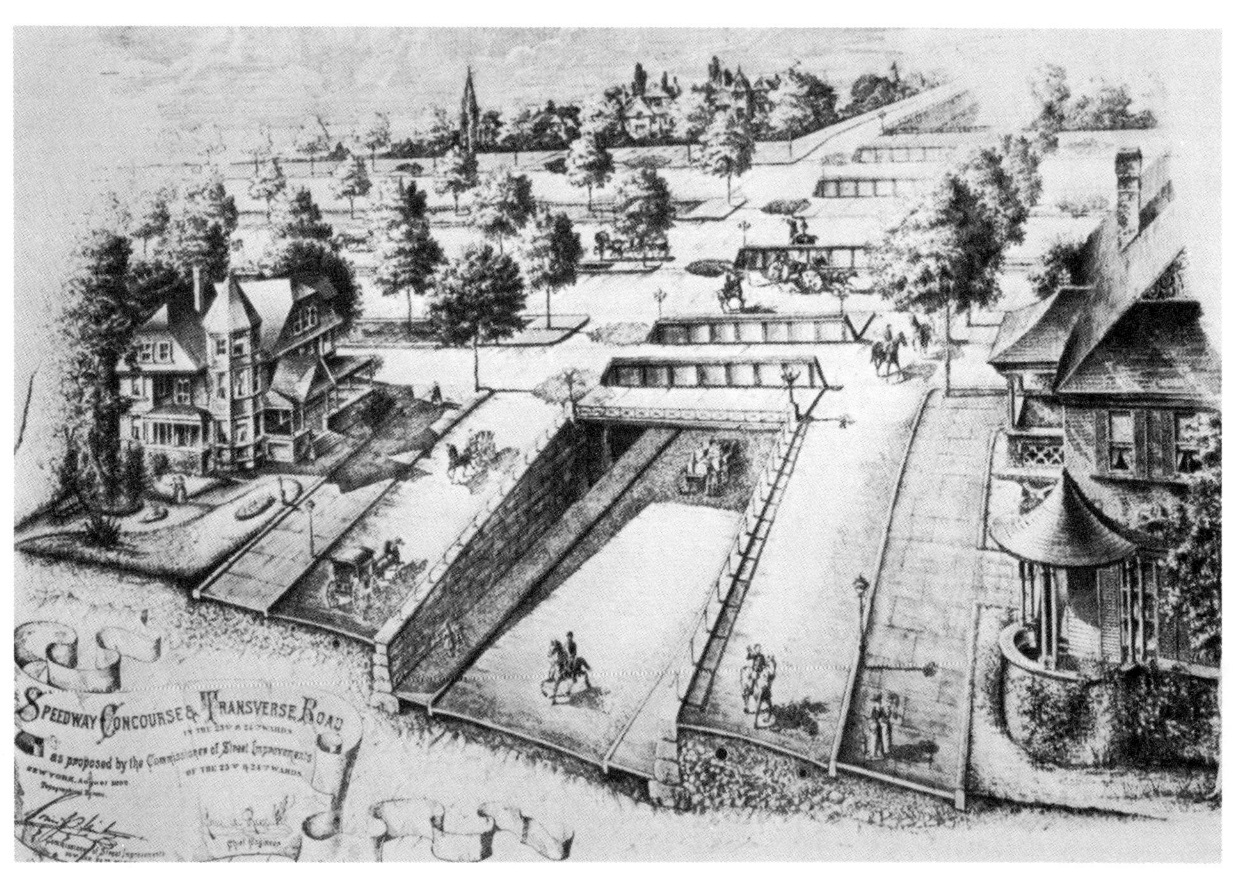

LEFT: A copy of the drawing Risse is holding in the picture above, showing the "Speedway Concourse & Transverse Road as proposed by the Commissioner of Street Improvements," and dated August, 1892. Designed as a "spacious and attractive driveway" linking Manhattan's park system with Bronx and Van Cortlandt parks, it provided for a central speedway carried across all major intersections on bridges, and flanked by a double boulevard, promenades, and bicycle paths.

. . . opening vast tracts of hitherto inaccessible land for real estate developments.

RIGHT: J. Clarence Davies (second from right) and his associates in front of his newly opened real estate office at 149th Street and Third Avenue, the Bronx, about 1900. Miss Alice M. Johnston is at his left. The others, from left to right, are William H. Harden, William G. Rule, Clarence W. Giesen, and Edward Lyons. Mr. Davies later formed one of the finest collections of historical prints and photographs of New York, which is now in the Museum of the City of New York. Many of the pictures in this volume are from his collection.

BELOW: Two photographs of Prospect Avenue, the Bronx, in 1895. The one at left was taken looking south from Westchester Avenue, where paving operations are under way. The other shows the avenue north from 162nd Street.

All pictures from J. Clarence Davies Collection, Museum of the City of New York

Linked to its neighbors by bridges and ferries, the island of Manhattan . . .

Author's collection

This unusual bird's-eye view of the city, looking southwest from above the Hell Gate railroad bridge, was drawn by Richard Rummell in 1907 and published in *King's Views of New York* in 1908. The Hell Gate span, properly called the New York Connecting Railroad Bridge, was shown as it would be, not as it was. Construction was not begun until 1914, and the bridge was not completed until 1917.

The view takes in Manhattan up to Harlem (at right) and shows the various East River bridges, including the almost completed Queensborough span at Blackwell's (now Welfare) Island. Just north of the island is the Edison power plant on Hallett's Point, Astoria. On Ward's Island (right foreground) is the Manhattan State Hospital for the insane. The tallest tower in the city, just over the center of the Queensborough Bridge, is the Metropolitan Life Insurance Co. building on the east side of Madison Square, designed by M. Le Brun & Son and completed in 1908.

. . . had become the focus of an expanding transportation network . . .

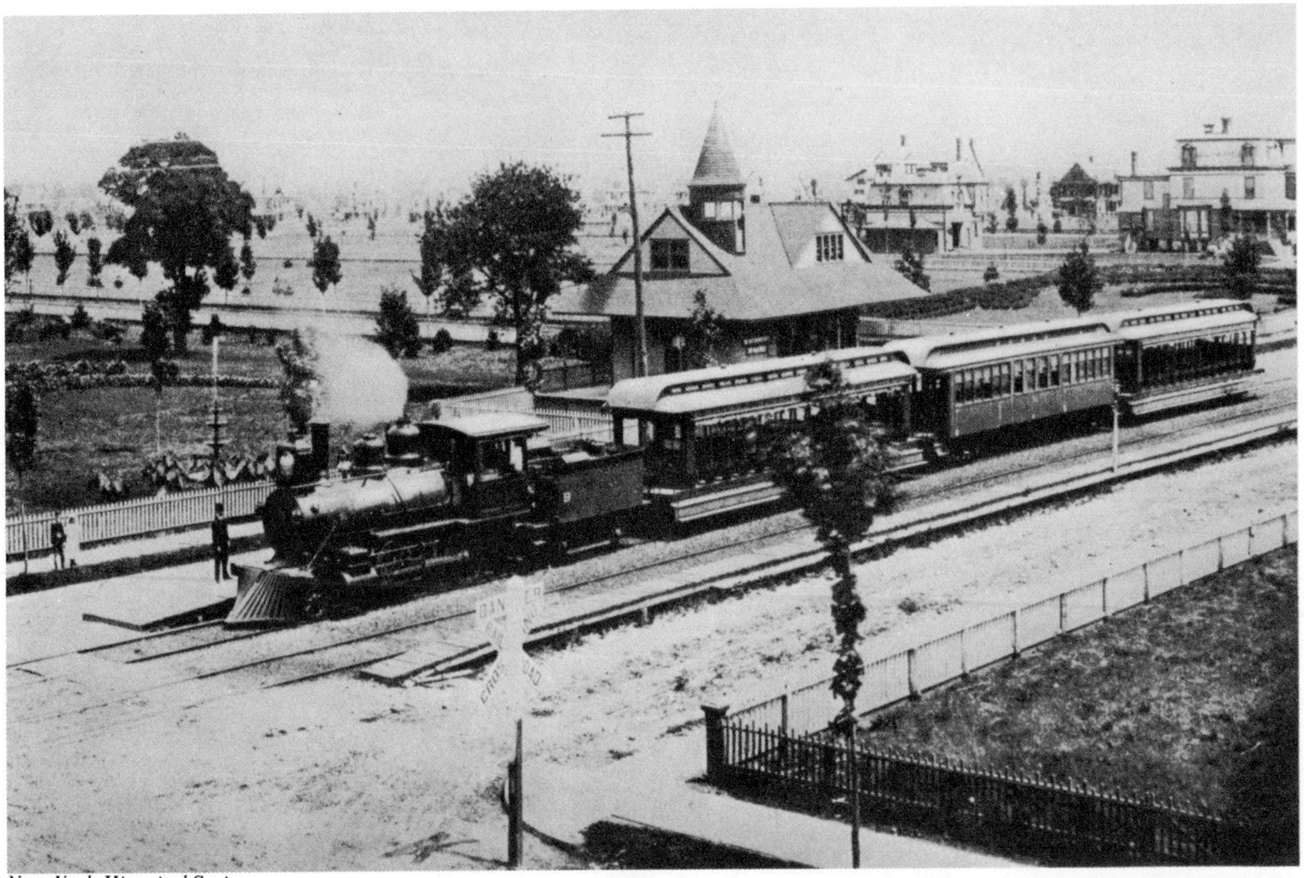

New-York Historical Society

In an article on "How People Come and Go in New York," *Harper's Weekly,* February 26, 1898, Richard Barry reported that the number of people who commuted daily to Manhattan was greater than the total population of a city the size of Cincinnati: 100,000 came by bridge and ferry from Brooklyn, another 100,000 or more by ferry from New Jersey, and a total of more than 118,000 arrived daily at Grand Central from Westchester and Connecticut.

ABOVE: A commuters' train at the Bensonhurst station of the Brooklyn, Bath Beach & West End Railroad in 1892. BELOW, LEFT: Commuters from New Jersey arriving at the West Twenty-third Street landing of the Erie Railroad's Pavonia ferry. The photograph was taken by Byron in 1896. BELOW, RIGHT: Cyclists on Bedford Avenue, Brooklyn, about to cross the tracks of the railroad on Atlantic Avenue. Photograph taken by Edgar S. Thomson in 1896.

Byron Collection, Museum of the City of New York

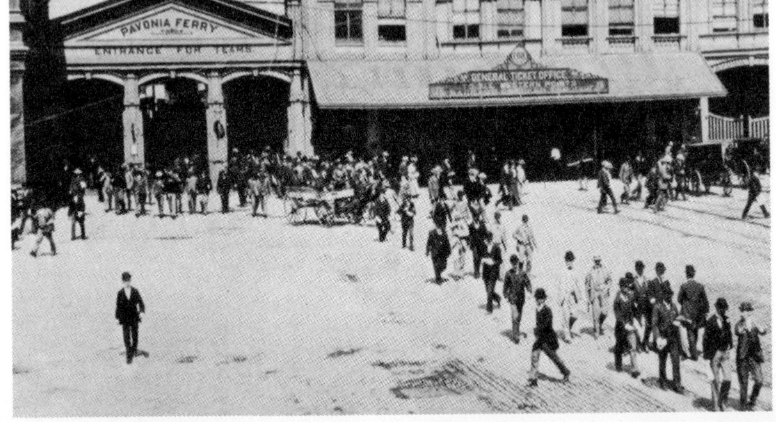

Brooklyn Museum

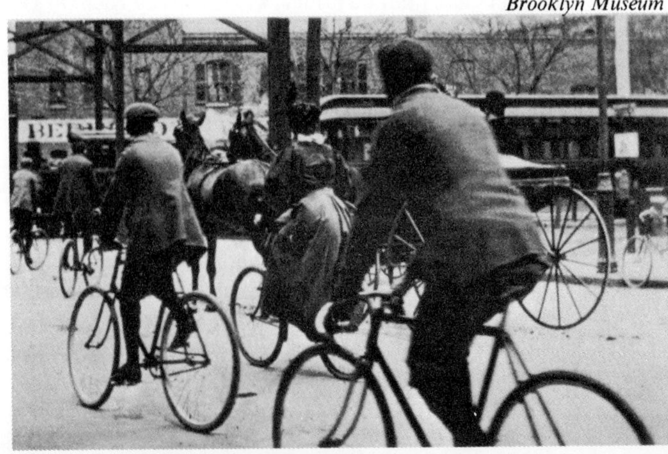

. . . which provided the real basis for the consolidation of the Greater City.

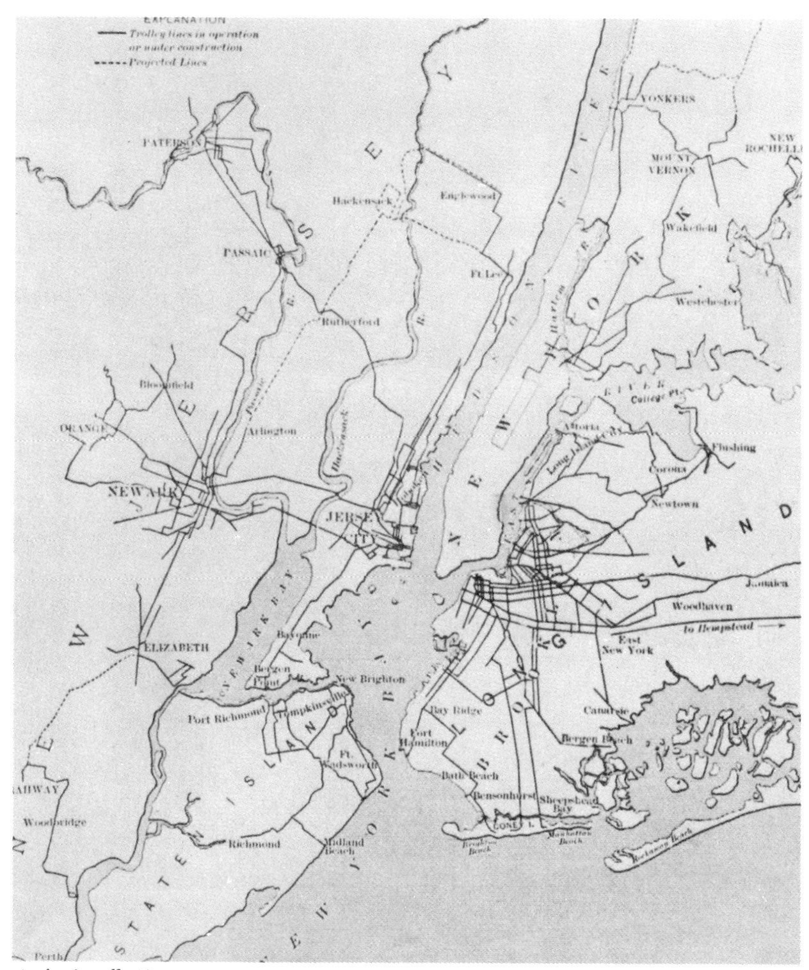

Author's collection

New-York Historical Society

The map of "Existing and Projected Trolley Lines Around New York" is reproduced from *Harper's Weekly,* August 1, 1896. The accompanying text pointed out that the trolleys brought shoppers to the city who had hitherto patronized local "village" stores, and gave city dwellers access to outlying real estate developments and parks. Instead of taking passengers away from the railroads, "the trolleys seem to have created a new patronage of their own. Travel has been stimulated, rather than diverted." The photograph above, showing the Manhattan-bound El train and trolleys moving onto the Brooklyn Bridge, was taken by George P. Hall & Son about 1898. The tall twin-capped skyscraper at extreme left is the Park Row Building (see pages 394 and 397).

LEFT: A photograph taken by Byron in 1899, during a trolley strike in Brooklyn.

Byron Collection, Museum of the City of New York

Though stages and horsecars still lumbered through the downtown streets . . .

Courtesy of Alfred Stieglitz Estate

. . . they were already outmoded enough to seem picturesque when Stieglitz photographed them in the early nineties . . .

Courtesy of Alfred Stieglitz Estate

"Winter-Fifth Avenue," reproduced on the opposite page, and "The Terminal" (above) were both taken by Alfred Stieglitz in February, 1893, a couple of years after his return from Berlin, where he had become interested in photography while studying mechanical engineering.

These were among the first of his photographs to be made with a hand camera. Unlike many of the early "Pictorial Photographers," who believed in the aesthetic values of photography, he did not regard the new, instantaneous cameras as beneath the dignity of serious workers.

("The Terminal" was taken in front of the Astor House, at the junction of Park Row and Broadway where the Harlem horsecars turned around on a loop of track—see page 401.)

. . . and a new era in urban transportation began early in the twentieth century . . .

Both pictures from Brown Brothers

Proposals for underground railroads had been made as early as the 1850s, and an experimental "pneumatic" subway, several blocks long, was actually built and operated for a couple of years in the early seventies. But it was not until 1900 that construction began on New York's first real subway. The picture above, at left, representing the station at Fourth Avenue and Twenty-third Street as it would look when completed, is reproduced from an advertisement put out in 1900 by Abbey's Effervescent Salt, "The Rapid Transit to Health." The gentlemen at right are setting out on an inspection tour (towed by handcars) of the first completed section in January, 1904. Mayor McClellan is in the front row at right, next to Alexander E. Orr, president of the Rapid Transit Commission.

RIGHT: It was in 1904, also, that the first tunnel under the Hudson was completed and work began on the Pennsylvania Railroad Station between Seventh and Eighth avenues and Thirty-first and Thirty-third streets. The completed structure, designed by McKim, Mead & White, is shown in a drawing by Hughson Hawley, published by the railroad in 1910. The new post office, by the same architects, straddles the tracks in the foreground.

Bella C. Landauer Collection, New-York Historical Society

. . . when rapid transit and the railroads went underground.

Both pictures from Culver Service

These pictures were taken in June, 1912, when work on the new Grand Central Terminal was nearing completion. The original building, erected in 1871, had been completely remodeled and much enlarged in 1899. But in 1903 the New York Central acquired the subsurface title to land north of the terminal, so that its train yards and tracks could be put underground, and in 1910 the old terminal was demolished. Work on the new structure, designed by Warren & Wetmore (architects) and Reed & Stern (engineers), began immediately, and it was opened in 1913.

The picture above, looking south along Park Avenue from above Fiftieth Street, shows the construction of the two levels of track below street grade.

The photograph below was taken from the middle of Park Avenue, above the northern entrance of the old Harlem Railroad tunnel, through which the streetcars ran underground to Thirty-third Street. The El station spanning Forty-second Street at right was at the end of a spur of track from the Third Avenue line. It was torn down when the bridge and ramps were built which now lift Park Avenue traffic across Forty-second Street and carry it around the terminal, through the New York Central office building, and down to street level again at Forty-sixth Street.

But the most portentous development in urban transportation at the turn of the century . . .

Both pictures from Staten Island Historical Society

The pictures on this and the following page were taken by Alice Austen, whose remarkable photographs of life in and around New York at the turn of the century were rediscovered two years ago. Miss Austen was born and spent most of her life on Staten Island. But wherever she went she took her camera with her, taking pictures which are startlingly direct and observant.

The photograph above, of a cabby and his hansom, was taken in Union Square, at Broadway and Sixteenth Street, in 1896. The one below, taken in October, 1888, shows Miss Julia Martin, a Staten Island neighbor, in her jaunting cart in front of the Martins' house.

Both pictures from Staten Island Historical Society

The two photographs on this page were taken by Miss Austen about 1910. In place of the hansom cab there is the taxi —the first of which had appeared on the city's streets in 1907. And in place of Miss Martin's jaunting cart there is the Pierce-Arrow touring car, shown in front of an unidentified house in Brooklyn.

Though the early cars were expensive, thousands were eagerly bought by city dwellers . . .

The photograph at top was taken by Van de Weyde in 1898, showing two of the electric cabs which had been introduced in that year. They are standing (one with a very flat tire!) in front of the Thirty-ninth Street entrance of the Metropolitan Opera House.

The first National Automobile Show, shown in the photograph at right, was held in Madison Square Garden in 1900. Many of the cars were electrics, and all of those shown in the picture had steering rods instead of steering wheels.

Below is a photograph taken by Byron at the opening of Smith & Mabley's new automobile salesroom at 1765 Broadway (west side, south of Fifty-seventh Street) in 1905. Proctor Smith got into the automobile business after he returned from Europe in 1900, bringing with him an 8-horsepower Panhard. Everyone wanted to buy it from him, it seemed, and he finally sold it for several thousand more than it had cost. Convinced that cars were the coming thing, he returned to Europe, made arrangements to represent Panhard and other European manufacturers, and returned to New York to open an automobile salesroom with his brother-in-law, C. R. Mabley, as partner. Their second shop, shown here, was one of the pioneers of New York's "Automobile Row," along Broadway north of Fifty-second Street.

J. Clarence Davies Collection, Museum of the City of New York

Brown Brothers

Byron Collection, Museum of the City of New York

. . . and motorized equipment was soon introduced in many fields.

Library of Congress, Division of Prints and Photographs

The photograph above, by the George Grantham Bain News Service, shows one of the four electric trucks put into service in New York in the U. S. Post Office's first experiment with mail delivery by automobile, about 1909.

BELOW LEFT: A photograph by George Grantham Bain of New York's first "Auto Street Cleaner," built in 1912 by convicts in the machine shop at Sing Sing Prison, from designs worked out by Magnus Butler, foreman of the shop.

BELOW RIGHT: An early motorized fire engine in New York, from a picture post card published in 1914. The first one had been introduced in the city four years earlier.

Library of Congress, Division of Prints and Photographs

Museum of the City of New York

The age of the horse was ending, and a new one —with problems of its own— had begun.

Library of Congress, Division of Prints and Photographs

The picture above is a still from Scene 16 of an early movie entitled *The Life of an American Policeman,* produced by Edwin S. Porter in 1905. From subsequent stills, filed with the copyright application, we learn that the car was overtaken farther up Riverside Drive by policemen mounted on bicycles. Porter's film was a companion piece to his *The Life of an American Fireman,* made in New York in 1903, which was the first narrative movie made in America. Unlike the fantastic narratives, such as *A Trip to the Moon,* that Georges Méliès had been making in France, Porter went in for realistic narrative. His second movie, *The Great Train Robbery,* was so popular that it has been credited with having established the moving picture industry on a permanent basis. From Porter's day to the present New York has been the setting of more movies than any other city. As Dennis Brogan has said, "thanks to the movies, it is better known to the world, visually at least, than any of its rivals from Babylon to London have ever been." The first movies ever publicly shown in the United States were exhibited at Koster & Bial's Music Hall, 115 West Twenty-third Street, April 23, 1896, when Edison's Vitascope was introduced, and New York remained the center of movie production until Hollywood superseded it in 1913.

At right is a photograph taken by Byron in 1906, in front of the Bide-a-Wee Home for Animals, 145 West Forty-eighth Street. Notice the motor express company office next door, and the car parked at the curb.

Byron Collection, Museum of the City of New York

Upon all these signs of material progress the prime movers and shapers of the city's destinies looked with assured confidence.

Museum of the City of New York

LEFT: This informal glimpse of J. P. Morgan in shirt sleeves, "Sketched from life" by Haydon Jones, is supposed to have been drawn from the window of a building across Wall Street from the Morgan office.

BELOW LEFT: A photograph taken about 1905 of the three men who did more than any others to create the neo-Renaissance façade of early twentieth-century urban grandeur: Charles Follen McKim (center), William Rutherford Mead (at left), and Stanford White, the architects of the Pennsylvania Station, Columbia University, the Hall of Fame, the Century and University clubs, and countless other famous buildings.

BELOW RIGHT: A photograph taken by Byron in 1898 of Chauncey M. Depew at his desk in his home on West Fifty-fourth Street. The maps behind him are of the railroad empire which he had helped Commodore Vanderbilt to create. A year after the picture was taken Depew gave up the presidency of the New York Central to become chairman of the board and United States senator from New York.

New-York Historical Society

Byron Collection, Museum of the City of New York

The onward march of prosperity seemed irresistible, in spite of occasional setbacks.

Culver Service

RIGHT: The Easter Parade on Fifth Avenue, early in the 1900s. At right is the Buckingham Hotel, where the Emperor and Empress of Brazil had stayed back in 1876, when the building's Eastlake Gothic interiors were fresh and new. Beyond St. Patrick's, on the northeast corner of Fifty-first Street, is the Union Club, where Best & Co. now stands.

BELOW LEFT: A photograph taken by Edgar S. Thomson showing the Business Men's Parade, or "Sound Money Demonstration," on Broadway a week before the election of 1896, in which McKinley defeated Bryan and the "free-silver" Democrats.

BELOW RIGHT: Four years later, when Bryan ran again (with Adlai E. Stevenson as his running mate), the city's businessmen organized another pro-McKinley parade. Counterpropaganda from the Democrats (which had little effect, apparently) is seen in this photograph of Fifth Avenue north from below Fortieth Street, taken by Raoul Froger-Doudement.

Brooklyn Museum

Brooklyn Museum

It was a time of imperial triumphs and—socially speaking—of delusions of imperial grandeur.

Museum of the City of New York

ABOVE: This splendid night-panorama of the city was made by a photographer named Butler from the roof of the Hotel Margaret on Brooklyn Heights during the celebration of September 29, 1899, in honor of Admiral Dewey, returned victorious from the Philippines.

Museum of the City of New York

LEFT: The original drawing by Frederick Burr Opper of a cartoon entitled "The Charge of the Four Hundred," inspired by the visit to New York of Prince Louis of Battenberg in November, 1905. It was for the Prince that the aging Mrs. Astor gave her last great banquet.

Byron Collection, Museum of the City of New York

LEFT: A photograph by Byron of the scene in front of the Gould mansion, northeast corner of Fifth Avenue and Sixty-seventh Street, on the day of Miss Anna Gould's marriage to the Count Boni de Castellane in 1894.

With the passing of the older generation of society's leaders . . .

RIGHT: Ward McAllister died in February, 1895—just five years after publishing his pompous memoirs of *Society as I Have Found It.* Byron's photograph shows the funeral procession moving south on Fifth Avenue past the Stewart mansion at Thirty-fourth Street, then the home of the Manhattan Club.

BELOW: Caroline Schermerhorn Astor—*the* Mrs. Astor—died in October, 1908, and in the mansion at Fifth Avenue and Sixty-fifth Street Carolus Duran's life-size portrait of her, before which she used to stand to receive her guests, was draped in black.

Byron Collection, Museum of the City of New York

Brown Brothers

. . . a new and racier set competed for the headlines.

Both pictures from Culver Service

"Society's amusements of the present day are exceedingly varied," Zeisloft reported in 1899. "At the private entertainments great ingenuity is displayed in providing new and startling diversions. Magnificence of display has almost reached the limit, and other realms are invaded to gratify the satiated tastes of the seekers for amusement." The stuffy Ward McAllister was succeeded by the petulant and cynical Harry Lehr (at whose instigation Mrs. Stuyvesant Fish gave a dinner in honor of a monkey, dressed in an evening gown, who sat in the place usually reserved for Mrs. Astor). In the photograph at left Lehr is seated at the left in J. Stewart Barney's surrey. BELOW: N. G. Lorillard and party at the Jerome Park race track in 1901.

As the photographers recorded it, New York at the turn of the century . . .

Culver Service

Author's collection

ABOVE: A scene on Broadway, just above Wanamaker's (formerly Stewart's) store, about 1905.

BELOW: "A Typical Scene on the Bowery," from Zeisloft's *The New Metropolis* (1899). Curtis & Heath's Grand Cake Walk and Minstrel Burlesque Company was performing at the Lyceum Concert Garden, just above Houston Street on the west side of the Bowery.

. . . was a place of striking contrasts and bewildering diversity.

Brown Brothers

Lewis W. Hine Memorial Collection

ABOVE LEFT: A photograph of Mrs. George Gould's pearls, about 1905. ABOVE RIGHT: An unidentified New Yorker photographed in 1906 by Lewis W. Hine. (For more of Hine's work, see pages 458-60.) BELOW LEFT: A typical flat in a respectable city tenement about 1905. BELOW RIGHT: Old Mrs. Benoit, an Indian, in her attic room on Hudson Street, 1897, from a photograph by Jacob Riis.

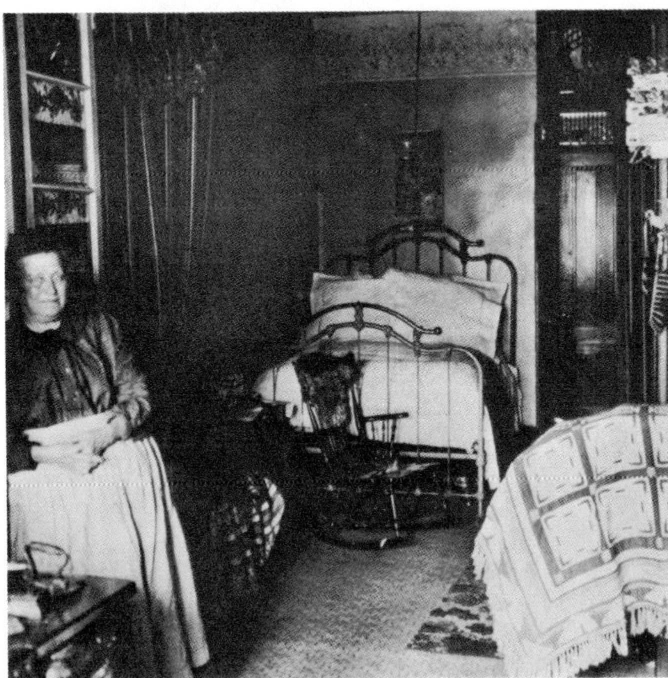

Library of Congress, Division of Prints and Photographs

Jacob A. Riis Collection, Museum of the City of New York

At one extreme were the bright lights . . .

Courtesy of Gottscho-Schleisner

This photograph of Luna Park, Coney Island, was taken on June 4, 1906, by a young man named Samuel H. Gottscho who was later to become known as one of the city's ablest and most devoted photographers (see pages 491-93, and other pictures in the final Group of this volume).

Thompson and Dundy's Luna Park had opened in 1903 (with Chauncey Depew riding the largest elephant in the triumphal procession) and had been a tremendous success. Even the brooding Russian novelist, Maxim Gorki, was overcome by the vision of Luna at night. "Thousands of ruddy sparks glimmer in the darkness," he wrote, "limning in fine, sensitive outline on the black background of the sky shapely towers of miraculous castles, palaces and temples. . . . Fabulous beyond conceiving, ineffably beautiful, is this fiery scintillation."

. . . and colorful elegance of the world of entertainment . . .

Museum of the City of New York

This water color of Madison Square Garden was painted about 1895 by W. Louis Sonntag, Jr., one of the most popular illustrators of the period. The view was taken from the corner of Twenty-seventh and Madison, looking south. The spire at right is the Madison Square Presbyterian Church at Twenty-fourth Street, facing the square on the site later occupied by the Metropolitan Life Insurance tower. (It was from the pulpit of this church that Dr. Charles Parkhurst in 1892 launched his savage attack on the "lying, perjured, rum-soaked and libidinous" politicians who "protected" vice and gambling in the city.)

The first buildings on the Madison Square Garden site were the depots of the New York & Harlem and New York, New Haven & Hartford railroads (see page 285). In 1873 P. T. Barnum and others leased the property for a concert garden, later known as Gilmore's Garden, where Moody and Sankey held their great revival meeting in 1876. In 1879 the name was changed to Madison Square Garden.

The original Garden was demolished in 1889 and replaced by the building shown here. Designed by Stanford White (who was murdered in its roof garden by Harry K. Thaw in 1906), the Garden was long one of New York's most famous landmarks. Saint-Gaudens' statue of Diana, which surmounted its Spanish tower, was probably the best-loved statue ever erected in the city. The building was torn down in 1925 to make way for the New York Life Insurance Co.'s skyscraper, and the present Madison Square Garden was erected on Eighth Avenue, between Forty-ninth and Fiftieth streets.

. . . and at another extreme, the solid respectability of quiet residential streets.

Library of Congress, Division of Prints and Photographs

Brown Brothers

ABOVE: Clinton Avenue, Brooklyn, in 1904; from a photograph by the Detroit Photographic Co. Baedeker's guide to the United States, published in the same year, described Clinton as the handsomest street in Brooklyn.

BELOW: Charlton Street in Greenwich Village, looking east from Varick Street toward Macdougal, about 1905. The horsecar was one of those on the crosstown line from the Chambers Street ferry to Avenue C and Eleventh Street.

On the outskirts of the city, life was much like that in a country village . . .

The pictures on this page were taken in the early 1900s by Mrs. Jeanette Bernard, a devoted amateur photographer who, for ten years or more, kept a detailed camera record of her family's life in their quiet neighborhood in the Borough of Queens shown at left. Mr. D. Jay Culver acquired hundreds of her glass negatives from a dealer in old glass about fifteen years ago—a collection which gives an unsurpassed picture of middle-class life at the turn of the century. Unfortunately he has no record of what street the Bernards lived on or who the people in the pictures are.

All pictures from Culver Service

. . . but in town, where more and more people lived in apartments and tenements, rather than in houses . . .

Collection of Albert M. Behrens; photograph courtesy of Museum of the City of New York

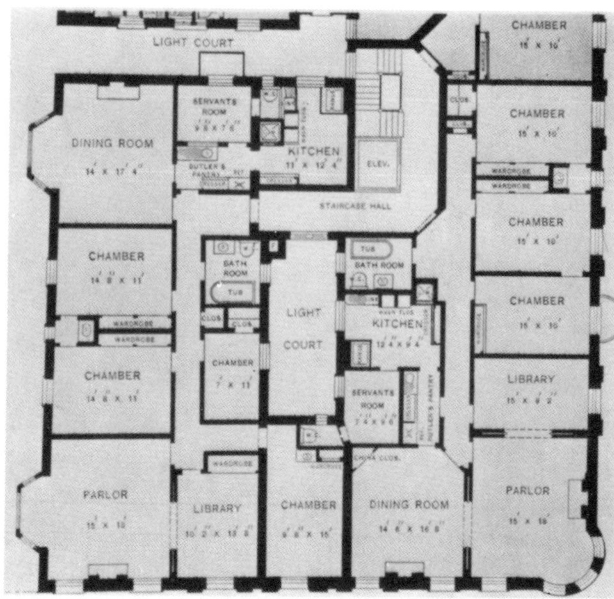

Author's collection

The first so-called apartment house in New York was the Stuyvesant, erected in 1869 on the south side of East Eighteenth Street, west of Third Avenue, from designs by R. M. Hunt. Despite objections by some of the stodgy older generation to what seemed to be merely glorified tenements, the idea caught on rapidly. In 1881 the huge Dakota Apartments (ABOVE LEFT) was built at Seventy-second and Eighth Avenue (now Central Park West), overlooking the park. The plans (ABOVE RIGHT), reproduced from Zeisloft's *The New Metropolis* (1899), show a group of three apartments in what was called a "high-class" house—probably the Navarro on Central Park South, southeast corner of Seventh Avenue. (Notice that no tub is provided for the servants' quarters.) BELOW LEFT: This picture of "The Return Home of a Working Girl After the Day's Work is Over" is reproduced from Zeisloft's chapter on "Classes in New York and their Ways of Living," in *The New Metropolis.* BELOW RIGHT: A drawing by Charles Rentz, architect, of the southwest corner of Thirty-second Street and Third Avenue, dated 1892, showing a new tenement house fronting on both streets.

Author's collection

Collection of Edward W. C. Arnold; photograph courtesy of Museum of the City of New York

. . . there was a bewildering diversity of urban modes of life.

All pictures from Byron Collection, Museum of the City of New York

ABOVE LEFT: David Belasco's den in his home at 247 West Seventieth Street, photographed by Byron in 1904. ABOVE RIGHT: An interior, photographed by Byron in 1894, identified only as "Mrs. Leoni's" parlor. BELOW LEFT: The library in the home of Miss Dodd, 231 West Twenty-first Street, photographed by Byron in 1898. The Rogers group, "Coming to the Parson," on the table by the bookcase, had been made in 1870. BELOW RIGHT: Dining room in the home of Miss Elsie de Wolfe, in the house on the southwest corner of Seventeenth Street and Irving Place where Washington Irving had once lived. Miss de Wolfe gave up a stage career to become the city's most fashionable interior decorator and—later still—Lady Mendl. Her newly decorated house was photographed by Byron in 1898.

The files of the professional photographers who worked in the city in the early nineteen-hundreds are full of amusing contrasts.

Byron Collection, Museum of the City of New York

The photograph at top right, taken by Byron in 1900, shows a group of students having tea in a dormitory room at Barnard College. Established in 1889, in a building at 343 Madison Avenue, Barnard moved uptown in 1897 to its present site between 116th and 120th streets, west of Broadway. In 1900 it was officially made a part of Columbia University, though it retained its independent financial status and its own faculty.

The photograph at center right was taken by Byron in 1904 in the "reposing room" of an unidentified Turkish bath for women.

BELOW LEFT: A photograph by George Grantham Bain of members of the Women's Auxiliary of the Typographical Union riding in a "Seeing New York" bus in the Labor Day parade, 1909.

BELOW RIGHT: One panel from a stereoscopic view entitled "Automobile Party of merry girls before Appellate Court Building, Madison Square, New York City," published by Underwood & Underwood, 1904. Baedeker's guide recommended the "Seeing New York" company's autobusses as "an excellent method of making a first general acquaintance with the city." The Appellate Court Building, designed by James Brown Lord, was erected in 1900 on the northeast corner of Madison Avenue and Twenty-fifth Street.

Byron Collection, Museum of the City of New York

Library of Congress, Division of Prints and Photographs

Library of Congress, Division of Prints and Photographs

*On the surface, at least,
it was a festive
era . . .*

Byron's photographs, at left, show us an evening bridge party at the home of Mr. John Farley, 303 West Ninetieth Street, in 1900; the bachelor apartment of Mr. Fox, a tailor, in 1903 or 1904; and a scene at Midland Beach, Staten Island, in 1898. The other photograph, below right, is reproduced from one panel of a stereoscopic view entitled "Ah there! Coney Island," published by Strohmeyer & Wyman in 1898.

All pictures from Museum of the City of New York; the three at left from Byron Collection

. . . when "conspicuous consumption" was everyone's delight . . .

These photographs are from a series Byron made in 1902 at Delmonico's fine new restaurant, designed by James Brown Lord, which had been erected in 1897 at the northeast corner of Fifth Avenue and Forty-fourth Street. RIGHT: The confectionery department, where the chefs are designing elaborate *pièces montées* of nougat, *pâte d'office,* and other confectioners' pastes. The creation at left is decorated with the seal of the Chamber of Commerce of New York. The photograph below shows a ladies' luncheon in one of Delmonico's elaborate dining rooms.

Both pictures from Byron Collection, Museum of the City of New York

. . . and gaudy but inexpensive grandeur was becoming available on a mass-produced basis.

REGULAR DINNER, 15 cts.

CONSISTING OF

Soup, Roast or Boiled Meats, Steak, Chops, Veal Cutlet, Fish, Two Vegetables, Pudding or Pie, Tea, Coffee, Milk, Ale or Beer.

Item	Price
Soup of all kinds	5
Beef, Mutton or Veal Stew	5
Pork and Beans	8
Ham and Beans	8
" " Cabbage	8
Boiled Ham	8
Corned Beef and Cabbage	8
Frankfurter and Sauerkraut	10
" " Potato Salad	10
Roast Turkey, Cranberry Sauce	15
" Chicken, " "	15
Chicken Fricassee	10
" Pot Pie	10
Small Steak	8
Small Steak with Onions	8
Yankee Pot Roast	8
All Roast Meats	8
Large Veal Cutlet Breaded, with Tomato Sauce & Fried Potatoes.	8
Coffee with Buns, Rolls or Crullers	5
Coffee and Three Butter Cakes	5
Coffee and Two Corn Cakes	5
Wheat or Buckwheat Cakes	5
Pies or Puddings	5
Two Eggs any Style	7
Three " "	10
Fried Sausages	8
Hamburger Steak	10
Mutton or Pork Chops	8
Liver and Bacon	8
Ham and Eggs	15
Bacon and Eggs	12
Fried Liver	5
Corned Beef Hash	5
Fish or Fish Cakes	5
Salt Mackerel to order	8
Large Bone Sirloin Steak, with Fried Onions & Fried Potatoes	15

Bread, Butter, Potatoes and Extra Vegetables served with all orders.

Commutation Tickets, $1.10 for $1 $1.65 for $1.50 $2.25 for $2. $3.35 for $3.

Author's collection

The facsimile of a menu, at left, was published in Zeisloft's *The New Metropolis* (1899) as an example of "The Kind of Dinner Eaten Daily by Thousands of New Yorkers" at the turn of the century.

The most popular chain of low-priced restaurants was Childs', whose tile and marble establishment at 47 East Forty-second Street is shown here in a photograph taken by Byron in 1899.

Byron Collection, Museum of the City of New York

Sports and games, whether gregarious . . .

Library of Congress, Division of Prints and Photographs

Lewis W. Hine Memorial Collection

This view of the Polo Grounds is reproduced from one panel of a stereoscopic photograph published by the H. C. White Co. in 1906. The printed title tells us that the picture was taken on "World's Pennant Day," when the Giants ceremoniously raised the pennant they had won in 1905.

RIGHT: Beginning in the 1890s, there was increasing agitation for small parks and playgrounds, to get the city's children off the streets. But as Lewis W. Hine's 1910 photograph reminds us, most New Yorkers continued to learn baseball on vacant lots and in blind alleys.

. . . or exclusive, were more popular than ever.

Byron Collection, Museum of the City of New York

ABOVE: A photograph taken by Byron in Central Park, winter of 1898.

BELOW: A group of tennis enthusiasts at the Staten Island Cricket Club, October 1, 1892. The photograph was taken by Alice Austen, whose notes identify those present as: the Roosevelts, Nellie Janssen, Gertrude Williams, and Mr. R. Walker.

Staten Island Historical Society

In the midst of the gaiety, nevertheless, there were eruptions of violence which gave warning . . .

Mayor William J. Gaynor, about to sail for Europe in 1910, was shot by a disgruntled city employee just as William Warnecke of the *World* was taking what he had thought would be merely a routine news picture of the mayor's departure (at right).

BELOW LEFT: When police refused to permit the Socialist Conference of Unemployed to hold a meeting in Union Square in March, 1908, a young anarchist named Selig Silverstein tried to kill some of them with a homemade bomb. It went off prematurely, fatally injuring Silverstein and his friend Ignatz Hildebrand. George Grantham Bain's gruesome photograph is marked "Taken 20 seconds after bomb thrown."

BELOW RIGHT: Silverstein had been an admirer and follower of Alexander Berkman, the anarchist who had served fourteen years in prison for his attempt to kill Henry Clay Frick at the time of the Homestead steel strike in 1892. George Grantham Bain's photograph shows Berkman addressing a crowd in Union Square on May Day, after Silverstein's death.

Brown Brothers

Library of Congress, Division of Prints and Photographs

Library of Congress, Division of Prints and Photographs

. . . that the city had need of all its resources of science and education . . .

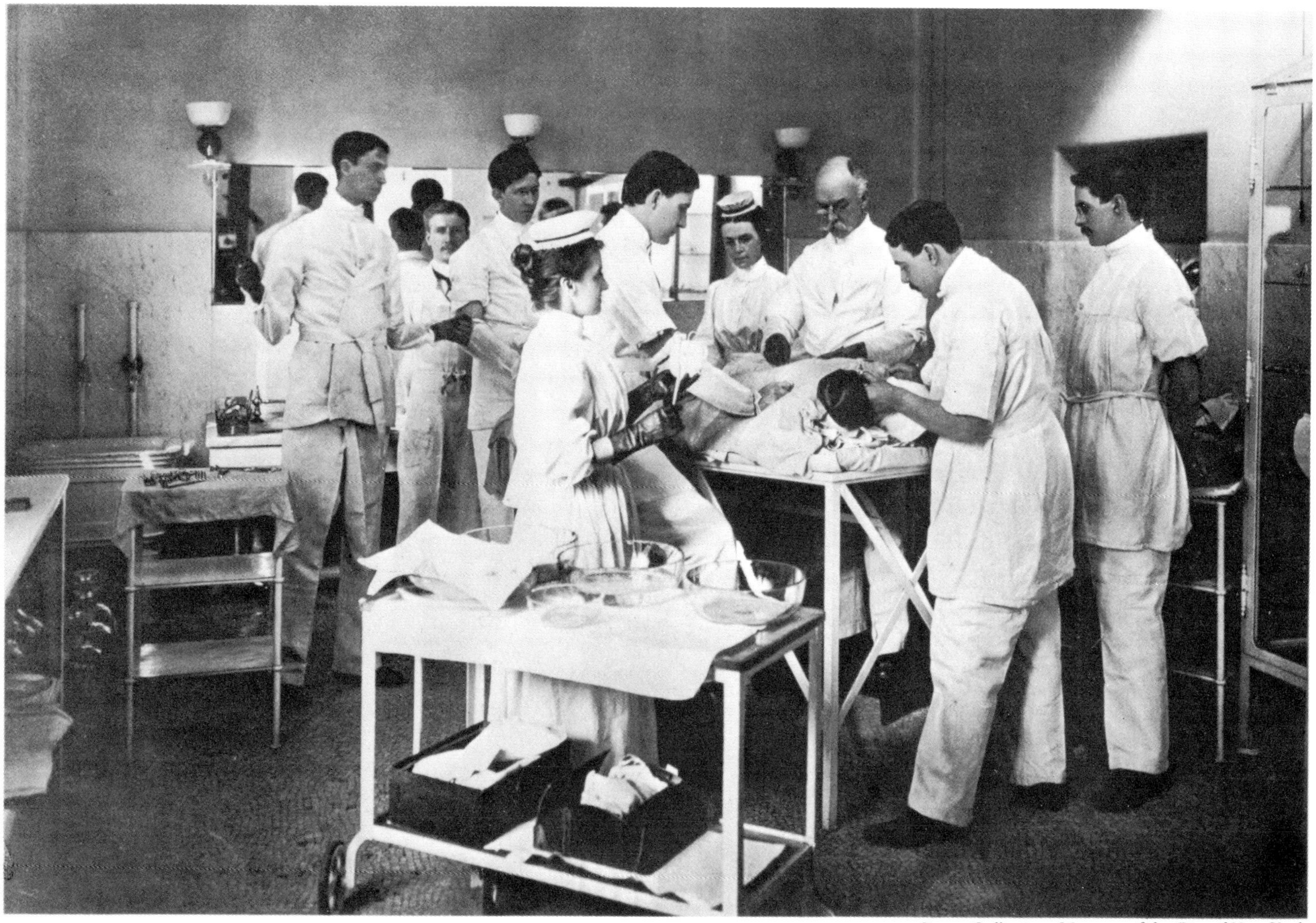

Byron Collection, Museum of the City of New York

ABOVE: Dr. Charles McBurney, distinguished graduate of the Columbia College of Physicians and Surgeons, operating at the Roosevelt Hospital, Ninth Avenue between Fifty-eighth and Fifty-ninth streets. The photograph was taken by Byron in 1900. BELOW: "School Duty—A frequent Scene at Seventh Avenue and One Hundred and Sixteenth Street," from Zeisloft, *The New Metropolis* (1899).

Author's collection

. . . if it were to succeed in molding its diversities into a workable human community.

Byron Collection, Museum of the City of New York

RIGHT: The People's Institute, at Cooper Union, carried on extensive programs of adult education and organized groups of youngsters in clubs which helped prepare them for responsible citizenship.

Byron's photograph was taken in the winter of 1905-6. (The sign held by the girls in center reads "Protectors of New York.")

BELOW LEFT: Arbor Day, May 5, 1905, at Public School 123, Brooklyn. By an unidentified photographer.

BELOW RIGHT: A photograph of the Virginia Day Nursery, 623 Fifth Street, south side, east of Avenue B.

New-York Historical Society

Byron Collection, Museum of the City of New York

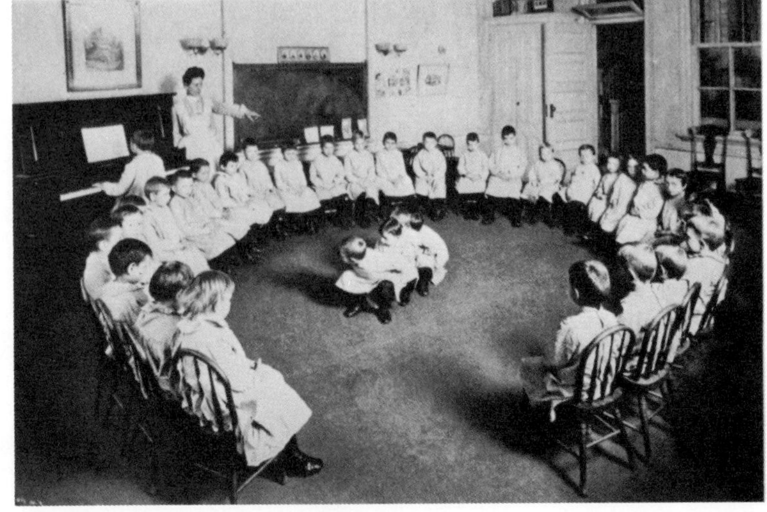

Wave after wave of immigrants
had been assimilated
in the past
half century,
but more continued
to come . . .

Museum of the City of New York

The young man standing in the background of this battered family tintype is Alfred Emanuel Smith, who was later to serve four terms as governor of New York State and be the Democratic nominee for President of the United States.

The tintype was taken about 1894, when Smith was twenty-one or so. Born in an Oliver Street tenement, in the slums south of Chatham Square, he had had various jobs—truckman's helper, fish peddler at Fulton Market, shipping clerk—but had not yet held any political office.

Seated in the front row are Smith's mother and Mr. and Mrs. Peter Mulvehill with their two children. The three young ladies behind them are Mrs. John J. Glyn (Smith's sister), Mary Hartley, and Catherine Dunn, who was later to become Mrs. Smith.

. . . and the city always seemed to be swarming with people who were bewilderingly or "picturesquely" foreign.

RIGHT: A group on Mott Street, photographed in 1898. No group in the city were more baffling to New Yorkers than the people of Chinatown. Even Jacob Riis, whose sympathy and understanding made him the champion of the city's immigrant poor, was worried by "the blank, unmeaning stare" he met among the Chinese. The Chinese had begun to settle in the region around Mott and Pell streets in the mid-seventies, and they continued to come until the Chinese Exclusion Act of 1882 put a stop to immigration.

Brown Brothers

BELOW: "The Italian Colony, Mulberry Bend," was drawn by W. Bengough and published in *Harper's Weekly*, June 29, 1895, as one of the illustrations for his series of articles on "The Foreign Element in New York." The text describes this as "the most picturesque, squalid, dilapidated, thoroughly interesting, and lively" foreign colony in the city.

Author's collection

Early in the twentieth century, however, pictures of immigrants began to reflect a deeper and more compassionate understanding.

Courtesy of Alfred Stieglitz Estate

In the preface to the catalogue of an exhibition of his photographs in 1921, Alfred Stieglitz stated his artistic creed: "Photography is my passion. The search for Truth my obsession." The picture which he considered to be his finest was this photograph of "The Steerage," taken in 1907.

The caricatured throngs of a half century earlier were transformed into crowds made up of human beings . . .

New York Public Library

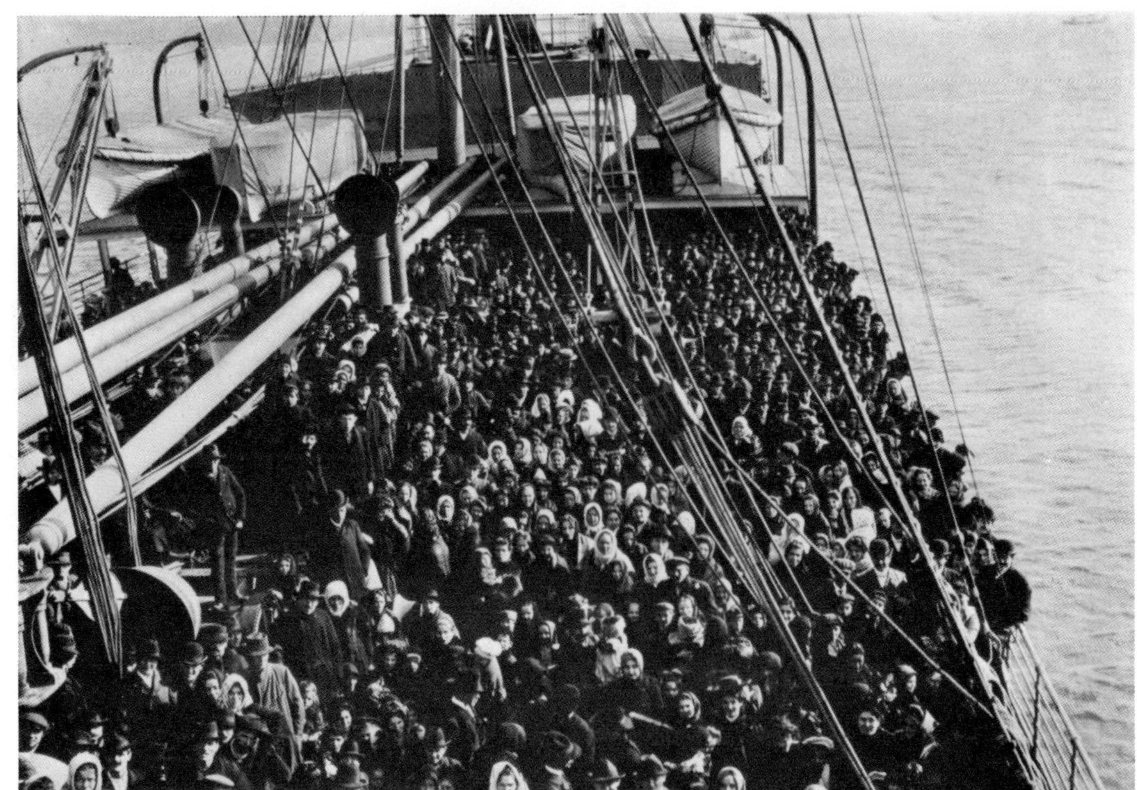

The anonymous wood engraving above was published in *Frank Leslie's Illustrated Newspaper,* January 12, 1856.

The photograph below, of immigrants arriving at Ellis Island on the S.S. *Patricia* in 1906, was taken by Edwin Levick.

Culver Service

. . . each of whom, individually, was worthy of being portrayed with candor and respect.

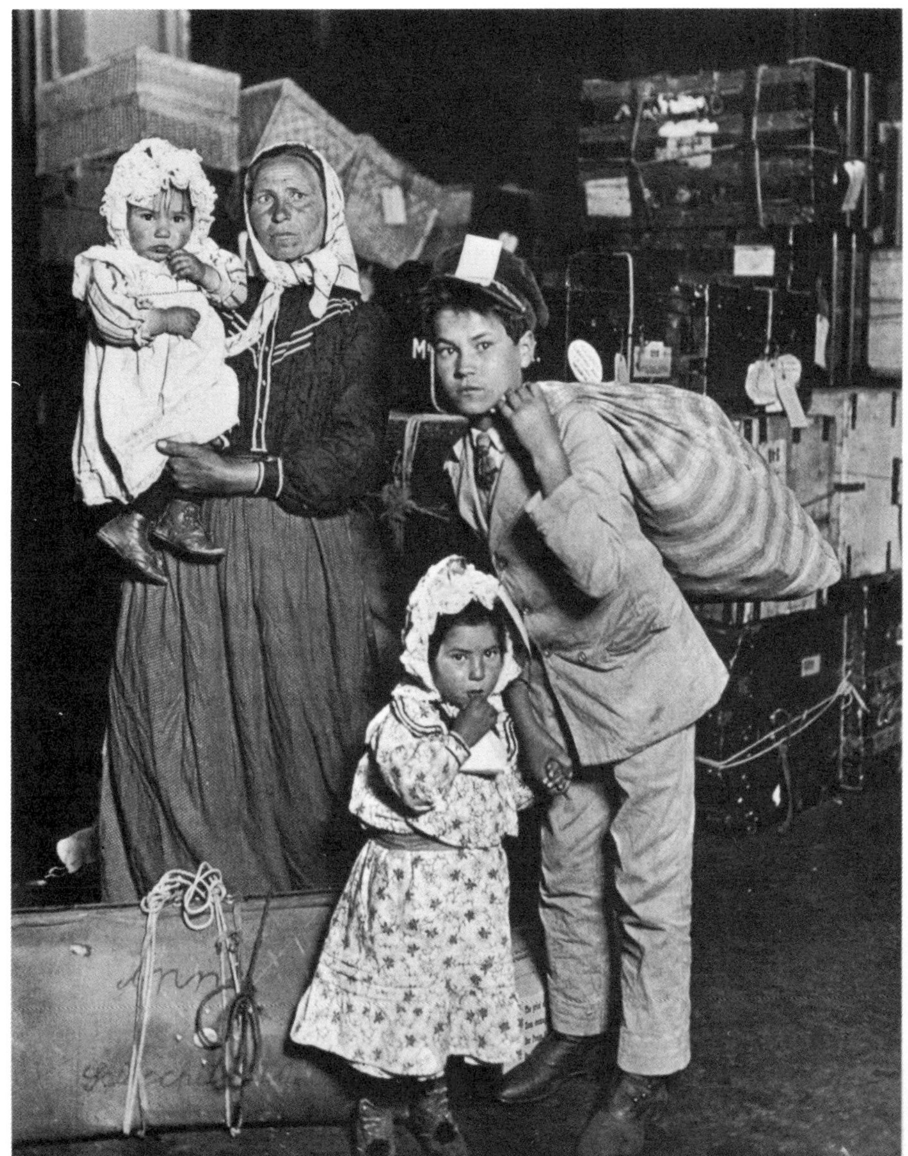

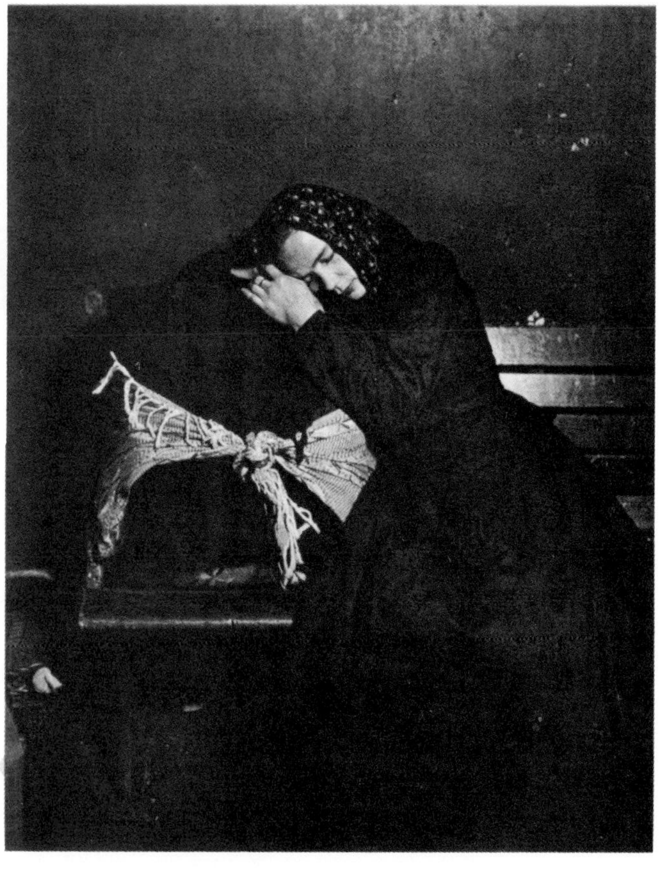

Lewis W. Hine, a sociologist trained at the University of Chicago, Columbia, and New York University, took up photography in the early 1900s as a tool for interpretive studies of life among the city's immigrant poor. The pictures on this page are selected from a series he made on Ellis Island in 1905.

(A photograph from a much later series by Hine, taken during the construction of the Empire State Building, will be found in the introduction to this book, page 18. See also pages 439 and 450.)

Both pictures from Lewis W. Hine Memorial Collection

And the documentary photographs made by Lewis Hine and others . . .

The photographs reproduced on this page are selected from the thousands Hine took during his investigations of tenement-house life and sweatshop labor from 1908 to 1910. Many of his pictures were published, with straightforward factual captions, in the reports of various investigating committees concerned with housing reform, child labor, and other industrial and civic problems.

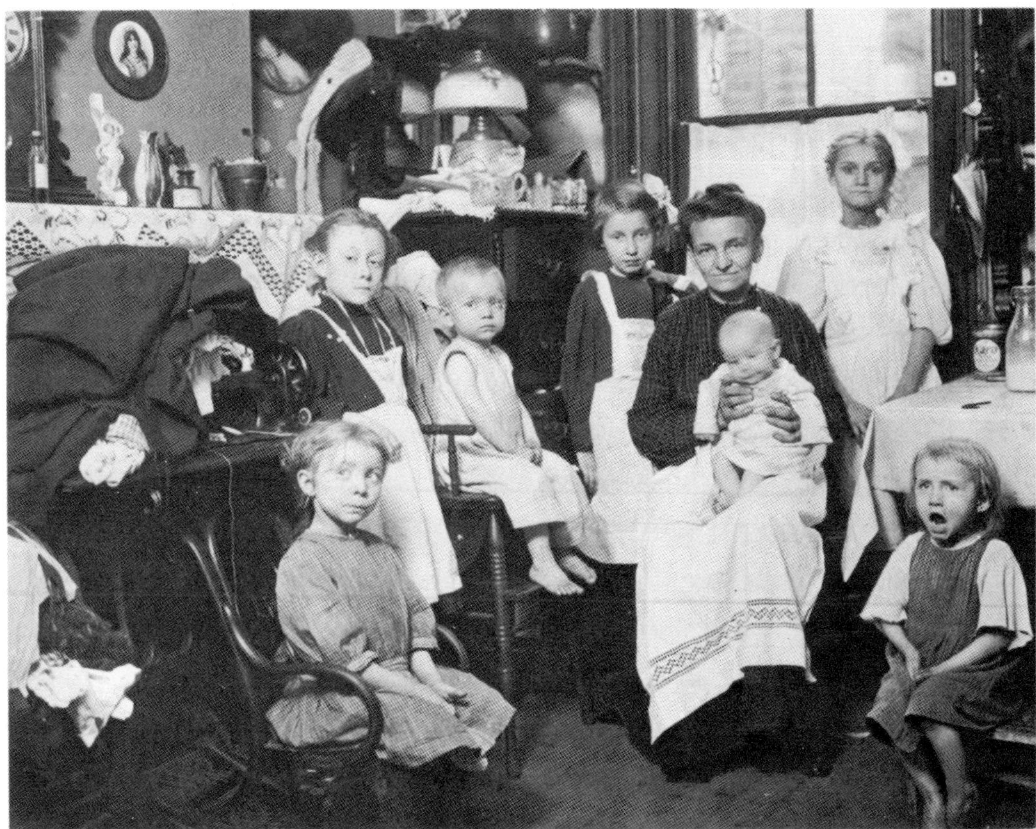

All pictures from Lewis W. Hine Memorial Collection

. . . became effective weapons in the successful fight for better housing and improved working conditions.

Author's collection

The unattributed picture of a laborer polishing buttons in a West Side factory is reproduced from one of the half-tone illustrations in the *Preliminary Report of the New York State Factory Investigating Commission* (Albany, 1912).

The commission, headed by Robert F. Wagner, with Alfred E. Smith as vice-chairman, had been set up by the legislature at the request of the Fifth Avenue Association and other civic groups after the disastrous fire at the Triangle Shirtwaist Company, on Washington Place in 1911, in which 145 employees —mainly women and young girls—lost their lives.

The commission's three-volume report covered all aspects of the factory system—sanitation, fire hazards, occupational diseases, child labor, factory inspection, the employment of women, and safety—and made many recommendations which were enacted into law. A number of photographs, many of them taken by Lewis Hine, illustrated the report.

This photograph of a bathroom in a New York tenement was taken in 1902 or 1903 for the Tenement House Commission. Photographer not identified.

Library of Congress, Division of Prints and Photographs

Though some of the popular illustrators still indulged a sentimental taste for the picturesque . . .

Courtesy of Mrs. Edward Hand

This charcoal drawing of "Elizabeth Street" was one of the illustrations in Francis Hopkinson Smith's *Charcoals of New and Old New York*, published by Doubleday, Page & Co. in 1912. Like many of his contemporaries, Smith was alternately fascinated and repelled by the flood of immigrants. On one page he laments the arrival, during 1911, of nearly a million "raw, untilled, unlettered and unkempt dumpings; most of them Goths, Vandals, and Barbarians." Yet he finds the scene on Elizabeth Street "enormously picturesque." Nowhere else in the city, he writes, "are the costumes so foreign and varied, and the facial characteristics so diverse."

. . . and though the older generation of pictorial reporters was being replaced by younger men, concerned less with factual detail . . .

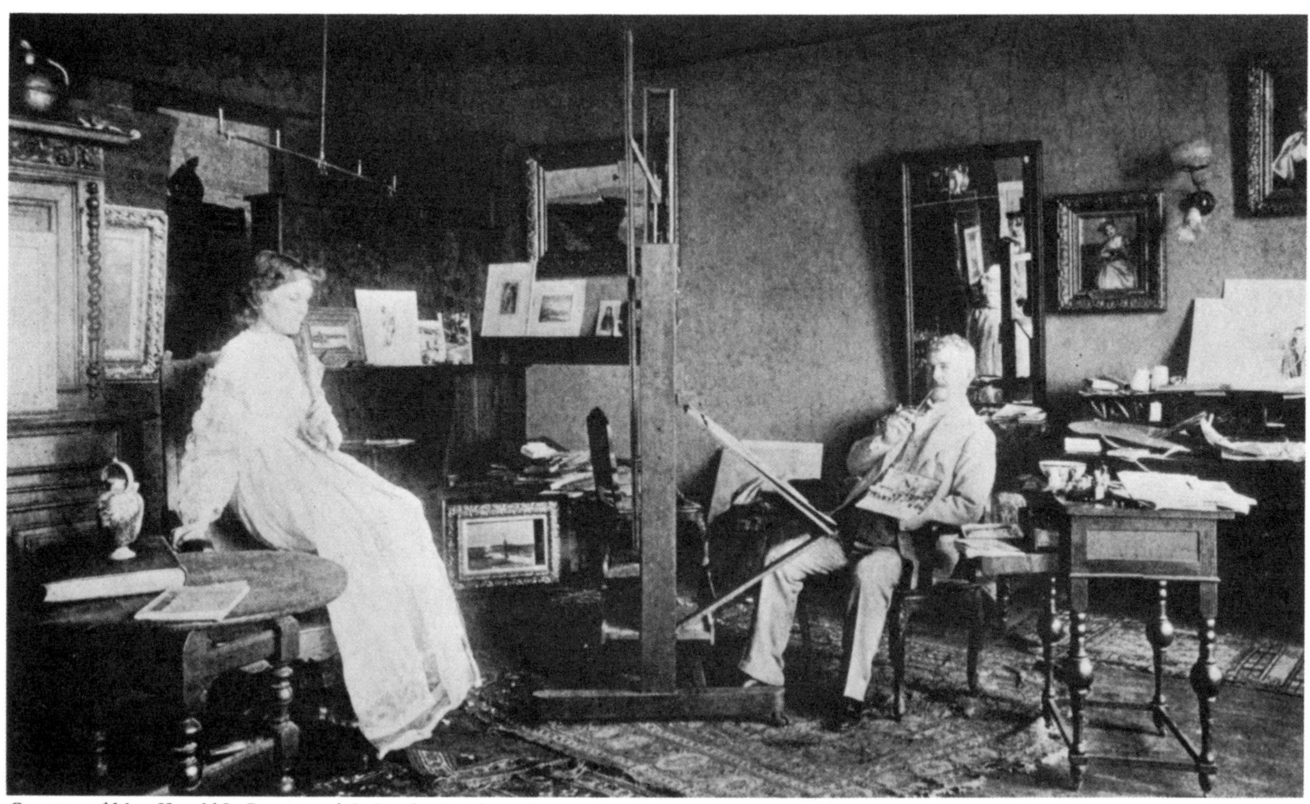

Courtesy of Mrs. Harold L. Bennet and C. Stanley Reinhart, Jr.

Author's collection

Charles Stanley Reinhart, shown above in his studio at 222 West Twenty-third Street in 1893, was probably the greatest of the reporter-illustrators of the last quarter of the nineteenth century. By 1900, however, the reportorial function which he and his colleagues had performed for the illustrated magazines and weeklies had been largely taken over by photography.

LEFT: One of the most popular of the younger generation of illustrators was Howard Chandler Christy, whose drawing of the entrance to Madison Square Garden on the night of the opening of the horse show is reproduced from *Harper's Weekly*, November 26, 1898.

Author's collection

After the introduction of the half-tone process for reproducing photographs, the artist's function in books and periodicals tended to be limited more and more to the illustration of fiction and to the creation of cartoons and other forms of social commentary.

The change is clearly reflected in the drawings published in the first *Annual of the Society of Illustrators* (New York, Charles Scribner's Sons, 1911). Here, for instance, is the drawing contributed by Charles Dana Gibson, whose "Gibson Girls" had for more than a decade epitomized the fashionable ideal of young womanhood. It was entitled "A Friend of the Society."

A number of the drawings in the first *Annual of the Society of Illustrators* reflected a serious concern with contemporary urban problems. Boardman Robinson's contribution was a savage drawing entitled "Beer" (at left, above). Art Young's was a caricature called "Successful Selfishness" (at right, above), which epitomized the current protest against monopolistic wealth. And Charles B. Falls gave expression to the hopeless misery of the slums in a drawing ironically entitled "Spring."

All pictures from author's collection

Author's collection

ABOVE: Gerrit A. Beneker's drawing, "A Drink of Water," is reproduced—as are the illustrations on the two preceding pages—from the first *Annual of the Society of Illustrators.* The steelworkers who built the city's great bridges and skyscrapers had already become romantic symbols of the constructive energies that were shaping the modern metropolis. The bridge represented under construction is, of course, the Manhattan Bridge, which was opened in 1909. In left background, beyond the Brooklyn Bridge tower, is the tower of the Singer Building.

In his early work as an illustrator Joseph Pennell had been in love with "the crumbling picturesqueness of an older, foreign world." But in the early 1900s he began his remarkable series of etchings of "The Wonders of Work" and in 1909 illustrated John C. Van Dyke's *The New New York.* This undated etching of "New York from Weehawken" reflects the change in his interests.

J. Clarence Davies Collection, Museum of the City of New York

In painting, too, there was a fresh awareness of the urban landscape, and in the first decade of the new century . . .

Corcoran Gallery of Art

The first "New York School" of painting was the group known as "The Eight," whose work was exhibited together for the first time in 1908. The group was composed of men of diverse talents and techniques (none of whom was a native New Yorker, by the way) whose only unifying bonds were a contempt for the sweet, decorous work approved by conventional taste and an unaffected and cordial interest in the urban scene.

One of the exhibitors was Ernest Lawson, whose painting, entitled "Boat House, Winter, Harlem River" (above), is one of a series he painted along the banks of the Harlem after his return from Paris, where he had become familiar with the work of the French Impressionists. Rising against the wintry sky on University Heights in the background is the Hall of Fame, designed by McKim, Mead & White and erected in 1901 on New York University's Bronx campus.

Another member of the group was William Glackens, a former Philadelphia newspaper artist who had covered the Spanish-American War for *McClure's Magazine*. His "Park on the River" (left) was painted in 1905.

Brooklyn Museum

. . . the leaders of the "Ash Can School" began exploring with affectionate gusto . . .

Metropolitan Museum of Art

Probably the most distinguished, certainly the best-known, member of "The Eight" was John Sloan. Like Glackens, Sloan had been a newspaper artist in Philadelphia, where he had also studied art with a disciple of Thomas Eakins. It was his relish for the rowdy and the ribald, for back yards and back alleys, which won for the group its nickname, the "Ash Can School."

"Dust Storm, Fifth Avenue" (above) was painted in 1906. "The Haymarket," painted in 1907, affectionately memorializes the famous (or infamous) café-dance-hall on the southeast corner of Sixth Avenue and Thirtieth Street, in the heart of the old Tenderloin district, where "Diamond Jim" Brady used to entertain.

Brooklyn Museum

. . . aspects of city life which the arts had hitherto ignored.

Whitney Museum of American Art

"Backyards, Greenwich Village," was painted by John Sloan in 1914.

The way had been prepared for fundamental changes in man's way of looking at the city.

Among the younger painters who followed "The Eight," Glenn O. Coleman was one of the most accomplished craftsmen. Like Sloan and Art Young, he drew for the old *Masses,* the voice of Greenwich Village radicalism during the years leading up to World War I. At right is his lithograph of "Minetta Lane," between Sixth Avenue and Macdougal Street. Below is his 1923 painting of "Fort Lee Ferry," looking northward from a point near which Archibald Robertson had drawn a very different scene a century and a half before (see page 76).

Whitney Museum of American Art

Brooklyn Museum

"THE SHAPES ARISE"
1910–1953

Shapes of democracy total, result of centuries,
Shapes ever projecting other shapes,
Shapes of turbulent manly cities,
Shapes of the friends and home-givers of the whole earth,
Shapes bracing the earth and braced with the whole earth.

Walt Whitman, *Song of the Broad-Axe* (1856)

This photograph of Manhattan from Governor's Island was taken by Samuel Gottscho, May 2, 1932 (see page 204).

Courtesy of Gottscho-Schleisner.

Courtesy of Gottscho-Schleisner

Pix Inc.

The photograph above, taken especially for this book by Gottscho-Schleisner, November 7, 1952, shows the oldest burial ground on Manhattan, south of Chatham Square on the east side of the New Bowery (or St. James Place) between Oliver and James streets. The plot has belonged to the Jewish Congregation Shearith Israel since 1682, and may have been part of the original burial ground granted to the Jews by Stuyvesant's Council in 1656. Many of the city's most eminent Jews of the colonial and Revolutionary periods were buried here. The photograph at left, taken in 1951 by Fred Stein, shows the headquarters of the Colonial Dames of America, at 421 East Sixty-first Street. For notes on the early history of the building, see page 92.

OPPOSITE: This photograph of Broadway, looking north from Bowling Green, was taken by John Harvey Heffren in 1948.

Museum of the City of New York

For two decades after 1910, the theme-signs in pictures of New York were "Building Coming Down" and "Will Move" . . .

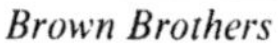
Brown Brothers

Brown Brothers

Courtesy of Gottscho-Schleisner

ABOVE LEFT: The northeast corner of Seventh Avenue and Forty-seventh Street in 1909.

ABOVE RIGHT: The site of the Woolworth Building, west side of Broadway above Barclay Street, in 1911. Woolworth's 792-foot "Cathedral of Commerce," designed by Cass Gilbert, was completed in 1913, and for almost twenty years was indeed the "highest in the world." At the left in the photograph may be seen a portion of the old Astor House (see page 196) with the spire of St. Paul's beyond.

RIGHT: The Audubon house, at 155th Street and the Hudson, photographed May 6, 1916, by Samuel Gottscho (see page 216).

. . . as old landmarks were destroyed to make room for taller and taller structures . . .

Brown Brothers

Culver Service

ABOVE: This photograph, looking northeast from the roof of a building on the south side of Fulton Street, was taken in 1913. The tower under construction at left is the Woolworth Building, and beyond it is the nearly completed tower of the new Municipal Building, designed by McKim, Mead & White, at Park Row and Chambers Street. In center foreground is the hollow square of the Astor House, and beyond it the old post office (demolished 1938–39) in City Hall Park. St. Paul's spire is in right foreground, and beyond it, up Park Row at Frankfort Street, is the domed tower of the Pulitzer (or New York *World*) Building.

ABOVE RIGHT: Nos. 121–31 West Fortieth Street, north side between Broadway and Sixth Avenue, in 1923.

RIGHT: This photograph of the stairway in the Brevoort-De Rham house, northwest corner of Fifth Avenue and Ninth Street, was taken by Tebbs & Knell, Inc., in 1925 while the house was being demolished (see pages 169 and 253). The Fifth Avenue Hotel was erected on the site.

Museum of the City of New York

. . . and the obsessive fascination with height reached its climax . . .

Courtesy of Consolidated Edison of New York

E. H. Suydam's drawing of "A Group of Lefcourt Buildings" was used, by permission of the Edison Company, as the frontispiece of Martin Clary's *Mid-Manhattan* ("The Multimillionarea"), published in 1929 by the Forty-second Street Property Owners and Merchants Association.

. . . as the booming twenties exploded into the thirties from the dizzy pinnacle of 1929.

Both pictures courtesy of Rockefeller Center, Inc.

These two photographs were taken from the Observation Roof of the RCA Building at Rockefeller Center. The one above was taken by Edward Ratcliffe, and the one below by Samuel Chamberlain. Among the skyscrapers which rise above the clouds the tallest, of course, is the 1250-foot Empire State Building, designed by Shreve, Lamb & Harmon, and erected in 1929-31 on the site of the old Waldorf-Astoria (see pages 411-12). Just left of it is the tip of the Metropolitan Life Insurance Co. tower at Madison Square. The tower with three vertical stripes in center foreground is 500 Fifth Avenue (also designed by Shreve, Lamb & Harmon), and at far left is the Lincoln Building, designed by J. E. R. Carpenter, and erected in 1929-30 on the south side of Forty-second Street between Madison and Park.

But in the early thirties, partly as a result of technical improvements in photography . . .

Library of Congress, Division of Prints and Photographs

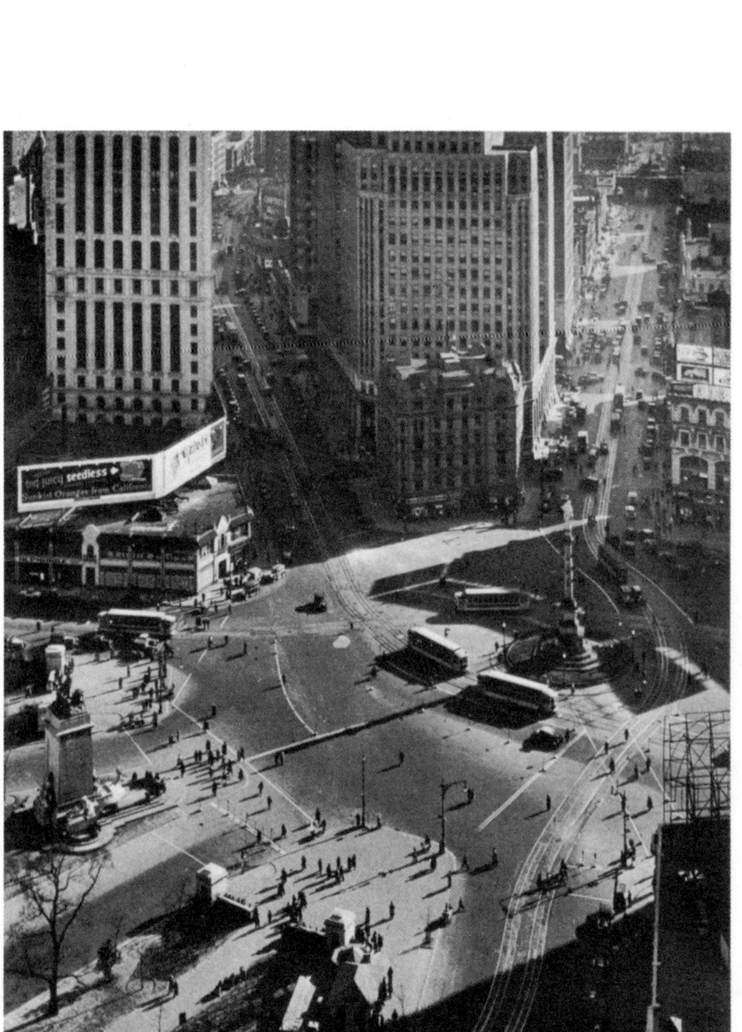

ABOVE: "Looking Down on the Flatiron Building, from the Metropolitan Tower," is reproduced from one panel of a stereoscopic view made by Underwood & Underwood in 1915. At extreme right is a corner of the Fifth Avenue Building, erected in 1909 on the site of the Fifth Avenue Hotel. Compare the vertical perspective in this picture with that in the photograph below.

LEFT: The photograph of Columbus Circle was taken by Gottscho-Schleisner from the roof of the Century Apartments on Central Park West, April 4, 1932. The view was taken looking south past the Columbus Monument down Eighth Avenue (right) and Broadway. The old hotel building on the south side of the Circle, between the two streets, was at one time occupied by the offices of the New York *Journal.* Behind it is the General Motors Building, designed by Shreve & Lamb and completed in 1928 (see page 294). The monument at left, at the entrance to Central Park, was erected in 1912 in honor of the men who lost their lives on the battleship *Maine* in 1898.

Courtesy of Gottscho-Schleisner

. . . and partly as a consequence of the sobering effects of the Great Depression . . .

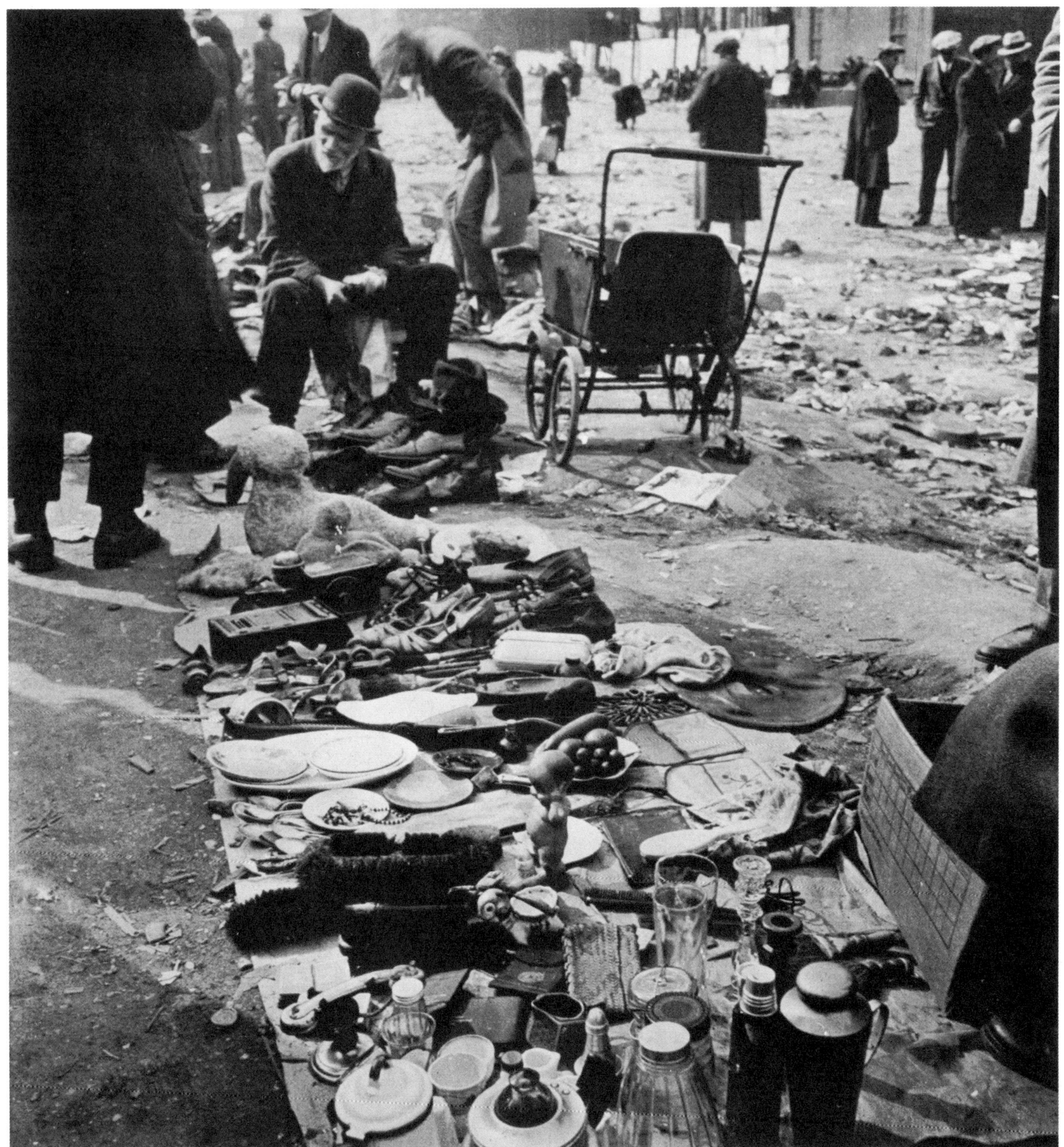

Courtesy of Gottscho-Schleisner

Samuel Gottscho's photograph of the Houston Street junk market was taken April 10, 1933.

Both pictures from Museum of the City of New York

The pictures on this page were taken in 1914 by Arthur D. Chapman, an amateur photographer who worked with an old view camera equipped with what he describes as a homemade meniscus lens "with practically everything wrong with it." A printer who worked nights for the New York *American* and the *Globe,* Mr. Chapman spent his afternoons wandering around Greenwich Village with his camera.

The picture above was taken in 1914 in Minetta Place, a narrow alley which formerly occupied the center of the block between Minetta Street and Sixth Avenue. The picture at left was taken in the same year, looking northwest on Greenwich Avenue from the El station at Sixth Avenue and West Eighth Street. The car tracks at lower left are curving southwest into Christopher Street. At right is the old Jefferson Market, built in 1877 and replaced in 1932 by a modern House of Detention for Women.

Courtesy of the photographer

Walker Evans was one of the most influential, and certainly one of the most accomplished, of the "straight photographers" whose work began to appear in the early thirties. His photograph of "South Street, New York," was taken in 1932.

The ideal of "straight photography," in contrast with the pictorial ideals of the earlier cameramen, was to present what Lincoln Kirstein has described as "the facts of our homes and times, shown surgically, without the intrusion of the poet's or painter's comment or necessary distortion." No one did it more forthrightly or with more unsparing clarity than did Evans in the magnificent series of photographs (of which "South Street" was one) which were published by the Museum of Modern Art in 1938, along with Kirstein's appreciative essay.

The soft focus which had lent charm to the affectionate camera studies of the "pictorial photographers" . . .

Museum of the City of New York

"Diagonals" was photographed by Arthur D. Chapman in 1914, looking down Christopher Street from the same El station from which he took the photograph of Greenwich Avenue that is reproduced on page 480.

The picture at left, looking southeast on Pike Street from the corner of Monroe to the Manhattan Bridge, was taken April 5, 1933, by Samuel Gottscho.

Courtesy of Gottscho-Schleisner

. . . was discarded for a sharper "documentary" vision which inquired more bluntly into the significance of urban forms.

Museum of the City of New York

ABOVE: Arthur D. Chapman's photograph of Clinton Court was taken in 1915. The entrance to the court was through a narrow passageway about halfway between Macdougal Street and Sixth Avenue on the south side of West Eighth Street.

The photograph at right was taken by Berenice Abbott, March 16, 1936, while she was making the documentary portrait of "Changing New York" from which a representative group of pictures is reproduced on the next seven pages. This picture was taken in the central court of the "model tenement," designed by Vaux and Radford, which had been erected in 1880-81 on First Avenue, between Seventy-first and Seventy-second streets, by the Improved Dwellings Association (see page 349).

Federal Art Project, "Changing New York," from Museum of the City of New York

It was in the early thirties, for example, that Berenice Abbott abandoned portraiture . . .

Federal Art Project, "Changing New York," from Museum of the City of New York

Returning in 1930 from France, where she had worked for six years as a portrait photographer, Berenice Abbott interested I. N. Phelps Stokes and Harding Scholle, director of the Museum of the City of New York, in her plan to make a comprehensive camera portrait of New York. Working at first with the museum's sponsorship and later under the sponsorship of the Federal Art Project, Miss Abbott produced a series of documentary photographs of the city which is rivaled in scope and intensity only by Brady's Civil War pictures and Atget's pictures of Paris. A selection from the series, with text by Elizabeth McCausland, was published by the Federal Art Project in 1939 in a volume called *Changing New York*.

The photograph above, of the Blossom Restaurant, 103 Bowery, was taken October 24, 1935. At right is Jimmy the Barber's shop, next door to the entrance of the Fulton Hotel (30 cents a night).

. . . and began to make the magnificent series of documentary photographs . . .

l pictures from Federal Art Project, "Changing New York," from Museum of the City of New York

Of the three pictures reproduced on this page only the one below at right, of Zito's Sanitary Bakery at 259 Bleecker Street (February 3, 1937), was included in the published volume of selections from Miss Abbott's series on "Changing New York."

At left, above, is the window of the A & P store at 246 Third Avenue, photographed March 16, 1936.

BELOW LEFT: Goldberg's Clothing Store, 771 Broadway, northwest corner of Ninth Street, May 7, 1937.

As Beaumont Newhall has pointed out (in *The History of Photography* [New York, 1949]), "Paradoxically, before a photograph can be accepted as a document, it must itself be documented—placed in time and space." Hence, of course, the frequency with which the photographers include in their pictures signs and billboards which provide documentation. But how different is the effect of the signs in Miss Abbott's pictures from that intended (and achieved) in the pictures of New York a century earlier (see pages 146-49).

. . . which make up her camera portrait . . .

Both pictures from Federal Art Project, "Changing New York," from Museum of the City of New York

ABOVE: Sumner Healey's antique shop, 942 Third Avenue (west side, between Fifty-sixth and Fifty-seventh), was photographed by Berenice Abbott October 8, 1936, shortly before Mr. Healey's death.

LEFT: This Victorian mansard house, just north of 158th Street at Riverside Drive, was built about 1860 by William A. Wheelock and was still occupied as a residence when Miss Abbott photographed it November 11, 1937.

"Their houses tell more about a people than their noses," Miss Abbott once said. "And besides, in a city as vast as New York, human beings are dwarfed by the colossal monuments of their hands."

Both pictures from Federal Art Project, "Changing New York," from Museum of the City of New York

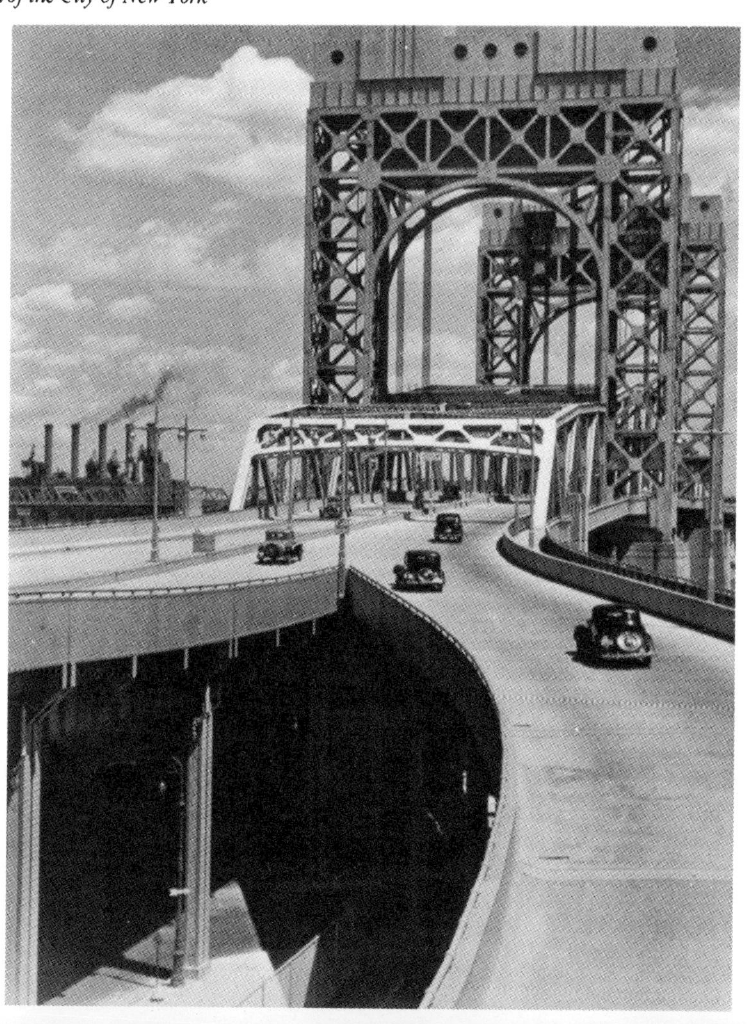

ABOVE: This photograph of "Gramercy Park West, Nos. 3 and 4," was taken by Miss Abbott November 27, 1935. No. 4 (at left) had been from 1848 until 1869 the home of James Harper, one of the founders of Harper & Brothers, publishers, and mayor of the city in 1844-45. The lamps in front of his house are the "Mayor's Lamps," by long custom placed outside the homes of those who held the office. No. 3 was the home of the Netherlands Club.

RIGHT: This photograph of the 125th Street approach to the Triborough Bridge was taken by Miss Abbott June 29, 1937. The bridge, with its nineteen-mile contributory system of ramps, viaducts, and cross-overs, was erected in 1929-36 to link the Bronx and Queens with Manhattan and with one another. O. H. Amman was chief engineer.

. . . the city's contrasts of wealth and poverty, new and old . . .

Both pictures from Federal Art Project, "Changing New York," from Museum of the City of New York

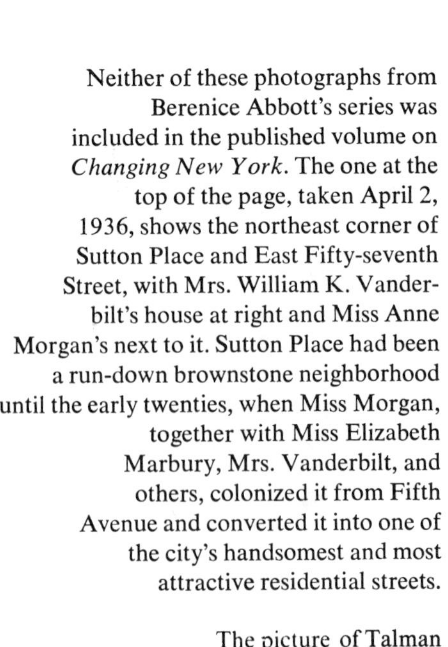

Neither of these photographs from Berenice Abbott's series was included in the published volume on *Changing New York*. The one at the top of the page, taken April 2, 1936, shows the northeast corner of Sutton Place and East Fifty-seventh Street, with Mrs. William K. Vanderbilt's house at right and Miss Anne Morgan's next to it. Sutton Place had been a run-down brownstone neighborhood until the early twenties, when Miss Morgan, together with Miss Elizabeth Marbury, Mrs. Vanderbilt, and others, colonized it from Fifth Avenue and converted it into one of the city's handsomest and most attractive residential streets.

The picture of Talman Street in Brooklyn (in the slums between Manhattan Bridge and the Navy Yard, near where the Farragut housing project has since been built) was taken May 22, 1936.

. . . and all its stubbornly insistent incongruities . . .

Both pictures from Federal Art Project, "Changing New York," from Museum of the City of New York

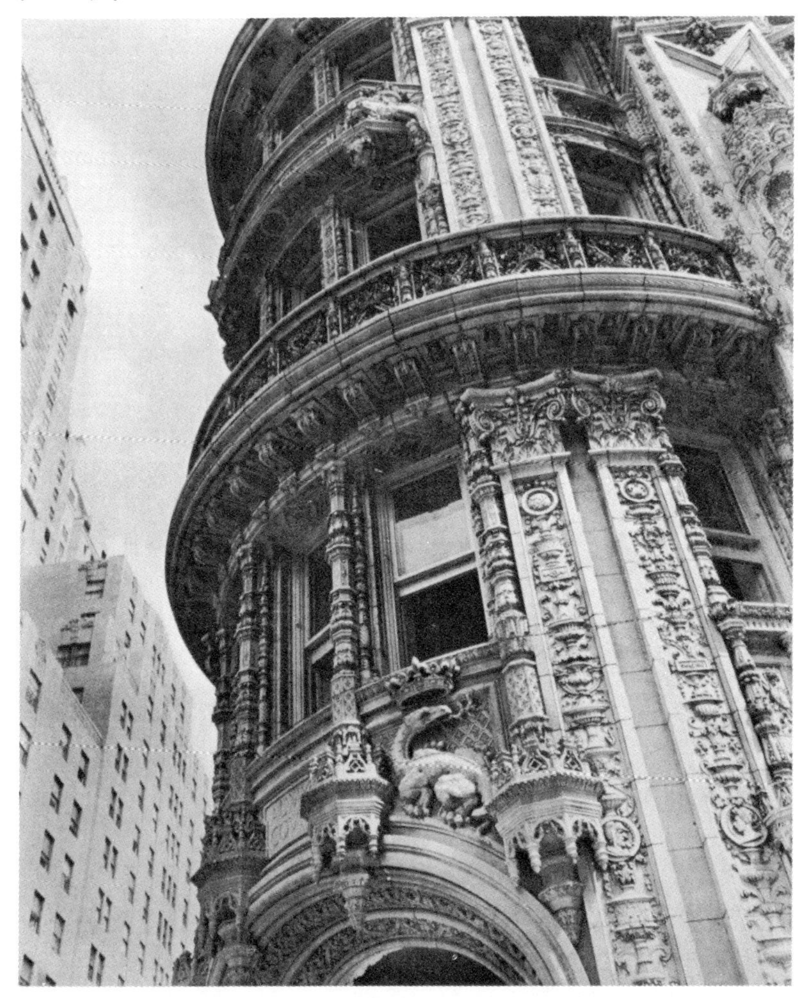

ABOVE: This photograph, looking southeast from West Street, was taken by Berenice Abbott March 23, 1938. The old white buildings in the foreground, at Nos. 117 and 118 West Street, just north of Cortlandt Street, were built in 1840. Above the roof of the one at left towers the Cities Service Building, designed by Clinton & Russell and erected in 1932 at 70 Pine Street, east of William Street. Just right of it, the tall, squarely blocked structure in the center of the picture is the Equitable Building, on the east side of Broadway between Pine and Cedar streets. Designed by Ernest R. Graham and erected in 1914, the unneighborly bulk of this monster office building was one of the final causes contributing to the adoption of the Zoning Resolution of 1916, the first New York ordinance regulating the height of buildings in relation to street width and restricting the percentage of the lot which may be covered (see page 496 for the effects upon city architecture).

RIGHT: This Berenice Abbott photograph of the façade of the Alwyn Court apartment house, on the southeast corner of Fifty-eighth Street and Seventh Avenue, was taken August 10, 1938. Built in 1908, from plans by Harde & Short, the building was remodeled in 1938, but its façade was left intact.

. . . are interpreted with uncompromising respect for fact.

Both pictures from Federal Art Project, "Changing New York," from Museum of the City of New York

ABOVE: Berenice Abbott's photograph of "Ye Olde Country Store" at 2553 Sage Place, Spuyten Duyvil, was taken October 11, 1935.

LEFT: The McGraw-Hill Building at 330 West Forty-second Street (south side, west of Eighth Avenue) is shown here in Berenice Abbott's photograph taken May 25, 1936. Designed by Raymond Hood and André Fouilhoux, and completed in 1931, this skyscraper was a landmark in the development of forms appropriate to steel and glass construction. Abandoning entirely the Gothic ornament which he had used in his prize-winning design for the Tribune Tower in Chicago (1922) and in the American Radiator Tower on Fortieth Street (1924), Hood here permitted the steel skeleton to express itself directly in bold and precise forms which owe nothing to any historical "order" of architecture. In the foreground is the Forty-second Street station of the Ninth Avenue El, demolished during the Second World War.

The clarity and precision of "straight photography," as it was called . . .

Both pictures courtesy of Gottscho-Schleisner

Both pictures on this page are from the studio of Gottscho-Schleisner, a partnership whose senior member, Samuel H. Gottscho, has long specialized in architectural photography (see page 440).

The photograph of the interior of St. Paul's Chapel, Broadway at Fulton Street, was taken by natural light on March 25, 1952. Built in 1764-66, probably from designs by Thomas McBean, St. Paul's was somewhat enlarged in the early 1790s, under the supervision of Major Pierre L'Enfant. One of the handsomest and best-preserved examples of colonial church architecture, St. Paul's is the oldest church building on Manhattan. The bright and spacious interior is almost unchanged since Washington worshiped here when New York was the capital of the United States.

The photograph below, showing Rockefeller Center under construction, was taken April 7, 1932, from the Goelet Building on Fifth Avenue. The excavation in right foreground is the present site of the sunken plaza and skating rink. The almost completed tower in background is the RKO Building at Sixth Avenue and Fifty-first Street. In the center of the picture the steel frame of the RCA Building is under construction.

. . . brought a fresh awareness of the unpremeditated beauty which had been unexpectedly created by the city's random growth . . .

Courtesy of Gottscho-Schleisner

This remarkable night photograph, looking north over Central Park from the completed RCA Building, was taken by Samuel Gottscho November 16, 1933. In the lower left corner is the Ziegfeld Theater at the corner of Sixth Avenue and Fifty-fourth Street, and at lower right (with the tip of its spire just lifting into the glow of light from Fifth Avenue) is the Fifth Avenue Presbyterian Church at the northwest corner of Fifty-fifth and Fifth.

In upper left background the sweeping roadway and cables of the George Washington Bridge span the Hudson, and off to the right are the distant lights of the Bronx.

. . . and made it possible to detect, beneath all the flagrant diversity of the urban scene . . .

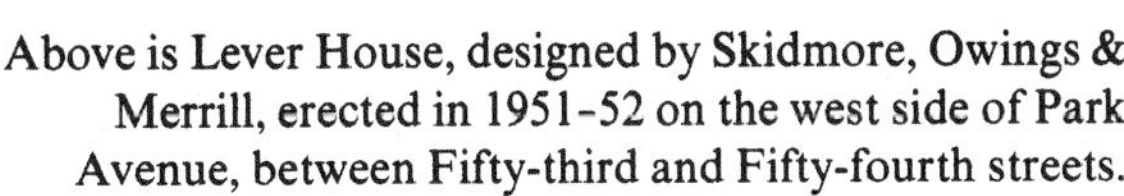

Above is Lever House, designed by Skidmore, Owings & Merrill, erected in 1951-52 on the west side of Park Avenue, between Fifty-third and Fifty-fourth streets.

At right is the building which James Bogardus erected at the northwest corner of Washington and Murray streets in 1848—the first iron building ever completed (see page 244).

The glass and steel architecture of Lever House, seen in juxtaposition with the massive Renaissance grandeur of McKim, Mead & White's Racquet and Tennis Club building (at left in the photograph above), looks like a complete break with the past. But one has only to observe the horizontal bands of glass in the Bogardus storehouses to be aware that Lever House, like Hood's McGraw-Hill Building (page 490), grows directly out of an urban vernacular tradition which has been developing, outside the realm of academic architecture, for more than a hundred years.

The two buildings on this page, photographed by Gottscho-Schleisner on two consecutive days in March, 1952, mark the beginning and the present culmination of the evolution of modern urban architecture.

Both pictures courtesy of Gottscho-Schleisner

. . . hitherto unnoticed continuities of industrial form . . .

Federal Art Project, "Changing New York," from Museum of the City of New York

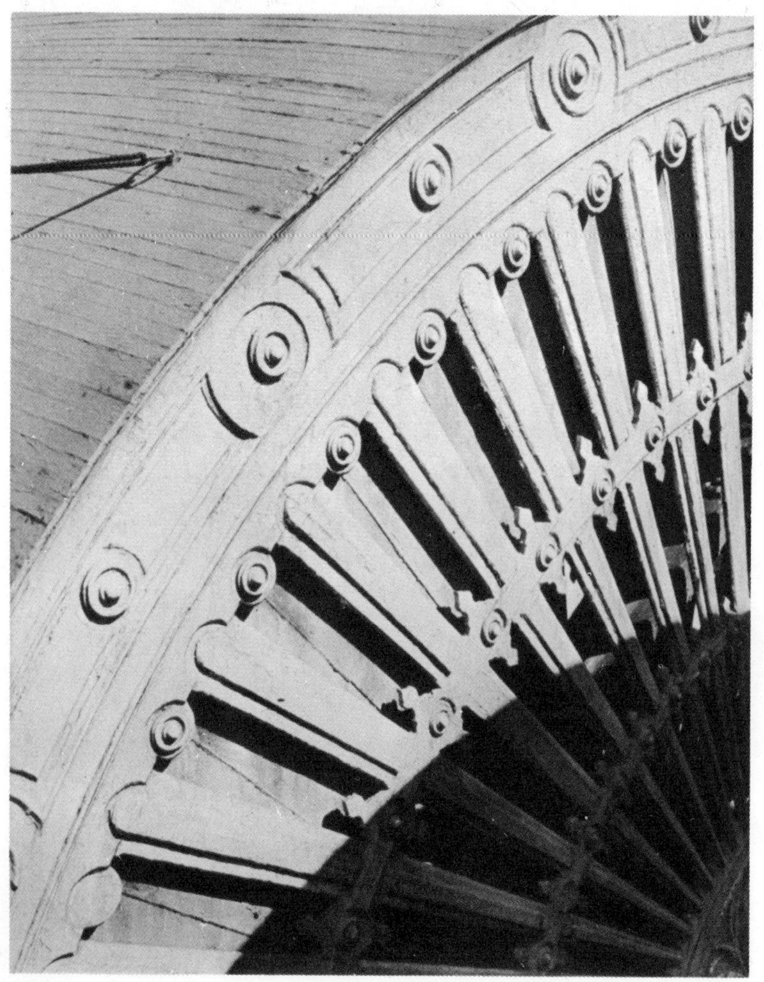

ABOVE: The New York tower of the Manhattan Bridge was photographed by Berenice Abbott November 11, 1936.

LEFT: This photograph of the paddle box of the Iron Steamboat Co.'s *Cephus* (which ran from Pier 1, at the foot of Battery Place, to Coney Island and Rockaway Beach) was taken in 1928 by George Platt Lynes.

Courtesy of the photographer

. . . which linked the city's past to its present . . .

Federal Art Project, "Changing New York," from Museum of the City of New York

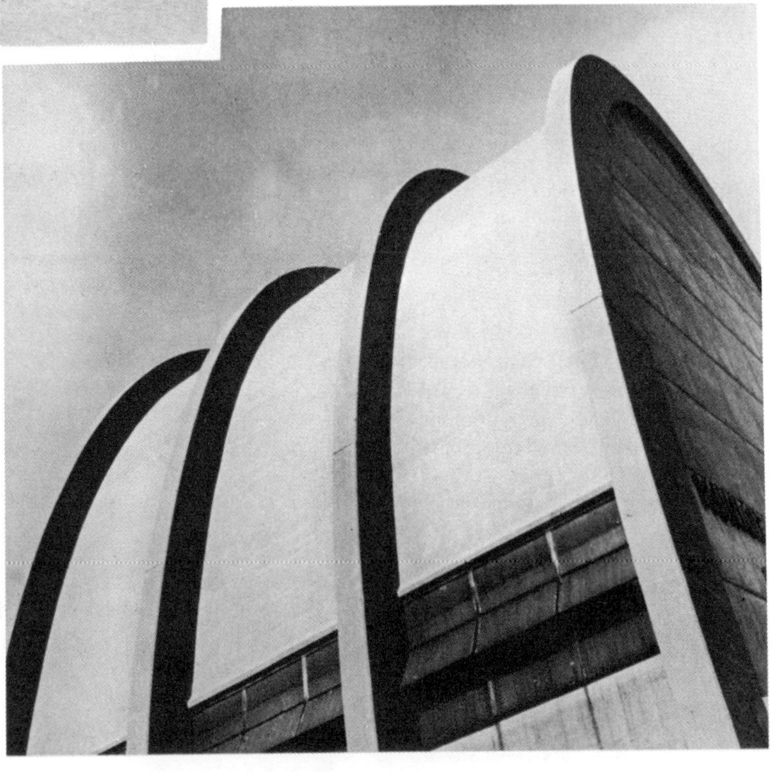

ABOVE: The coffee warehouse, built about 1884 by Arbuckle Bros. at Water and Dock streets in Brooklyn, was photographed by Berenice Abbott, May 22, 1936.

RIGHT: The photograph of the Municipal Asphalt Plant, on Franklin D. Roosevelt Drive near Ninety-first Street, was taken about 1950 by Fred Stein.

Pix Inc.

. . . and permeated all aspects of the city's life.

Courtesy of Gottscho-Schleisner

The photograph at the top of the page is an enlarged detail of a picture taken by Samuel H. Gottscho April 22, 1932, looking northeast from the Chrysler Building on the northeast corner of Lexington Avenue and Forty-second Street, showing the setback architecture, rising in steps from the street, which had resulted from the 1916 Zoning Resolution. The law required that, above the street wall, each building set back one foot for each four feet of additional height.

The Third Avenue El (now—1953—the city's last surviving elevated line) slants across the foreground of the picture. In right background, along the East River shore, are the abattoirs and other buildings which were demolished to provide the site for the United Nations headquarters (page 517).

The picture below is a detail from a photograph, published in the New York *Times*, May 9, 1952, showing workers at the Bohack Terminal candling eggs.

New York Times Studio

Forms and patterns which had seemed alien and strange when the paintings at the Armory Show first called public attention to them . . .

Courtesy of Walter Pach

This unattributed photograph shows the interior of the Sixty-ninth Regiment Armory at Lexington Avenue and Twenty-fifth Street during the famous Armory Show of 1913. Organized and presented by the newly formed Association of American Painters and Sculptors, which included all but one of "The Eight" (see page 467) and many younger and more experimental artists, the show brought together, for the first time in America, a representative cross section of the modernist movements in art, including cubism, futurism, fauvism, post-impressionism, and all the other brand names which were furiously attacked and defended for the next dozen years. Rouault's and Picasso's paintings, Brancusi's sculpture, and hundreds of other examples of what Royal Cortissoz in the *Century* contemptuously called "Ellis Island Art," attracted throngs of bewildered but fascinated New Yorkers from every social level.

. . . have since become familiar to everyone . . .

Federal Art Project, "Changing New York," from Museum of the City of New York

ABOVE: Berenice Abbott's photograph, looking east on Exchange Place from William Street, was taken May 12, 1936. At the left is the rear elevation of the National City Bank, the lower stories of which had been built in 1842 as the Merchants Exchange (see page 171). At right is the City Bank Farmers Trust Co. building, and in the background the Hanover Street front of 63 Wall Street.

LEFT: John Marin's water color, "Movement, Fifth Avenue," was painted in 1912, the year before the Armory Show (preceding page), at which he was one of the least conventional Americans to exhibit.

Art Institute of Chicago, Alfred Stieglitz Collection

. . . as photographers and painters alike . . .

Pix Inc.

ABOVE: "Brownstone House Entrance" was photographed by Fred Stein in Greenwich Village about 1951.

RIGHT: John Marin's water color, "A City Seeing," was painted in 1928.

The Miller Company Collection, "Painting Toward Architecture"

. . . have explored the city's austere geometry . . .

Federal Art Project, "Changing New York," from Museum of the City of New York

Berenice Abbott's photograph of Nos. 4, 6, and 8 Fifth Avenue (southwest corner of Eighth Street) was taken March 6, 1936. No. 8, at right, was built in 1856 for John Taylor Johnston—the first marble house in New York. Johnston was a wealthy art patron, who maintained, above the stable in the rear of the house, an art gallery which was open to the public one day each week. When the Metropolitan Museum of Art was organized in 1870, Johnston was its first president.

. . . of intersecting planes of light and shadow . . .

Courtesy of Mrs. Earl Horter

"Church Street El" was painted by Charles Sheeler in 1921. Like Marin, Sheeler was one of the American painters whose work had attracted attention at the Armory Show (page 497). This semi-abstract canvas was painted in the same year in which Sheeler —a first-rate photographer as well as a painter—collaborated with Paul Strand in making the moving picture called *Manahatta,* with captions from Walt Whitman.

. . . and discovered new patterns of order . . .

Both pictures from the Newark Museum, Newark, New Jersey

The pictures reproduced on this page are two of the five panels entitled "New York Interpreted" which Joseph Stella painted in 1923 after his return from Europe, where he had become familiar with the work of Picasso, Modigliani, and the Italian futurists.

. . . in the thrusting verticals of the city's towers.

Both pictures courtesy of Gottscho-Schleisner

These two photographs by Samuel H. Gottscho were taken four years apart—the one above on January 4, 1928, and the one below on June 11, 1932. Both were taken looking south from the roof loggia of the Barbizon Hotel for Women, Lexington Avenue and Sixty-third Street.

In the 1928 picture the skyline is dominated by the forty-two-story Ritz Tower hotel (center arch), erected in 1925 at the northeast corner of Fifty-seventh and Park from plans by Emery Roth and Carrère & Hastings. The tallest building visible through the left-hand arch is the Shelton Hotel, erected in 1923, at the southeast corner of Lexington Avenue and Forty-ninth Street. The Shelton, designed by Arthur Loomis Harmon, was the first important skyscraper to be built after the 1916 Zoning Resolution was adopted, and its bold, stepped-back outline exerted a wide influence on subsequent buildings.

Four years later the Shelton had been dwarfed by the 1046-foot Chrysler Building (directly behind it, at Lexington and Forty-second Street), erected in 1929 from plans by William Van Alen. The other very tall tower visible through the left-hand arch is the General Electric Building, at Lexington and Fifty-first, completed in 1931 from plans by Schultze & Weaver. Between them is the Chanin Building, designed by Sloan & Robertson and built in 1929. In the center arch, the Ritz Tower has been flanked by the Empire State (see page 477) and by the tower at the northwest corner of Fifth Avenue and Forty-seventh Street.

But the complexity of urban forms . . .

. . . has been revealed most strikingly in aerial photographs.

New York Times Studio

The airplane view, above, was taken October 31, 1952, and first published in the New York *Times* three days later. The picture was taken from a point above the Bronx Terminal Market (foreground) and the Major Deegan Expressway, looking north along the Harlem River and across upper Manhattan toward the George Washington Bridge and the Columbia-Presbyterian Medical Center (just left of the bridge tower). Part of the Yankee Stadium appears at lower right, and across the river are the Polo Grounds and the Colonial Park housing development. Crossing the Harlem in foreground is Macomb's Dam Bridge, and part of High Bridge is visible at upper right (compare the earlier views of this region on pages 210 and 416).

OPPOSITE: Margaret Bourke-White's photograph was first published in *Life,* April 14, 1952, with several others, taken in various parts of the United States, which revealed the striking patterns visible from a helicopter. The picture was taken from a point in mid-air about Thirty-ninth Street and Eleventh Avenue, looking eastward. At upper left is the Port of New York Authority's new Bus Terminal (1950) on the block bounded by Eighth and Ninth avenues and Fortieth and Forty-first streets, and in left foreground the entrance to the Lincoln Tunnel.

From a plane it was possible at last to see . . .

Fairchild Aerial Surveys, Inc.

This aerial photograph of Manhattan and its surroundings was taken January 26, 1953. It should be compared with such earlier pictures as the "balloon view" on pages 330-31 and the bird's-eye views on pages 240 and 189.

The Fairchild people have been taking aerial photographs since 1922, and their files provide an unparalleled record of the changing city as it can be seen from the air. The first airplane flights over New York were made by Wilbur Wright during the Hudson-Fulton Celebration in 1909, but it was not until the First World War that aerial photography was sufficiently perfected to be of practical use.

Both pictures from Fairchild Aerial Surveys, Inc.

The photograph at the top of this page was taken February 3, 1950, from a point in mid-air somewhat west and north of the imaginary point from which Theodore R. Davis portrayed the city in the bird's-eye view reproduced on page 332. In center foreground, in line with the end of the approach to the Brooklyn Bridge, is the Municipal Building, straddling Chambers Street at Park Row. To the right, about halfway between it and the Woolworth Building, is City Hall; to the left, between it and the hexagonal County Court House, is the 32-story U. S. Court House, which just hides from view St. Andrew's Church (see Davis' picture). Just north of the bridge, where some of the foulest slums used to be, are the Alfred E. Smith Houses. At extreme right is the double ribbon of the Miller elevated highway on West Street, leading south to the Battery and the entrance to the almost completed Brooklyn-Battery Tunnel, at whose Brooklyn end, just left of Governor's Island, can be seen the sweeping curve of the Belt Parkway's Gowanus link.

The air view at the bottom of the page, looking north across the massed apartments of Jackson Heights toward La Guardia Field and Flushing Bay, was taken January 26, 1953. The wide street slanting from the lower left corner of the picture to middle right is Roosevelt Avenue, along which the elevated tracks of the IRT subway run out to Flushing in upper right corner. The gash which cuts slantwise across the foreground is the right of way of the New York Connecting Railroad, linking the Pennsylvania and New Haven lines by way of Hell Gate Bridge.

. . . in comprehensive bird's-eye perspectives . . .

. . . which in the past had been only imagined.

This aerial view, looking west from a point above Flushing Bay, was taken March 17, 1952. In the foreground is La Guardia Field, built in 1935-39 on filled land made with debris and ashes transferred from the old dump on Riker's Island, just to the right, where the Penitentiary was erected in 1935 (to replace the obsolete Welfare Island prison). Just beyond Riker's Island are South Brother and North Brother islands, the latter the site of the Riverside Hospital for communicable diseases.

Left of the airport, Grand Central Parkway curves south to meet Astoria Boulevard, running in a direct line from lower left to the Astoria end of the Triborough Bridge. Curving across the boulevard from center left are the elevated tracks of the New York Connecting Railroad, leading up onto Hell Gate Bridge (see page 421).

Beyond lies upper Manhattan, from about Fifty-ninth Street (whose tall hotels are seen south of Central Park, at left) to about 160th Street. The horseshoe shape of the Polo Grounds and a portion of the Colonial Park Houses (see page 505) are just distinguishable at extreme right.

Fairchild Aerial Surveys, Inc.

And with the new angle of vision came new understanding of urban reality . . .

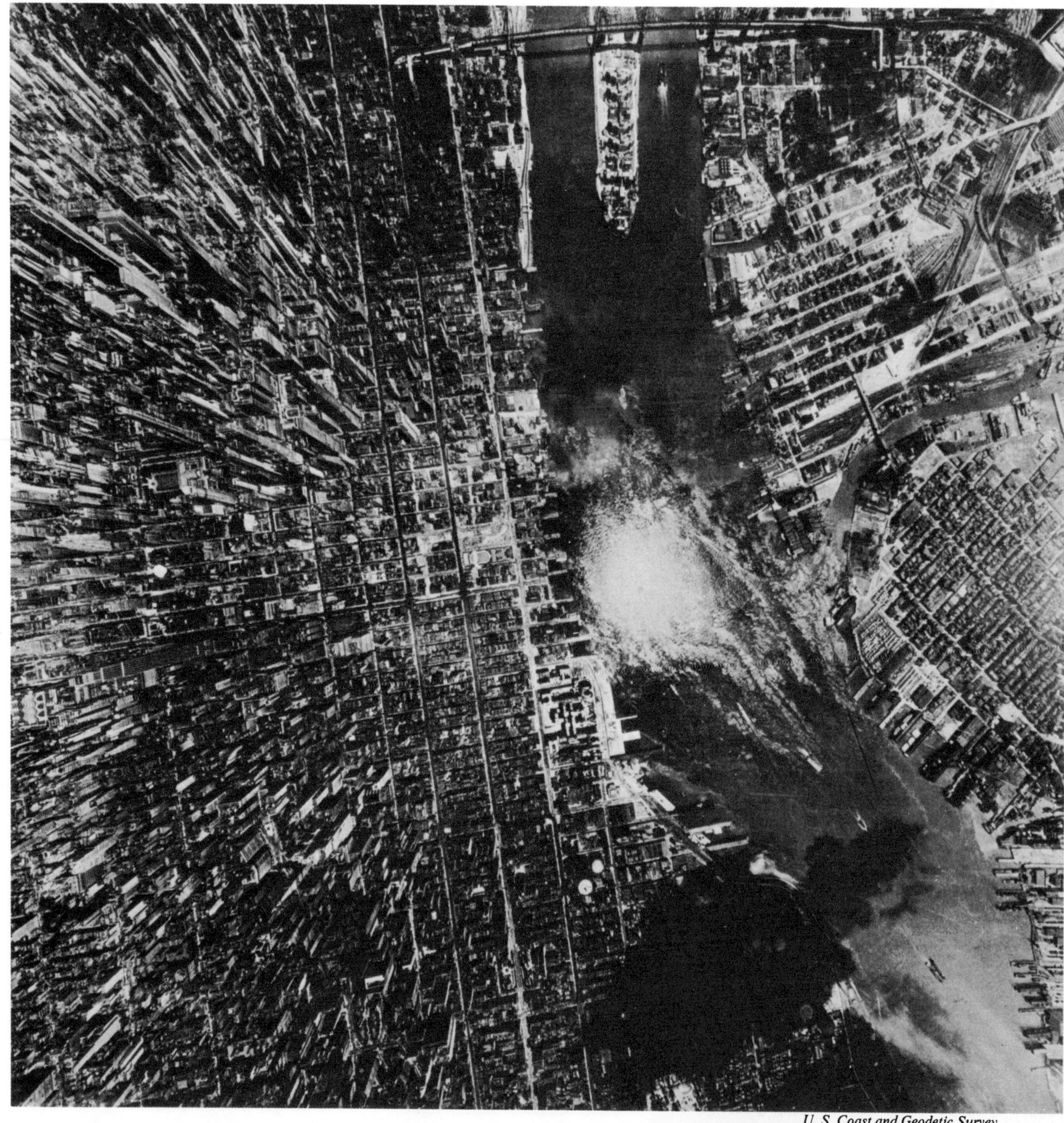

U. S. Coast and Geodetic Survey

This photograph, taken July 5, 1940, was made for the U. S. Coast and Geodetic Survey by an Army Air Force photographer using a nine-lens camera developed for aerial map-making.

. . . at once broader in scope and more detailed than ever before . . .

U. S. Geological Survey

The map at left, covering approximately the area shown in the photograph opposite, is composed of parts of two separate sheets of the U. S. Geological Survey's maps, published in 1943 and based in part on data derived from the photograph. The picture centers, of course, on a part of town which has been largely transformed since it was taken. What the changes have been is made clear in the photograph which is reproduced on the following page (see caption below).

NEXT PAGE: In the course of working on this book, the author wrote to Park Commissioner and City Construction Coordinator Robert Moses, asking him if there were any single map or drawing or photograph which would convey his over-all view of the relationships between the geography, buildings, and people which make up the city. The picture he selected is the aerial photograph on the next page, which symbolizes, as he expressed it, "the tremendous complexity of the city, its waterways, highways, offices, the homes and institutions of its people, their work, ideas, and recreation." The photograph, taken about 1951, shows Manhattan from below Corlaer's Hook, north to the United Nations building and west to Times Square, a neighborhood which, as Mr. Moses says, "is being completely reclaimed, rebuilt, and modernized."

At lower left, just west of the south end of the new East River Park, are the Vladeck Houses, and just above them, the housing development built by the Amalgamated Clothing Workers Union. (For the early development of this region, see page 68.) Following the Franklin D. Roosevelt Drive north along the river front, we come, in order, to the site cleared for the Baruch Houses (just above the Williamsburg Bridge), the Lillian Wald and Jacob Riis houses, Stuyvesant Town and Peter Cooper Village (financed by the Metropolitan Life Insurance Co.) in what used to be the Gashouse district, the Veterans Hospital, Bellevue, and the site for the New York University medical center, the United Nations headquarters, and finally, at upper right, Beekman Place and Sutton Place.

. . . to aid in planning and controlling the city's future growth.

Office of the New York City Construction Coordinator

See preceding page for data on this picture.

But New York is not the planner's or builder's city any more than it is the sight-seer's.

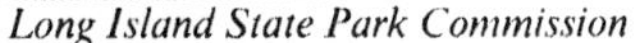
Long Island State Park Commission

Courtesy of Rockefeller Center, Inc.

New York Times Studio

ABOVE LEFT: Former Governor Alfred E. Smith and Commissioner Robert Moses at the celebration of the tenth anniversary of Jones Beach State Park in 1939.

ABOVE RIGHT: John D. Rockefeller, Jr., driving the final rivet at the ceremony celebrating the completion of Rockefeller Center, May 1, 1939, assisted by M. L. Carpenter, steel foreman on the job.

LEFT: A group of sight-seers from Ohio, photographed March 21, 1952, by Edward Hausner for a feature story in the New York *Times* the following day. More than 13,000,000 people visit New York in a year. Every minute of the day a passenger train arrives; a plane lands or takes off at La Guardia Field every three minutes (to say nothing of Idlewild, Newark, and the other metropolitan airports); and a boat of some sort docks every half hour.

In one sense it is millions of separate cities . . .

Contemporaneously with the rise of "documentary" photography during the thirties (see page 481) came the development of "candid cameras," which made it possible to take instantaneous, unposed pictures, indoors and out, under conditions which would previously have required flash bulbs or time exposures. The "candid" shots on this and the following two pages were made between 1948 and 1952. RIGHT: Ed Feingersh took this picture in Times Square in 1951. BELOW LEFT: One of a series of pictures taken by Suzanne Szasz at the Port of New York Authority's Bus Terminal, Fortieth Street and Eighth Avenue in February, 1951. BELOW RIGHT: Another photograph by Suzanne Szasz, taken in 1950 in the CBS television studio after a tough rehearsal. The young lady was an international exchange student who was a guest on the Faye Emerson Show.

Pix Inc.

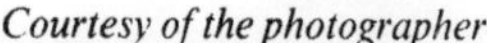

Courtesy of the photographer

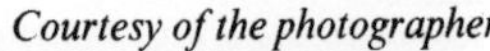

Courtesy of the photographer

. . . each created by one of the millions of people . . .

Courtesy of the photographer

ABOVE: The woman testing a loaf of bread was photographed by Suzanne Szasz in an A & P store on Seventy-ninth Street in 1950. RIGHT: Erich Hartmann photographed the dealer at the American Fruit Exchange, Second Avenue at Eleventh Street, in 1952. BELOW LEFT: Bob Schwalberg photographed the longshoremen at Pier 34 during the dock strike in 1951. BELOW RIGHT: The woman using her mirror to see over the heads of the Easter Parade throng was snapped by George Cserna on Fifth Avenue in 1952.

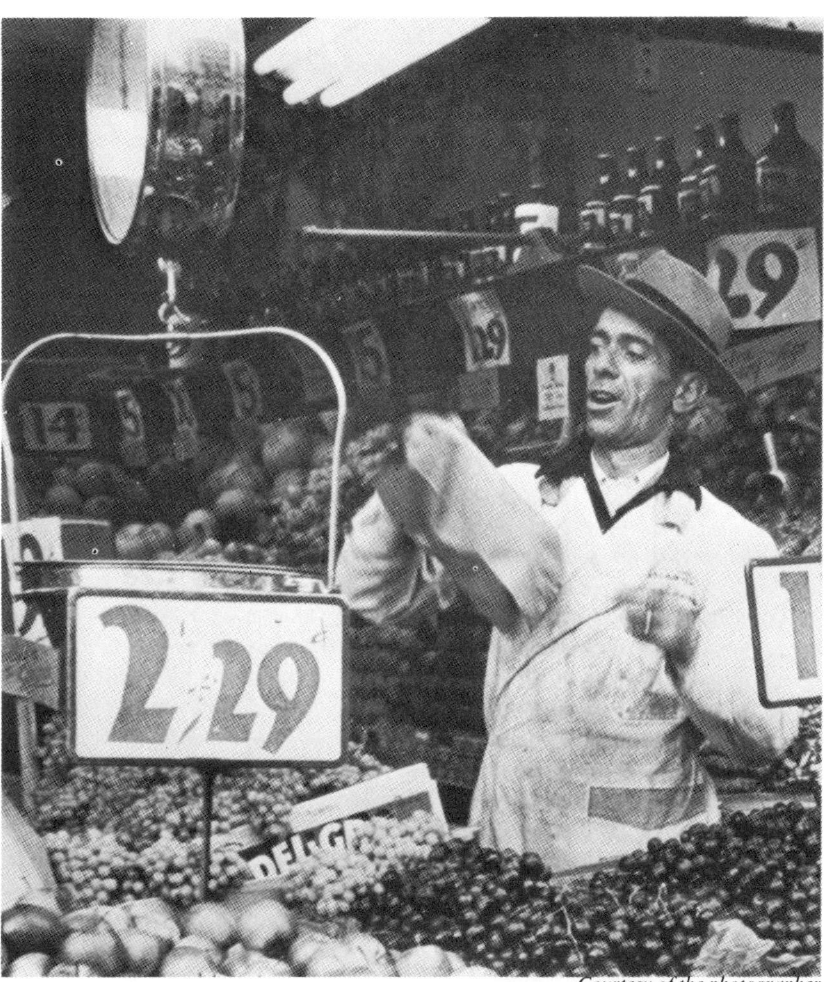

Courtesy of the photographer

Pix Inc.

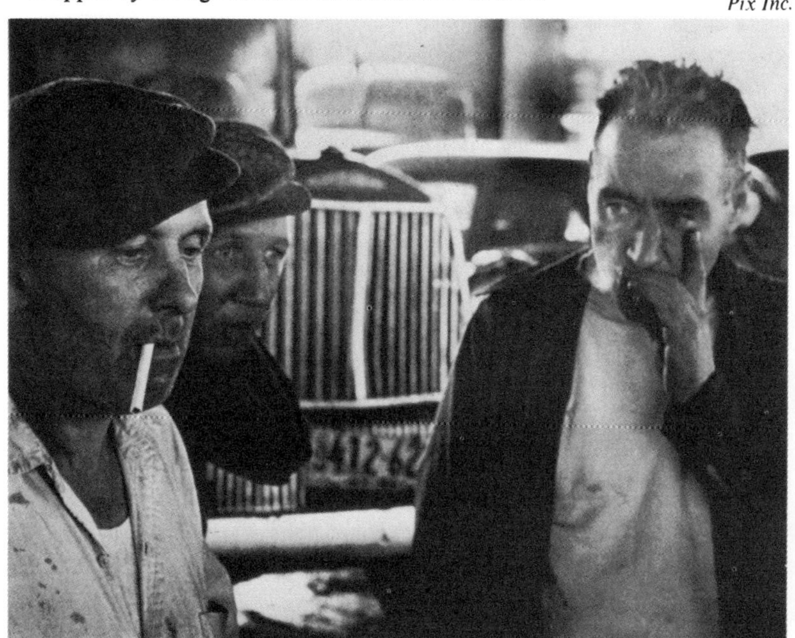

Courtesy of the photographer

. . . who make worlds of their own in its crowded privacy.

Pix Inc.

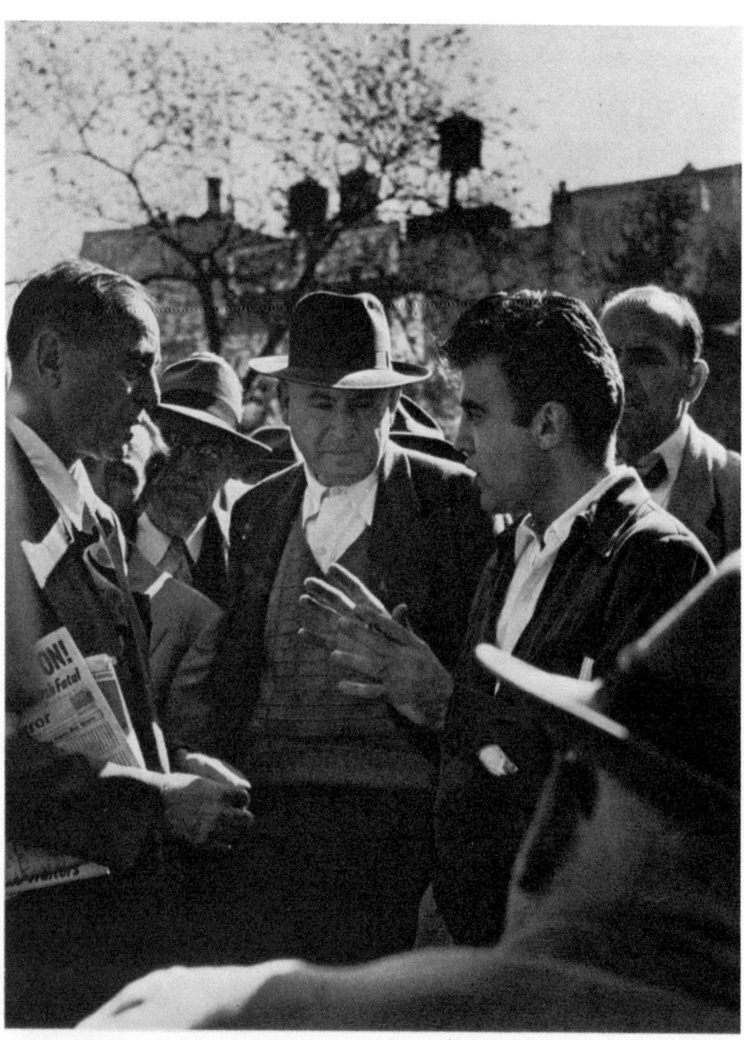

ABOVE: Ed Feingersh found the three girls chatting on Third Avenue, about Twenty-ninth Street, in 1948.

LEFT: The political discussion (or was it baseball?) in Union Square was photographed by Erich Hartmann on a Saturday morning in September, 1952.

Courtesy of the photographer

*And perhaps for that very reason
it is, in another sense,
everybody's city.*

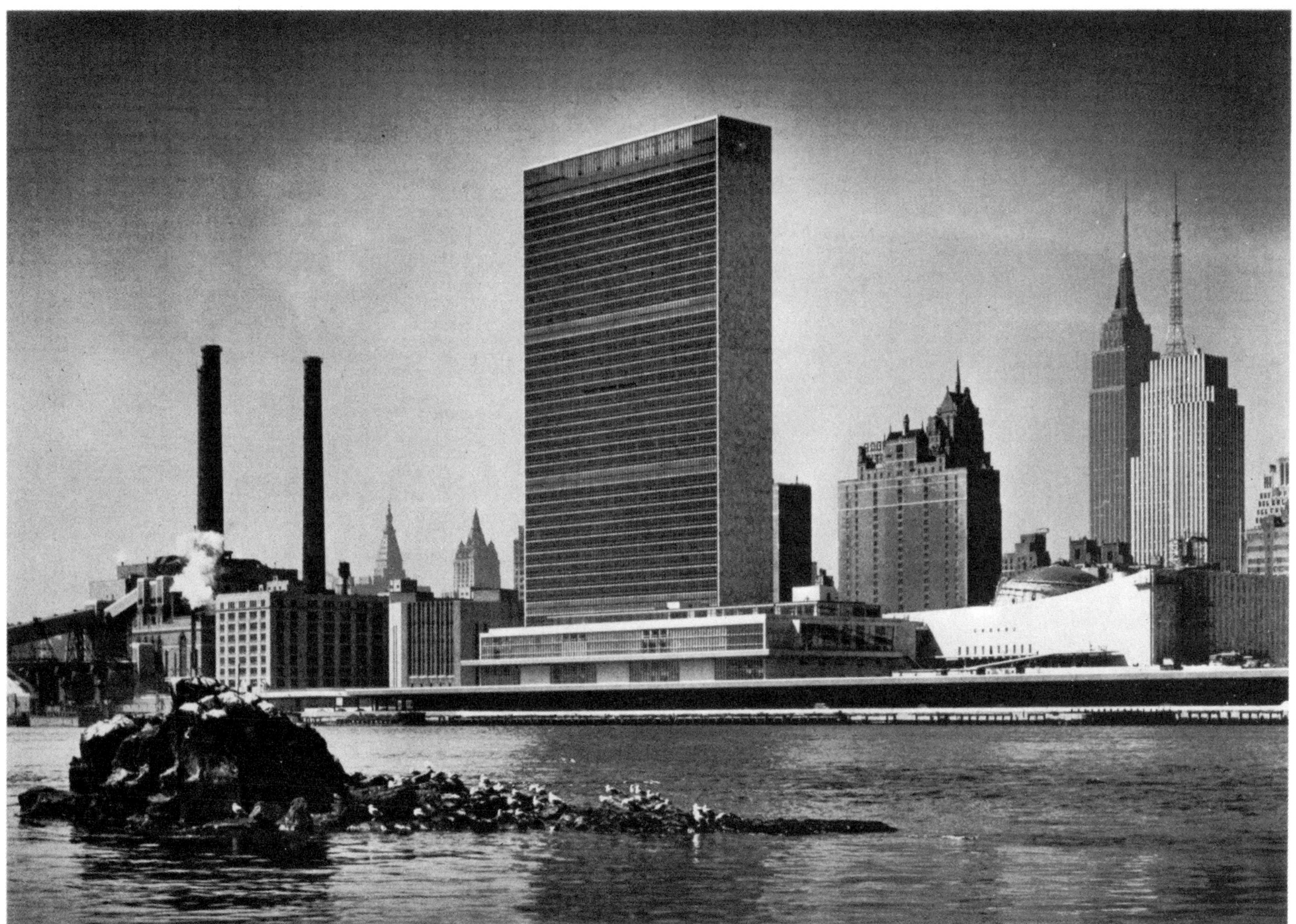

Courtesy of Gottscho-Schleisner

This photograph of the United Nations headquarters was taken by Gottscho-Schleisner on March 18, 1952, from the southern tip of Welfare Island in the East River. Actually, of course, the United Nations buildings are not in New York at all, since the seventeen-acre plot on which they stand, east of First Avenue between Forty-second and Forty-eighth streets, is United Nations territory.

The chief designers of the UN group, built in 1949–52, were Wallace K. Harrison and his deputy (and partner), Max Abramowitz, working with an international Board of Design Consultants including France's Le Corbusier, Brazil's Oscar Niemeyer, the Soviet's Nikolai Bassov, and Sweden's Sven Markelius. In the photograph the towering glass and marble Secretariat building is flanked at the left by the stacks of the Consolidated Edison power plant, the Metropolitan Life tower at Madison Square, and the New York Life Insurance Building; and at the right by Tudor City, the Empire State, and the *Daily News* building, erected in 1930 from designs by Raymond Hood and John Mead Howells.

No single way of looking at New York . . .

This photograph of Fifth Avenue traffic, taken with a camera equipped with a telescopic lens, was made by Andreas Feininger for *Life* in 1949.

The foreshortened perspective produced by the telescopic camera (notice the street numbers on the lampposts) dramatically overstates the congestion of busses, trucks, taxis, and cars which has become one of the city's most pressing problems.

. . . is adequate to comprehend
either its surface chaos
or its underlying
order . . .

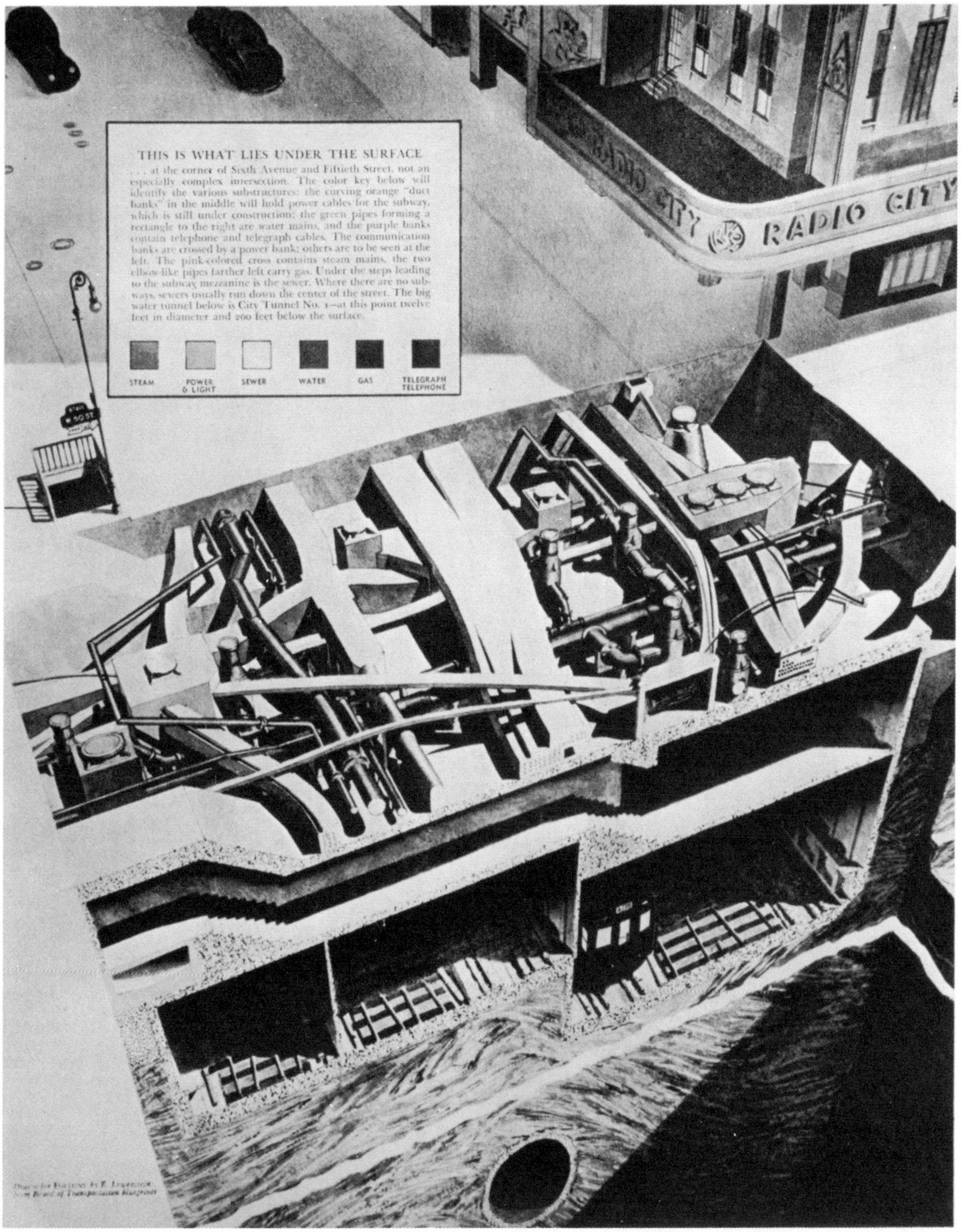

Fortune Magazine

This schematic drawing of "What Lies under the Surface" at Sixth Avenue and Fiftieth Street was made by Emil Lowenstein from Board of Transportation blueprints. It is reproduced here from page 126 of *Fortune's* special New York City issue, published in July, 1939, at the time of the New York World's Fair. In spite of the absence of color in the present reproduction, the inset caption and key make it possible to identify most of the pipes, ducts, and tunnels which are shown.

. . . and no selection of pictures can do more than suggest . . .

This photograph was taken in 1951 by Roy de Carava from the platform of the 165th Street station of the Third Avenue El.

Courtesy of the photographer

. . . the dissonant variety of personal attitudes and interests which are reflected . . .

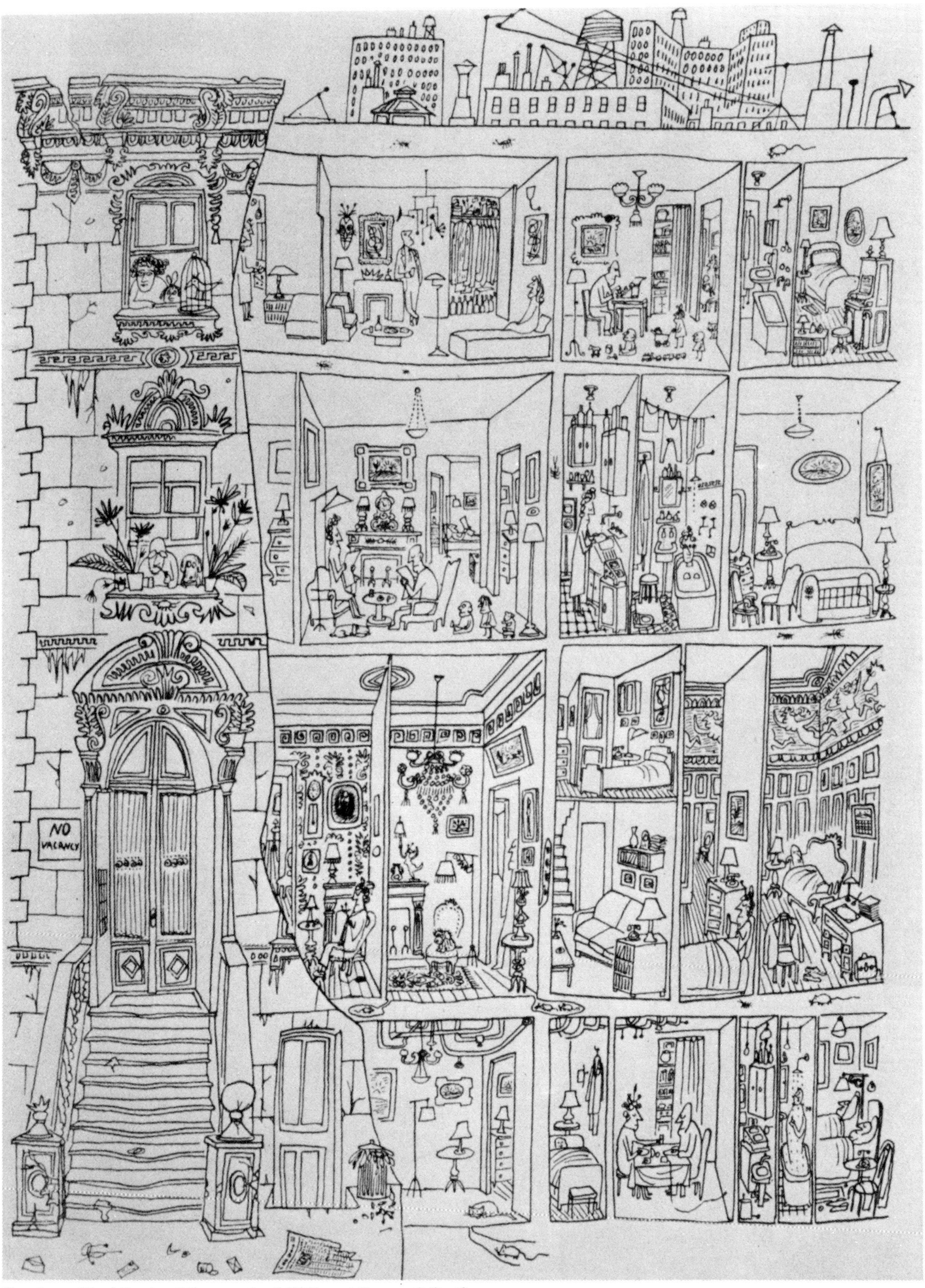

Courtesy of Architectural Forum, *April 1946, and Harper & Brothers*

Saul Steinberg disconcertingly cuts away the shabbily ornate wall of a brownstone front in this drawing from his book, *The Art of Living* (1949).

. . . in the work of contemporary artists and photographers.

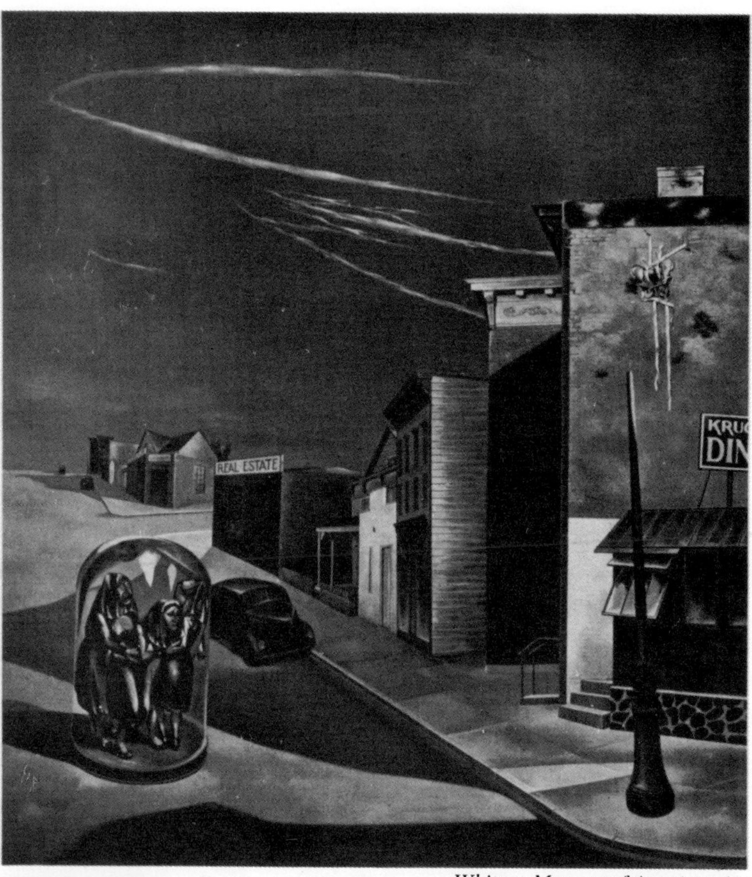

Whitney Museum of American Art

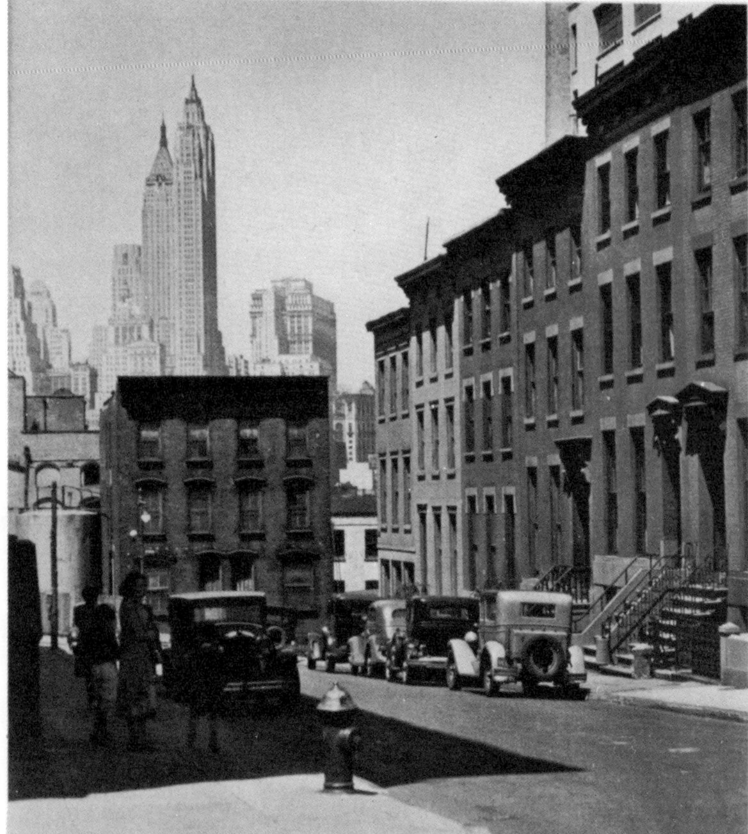

"Terror in Brooklyn," by Louis Guglielmi, was painted in 1941.

Berenice Abbott's photograph, looking east down Poplar Street from Willow Street on Brooklyn Heights, was taken May 14, 1936.

Federal Art Project, "Changing New York," from Museum of the City of New York

But the recurring images . . .

Walker Art Center, Minneapolis

LEFT: Abraham Rattner's "City Still Life" was painted in 1943.

BELOW: Roy de Carava's photograph was taken on 103rd Street, between Lexington and Third avenues, in 1950.

Courtesy of the photographer

Wadsworth Atheneum, Hartford

Ben Shahn's "Vacant Lot," painted in 1939, was his response "to the attraction and the sense of loneliness" of the space created when an old building was torn down at the corner of Greenwich and Bethune streets, next to his studio.

. . . are the architectural forms in which its loneliness and aspiration . . .

Midtown Galleries

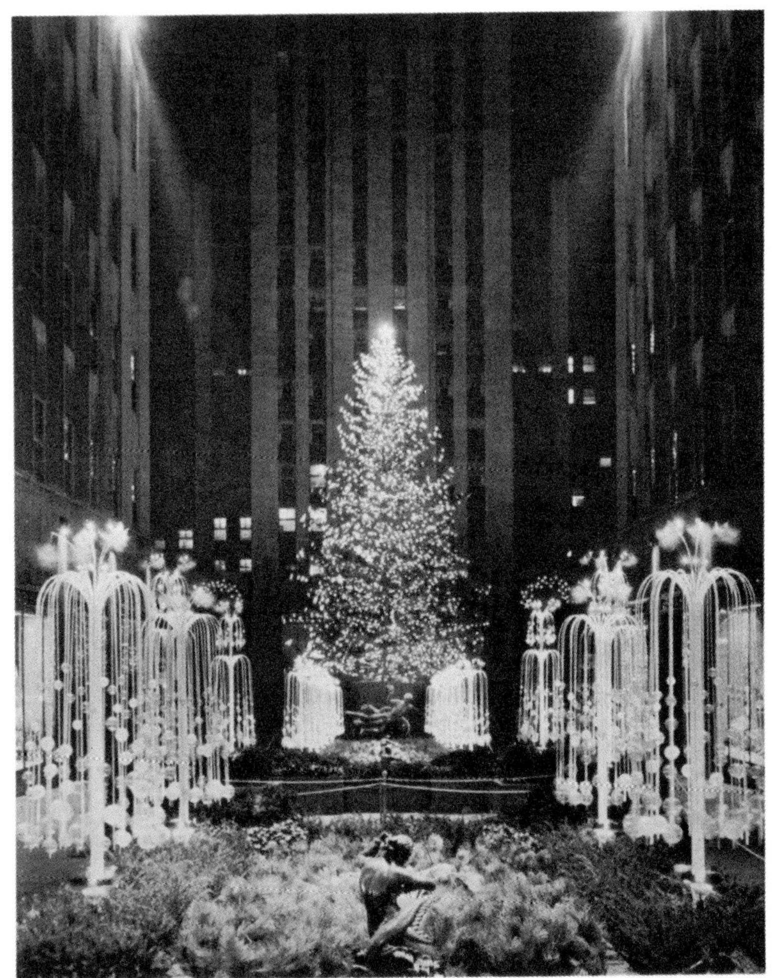

"The Architect," by Paul Cadmus, was painted in 1952.

This photograph of the 1951 Christmas tree at Rockefeller Center was taken by Edward Ratcliffe.

Courtesy of Rockefeller Center, Inc.

Courtesy of Rockefeller Center, Inc.

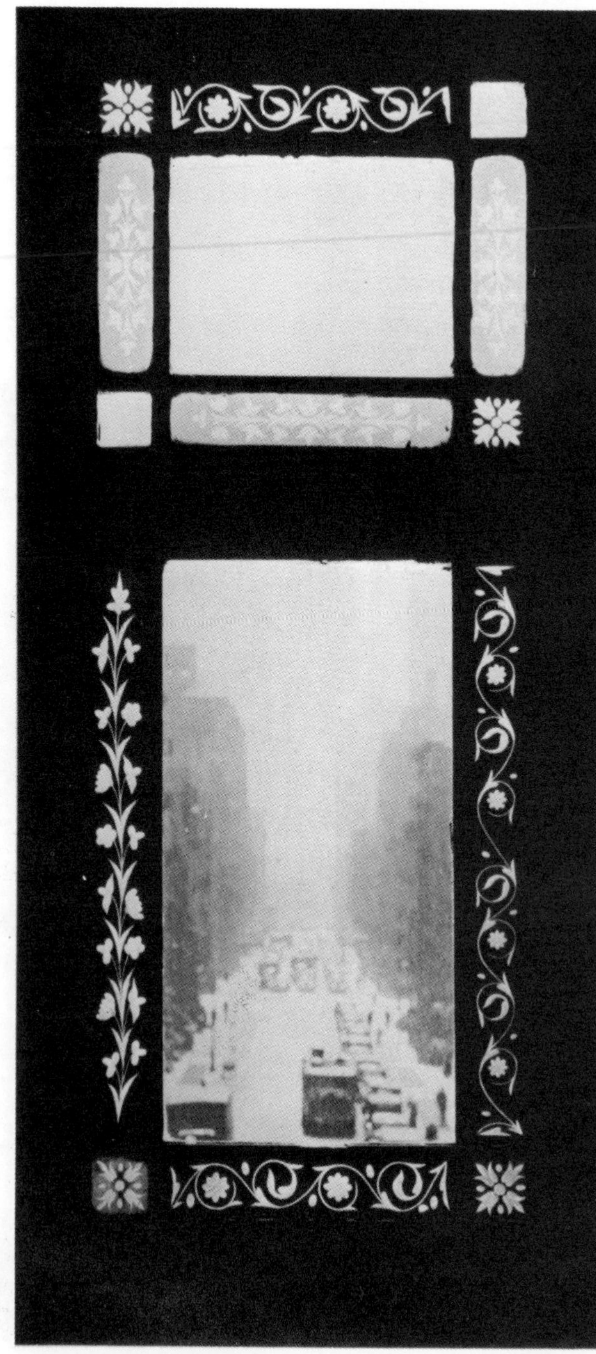

The photograph at left was taken by Godfrey Frankel in 1948, through the window of the Fifty-third Street station of the Third Avenue El. The one above, by an unidentified photographer, was taken December 26, 1933, looking east from the Associated Press Building at Rockefeller Center (before the International Building, which now blocks the view, had been built). The skyscraper whose tower rises between the spires of St. Patrick's is the General Electric Building, to the right of which is the new Waldorf-Astoria on the east side of Park Avenue between Forty-ninth and Fiftieth, completed in 1931 from designs by Schultze & Weaver.

Courtesy of the photographer

. . . have found their most concrete expression.

Courtesy of the photographer

Roy de Carava's photograph, above, was taken in 1951, looking north from below 126th Street, in mid-block between Seventh and Eighth avenues. In the background the first units of the St. Nicholas Houses are going up on the blocks between 127th and 129th streets.

Fred Stein's photograph, at right, was taken about 1945 from a building on the north side of Fifty-second Street, looking south through the channel of Rockefeller Plaza to the Empire State. At left is the International Building, and at right the Associated Press Building with the RCA tower beyond it. The houses in the foreground have since been demolished to make way for the Esso Building.

Pix Inc.

And as New York begins its fourth century, it is primarily Manhattan's fantastic skyline . . .

New York Times Studio

ABOVE: This photograph of the new Queen of the Seas, the liner *United States,* being welcomed to her home port June 23, 1952, was taken by George Alexanderson for the New York *Times.* The picture should be compared with the one at the top of page 396.

LEFT: This photograph of Manhattan's skyline was taken by Roger Higgins of the *World-Telegram and Sun,* November 17, 1947, from the Independent Subway's elevated platform at Smith and Ninth streets in South Brooklyn, not far from the place at which the view on page 123 was made more than a century earlier.

New York World-Telegram and Sun

. . . rising like a Phoenix from the ashes of its own past . . .

Courtesy of Editions Verve *and Simon & Schuster*

The photograph above, by the French photographer Henri Cartier-Bresson, was one of those included in his volume called *The Decisive Moment* (New York, Simon & Schuster, 1952). His caption for it was simply: "New York 1947. After a fire on a pier shed in freezing weather, Manhattan across the Hudson River seems to rise like a Phoenix."

*. . . which dominates men's vision of the city.
Those implausible
towers . . .*

. . . massed in ragged and anarchic Sierras
at the eastern edge of the
continent . . .

This photograph of New York's skyline, as seen with a telephoto lens from eight miles away in New Jersey, was taken by Andreas Feininger and first published in *Life,* March 31, 1947.

The picture was taken from near Bendix, New Jersey, looking southeast across the valley of the Hackensack River. The highway in the foreground (actually about a mile from the camera) is a stretch of Routes 46 and 6. On the ridge in the middle distance are parts of the towns of Guttenberg and West New York. And across the Hudson in the background are the towers of mid-Manhattan, from Rockefeller Center, at left, to the New York Life Building, Madison and Twenty-sixth Street, at right. The southeast perspective will be clear if the reader notices that the Chrysler Building and the next three very tall towers to the right of it—Chanin, Lincoln, and 500 Fifth Avenue (with mast)—are all on Forty-second Street, running westward across town.

Courtesy of the photographer

. . . have come to symbolize far more than the industrial power of the civilization that is focused in them.

New York Times *from Socony*

This photograph, taken by an unidentified photographer in 1952, shows an oil barge traveling westward toward the East River on Newtown Creek, the boundary between Brooklyn and Queens (see page 511). The creek is one of the busiest waterways in the country, carrying more freight in a year, it has been said, than the Mississippi. The Empire State Building towers in the center, just above the bridge which spans the creek from Greenpoint's Manhattan Avenue (at left) to Vernon Boulevard in Long Island City.

Against all logic, and without anyone's planning it that way, they have become a symbol of man's aspiration . . .

United Press Associations

This night photograph of the Manhattan skyline as seen from Calvary Cemetery in Queens was taken in December, 1952, by an unidentified United Press photographer. The tower topped with a glowing light near the left margin is the Metropolitan Life Building at Madison Square. In the center is the United Nations building, with the Chrysler spire behind it. The buildings at extreme right are at about Seventy-second Street.

. . . even though, like any towers man is likely to build, they stop well short of heaven.

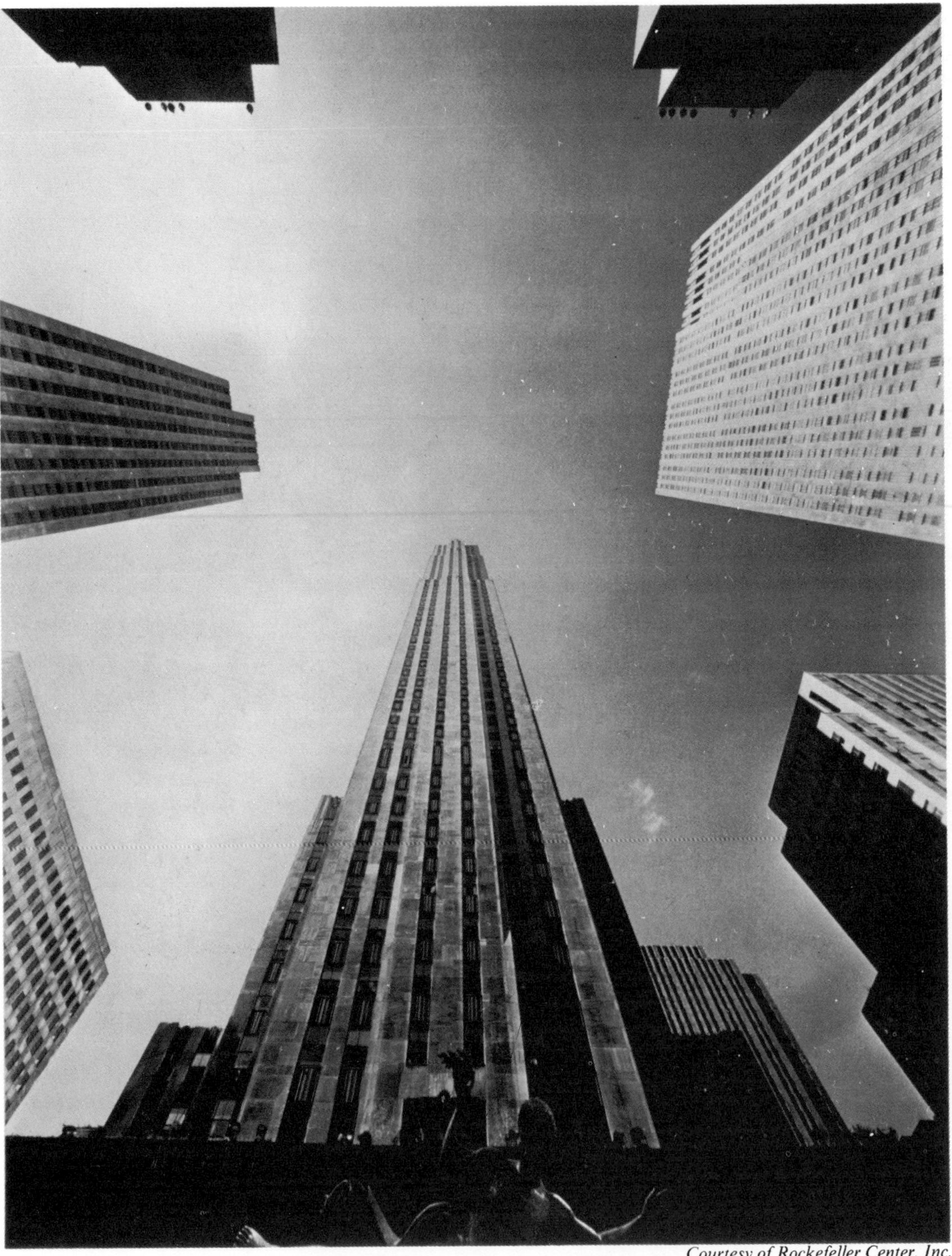

Courtesy of Rockefeller Center, Inc.

This vertical photograph, made with a wide-angle hypergon lens, was taken by Wendell MacRae about 1940, looking straight up from the lower plaza of Rockefeller Center, where the skating rink is in winter and where people dine outdoors in summer. Starting with the RCA Building in lower center and moving clockwise, the buildings are, in order, the Time and Life Building, La Maison Française, the British Empire Building, the International Building, and the Associated Press Building.

ACKNOWLEDGMENTS

Though the author alone is responsible for the selection and arrangement of pictures in this book, and for the comments about them, he is indebted to many people for encouragement and help. First of all he would like to thank the Columbia University Bicentennial Committee, under the chairmanship of Arthur Hays Sulzberger, for sponsoring the volume in connection with the bicentennial celebration. While the Committee's support has been wholehearted, at no time has any representative of the University sought to influence in any way the book's scope or editorial program.

No one who reads the book can fail to recognize my indebtedness to others who have written about the city of New York. My greatest debt, of course, is to I. N. Phelps Stokes' *Iconography of Manhattan Island* (1915-28), but I have read or frequently consulted more than two hundred others. Some of these are mentioned in the text; others, such as Agnes Rogers' and Frederick Lewis Allen's *Metropolis* (1934) or John A. Krout's *The Greater City* (1948), for example, have simply been absorbed into my general awareness of the city and its history.

Many generous and friendly people have guided me to useful material and have done what they could to help me avoid errors of judgment or fact. To all of them, including the owners and custodians of the pictures reproduced in these pages, I am greatly obliged. My particular thanks go to Constance A. Foulk, for resourceful and painstaking picture research and for handling most of the complex details of permissions and credits; to Grace M. Mayer, curator of prints at the Museum of the City of New York, for expert guidance and for unfailing helpfulness at every stage of the research; to Alma Reese Cardi for combining thoughtfulness and patience with imagination and taste in working out the intricate problems of layout, typography, and design; and to my wife, Eleanor Hayden Kouwenhoven, and our children, Ann and Gerrit, for help and consideration of every conceivable kind.

The majority of the black-and-white reproductions were made from photographs of the original pictures taken by John Harvey Heffren, and the color plates were made from Ektachromes taken by Francis G. Mayer of Art Color Slides, Inc. Others to whom I am grateful for a variety of favors include: Frederick Lewis Allen, Oliver E. Allen, Douglas M. Black, Harry MacNeill Bland, Walter I. Bradbury, C. C. Brinley, Allen S. Davenport, Marshall B. Davidson, Douglas Gorsline, Oliver Jensen, Eric Larrabee, Russell Lynes, Catharine Meyer, Agnes Rogers, M. Lincoln Schuster, Milton Halsey Thomas, Kathryn C. Tebbel, and Paul Vanderbilt.

J. A. K.

GENERAL INDEX

STREET INDEX

72 73 74 75 12 11 10 9 8 7 6 5 4 3 2 1